Trade and Security

Trade and Security:
The United States and East Asia, 1961-1969

By

Charles M. Dobbs

CAMBRIDGE
SCHOLARS
PUBLISHING

Trade and Security:
The United States and East Asia, 1961-1969,
by Charles M. Dobbs

This book first published 2010

Cambridge Scholars Publishing

12 Back Chapman Street, Newcastle upon Tyne, NE6 2XX, UK

British Library Cataloguing in Publication Data
A catalogue record for this book is available from the British Library

ISBN (10): 1-4438-1990-5, ISBN (13): 978-1-4438-1990-9

Dedicated to my family, past and present

TABLE OF CONTENTS

FOREWORD

Every scholarly researcher incurs the usual debts that deserve a greater expression of appreciation than several lines in the "foreword." I benefitted from outstanding archivists at the John F. Kennedy Library, the Lyndon Baines Johnson Library, and the National Archives II. They all have this wonderful ability to bring together one's not entirely formed ideas [and thus requests for materials] and their respective archive's holdings into a productive research trip. I also want to thank Ed Goedeken, the History Subject Librarian at Iowa State University and the Interlibrary Loan Office at ISU for helping me secure needed materials. Colleagues at Iowa State University and other institutions were kind enough to offer advice, not always appreciated at the time they gave it, and necessary suggestions for improvement.

I also want to thank more than thirty years of students at my previous and current institutions. You all have served as test subjects for my ideas and my efforts to organization time, themes, and geography into consistent, compelling "wholes." It's been a great run!

My dissertation supervisor was a towering figure in the field of American diplomatic history. Robert H. Ferrell was the scholarly equivalent of a US Marine Corps drill instructor. First, he broke us down to rid us of our bad habits and then he built us up in the image he wanted. We all were so stamped that for decades the "Ferrell treatment" meant high praise. Others at Indiana at that time strongly seconded Mr. Ferrell's efforts. John Edward Wilz, David Pletcher and Richard Kirkendall combined to make a tremendous, unofficial research group in U.S. diplomatic history.

I have to thank Amanda Millar and Carol Koulikourdi at Cambridge Scholars Publishing. I was not always the most responsive of authors, and they showed kindness and support when it was most needed.

Finally, I want to thank my family. My mother, Lily Dobbs Lane, proudly shows off my publications to her friends; my sister, Debra Dobbs Satter, smiles at me with that knowing look. My brother-in-law, N. Douglas Raber, reads what I write and generally approves, which is kind of him. My in-laws, Nevin and Dorothy Raber, never seem satisfied, and always ask about the "next" book before I have time to enjoy recent publication of the current one. Our children, Hannah and Jonathan, each of whom is an adult, try to decide which is worse, my love of history or my love of chess. And, of course, I owe the greatest debt to my wife, Ann, who has always been supportive, encouraging, and helpful – my best friend for the ages.

CHAPTER ONE

THE SITUATION IN 1960-61

On January 20, 1961, John F. Kennedy became the nation's 35th president, and he intended to act firmly in foreign affairs, particularly in the Cold War confrontation with the Soviet Union and the People's Republic of China. As Robert Schulzinger has written, "Harry Truman's containment policy seemed too defensive, Secretary of State John Foster Dulles's 'brinkmanship' too blustery, and Ike's appeals to end the arms race too defeatist for the Democrats who took over in January 1961." Richard Walton three decades ago characterized John Kennedy's foreign policy as "Cold War and Counterrevolution." Thomas Paterson has called it "Kennedy's Quest for Victory."[1]

Kennedy and his advisors perceived a dangerous world in which America had to resist Soviet and Soviet-sponsored aggression. As Kennedy proclaimed in his inaugural address, "Let every nation know, whether it wishes us well or ill, that we shall pay any price, bear any burden, meet any hardship, support any friend, oppose any foe, in order to assure the survival and the success of liberty." The Soviet Union seemingly sought nuclear parity or even supremacy to complement its presumed conventional warfare superiority. The People's Republic of China seemed a threatening, revolutionary state, committed to destroying the existing order in Southeast and East Asia. There were challenges occupying the attention of the new administration: Berlin, Cuba, Laos, tension in the Middle East, on the Indo-Pakistani border, and elsewhere. The stronger rhetoric reflected a more apocalyptic view, and a simplification of complex situations to fit into the world construct of the new administration.

---

[1] Robert D. Schulzinger, *American Diplomacy in the Twentieth Century, Third Edition,* New York, Oxford University Press, 1994, p. 259; Richard J. Walton, *Cold War and Counter Revolution: The Foreign Policy of John F. Kennedy,* New York, Viking Press, 1972; Thomas G. Paterson, Editor, *Kennedy's Quest for Victory: American Foreign Policy, 1961-1963,* New York, Oxford University Press, 1989.

These confrontations overwhelmed other foreign policy matters at the highest levels of the United States government. More importantly, foreign policy considerations had precedence over foreign economic policy considerations, as the Cold War and the Soviet-American and Sino-American rivalries dominated foreign policy formulation and execution. That is, issues from specific areas across the globe and such matters as economic development, trade legislation, and alliances all passed through the prisms of these rivalries and became distorted after such passage.

The Cold War in East Asia still dominated U.S. foreign relations towards the region. The Council on Foreign Relations' annual publication, *The United States in World Affairs, 1961,* reported that "where direct Communist pressure or infiltration was not a major problem, the United States was free to concentrate on its basic policy of assisting the Asian countries in developing their own potentialities and increasing others' long-term ability to resist totalitarian aggression or seduction." As the CFR report noted, the government in Washington applied this policy to non-aligned countries as well as U.S. allies.[2]

Along with the general confrontation with the Soviet Union, the government in Washington viewed the looming presence of the People's Republic of China. The CFR report further noted that "Communist China overshadowed the Soviet Union as a long-term threat to security in Southeast and East Asia." In fact, "there were few countries in this part of the world that had not already felt the diplomatic and military weight of Communist China" and "the Chinese People's Republic would represent an even more potent international force in years to come." National Intelligence Estimate 1-61, "Estimate of the World Situation," found that "during the past two or three years the Chinese Communist regime has been exhibiting a growing self-confidence." Interestingly, "the most striking characteristic of Communist China is not its economic progress but its great revolutionary élan." Thus, the "Chinese Communist drive and sense of mission" appears in its foreign policy outlook. "The Chinese Communists' view of the world situation is extremely doctrinaire" and that "the emerging peoples in Asia, Africa, and Latin America are ripe for Communist revolution, if only they are actively supported to this end." Analyses within and without government largely agreed on the menace that Beijing represented, and whether that view was accurate, it influenced the view of American policymakers towards issues in East Asia.[3]

---

[2] Richard Stebbins, *The United States in World Affairs, 1961,* New York, Council on Foreign Relations, 1962, pp. 207-208.

[3] Stebbins, *Ibid.,* p. 219; DCI, NIE 1-61, Estimate of World Situation, 17 January 1961, www.foia.cia.gov/browse, paragraphs 20, 23, 24.

The regimes in Beijing and Taipei were mutually hostile. The People's Republic remained committed to "ousting the rival Chinese Nationalist government from its American-protected home on the island of Formosa." Taipei, still dominated by Guomindang refugees from mainland China rather than native Taiwanese elites, in turn, criticized "Communist mismanagement, unworkable agricultural policies, and the commune system [which] have brought serious food shortage to the Chinese people." "The Communist regime cannot meet the genuine needs and desires of the Chinese people for economic and social progress."[4]

At times, it seemed the People's Republic of China might attack Nationalist-held islands near the mainland. "Quemoy and the other Nationalist island outposts between Formosa and the mainland were still being subjected to an intermittent Communist bombardment which had been going on ever since 1958." These Nationalist-held islands only eight miles from the Chinese mainland potentially threatened nearby Chinese ports and coastal shipping, and thus remained a constant irritant to the government in Beijing. In 1954-5 and again in 1957-8, mainland artillery shelled the islands bringing a predictable announcement of U.S. support, which may have been Jiang Jieshi's purpose each time in provoking the crises.[5]

Similarly, Jiang Jieshi sought U.S. military support to "liberate" the mainland. *Newsweek* reported "President Chiang still dreams of a return to the mainland" but he realized that "the U.S. represents both their defense against Communist invasion and their only hope of someday regaining the mainland." He and his government regularly informed Washington of problems on the mainland, and sought assurances of American support for a return without which a return was impossible.[6]

Conditions on the mainland were – admittedly – difficult to understand. Since gaining power in 1949 Mao and his leadership group provided little respite and recovery for the Chinese people. War with the United States in Korea, the regaining of Tibet and China's non-Han ethnic border areas cost lives and scarce resources. Then Mao turned to remaking the Chinese people after the "One Hundred Flowers" campaign in 1951-52. Later in the 1950s, Communist cadres reorganized traditional village structures into a series of production teams, brigades, and communes – the collectivization of agriculture; communes had communal kitchens, mess

---

[4] Stebbins, *Documents, 1961,* p. 221; Richard P. Stebbins, Editor, *Documents on American Foreign Relations, 1961,* New York, Harper & Brothers, 1962, pp. 325-6.

[5] Stebbins, *Ibid.,* p. 221.

[6] *Newsweek,* June 20, 1960, pp. 45-6.

halls, and nurseries. Mao sought to destroy traditional family ties and create the new Chinese man and woman. Widespread famine and the deal of untold millions soon followed. Beijing was unwilling to admit the disaster it caused and thus to accept foreign food assistance. Similarly, in "The Great Leap Forward" campaign, Mao promised to catch Great Britain in industrial production by 1962, but "backyard" steel furnaces produced inferior product, which was symptomatic of the entire campaign. The result was overproduction of inferior goods, deterioration of industrial plants, and exhaustion of factory workers and farm laborers. Meanwhile, foreign leaders could not understand why Beijing continued to cause such widespread suffering for its own people.

Nationalist raids only added to the tension and confusion, while doing little to weaken Communist control of China. Jiang Jieshi was utterly committed to the belief that Chinese on the mainland were waiting for him to return so they could overthrow the yoke of communist oppression. He believed that Mao's heavily flawed policies provided conditions for such a successful return, and he regularly sought reassurances of U.S. support. He threatened and sometimes launched small raids against coastal provinces but they achieved little save for the capture and deaths of the intelligence agents dropped into China. In April 1960 the CIA wrote the Defense Department that "the government of the Republic of China plans for paramilitary action;" it proposed to "drop 200 man teams into mainland" and "smaller 20 man teams." Taipei wanted U.S. government support, which Washington carefully avoided any hint of providing. Communist control and perhaps memories of Nationalist corruption combined to frustrate Jiang's hopes to create unrest from within.[7]

Meanwhile, Beijing continued its anti-American rhetoric and showed little interest in improving relations. The Sino-American ambassadorial talks in Warsaw, Poland, one of the few regular exchanges between Beijing and Washington, soon deteriorated into a forum for political attack once the original purpose of facilitating exchanges of prisoners from the Korean conflict was resolved. One observer commented that "the special hostility of Peking toward the United States is primarily a consequence of American support for the large and well-equipped military forces of the Republic of China."[8]

The Korean peninsula remained an armed camp long after the armistice agreement in summer 1953. The peninsula had always fit

---

[7] Department of State, *Foreign Relations of the United States, Volume XIX, China*, Washington, DC, GPO, 1996, Document 330, April 18, 1960, p. 657.

[8] Wayne Ayres Wilcox, *Asia and United States Policy,* Englewood Cliffs, NJ, Prentice-Hall, Inc., 1967, p. 50.

together as an economic whole, and the division near the 38th parallel posted difficult economic challenges as well as the continuing threat of renewed fighting. As Richard Stebbins summarized, "the really critical problem for the United States" was "encouraging development in South Korea of a national life sufficiently vigorous to overcome the country's natural handicaps and enable it to resist either domination from without or subversion from within." Military spending to protect against North Korea distorted economic, social, and political priorities.[9]

Kim Il-song in Pyongyang seemed unpredictable, and perhaps was preparing for another effort to conquer the south. Kim likely was a Korean expatriate from Siberia, a Soviet World War II Red Army veteran who may have fought at Stalingrad, who needed to ensure his nationalist credentials by unifying the peninsula. He had tried once in June 1950, and very nearly had succeeded. Infiltrating guerrilla units into the south and maintaining an army far larger than needed for defense kept the government in Seoul focused on defense matters and not political maturation, economic development, and social cohesion.

At the same time, South Korea lacked effective political and economic systems. By 1960, Syngman Rhee's regime, which had come to power during the American occupation in the late 1940s, was nearing collapse. While he served as a symbol of Korean nationalism in the 1920s and 1930s, Rhee selected his advisors poorly and cronyism and corruption characterized his government. The result was a new government led by Dr. John M. Chang, who campaigned against the corruption and mismanagement in Korean politics and economy. However, senior military officers, while appreciating his commitment to honesty and efficiency, found him insufficiently patriotic and not sufficiently committed to increasing military spending. In September 1961, General Park Chung Hee led a coup that replaced Korea's elected government with a military junta. It seemed a step backward to many outside analysts. During this period, American experts – diplomatic and military – worried about a new outbreak of hostilities perhaps preceded by a guerrilla campaign of destruction and intimidation.

The deteriorating situation in Southeast Asia occupied the new Kennedy Administration. What appeared to be a Hanoi-organized and –led guerrilla campaign threatened the regime of Ngo Dinh Diem in South Vietnam; other guerrillas took advantage of instability in neighboring Laos. The government in Washington believed that Beijing was behind these threats to stability and might topple the remaining mostly weak and

[9] Stebbins, op. cit., pp. 230-1.

developing governments in the region. Perhaps this "red tide" might spill over into Cambodia and Thailand eventually to Malaya [as it was then named] and Indonesia, controlling the shipping bottleneck through the Molucca Straits in that region.

Beginning in 1959, a guerrilla movement increased the tempo of its operations in South Vietnam. For three years after Saigon refused to participate in the nationwide elections which the Geneva Conference established to end the French-Viet Minh conflict, Hanoi appeared to concentrate on securing absolute control over North Vietnam In 1959, the Politburo created three groups to aid the infiltration of men and materiel by land into neighboring Laos, then, with the infiltration route secure, down to Vinh in North Vietnam and along the Laotian and Cambodian borders, the famed Ho Chi Minh Trail into South Vietnam, and finally by sea to the Cambodian port of Sihanoukville to contest Saigon's control of the Mekong Delta. In the next several months, Communist guerrillas engaged in a campaign of assassination in the South Vietnamese countryside.

By the time of the Kennedy inauguration, the insurrection had upset the tempo of life in South Vietnam. *Time* reported "For the first time since 1954, the Reds are operating in bands of more than 50 men. Some are old Red cadres left behind at the time of partition; others are newly infiltrated guerrillas sent down from North Viet Nam through neighboring Laos or Cambodia, or put ashore from small fishing boats in the Gulf of Thailand. Their total strength is now estimated at 3,000 to 5,000 men, concentrated in the swampy Mekong Delta—"a diseased part of the body," one U.S. observer calls it. It is a secret, hushed war of stealth and secrecy." *Time* noted that the guerrillas' "special targets have been civil officials, and in recent months they have managed to murder an average of ten a day."[10]

A Chinese Communist-inspired insurgency appeared about to take over Laos, and the options for American policymakers were equally unattractive. The situation deteriorated seemingly so quickly that Admiral Harry D. Felt, U.S. commander in chief in the Pacific, warned "the Southeast Asian peninsula is a target for Communist China, and Laos is the first point of entry." By summer 1960, news magazines were reporting regularly on the expanding civil war. In late December, *Time* reported that "the fight for Vientiane was the long-postponed showdown between armies of the left and right in Laos. Ever since his coup in August, the city had been controlled by pro-Communist Captain Kong Le with a battalion of paratroops. Much of the rest of the country has remained in the hands of

[10] *Time,* May 2, 1960, "The Sunset War," *Time* on line archive.

pro-U.S. General Phoumi Nosavan, the closest thing Laos has to a strongman." *Time* concluded "the stage was set for trouble." "The spectacle of one pro-Communist captain with a nucleus of only 300 paratroopers standing off a 29,000-man army nurtured and trained by the U.S. was bad enough." "The government of Premier Boun Oum was even talking of moving south out of Vientiane, which was won from Kong Le just last month." *Time* concluded that "about all that the new U.S. administration could initially offer on Laos was a new look by new men" and that "Laos offered the unattractive choice between a difficult peace and an impossible war."[11]

The hostilities in Laos and South Vietnam affected America's ally, Thailand. The Thai leader, [former field marshal turned premier] Sarit Thanarat, regularly expressed his concern. During the Second World War, Thailand had warred briefly with Cambodia, and was interested in reversing the centuries-long expansion of the Vietnamese state from the Red River delta, down the coastline into the Mekong delta and then westwards into Cambodia. Fear of communist subversion combined with a long-standing Vietnamese-Thai rivalry to define Bangkok's foreign policy and its need for reassurances of U.S. support. As Sarit told reporters, "Thailand is the pivot of the free-world alliance in Asia. If one of our neighbors becomes dominated by Communists, rocket bases will be an absolute necessity." He later noted "We are prepared to meet steel with steel anytime."[12]

Kennedy made this region the test case for new theories of nation-building and warfare. Kennedy had decried the policies of the Eisenhower years, especially the reliance on massive retaliation which appeared to concede the military initiative to the Soviet bloc. There was an implicit criticism of the longstanding containment policy since it was both passive and defensive. Kennedy was enthralled with the U.S. Army's Special Forces and the tactical opportunities presented by combat helicopters and other new technologies. He favored meeting insurgencies more directly, and was more willing to expend America's military strength – and Vietnam became [perhaps] the [unintended] test case.

Meanwhile, there were communist guerrilla operations of varying effectiveness in the Philippines, Malaya, and Indonesia. While not in any direct line of fire, other governments in Southeast Asia had their respective insurgencies and threats to confront. Waves of imperialism over the centuries had divided the Philippines into primarily Catholic [and Spanish-

[11] *Time,* June 6, 1960, "Red Alert;" December 26, 1960, "Battle for Vientiane;" and January 27, 1961, "Unattractive Choice," all *Time* on line archive.
[12] *Time,* August 1, 1960, "Pivot—with Rockets," *Time* on line archive.

speaking] northern islands and mostly Moslem peoples in the south. That helped define the challenge the government in Manila in northernmost Luzon faced in asserting control over distant southern islands. Malaya had been the site of *the* great anti-guerrilla success – Sir Robert Thompson's effort beginning in the late 1940s – but that reflected tension between majority Malays and minority ethnic Chinese, a tension that would be both eased and exacerbated as Singapore joined and broke with the larger Malay state. Indonesia, in some ways, consisted of Java dominating other islands in a Republic stretching across 3,000 miles of water, while the government in Jakarta argued with The Netherlands about West Irian, the Portuguese about Timor, and its neighbors over Sabah on the island of Borneo.

It was easy though largely mistaken to see the People's Republic behind each of these challenges to the existing order. Beijing called for revolution to overthrow what it viewed as a U.S.-inspired, capitalist encirclement that continued colonialism and imperialism in new guises. In the same way the Beijing likely viewed the world through the prism of its rather rigid ideology, the new administration in Washington also understood a complicated and complex region of the world through the prism of the Chinese threat to regional stability rather than the stresses and tensions that reflected centuries of history, development, war, and other factors.

As the Cold War in Asia seemingly moved from conventional to guerrilla – i.e., asymmetrical – conflict, there was the continuing challenge of constructing a stable world economy, ensuring a prosperous American economy, and strengthening the economies and polities of nations in eastern Asia. When the Second World War ended in 1945, the United States held 45% of the world's diminished productive capacity. The Marshall Plan helped revive Western Europe and Japan and helped Canada to adjust to Britain's decline as the central point for the Commonwealth's economy. But the revival and growth of what had been pre-Second World War industrial states posed new challenges. U.S. trade policies had given preferences of various sorts to trading partners to assist their recovery; that is, while trading partners erected barriers – both formal and informal – to American exports, the government in Washington largely allowed imports to enter unhindered. By 1961, American producers were complaining about these unfair advantages at home and abroad, and calling for action to equalize tariff and trade barriers. Meanwhile there were regions with weak economies and large numbers of impoverished citizens in Latin America, newly independent sub-Saharan Africa, and Southeast Asia seemingly ripe for Communist subversion. There was great need for a complex balancing act between foreign policy and foreign economic policy and the needs of the domestic U.S. economy and needs of developing regimes in East and Southeast Asia.

American policymakers concentrated on GATT [General Agreement on Tariffs and Trade], the World Bank, and the International Monetary Fund, with a view towards trade with Europe and foreign aid for Third World nations, including some in southeastern and eastern Asia. NIE 1-61, "Estimate of the World Situation," concluded that "the harmonization of economic policies among the industrial nations of Western Europe, and of these policies with those of the US, will be a major problem of the forthcoming decade." However, "Western European economies are booming" and "Japan enjoys a flourishing economy, but is passing through profound political and social changes."[13].

The United States faced a troubling balance of payments deficit, a narrowing balance of trade surplus, and foreign tariff and trade barriers that constrained growth in the U.S. economy. The balance of payments deficit reflected the narrow trade surplus and transfers of U.S. funds abroad. The trade surplus narrowed as other nations produced goods including textiles, electronic gadgets, and automobiles that Americans wanted while their foreign counterparts either did not want American goods or trade barriers made such goods uneconomic.

America's balance of trade surplus continued to narrow. In April 1960, *Time* quoted James Chapman, president of the American Cotton Manufacturers Institute, that "no industry in America is safe from damage by foreign goods." An increasing number of companies were "asking the government to check foreign competition." "Many US industries complain that foreign nations are moving far too slowly to ease trade barriers." One of the real challenges was imports produced in US-owned overseas plants competing with production at home. *Time,* in late June 1960, reported that "Chambers of Commerce often consider it downright 'disloyal'; unions complain that it 'exports' US jobs." *Newsweek* in October 1960 focused on the US international trade position and reported that "with Western Europe and Japan booming, American industry is finding itself matched in many of its time-tested skills and outmatched in more and more markets by aggressive, talented foreign competitors."[14]

---

[13] DCI, NIE 1-61, Estimate of World Situation, 17 January 1961, www.foia.cia.gov/browse, paragraphs 13, 11.

[14] *Time,* April 18, 1960, "A Rise in Imports," and June 27, 1960, "Business Goes Abroad to Sell in the U.S., *Time* on-line archive; *Newsweek,* October 17, 1960,

The automobile industry seemed symptomatic of the challenges. In mid-April 1960, "for the first time in history, the US auto industry went to the government to complain about foreign tariffs." Earlier, in February 1960, *Newsweek* noted the rise of compact cars, calling them "a revolution in the auto business." Two months later, the news weekly noted the Fourth International Auto Show and that "six spanking-new American-made compact cars will be lined up grille to grille against entries from nine countries around the world." Two months later, *Newsweek* reported that "foreign automakers pranced off with 12.7 per cent of the U.S. new-car market last December . . . a whopping 61 per cent increase over 1958." *Newsweek* believed that US automakers were responding with competitive compact cars that would sell at home and abroad and in October it noted the Detroit annual auto show and that "all the new entries are carefully tuned for the hot sales battle among themselves and against the imports." The fear was European automobile exports, for the beginning of the great wave of Japanese car exports was just over the horizon.[15]

A balance of payments deficit was equally difficult to reverse. There were a series of factors. As *Time* magazine reported in early November 1960, the chief reason for the increase in the deficit was "a flood of uneasy dollars that are always seeking the highest interest rates around the world." Add to the outflow of investment dollars were expenditures on troops and dependents overseas, foreign economic assistance, foreign military assistance, and more American tourists traveling abroad than foreign tourists visiting America. The Eisenhower administration had tried various measures, including limiting financial support for overseas dependents, encouraging tourism to America, and urging that U.S. companies invest their surplus funds at home – but to little avail.[16]

The result was real and continuing pressure on the U.S. dollar and U.S. gold reserves. *Time* in late November reported that Treasury Secretary Robert Anderson and Defense Secretary Thomas Gates interrupted President Eisenhower's vacation to discuss "the U.S.'s nagging deficit in international payments and the resulting drain on U.S. gold reserves, eroding international confidence in the soundness of the dollar." The issue was "the dollar's ability to go on serving as the free world's basic

---

"The U.S. in the World Market," pp. 92-94 and November 28, 1960, "Our Salesmen Overseas," pp. 72-73.

[15] *Time,* April 18, 1960, "A Rise in Imports," *Time* on-line archive; *Newsweek,* February 8, 1960, pp. 81-82; April 18, 1960, pp. 99-101; June 27, 1960, p. 78; October 10, 1960, p. 86.

[16] *Time,* November 7, 1960, "U.S. Allies Must Help Solve It," *Time* on-line archive.

currency, a state of affairs on which, as the allies well knew, the health of their own booming economies depended." Even Soviet leaders worried about the dollar, and changed the valuation of the ruble to gold to help stabilize the U.S. currency. *Time* worried about the flight of gold, and quoted David Rockefeller of Chase Manhattan Bank who said it was "perhaps the most serious international economic problem this country faces." *Newsweek* quoted Raymond Cartier writing in *Paris-Match* after the U.S. presidential election that "please, Mr. Kennedy, save the dollar."[17]

Some of the most reasonable prescriptions to meet America's economic woes would have spelled disaster to developing world economies. The government in Washington faced a dilemma: was it more important to support Free World and developing world economies to help them resist the lure of communism or to maintain the strength of the American economy and the soundness of the U.S. dollar. As the 1960s wore on, the dilemma would become increasingly stark.

Castro had seized power in Cuba and soon thereafter aligned his regime with the Soviet bloc. In early January 1960, *Time* reported that "only seven months after its creation," Castro's dictatorship had taken control of the economy, authorized expropriation of large land holdings, and had begun to focus on private business. Two months later *Time* worried about "Russia's deepest penetration of the Hemisphere" – a broad trade-and-aid agreement with Cuba. In June, *Time* reported on "The Marxist Neighbor," and noted that "the jargon in Castro's speeches and in his captive press these days is increasingly Marxist." It also drew attention to the "herding of Cubans" into mass institutions – militias, cooperatives, government youth groups, and labor unions. By mid-October, *Time* noted that "Fidel Castro last week placed his country on the Soviet side."[18]

Besides direct [and sometimes comical] anti-Castro measures, the U.S. government worried over Latin America economic growth, eventually announcing the Alliance for Progress. As John Kennedy became President, senior aide Walt Rostow was gathering information about Third World

---

[17] *Time,* November 28, 1960, "End of an Easygoing Era," and November 28, 1960, "Redressing the Balance," September 26, 1960, "The Flight of Gold," *Time* on-line archive and *Newsweek,* December 5, 1960, pp. 48-49. See also, Francis J. Gavin, "The Gold Battles within the Cold War: American Monetary Policy and the Defense of Europe, 1960-1963," *Diplomatic History, Vol. 26, No. 1, Winter 2002,* pp. 61-94.

[18] *Time,* January 4, 1960, "Animal Farm;" February 29, 1960, "What Should the U.S. Do;" June 20, 1960, "The Marxist Neighbor;" October 10, 1960, "Red All the Way;" *Time* on-line archive.

economies, and making plans to help improve economic performance. Kennedy made clear the American commitment in his inaugural address: "to our sister republics south of our border, we offer a special pledge to convert our good words into good deeds in a new alliance for progress to assist free men and free governments in casting off the chains of poverty." Making clear the relationship between this commitment and Castro's communist regime in Cuba, Kennedy continued "but this peaceful revolution of hope cannot become the prey of hostile powers." A month later, Kennedy formally announced the Alliance for Progress in an article he authored for *Life en Español*. Sadly the flawed and failed Bay of Pigs invasion in April undid whatever good will the mere announcement of an economic assistance plan generated.[19]

Washington also worried about the future of Africa. The high tide of European colonialism on the continent was rapidly retreating, and Africa's crushing poverty and economic inequities made the continent ripe for Communist penetration. Time magazine reported on efforts in Mauritania, with World Bank financial support, to develop its iron ore reserves to finance economic development. But there were concerns elsewhere. Again, *Time* reported that, in the aftermath of the French withdrawal from Guinea, the capital, Conraky, "was rife with tension." *Time* claimed the Guinean leader was communist leaning, charging that Sékou Touré was fast becoming the captive of those who tilted toward Moscow. Meanwhile, the Republic of Congo, Mali, Senegal, Sudan, Somalia, and Malagasy Republic all gained their independence. United Nations officials pointed out that, "in the next [UN] General Assembly, the African-Asian group will be the U.N.'s largest single voting bloc."[20]

And, not unnaturally, official Washington looked eastward across the Indian Ocean to Asia, where the prospects were less sanguine. *The New York Times* reported in November 1960 that the annual report of the Colombo Plan contained "numerous continuing economic problems of the under-developed countries of Asia." In Indonesia, for example, in 1959 a National Intelligence Estimate concluded that "the situation holds little prospect for stability and progress." The intelligence analysis also noted that "the economic deterioration of Indonesia continues," relations with the Dutch will remain near the breaking point," but "relations with most of

---

[19] *Time,* January 27, 1961, "Excerpts from President Kennedy's inaugural address," February 24, 1961, "Alliance for Progress," March 17, 1961, "Two Views South," and May 5, 1961, "The Shock Wears On," *Time* on-line archive.

[20] *Time,* April 18, 1960, "Hope in the Desert," June 6, 1960, "Coffins & Broken Backs," July 11, 1960, "For History and Pride," and July 18, 1960, "First Among Equals," *Time,* on-line archive.

the Communist bloc will probably remain cordial." Several months later, a report from the Embassy in Jakarta noted "the political atmosphere is probably more tense than at any time since early 1958."[21]

Matters improved little as Eisenhower's presidency drew to a close. A Special National Intelligence Estimate concluded that "political power in Indonesia has become increasingly polarized between the Army and the Indonesian Communist Party. The economy is in a sad state and popular discontent, particularly in urban areas, is increasing." By October, the State Department informed President Eisenhower that it had a "number of disquieting reports which suggest that the Indonesian government believes that the United States does not wish true independence for Indonesia since the United States fears that Indonesia would then adversely influence our SEATO allies and since a strong Indonesia might stifle United States economic interests in that country." Thus, in mid-December, a National Security Council Report concluded that "the chief danger confronting US policy with regard to Indonesia is that a combination of domestic instability, burgeoning Sino-Soviet bloc economic and military aid, and substantial local Communist strength may lead to a Communist takeover or to a policy increasingly friendly toward the Sino-Soviet bloc."[22]

America's former colony, the Philippines, also suffered from a weak economy, government inefficiency and corruption, and political instability. As an embassy report, "Comprehensive Economic Assessment of the Philippines," commented, "no progress has been made toward eliminating the graft ridden and uneconomic system of imports and exchange controls." Another report warned that "with the Philippine economy undergoing steady diversification, the United States remains a major trading partner ... therefore any major change in the U.S. economic situation or policy would affect the Philippines."[23]

---

[21] *The New York Times,* November 18, 1960, p. 3; Department of State, *Foreign Relations of the United States, 1958-1960, Volume XVII, Indonesia,* Washington, DC, GPO, 1994, Document 234, NIE 65-2-59, December 8, 1959, pp. 456-457; Document 246, March 29, 1960, p. 474.

[22] *FRUS, 1958-1960, Volume XVII,* Document 252, SNIE 65-60, May 3, 1960, p. 482; Document 285, Acting Secretary of State C. Douglas Dillon to President Eisenhower, October 5, 1960, p. 553; Document 293, NSC 6023, December 19, 1960, p. 571.

[23] Department of State, *Foreign Relations of the United States, 1958-1960, Volume XV, South and Southeast Asia,* Washington, DC, GPO, 1992, Document 449, Embassy to State Department, March 11, 1960, p. 958; Document 456, Embassy to State Department, December 24, 1960, p. 975.

Thailand was a more interesting situation. The Operations Coordinating Board in Washington concluded that "Thailand is the hub of U.S. security efforts in Southeast Asia;" it recommended that U.S. policy should seek to establish a stable, representative government, a strong and healthy economy, and a society all ready to resist communist subversion. But, a month later, the Bureau of Intelligence and Research informed Secretary Christian Herter that the Thai government leaders were generally "resentful over what they have considered shabby treatment of Thailand in apportionment of U.S. economic aid." They were particularly upset with "the commitment by the United States to supply very large quantities of wheat and rice to India which will cut into Thailand's own market for its predominant export earner, rice." This small crisis illustrated a larger challenge for the U.S. government, for actions to assist economic development in one country might very well negatively affect the economy in another. Nonetheless, Thai leaders were committed to economic development. *The New York Times* gushed in January 1960 that "the year 1959 may be remembered as the year the dam broke and Thailand started on her long-delayed march to becoming a modern economic state." By May 1960, World Bank officials evaluated Thailand's finances and currency as "in a strong and sound condition" and found "the economy of the country is active and growing."[24]

Governments in Taiwan and Korea focused on military preparedness, and assumed the government in Washington would provide economic assistance as needed. The American embassy in Taipei wrote the State Department in late December 1959 that it had spoken with Republic of China officials "of the U.S. interest of embarking on an accelerated development program in Taiwan." Embassy officials invited the Republic of China "to submit proposals." They wanted to "encourage the GRC [Government of the Republic of China] to take positive action for constructive economic, fiscal policy and provide foreign exchange necessary to support growth." The next year Taipei accepted the need to focus on economic self-strengthening, and committed itself "to live without United States economic aid by the end of 1964."[25]

---

[24] *FRUS, 1958-1960, Volume XV,* Document 548, Report Prepared by the Operations Coordinating Board, Undated, pp. 1118-1119; Document 549, Deputy Director of the Bureau of Intelligence and Research to the Acting Secretary of State, May 13, 1960, p. 1130; *The New York Times,* January 12, 1960, p. 57; May 24, 1960, p. 53.

[25] *FRUS, 1958-1960, Volume XIX,* Document 323, Embassy Taipei to State Department, December 31, 1959, pp. 643-644; *The New York, Times,* June 19, 1960, p. 21.

American pressure bore fruit. Taipei produced a plan in 1960 that if successful would "enable Taiwan to live without United States economic aid by the end of 1964." Since the economy had been expanding for some years, the key, "though not openly admitted, is a de-emphasis of the armed forces." Jiang was changing his thinking to hope that a prosperous Taiwan would contrast with the hardships on the mainland and thus create popular hope for a Nationalist return.[26]

South Korea faced even greater challenges than Nationalist China. A National Intelligence Estimate concluded that "the major, long-term problem confronting the ROK [Republic of Korea] is and will remain the poverty of its economy. In fact, because of the paucity of basic resources in its territory, the military burden, and the division of the country, the ROK is not able to achieve a self-supporting economy in the foreseeable future." The report concluded that the ROK "will almost certainly continue to require large-scale foreign aid." The South Korean government agreed, and indicated it would "seek President Eisenhower's support in solving its critical problems – including questions of unification and economic and military aid – during his twenty-eight hour visit."[27]

The government in Seoul was not entirely blameless. A Congressional staff report criticized South Korea's monetary and trade policies, claiming they "are blocking economic recovery." The report further noted that "South Korea's monetary exchange rate and its refusal to trade with Japan were offsetting the economic aid being given by the United States." At about the same time, *The New York Times* reported the Korean cabinet rejected a US proposal for a joint budget study plan. Cabinet members claimed the proposal "constituted intervention by the United States in Korea's domestic affairs." Still, by summer 1960, the Seoul government announced a program to stabilize the national economy.[28]

Another challenge was economies largely based on natural resources, resource extraction, and changing trading relationships as the former colonial powers continued to recede. European colonial empires treated colonies as sources of raw materials and consumers of the finished goods of the mother country. Even though the high tide of colonialism had largely receded in Southeast and East Asia, the nature of the economies of

---

[26] *The New York Times,* April 3, 1960, p. 19.

[27] *FRUS, 1958-1960, Volume XIX,* Document 333, NIE 42.1-2-60, November 22, 1960, "Prospects for ROK," p. 697.

[28] Department of State, *Foreign Relations of the United States, Volume XVIII, Japan; Korea,* Washington, DC, GPO, 1994, Document 333, NIE 42.1-2-60, November 22, 1960, "Prospects for ROK," p, 697; *The New York Times,* July 9, 1960, p. 4; July 7, 1960, p. 6; May 6, 1960, p. 5.

these former colonies and dependencies had not yet changed to greater self-sufficiency and to interregional trade and cooperation.

Japan was the linchpin. As the European colonial empires retreated around the world, many newly independent and developing nations needed new trading partners and trade patterns, access to manufactured goods, economic assistance, and manufacturing and other advice. Japan's effort during the Second World War – the Greater East Asia Co-Prosperity Sphere – remained a hot button issue to many nations in the region, but Japan was a key to any U.S.-led effort to strengthen regional economies and thereby polities and societies to resist pressure from or the lure of the People's Republic of China. Moreover, Japan was setting a rather remarkable example – truly a phoenix risen from the ashes of the utter destruction symbolized by the aftermath of the fire bombings of most major Japanese cities and the atomic bombings of Hiroshima and Nagasaki.

By 1960, Japan was astounding its neighbors and the industrialized nations elsewhere. In June 1960, *Newsweek* reported on "Japan Today – the Paradox." Reporter Rafael Steinberg found a country somewhat free "of the old restraints, disciplines, and rituals" and thus with "a gaping void." "The struggle between old and new, western and Oriental," Steinberg noted, "permeates the daily life of almost every Japanese."[29]

A dramatically expanding economy seemed to provide the bedrock for a stable political and social system. A dramatic strike against Nissan in the early 1950s led to the rise of company unions, lifetime employment in large firms, and adoption of manufacturing theories of such individuals as W. Edward Deming, including "just-in-time" manufacturing, an emphasis on quality and eliminating defects, and lean production techniques. This led to near double digit increases annually in the Gross National Product and a "growing export stream." *Newsweek* reported in January 1960 that "Japan was booming as never before." Steel manufacturing had increased, exports had jumped, and "for the first time in its history, Japan had become a creditor instead of a debtor nation." To continue to expand, Japan needed access to the US economy, and this of course resulted in a dilemma for US officials. In 1960, Japan exported textiles, electronics, cameras, large cargo ships, and toys and its success threatened competing American industries. Japan faced increasing calls in the United States for

---

[29] *Newsweek,* June 20, 1960, pp. 51-56.

higher tariff barriers and import restrictions; in Southeast Asia, it faced demands for foreign aid based on war reparations and war guilt.[30]

The riots accompanying the forced renewal of the U.S.-Japan mutual security treaty surprised many foreign observers. The 1951 treaty had a ten year term, and negotiators had seemingly completed a new treaty for ratification in 1960 to begin the next year. While the treaty reduced U.S. rights in Japan, it also kept Japan firmly within the U.S. security system in East Asia. For many Japanese, the treaty forced Japan between the two superpowers, and perhaps could "drag Japan into someone else's war." For more than a week there was rioting in Tokyo and as the time for the Japanese Parliament – the Diet – to ratify the treaty neared, some 300,000 demonstrators gathered in Tokyo. Japanese Prime Minister Nobusuke Kishi forced the treaty through the Diet dominated by members of his Liberal-Democratic Party and the riots became more violent. As *Newsweek* commented, "On June 19 President Eisenhower arrives in Tokyo. If the treaty is still not ratified by that date, Kishi would lose a lot of face." Foreign commentators realized the treaty opposition more reflected internal politics than latent anti-Americanism. *Newsweek* called it "a domestic row between Prime Minister Nobusuke Kishi's conservative-minded Liberal-Democrats and the Opposition Socialists." The power play upset many in Japan who complained of "Kishi's ramming tactics." *Time* stated "Japan was facing its biggest political crisis since the war."[31]

It also led to cancellation of President Dwight Eisenhower's cherished plans for a state visit to Japan. In the end, an embarrassed Kishi had to ask Eisenhower to cancel the visit owing to "security concerns." *Newsweek* had called Eisenhower's trip a "risky journey to the east," and once the visit to Japan [part of a five nation state visit] was cancelled, *Newsweek* titled its report "The debris of a mission." Student rioters chanted "We won! We won!" Editorialist Ernest Lindly called it "the lessons of Japan" and noted "Japan's prestige has suffered a blow," and the "United States cannot let Japan retreat to pacifism or let less advanced nations of Asia not trade with Japan."[32]

---

[30] *Newsweek,* January 25, 1960, "Growing Export Steam," pp. 72-73; January 25, 1960, "Friendly, Savvy Salesman from Japan," pp. 39-40.

[31] *Newsweek,* June 27, 1960, p. 25; May 9, 1960, pp. 43-44; *Time,* "Delaying Tactics," May 9, 1960, *Time* online archive *Newsweek,* May 30, 1960, p. 44; *Time,* June 6, 1960, "The Anti-Kishi Riots," *Time* online archive.

[32] *Newsweek,* June 13, 1960, pp. 27-29; June 23, 1960, pp. 23-30; *Time,* "The Expendable Premier," June 27, 1960, and June 6, 1960, "The Anti-Kishi Riots," *Time* online archive; *Newsweek,* June 23, 1960, p. 36.

But growth was not without tension. During an official visit to Washington, Japanese Prime Minister Nobusuke Kishi told President Dwight Eisenhower, commenting on "the rapid improvement in Japan's balance of payments with the United States," that "Japan is doing everything possible to assure orderly marketing and to exercise self-restraint and control in its exports to the United States." In turn, Kishi hoped the United States would appreciate Japan's efforts to "contribute to a healthy growth of bilateral trade with the United States." In October, the Commerce Department asked Japan "to move speedily toward a general lifting of restrictions on United States products."[33]

Yet the United States could not press Japan too hard to change. National Intelligence Estimate 41-60 concluded "Japan's continued dependence upon US for defense and on non-Communist world for trade will continue to be a powerful deterrent to any significant shift in Japanese foreign policy." A subsequent National Security Council Report stated that "Japan's dramatic recovery emphasizes its importance to US and Free World" and that "Japan has one of the fastest rates of economic growth in the world, enjoying unprecedented prosperity with new highs in nearly all sectors of the economy."[34]

As John Kennedy and his foreign policy and foreign economic policy teams assumed office in January 1961, they faced challenges in East Asia. The Soviet Union and Cold War issues that dominated discussions about Europe appeared distant and generally irrelevant. The People's Republic of China was a looming presence, though, to be sure, momentarily a stumbling rather than a sleeping giant. The economies of Southeast Asia were weak, and perhaps susceptible to communist subversion. Japan had enjoyed a spectacular decade of development, spurned initially by U.S. spending there during the Korean War and afterwards by the reorganization of the Japanese economy and enforcement of labor peace after the Nissan strike early in the decade. Still, Japan needed exports to expand its economy and either the United States had to grant its ally preferential access or it had to strengthen regional economies to absorb surplus Japanese production.

It was reasonable for the new Kennedy teams to conclude the challenges were great. In January 1961, the futures of the Republic of

---

[33] *FRUS, Volume XVIII,* Document 139, Memorandum of Conversation, January 19, 1960, pp. 268-9; *The New York Times,* October 7, 1960, p. 49.

[34] *FRUS, Volume XVIII,* Document 150, NIE 41-60, "Probable Development in Japan," February 9, 1960, pp. 286-287; Document 175, NSC Report 6008/1, "US Policy Toward Japan," June 11, 1960.

Korea and the Republic of China were not clear. Insurgencies in Laos and South Vietnam threatened Southeast Asian stability. Governments in Kuala Lumpur, Manila, and Jakarta still had to secure the allegiance of far flung populations while learning to co-exist with one another amidst all the island chains in the Southwest Pacific. Sadly, Beijing had no more knowledge of what motivated the government in Washington than Washington had of the government in Beijing.

The issues were remarkably complex, and the Kennedy foreign policy teams had little prior knowledge of the area or of its complexities. Regional leaders in time would learn how to manipulate symbols and values to produce desired American decisions. For men in senior policy positions in 1961, they had attended college and matured in an era of declining European colonialism and they still used that prism to understand many issues. For example, they regularly – and likely more comfortably – consulted with foreign European colonial powers [and current U.S. allies] than the new and somewhat impatient leaders in Asia. But European colonialism was a shell superimposed onto the continuing realities of the region – neither relevant nor irrelevant, just a shell.

Walt Rostow, a Kennedy advisor, had great influence over economic development issues. Years earlier, Rostow, an economic historian, had authored *The Process of Economic Growth* [1952] and during the remainder of the 1950s had written about Free World, Communist, and Third World economic development. He exported his theories and his understanding of economic development to Kennedy Administration policy planning around the world. Differences in topography, natural resources, populations and other variables made such exporting difficult. But Rostow was influential, along with diplomats of the former colonial powers, and corporate executives active in the region.[35]

One other basic tenet was the so-called domino theory. In many ways it was a poor choice of words, because it implied a more immediate action than theory proponents meant. That is, we all have seen someone take hours and hours to line up hundreds and thousands of dominoes and then topple the first one and within minutes all of the dominoes have fallen. Theory proponents, and this included most governments in the region, believed that absent a strong U.S. presence, one by one the countries of the region would over time succumb to the pressure, lure, and presence of the People's Republic of China – a slow acting series of dominoes. But the outcome, if one accepted the theory and most Southeast and East Asian

---

[35] Rostow, Walt W. *The Process of Economic Growth,* New York, W.W. Norton & Co., 1952.

leaders did, would be the same – a Communist leaning, critical region of the world.

China was the eight hundred pound gorilla on the sidelines of virtually every conversation about East Asia. Complicating such conversations was the continuing retreat of European colonial empires. In 1961, emerging polities and weak economies susceptible to internal unrest and external pressures characterized most countries in Southeast and East Asia. Isolation of China seemed to be a tenet of U.S. foreign policy.

Most governments in the region perceived the government in Beijing as the common factor behind most of the challenges in the region. South Korea not unnaturally worried about a re-starting of fighting on the peninsula as well as continuing guerrilla subversion; the government in Seoul believed that Kim Il-song in North Korea would not attack or ramp up the guerrilla effort without support from Beijing and Moscow. Jiang Jieshi on Taiwan worried that the United Nations would choose either to recognize the government in Beijing as part of a "two Chinas" arrangement or, worse, to substitute that government for his in China's UN "seat." Japan was concerned about Chinese aggression but also wanted some level of government contact to increase Sino-Japanese trade. Governments in Southeast Asia confronted internal security threats of varying severity and believed that Beijing offered leaders of those movements financial and military support as well as advice and guidance. And there was always concern, likely unfounded, about the loyalty of the substantial Chinese ethnic minority populations in these countries.

This view particularly affected the common wisdom concerning the worsening conflict in South Vietnam. Although the government in Hanoi made the decision in 1959 to recommence the effort to conquer the south, and it sent men and material southward by land and sea, governments in the region and the government in Washington believed that Hanoi looked to Beijing for support and advice, and that Beijing was a key to containing North Vietnam's expanding aggression. If Beijing was the driving force behind Hanoi's aggression, where would the Chinese agree to a halt? Along with the situation in South Vietnam, there was the conflict in Laos, where a Communist insurgency clearly received support from Hanoi and likely from Beijing.

Most nearby governments accepted a modified domino theory, seeing themselves, in the worst case, in the long term grip of the People's Republic of China. Again, as noted in the previous chapter, they did not believe that they would topple immediately, the standard image of a line of dominoes, but over time, the pressure from China would overwhelm their capacity to resist falling into the Chinese sphere of control unless the

United States provided a resolute shield behind which they could strengthen their polities and economies.

The issue of Chinese representation in the United Nations forced consideration of relations with the government in Beijing. Chinese Nationalist leader, Jiang Jieshi, worried about U.S. support for a "two Chinas" policy at the UN. He needed regular reassurance of US support for his government as the government of all China. Ambassador Everett Drumright in the embassy in Taipei in mid-March 1961 reported that "GRC authorities are deeply disturbed because they consider new administration has not come out unreservedly in support of GRC on the [Chinese representative] issue." They fear the U.S. government is "prepared to toss in [the] towel." Again, in mid-May, a joint communiqué stated "the United States has no intention of recognizing the Peiping regime" and "opposes seating the Peiping regime at the United Nations." For example, in June 1961, Secretary of State Dean Rusk cabled the U.S. embassy in Taipei to inform Jiang that "Department [is] distressed by evident misunderstanding [of] United States policy and suspicions [of] United States motives," and that the "United States has no intention of forcing GRC [Government of the Republic of China] into "two Chinas" or any other arrangement, nor do we want seating of Communist China in United Nations. Rusk did indicate that the "United States must retain freedom and flexibility to make decisions in interests of our own and free world security." President John Kennedy had to write Jiang in mid-July 1961, again to reassure him and followed up in a meeting with Taiwan Vice President, General Ch'en Ch'eng on July 31, 1961, noting that if Beijing gained admission to the United Nations, it "would be a very damaging blow to United States prestige."[36]

Other governments were more conflicted. On the one hand they questioned the logic of denying the existence of a government clearly

[36] Taipei, #571, to Secretary of State, March 20, 1961, China Cables, 2-8/61, National Security Files, Box 25, John F. Kennedy Library; Document #463, May 15, 1961, China, General, 8/1/61-8/23/61, NSF Files, Box 22, JFK Library; Rusk to American Embassy Taipei, #715, June 30, 1961, "China, Cables, 2-8/61," NSF, Box 25, JFK Library; Memorandum for McGeorge Bundy, July 14, 1961, China, General, 7/8/61-7/14/61, NSF Files, Box 22, JFK Library; Memorandum of Conversation, August 10, 1961, China, General, 8/1-10/61, NSF, Box 22, JFK Library. For more examples of the time devoted to the Chinese recognition issue in 1961 alone, see Department of State, *Foreign Relations of the United States, 1961-1963, Volume XXII, Northeast Asia,* Washington, DC, GPO, 1996, pp. 1-175, *passim.*

ruling more than six hundred million people, yet they were unwilling to recognize the PRC or deal with it owing to Beijing's revolutionary rhetoric and rejection of the status quo. India found itself in an unwanted rivalry with China, and was "hostile to China's efforts to extend her influence to Laos, Cambodia, Burma, Malaya, and Indonesia, all states which India has firm cultural ties."[37]

Beijing rejected the "two-Chinas" formula before Washington considered supporting it. Communist leaders viewed Taiwan as an integral part of a China they controlled; they accepted that they could not cross the Straits to force a violent resolution of the still unfinished Civil War, but they did not accept the independence of any government located in Taipei. They forced most governments considering recognition of their regime to sever relations with Jiang's government. The matter arose regularly, including President Kennedy's meeting with Soviet Premier Nikita Khrushchev in Vienna and in meetings with various Allied leaders.[38]

Complicating the issue was the continuing retreat of European colonial regimes, especially in sub-Saharan Africa. In the 1960s, such new nations as Togo, Mali, Senegal, the Congo, Niger, Chad, and the Cote d'Ivoire, Nigeria, and Sierra Leone joined Egypt, Libya, Morocco, Tunisia, and Ghana as independent nations and members of the United Nations. Leaders of these new nations frequently had great sympathy for the leaders of the PRC. Some viewed Jiang as an American puppet while they respected the long revolutionary conflict that resulted in the overwhelming victory of Mao and his fellow Communists in 1949. Given the problems these leaders faced, they were willing to trade votes, in a way, for economic and military assistance and advice.

During the 1960 campaign, Kennedy advisors considered "the China problem." They believed that the independence movement in Africa would tip the balance on the China recognition issue. They considered strategies to moderate Beijing's behavior, as they saw it, yet they wanted to maintain a strong front if China refused to tone down its rhetoric and its support for

---

[37] *The New York Times,* "India vs. China in Southeast Asia," November 26, 1961, p. E4.

[38] Robert Komer on the National Security Council Staff wrote McGeorge Bundy to suggest the "two Chinas" policy for the China UN seat it might "make Peiping refuse UN membership, thus gaining us credit for being reasonable while shifting onus to intransigent CFR. See *FRUS, 1961-1963, Vol. XXII,* Document 9, March 3, 1961, pp. 20-22, Document 13, March 14, 1961, pp. 28-30; Document 18, April 5, 1961, pp. 42-44; Document 29, Editorial Note, pp. 70-72 [the Kennedy-Khrushchev talks] for examples of discussions of the two Chinas issue with world leaders.

violent, revolutionary change. They also believed that issues were related, and that weakness in some confrontation with China might cause the Soviet Union to expect weakness over Berlin, for example.

Kennedy seemed unwilling to revisit China policy. John F. Kennedy told key advisors that he would postpone efforts to improve relations with the People's Republic until a second term. His razor-thin popular vote margin over Richard Nixon gave him little political capital. His predecessor, Dwight Eisenhower, told him at a meeting on January 19, 1961, the day prior to inauguration, that he, Eisenhower, would support his successor in foreign policy save for a change in policy towards China. Given these constraints, Kennedy met with his new Secretary of State, Dean Rusk, and warned that "I don't want to read in *The Washington Post* or *The New York Times* that the State Department is thinking about a change in our China policy!" Rusk, ever the loyal subordinate, took the blame from many State Department diplomats for intransigence and stubbornness when he was only following the orders of his president. Rusk believed that reaching out to China might please the Democratic Party's liberal constituency but do little to affect Beijing's policy toward Washington, and it would dishearten America's allies in the region. Or, as Rusk concluded in his memoirs, "the Chinese Communists didn't seem interested in improving U.S.-Chinese relations." Walt W. Rostow, head of the Policy Planning Staff in the State Department in 1962, and later to become Johnson's National Security Advisor, urged that the United States retain "a capability for directly harassing Communist China" for he "saw little chance that [Beijing's] belligerence toward the West would soon diminish."[39]

Despite Kennedy's admonition, in 1961 and into 1962, State Department and National Security Council analysts reviewed US policy towards China. In March 1961, a State Department analysis noted that "we are faced by the widely presumed need to negotiate with the Peoples Republic of China, the looming question of Chinese membership in the UN, the continued dangerous confrontation around the offshore islands, and the requirements of Taiwan's long-term survival in the face of growing

---

[39] See Dean Rusk, *As I Saw It,* New York, W.W. Norton & Company, 1990, pp. 283-4; Thomas J. Schoenbaum, *Waging Peace and War; Dean Rusk in the Truman, Kennedy, and Johnson Years,* New York, Simon and Schuster, 1988, pp. 387-8; Walt W. Rostow, "Basic National Security Policy," March 26, 1962, pp. 190-196 as quoted in Gordon Chang, *Friends and Enemies,* Stanford, CA, Stanford University Press, 1990, pp. 258-259.

Chinese Communist power." Fundamentally, the authors proposed a "two-Chinas" solution that satisfied neither Beijing nor Taipei.[40]

For the next several months, James Thomson and others continued to promote this "two-Chinas" theme to permit the U.S. government to "negotiate with the PRC bi-laterally" while assuring "continued independence and security of a GRC governed Taiwan with as wide recognition as possible" and "with a minimum of tension between it and PRC." Another analysis called for "an early review of China Policy," noting, however, such a review must take into account our whole Far East policy, because our policy in Southeast Asia, the Japan-Korea area, or vis-à-vis India or the USSR will affect, and be affected by, our attitude toward Peiping." The paper stated ominously that "*time is not working in our favor in the Far East*" [italics in original]. It found a "growing power base" and "the likelihood of continued CPR aggressiveness over at least the next several years." It called for "a strategy which faces up to containing the outward thrust of ChiCom power for the indefinite future." *Newsweek* reported that the Berlin crisis absorbed Secretary of State Dean Rusk's attention, and Undersecretary Chester Bowles was overseeing preparation of a series of proposals seating both Beijing and Taipei in the General Assembly, but leaving Jiang in possession of China's Security Council seat.[41]

Diplomats and analysts did not test their assumptions about an aggressive Chinese government. A draft proposal for a "Far Eastern Aid Strategy" noted that "we can be sure that China's present leadership is

---

40 "Subject: US Courses towards China," March 30, 1961, Papers of James C. Thomson, Jr., Box 14, Far East, Communist China, General, 1/61-6/61, John F. Kennedy Library.

41 "Subject: US Policy Towards China," April 3, 1961, Thomson Papers, same box and folder, JFK Library; "A Strategic Framework for Rethinking China Policy," April 7, 1961, NSF Country File, Box 22, China, General, JFK Library. A Policy Planning Council Paper highlighted the dilemma of approaching the government in Beijing while seeking to guarantee the continued existence of the government in Taiwan: see "United States Policy towards China," Papers of James C. Thomson, Jr., Box 14, Far East, Comm China, General, 1/61-6/61, JFK Library; *Newsweek*, "A New China Policy in the Making," July 10, 1961, p. 22. Interestingly, Beijing attacked Walt Rostow and his work in economic development theory. The *Kuang-Ming Jih-pao* of March 28, 1961 published an article titled "A Reactionary Economic Theory that Serves the US Ruling Clique." It claimed to expose "absurdities in Rostow's *Stages of Economic Development.* Apparently Beijing rejected Rostow's view that China was at the "take-off" stage, NSF Country File, Box 22, China, General, 6/13/61-6/27/61, AmConGeneral, Hong Kong, #860, to State, May 24, 1961, JFK Library.

bent on recouping the lost centuries of China's inferiority within a matter of decades." It called for continued economic development of nations in the region, continued increase in "their cohesion in the region, and increased association of regional strength with Western power." A Special National Intelligence Estimate believed that "in 1971 mainland China will probably continue to be under the control of a ruthless, determined, and unified Communist leadership which remains basically hostile to the US." Given increasing population and economic strength, the PRC "will become even less restrained in taking political or military action independent of the USSR."[42]

In late 1961, the State Department's Policy Planning Council began reviewing policy – a process that required several months. It noted that U.S. policy sought to preserve Free World countries against "further Sino-Soviet bloc expansion and subversion," limit "Communist China's growth" and reduce its "power and prestige," and "eventual reunification under free governments of divided countries of the area." A subsequent SNIE concluded that "Communist China's leaders believe that they can eventually achieve their objectives in the area at far less cost and risk through the techniques of Communist political warfare." "In any case, the Communist Chinese will seize every opportunity to undermine US standing and to generate anti-American feeling in the Far East." In April, State Department staffers urged Chester Bowles to meet with Kennedy and his key advisors on the analysis. None of these analyses were able to view the region from Beijing's viewpoint.[43]

---

[42] "A Draft Proposal: Multi-year South Asian and Far Eastern Aid Strategy within the framework of a long term China Policy," Thomson Papers, Box 14, Far East, Communist China, General, 7/61-12/61 and undated, JFK Library; Document 62, SNIE 13-2-61, "Communist China in 1971," September 28, 1961, pp. 138-139.

[43] "US Policy Toward China," October 26, 1961, Thomson Papers, Box 14, Far East, Communist China, "S/P-61159: US Policy Toward Communist China," 10/26/61, JFK Library; Thomson to Bowles, May 4, 1962, Thomson Papers, Box 15, Far East, Comm China, S/P Study, 11/15/62, JFK Library; *FRUS, 1961-1963, Vol. XXII,* Document 80, "Chinese Communist Capabilities and Intentions in the Far East," November 30, 1961, p. 175. Discussion continued into November: see "Notification of Secretary's Policy Planning Meeting," November 15, 1962, Thomson Papers, same box and folder; "A US Policy Toward Communist China," November 15, 1962, Thomson Papers, Box 2, China, General, "A US Policy Towards Communist China;" Rostow to Members of the Planning Group, November 28, 1962, NSF Box 23, China, General, 9/62-12/62; and Thomson to Ambassador Reischauer, November 30, 1962, Thomson Papers, Box 15, Far East, Comm China, S/P Study, 11/15/62, all JFK Library.

Even if the U.S. government was willing to reconsider policy, the Chinese government seemed set on retaining the United States as its main enemy and object of its vitriol. It was not unreasonable for Beijing to fear the U.S. policy of isolating China as a prelude to possible invasion. After Lyndon Johnson became president, policy towards China changed little.

For those diplomats and opinion makers needing proof of Beijing's threat to a fragile order in the region, they had only to look at the situations in Laos and South Vietnam. *Newsweek* found similarities between Laos and Korea ten years earlier. It compared Chinese intervention in Korea with seven North Vietnamese battalions crossing onto the Plain of Jars. *Newsweek* also worried that the jungle war that embroils Laos threatens to spread."[44]

Laos was rapidly disintegrating into several armed camps. After the failure to integrate Communist formations into the Royal Laotian Army in 1959, fighting resumed, and in December 1960 the pro-American forces under Phoumi lost control of the strategic Plain of Jars bordering North Vietnam. When Kennedy became president, the CIA began supplying an indigenous mountain people, the Hmong, with arms to contest Pathet Lao and North Vietnamese control of the plain. Finally, the members of the International Control Commission, Canada, India, and Poland, were able to secure a cease-fire in early May 1961. The next year, as the Vietnam conflict widened, there began a decade long battle between Laotian forces respectively loyal to and receiving support from China and North Vietnam and also the United States and Thailand.

The stakes in Laos in this heyday of the domino theory were terrible. George Herring has recounted that, "in 1961, the world appeared to be entering the most perilous stage in its history." If the United States failed to meet the challenge, Kennedy claimed that "the whole world, in my opinion, would inevitably begin to move toward the Communist bloc." Kennedy worried that Khrushchev might misinterpret an American failure to make a stand in Laos but also wondered how to convince the American people to make a stand in far-off Laos and not in nearby Cuba after the Bay of Pigs fiasco in April 1961. That is, as a domino, Laos mattered potentially not only in Southeast Asia but across the entire range of Soviet-American and Sino-American rivalries.[45]

When the truce in Laos appeared to collapse in January 1961, the Pentagon ordered the aircraft carriers *Lexington* and *Bennington* to cut

---

[44] *Newsweek,* "Laos: Another Korea," January 9, 1961, p. 30, 31.

[45] George C. Herring, *America's Longest War, Fourth Edition,* New York, McGraw-Hill, 2002, p. 89, 93, 94.

short a rest stop in Hong Kong to take up positions in the South China Sea; an entire complement of support ships, including troop ships full of marines, accompanied the two carriers. *U.S. News* reported that "the march by Communists toward a takeover in Southeast Asia is underway again. The goal is to maneuver U.S. power out of that part of the world. The other prize: access to food, oil, rubber, other riches lacking in Red China." The news magazine also noted that "the Red strategy in Asia: outflank US in the Pacific, threaten India." It also noted that "Russia appears to be the big winner and the United States the big loser in the Laos crisis." It further claimed that "the far-reaching effects of any U.S. retreat in Laos will not be fully measurable for months." Five weeks later *U.S. News* reported that "in Southeast Asia, the Communists are building a new empire," that "Khrushchev is ahead" and that "Kennedy is losing." As with other reports in news weeklies, this report claimed the Communists would move from Laos to South Vietnam, then to Thailand and eventually to critical resource-rich countries of Malaya and Indonesia. Sadly, "no one in this part of the world has found the answer to Communist infiltration, subversion and guerrilla warfare." As *Time* reported in late March 1961: "And yet, if the finger of Laos goes, so too goes the rest of the hand: a complete Communist takeover would endanger Burma, Thailand, Cambodia and South Viet Nam, all of which share Laotian borders. With those countries under the Red flag, India would be dangerously outflanked—pinned down to the east, as it is already bedeviled to the north by Red China. Indonesia, already softened by Communist incursions, would be easy plucking. Malaya and Singapore could become steppingstones for further Communist expansion, to the ultimate peril of Australia and New Zealand." *Time* noted the Soviet Union provided Pathet Lao armies with forty five tons of material every day: "Gorky trucks, armored cars, assault rifles, carbines, light and heavy machine guns, 105 mm howitzers, [and] long-barreled 85-mm cannon." *U.S. News* reported "it looks like one more country going to the Communists." And, "control of Laos is one of the keys to the Communist drive to take over South Vietnam." There was more bad news in early May. *Time* headlined: "Collapse." *Time* reported that "the slipping Western position in Laos became a near collapse last week." *Time* worried that "the ruin may well spread beyond the confines of Laos." "There was small inclination among the U.S.'s allies to save Laos on the battlefield," and "the U.S. military had no inclination to commit U.S. fighting men to a wasting guerrilla war in the Laotian jungles." *Newsweek* titled one report: "Holding the Line after Laos." It quoted the Chairman of the US Joint Chiefs of Staff, General Lyman Lemnitzer: "The U.S. has lost the battle of Laos." In another report, *Newsweek* showed a "giant iron wedge" as "Communist power crashed its way down the valley of the Mekong," next threatening Thailand and South Vietnam, the next dominoes in line. *U.S. News* claimed that "here in an isolated part of Southeast Asia that Khrushchev has picked his spot to test the nerves of John Fitzgerald Kennedy." It further stated that "the Reds want Laos as a new base for conquest."[46]

There was a critical, untested assumption that China was the real threat in East and Southeast Asia and it was following a script of sorts that the Soviet Union dictated. Cuba, Berlin, and Laos blended into one large Communist effort to take over the world. Few American strategists had studied Vietnamese history, for example, to realize that, for more than a thousand years the Vietnamese people had contested Chinese power and having blunted such power began to exercise their own "manifest destiny" over several centuries, moving from the Red River valley down the narrow coastal plain and eventually into the Mekong River valley where the arrival of the French in the 19th century stopped their colonization and expansion against the Khymer people. Perhaps Hanoi was only acting out long frustrated dreams of the Vietnamese to take over Indochina unrelated to the Cold War issues of Soviet or Chinese aggression.

Many American strategists and news analysts viewed Soviet Premier Nikita Khrushchev behind the problems in the region and elsewhere in the world. In January 1961 *Newsweek* commented that behind "Mr. Kennedy's most urgent foreign problems – Laos and Cuba, the Congo and Algeria – the tides of Communist power were flowing." There was a several page world map with hotspots on fire under the titles "A world of surging Soviet power," "The hungering billions," and "Chinese on the March." In mid-May, *Newsweek* noted Soviet press "attacks on Mr. Kennedy's 'hypocrisy.'" The news magazine opined that Khrushchev was "probing the West's defense perimeter." It claimed that "the Communists are going all-out to bring down the pro-Western governments of Thailand and South Vietnam." In June *U.S. News* told readers to "look at Asia. There you find the Communists on the offensive moving ruthlessly, building up an image of irresistibility." *U.S. News* went on to state that

---

[46] *Time,* January 13, 1961, "The Three-Front War;" www.time.com/archive; *U.S. News & World Report,* January 16, 1961, p. 46; *Time,* March 31, 1961, "Laos: Background for Battle," www.time.com/archive; *U.S. News & World Report,* March 27, 1961, pp. 52, 53; "Southeast Asia on the Road to a Communist Take-Over," April 10, 1961, p. 39; "Southeast Asia: Down The Road to Communism," May 15, 1961, p. 41; *Time,* May 5, 1961, "Collapse," *Time* on-line archive, www.time,com/archive; *Newsweek,* May 22, 1961, p. 35; "Then There Were Two," May 15, 1961, p. 42, 44.

"the Communist bloc is winning in Asia because its leaders are tough-minded, willing to take reasonable risks, and are riding the wave of revolutionary nationalism that is dominant in the newly independent countries." By contrast, the United States "is losing in Asia because its allies and friends are, for the most part, weak and small, and disunited."[47]

The Vienna summit in June 1961 did little to alter their perception. *U.S. News* headlined "did Khrushchev win at Vienna," and answered "Yes." It claimed "the Soviet boss exuded triumph" and "Communist-led forces blasted away a ceasefire" in Laos. By October *U.S. News* was reporting on "Khrushchev's Master Strategy." It claimed that "the Soviet strategy, tried and tested, has a single objective: a world dominated by Communism." The method: "to chip away at one weak spot after another." Japanese leaders told *U.S. News* the U.S. needs to be "tough-minded." "In South Vietnam, for example, the U.S. can recover some of its show of weakness in Laos by holding the line against the Reds. But the loss of South Vietnam would cause irreparable damage to US prestige in Asia." *U.S. News* quoted extensively from a Dean Rusk statement, highlighting his comment that "our survival is at stake."[48]

As 1961 moved to a close, the government in Washington was willing to accept a negotiated arrangement in Laos despite the negative impact on allies in the region. *U.S. News & World Report* showed the communist "strategy of conquest as Laos goes red," with a two page map of the region and a dramatic line running from North Vietnam to Laos, South Vietnam, Cambodia, Thailand, Burma, and Malaya with the caption "after Malaya, Reds can go into Singapore, Indonesia" – a clear statement of the "domino theory." *Business Week* reported that "the potential loss of Laos to Communist domination means a new political and military equation in Southeast Asia, a shifting of the balance of power toward the Communists." The caption on the accompanying map of the region noted "Laos is an open corridor for invaders or infiltrators into the rest of Southeast Asia." *Business Week* speculated that "the US may negotiate with the Russians to set up a belt of 'neutral' states, stretching from South Vietnam across Southern Asia to Turkey." "It is a vicious cycle of distrust feeding upon itself." *U.S. News* followed up a few weeks later "After Laos-Red Strategy for Takeover in Asia." It quoted an anonymous "American authority" that "the real objective is Malaya, which could be highly vulnerable to a Red

---

[47] *Newsweek,* January 23, 1961, pp. 28-29; "Putting on the Pressure," May 15, 1961, p. 41; *U.S. News & World Report,* "Why Russia Keeps on Winning," June 12, 1961, pp. 44-45.

[48] *U.S. News & World Report,* June 19, 1961, pp. 37-38; October 23, 1961, pp. 39-40, 42; U.S. News, July 24, 1961, p. 69.

Chinese invasion and then the wealth of Indonesia which Red China wants badly" for "Indonesia's resources of rubber, tin, lumber, and oil are coveted by Mao Tse-tung." The so-called authority closed the loop: "Indonesia now carries on a heavy trade with Japan, which would be cut off if the Reds took over," "so, it's important for the U.S. to make a stand somewhere soon in Southeast Asia." *Time* magazine described the cease-fire in May as "a cold war defeat for the U.S," claiming that "almost visibly, the U.S. was falling back in Southeast Asia." Western experts agreed, that Laos "will go quickly behind the Iron Curtain." This discouraging situation came only seven weeks after Kennedy stated that "the security of all Southeast Asia will be endangered if Laos loses its neutral independence." As *Time* concluded, "with Laos all but written off, the Administration is confronted with deciding whether or not to take a stand in Communism's next Southeast Asia target: South Viet Nam." But, as *Time* noted in another report, "in South Viet Nam, a pro-Communist Laos will mean an increasing flow of guerrillas and supplies transiting Laos over the old Ho Chi Minh Trail." Five months later, *Time* reported that "in Laos, the decay of the U.S. position has gone ever further."[49]

The situation in Vietnam also was worsening in that first year of the new presidential administration. Failure in Laos raised the stakes in Vietnam. Kennedy believed that Khrushchev "just beat the hell out of me" at Vienna in their face-to-face meeting in June, and in August Soviet and East German forces constructed the initial Berlin "wall." He and his advisors it was time for a stand, and the place was Vietnam.[50]

As pressures mounted for decisive action, the situation in South Vietnam continued to deteriorate. *Time* warned that the "Communists" were switching their attention from Laos to South Vietnam: "The Communists pushed supplies and reinforcements [along the Ho Chi Minh Trail] to the jungle fighters who are battling to take over South Viet Nam – a far richer prize than Laos." "The Viet Cong burn villages, capture rice barges, mine roads, and extort money and food from peasants. Last year in thousands of little quick strikes, they blew up 284 bridges, killed 4,000 officials, village elders, soldiers and farmers." A month later *Time* reiterated that "in South Viet Nam, a pro-Communist Laos will mean an

---

[49] *Time,* "A Price Too High," May 12, 1961; "The Rains Went," October 20, 1961, www.time.com/archive; *U.S. News & World Report,* May 15, 1961, p. 43; *Business Week,* May 27, 1961; *U.S. News,* June 5, 1961, p. 72; *U.S. News & World Report,* April 3, 1961, p. 42; *Time,* "Falling Back," May 12, 1961, www.time.com/archive. See also *Newsweek,* "The Cruelest Decision," May 8, 1961, p. 41.

[50] Herring, p. 96.

increasing flow of guerrillas and supplies," while a North Vietnamese spokesman stated that "the people's revolutionary struggle [in South Vietnam] has entered a new stage."[51]

Kennedy was concerned, and his Vice President, Lyndon Johnson, reported after an official visit to Asia, including Vietnam, that the United States had to resist Communist aggression in South Vietnam or retreat to America's west coast. *Time* reported that, "faced with the Communist challenge, the U.S. has made a major decision: South Viet Nam must be defended at all costs." Kennedy later authorized the US Army's Special Forces, the so-called Green Berets, to develop a counterinsurgency effort to hold on in South Vietnam. By 1961, South Vietnamese had tired of their leader, Ngo Dinh Diem, his family, and the corrupt of his rule. Meanwhile, American advisors had tired of Diem's continuing resistance to making necessary reforms. In the countryside, the Viet Cong terror campaign – assassinating village chiefs and other leaders guilty of cooperating with Diem's government or U.S. advisors – had largely severed the tenuous loyalty of the Vietnamese people to their government.[52]

There were no easy solutions. The continuing commitment to the domino theory caused Kennedy and his advisors to increase America's involvement in South Vietnam. Military experts advocated both counterinsurgency in the south, and Kennedy agreed to increase the South Vietnamese military by another 20,000 troops. Early tests of South Vietnamese forces were not always favorable. A Viet Cong attack on the provincial capital of Phuoc Thanh demonstrated the unwillingness of SVA soldiers to fight and citizens to resist the VC. Advisors proposed, but Kennedy did not yet accept an ill-defined graduated response against North Vietnam to convince Hanoi to halt its support for the Viet Cong. Social scientists believed in nation-building projects that had little relevance for Vietnamese in the Mekong Delta or the Central Highlands. Still, Kennedy accepted a top secret report from Stanford economist Eugene Staley that "would commit the U.S. to the most detailed program of economic and social reform that the U.S. has ever undertaken in Southeast Asia." Others hoped Diem, a minority Catholic, would reach out to the largely Buddhist bureaucracy and officer corps. Still, Diem "remains

[51] *Time,* "Richer Prize," April 14, 1961; "Falling Back," May 12, 1961, "Welcome to Saigon," July 14, 1961, *Time* on-line archive, www.time.com/archive.

[52] *Time,* "The Right to Intervene," May 19, 1961, "Decisions of Magnitude," July 21, 1961; "The Firing Line," August 4, 1961, *Time* on-line archive, www.time.com/archive.

aloof from the masses in the tradition of a mandarin who follows the ancient Confucian code of a divinely guided prince."[53]

A fact finding mission by General Maxwell Taylor typified the challenges. Taylor traveled to Vietnam for a week on the sixth such mission that a nervous John Kennedy had sent to Vietnam. Taylor found that "Diem has internal political problems far greater than he had supposed" and they hindered the fight against the Viet Cong. The army needs to improve its logistics, and the US must help interdict the increasing logistical ability of the Viet Cong along the Ho Chi Minh Trail. The key question, given the importance the U.S. accorded to Vietnam and the disarray within the country, was whether to send American troops to Vietnam. *U.S. News* reporter Robert Martin provided an eyewitness account of the jungle warfare the South Vietnamese army was losing. A week later, *U.S. News* followed up with another report "on the 'hot war' the Communists are winning, so far." A month later *Time* reported "disenchantment with Diem." The news weekly noted that "Washington lately has become increasingly disenchanted with Diem." The U.S. government was particularly troubled by Diem's view that "nothing should or could be done in the way of domestic reforms before the military situation has been improved." Despite such concern, Washington had few levers to cause Diem to change.[54]

As 1961 drew to a close, various pressures combined to make an increased commitment to Vietnam a path of least resistance. *U.S. News* reported that "new and stronger U.S. moves in Southeast Asia are being predicted now." While the news magazine predicted Taylor's report would stop "short of recommending early use of U.S. combat troops in the jungles of South Vietnam to fight the Communist rebels." It noted that Taylor believed that, "if the U.S. does not come to the help of South Vietnam, the U.S. will be finished in the whole area of Southeast Asia."[55]

If many in the region view China as a threat, the United States also had to deal with challenges in America's international trade and gold situations. When Kennedy took office, the United States already had a

---

[53] *Time,* "The Firing Line," August 4, 1961; "Night War in the Jungle," September 29, 1961, *Time* on-line archive, www.time.com/archive.

[54] *Time,* "Report from Vietnam," November 3, 1961; www.time.com/archive; *U.S. News & World Report,* October 30, 1961, p. 54; November 6, 1961, p. 39; *Time,* "Disenchantment with Diem?", December 8, 1961, *Time* on-line archive, www.time.com/archive.

[55] *U.S. News & World Report,* "Coming Strategy on the Asiatic Front," December 4, 1961, p. 31.

balance of payments deficit. The U.S. sold more goods abroad than it imported through the 1950s [there has been a long-term challenge in evaluating "services" in this equation], and thus enjoyed a balance of trade surplus. However, American military stationed abroad purchased goods and services with US dollars; their dependents living with them did the same; more American tourists traveled abroad than foreign tourists visited America; American companies invested domestic profits overseas because they could make more money in that way; America foreign aid also contributed to the problem. *The New York Times* noted that there was "no quick solution sighted for the payments deficit of the United States." Costs were significant. *Time* noted that US "textile companies had closed down more than 800 mills employing 250,000." Angry textile manufacturers, employees, and their representatives in Congress on one side and textile exporting nations in Asia on the other pressed the Kennedy Administration.[56]

Two weeks after inauguration, Kennedy told the Congress about the balance of payments and gold outflow challenges. He stated that the balance of payments "has become one of the key factors in our national economic life," and because of the deficit "we have lost gold." "Any potential weakness in our dollar spells trouble, not only for us but also for our friends and allies," since "we are the principal banker of the free world." Kennedy then proposed a series of measures both short- and long-term to "correct the persisting basic deficit in our balance of payments." *U.S. News* praised Kennedy's program on America's balance of payments deficit, and particularly the measures he took to strengthen the dollar's value in gold. By year's end, *The New York Times* reported that the Kennedy Administration was ready "to go to Congress in January [1962] with a revolutionary trade program." Kennedy wanted to forestall the rise of trading blocs among Western nations by dramatically lowering tariffs across-the-board, what would come to be called after his death "The Kennedy Round."[57]

A noted financial leader offered his prescription. In a long article in the magazine section of *The New York Times,* James Warburg offered his prescription to solve America's balance of payment and gold drain problem. He counseled against measures that would unfavorably affect the Third World to deal with deficits in trade and payments with Western

---

[56] *The New York Times,* "Trade Problem Seen Continuing," January 1, 1961, p. F1; *Time,* "Half-Free Trade," June 30, 1961, www.time.com/archive.

[57] Robert P. Stebbins, Editor, *Documents on American Foreign Relations, 1961,* New York, Harper & Brothers, 1962, pp. 26, 27, 31; *U.S. News & World Report,* "A 'Strong' Dollar Now?", February 20, 1961, pp. 33-34; *The New York Times,* "President Ready for Early Move on Freer Trade," November 13, 1961, p. 1.

Europe. He believed America's allies could help America in this challenge by absorbing more of our industrial production and helping more with the costs of mutual defense. He wanted to discourage the outflow of investment capital from America owing to short-term interest rate advantages abroad. He hoped to strengthen key American industries so they could meet the foreign challenge and export. His comments, given wide publicity, were no different from the prescriptions of Kennedy's economic advisors, but they ran squarely into foreign policy considerations, and foreign policy trumped foreign economic policy in the 1960s.[58]

As John Kennedy took the oath of office, his new administration had largely determined the outline of U.S. policy towards the free nations of East Asia. He and his advisors focused on the Soviet-American confrontation and the seeming threat of the People's Republic of China – of Soviet pressure in Third World areas, a sense of American defeats after Castro's victory in Cuba and the Berlin Wall. They believed in the domino theory and that regimes in East Asia needed time to develop economically and to gain a measure of support or, at the very least, acquiescence from their respective peoples to withstand the spread of Communism. Thus, the Kennedy accepted an increasing commitment to the anti-communist struggle in Indochina both to halt what he viewed as communist aggression and to buy time for an equally important effort to use the U.S. economy to help prop up weak regimes in the region. The administration committed the U.S. economy to this battle without a process to regularly check at what point such propping up of these economies had succeeded and measuring those successes against damage to the U.S. economy from unfair trade privileges.

---

[58] James P. Warburg, "The Gold Crisis – An Analysis," *The New York Times,* January 8, 1961, pp. SM10+.

CHAPTER TWO

THE ECONOMY COMPLICATES FOREIGN POLICY

As the Kennedy and Johnson administrations confronted the Soviet Union, the People's Republic of China, and their allies, the U.S. economy threatened America's position as undisputed leader of the Free World. In the 1950s, the United States developed a troubling balance of payments deficit that proved stubbornly resistant to corrective measures. As it continued into the 1960s, it weakened the dollar internationally and limited the ability of the government in Washington to press allies in this still tense era of the Cold War confrontation with the Soviet Union.

Despite moral suasion and a series of laws and actions, the government in Washington was unable to reverse the balance of payments deficit. The Kennedy and Johnson administrations issued messages, proclaimed improvements, sought legislation, cajoled business and the general population, and approached allies to little avail. More importantly, largely unaccounted for spending on the expanding war in Vietnam placed added pressure on the balance of payments, increased the deficit, and weakened the domestic economy by encouraging inflation and significant import substitution for what previously was domestically produced goods.

Policymakers concluded that both America's international position and the needs of developing countries required a dramatic lowering of formal and informal restrictions on trade. Kennedy and his advisors soon concluded there was need for an across-the-board 50% reduction in tariffs worldwide to spur international trade, open markets somewhat closed to U.S. exports, and assist the economic development of Third World nations. He proposed these talks through GATT and Johnson saw them to a successful conclusion, although securing passage of the so-called Kennedy Round tariff cuts did not resolve problems facing the U.S. economy.

Success in the so-called Kennedy Round at the GATT talks could not compensate for other factors affecting America's international economic position. The U.S. economy remained so large that developing nations looked to exporting into it to create their own economic boomlets. Moreover, the Cold War rhetoric that the Kennedy and Johnson administrations both embraced made reasonable sacrificing the U.S. economy to help Southeast and East Asian economies develop and their polities better able to resist Communist expansion. Finally, spending on the Vietnam War was the insufficiently acknowledged factor in too many issues concerning the U.S. economy.

By 1960 government and academic experts and the media had focused on the stubborn and worsening balance of payments problem. Robert Anderson explained the trends since the end of the Second World War, and noted that "we have been running an overall deficit for ten years and it has become relatively large in the past two years." But Anderson stated that, "as a great power with far-flung responsibilities and with worldwide financial and economic interests, both public and private, the United States to a surprising extent must depend on a reasonable equilibrium in its balance of payments to carry out its responsibilities and to accomplish its political and economic aims." Richard Gardner noted the dilemma for American policymakers: "we could strike a balance by drastically curtailing foreign military spending and economic aid, restricting our imports and our private foreign investment, or painfully deflating our domestic economy. But these measures would solve our balance of payments at the cost of our security and prosperity and that of the entire free world." Gardner argued that, to have an expanding free world economy, monetary reserves must grow at about the same rate as international trade." Since such reserves did not increase proportionately in the 1950s, "the rest of the reserve needs of the free world outside the United States were met from the deficit in the U.S. balance of payments." There was no immediate, painless solution. Francis Gavin has quoted George Ball that Kennedy was 'absolutely obsessed with the balance of payments" and that Kennedy saw this challenge as "inextricably linked" with nuclear weapons and the confrontation with the Soviet Union.[1]

[1] Robert B. Anderson, "The Balance of Payments Problem," *Foreign Affairs,* Vol. 38, No. 3, April 1960, pp. 423, 425; Richard N. Gardner, "Strategy for the Dollar," *Foreign Affairs,* Vol. 38, No. 3, April 1960, pp. 433, 434. *The New York Times* editorialized on "'expanding our foreign trade," August 18, 1960, p. 26; Francis J. Gavin, *Gold, dollars, and power: the politics of international monetary relations, 1958-1971,* Chapel Hill, University of North Carolina Press, 2004, p. 59 and Chapter Three, "The Gold Battles within the Cold War," *passim.* For a review of the period more generally, see Richard Holt, *The Reluctant Superpower: A history*

The problem continued into 1961. *The New York Times* stated there was "no quick solution sighted for payments deficit of the United States." *The Times* reported that "this country has been economically dependent on a broad range of imported materials . . . hundreds of items of strategic and industrial importance." *U.S. News* commented that "with the dollar in trouble almost everywhere . . . much depends on foreign confidence in the dollar." *Newsweek* reported "the bulging deficit in the U.S. balance of payments ranked as the nation's No. 1 economic problem only a few months ago," but improvement in the nation's international accounts might cause some to believe the issue was resolved. *U.S. News* agreed. But by November the optimism of early spring had faded: "another big balance of payments deficit is in prospect this year. And it may very well be bigger next year." By year's end *U.S. News* gloomily reported that "U.S. prosperity will stimulate imports" and "major exporting nations in Europe, as well as Japan, will probably be putting extra steam behind their export efforts in the U.S. market."[2]

Were there additional, perhaps manageable dimensions to the challenge? *Business Week* reported that "since 1953, export prices of U.S. manufactured goods have been rising faster than those of other countries" and "the U.S. share of the world market for manufactures has slipped." "The real explanation seems to be a much slower improvement in productivity." *Time* used the textile industry to illustrate the problem: "one of the chronic afflictions of the U.S. economy is the limp state of the nation's textile industry." Part of the problem was "obsolete equipment and the loss of markets to plastics, paper and synthetic fibers," but also there were "textile producing areas with low labor costs" flooding "an already glutted world textile market."[3]

The situation of cotton textile imports helped illustrate the American dilemma. Several Asian economies relied on exports of cotton textiles – cloth and various finished products – to earn foreign capital to purchase needed imports. They needed easy access to the American market. For

---

of America's global economic reach, New York, Kodansha America, Inc., 1995, pp. 181-187.

[2] *The New York Times,* "Trade Problem Seen Continuing," January 1, 1961, pp. F1, F9; *U.S. News & World Report,* "Business Around the World," February 6, 1961, p. 96; *Newsweek,* "The Dollar Gap: Hunky Dory," April 24, 1961, pp. 75-76; *U.S. News & World Report,* "Business Around the World," April 24, 1961, p. 113; November 6, 1961, p. 107; December 11, 1961, p. 111.

[3] *Business Week,* "Why the U.S. has lost export sales," June 24, 1961, p. 63; *Time,* "Half-Free Trade," June 30, 1961; "Optimism for Exports," November 10, 1961, both www.time.com/archive.

American policymakers, they wanted to strengthen these economies to help those countries resist Communist aggression, yet they recognized the pain that such imports caused in those states and localities with textile plants. In May 1961, the Kennedy administration sought an international conference to convince developed countries to import more cotton textiles from key producers in Southeast and East Asia. *The New York Times* reported that success could mean a general increase in Hong Kong's cotton textile exports but a 9% drop in exports to the United States. Several months later, the administration continued to press allies to accept more cotton textile imports from developing countries, but Germany, France, and Italy restricted imports and Britain gave preferences to Commonwealth producers. At the same time, Japanese textile manufacturers protested voluntary quotas their government had accepted. Hong Kong received support from the British government to protest limitations on exports to the United States. However, *U.S. News & World Report* stated "U.S. textile industry is agitating for import quotas" and the "U.S. is not willing to bear the brunt of the impact from increasing textile imports."[4]

The next year, the situation continued along similar lines. In early 1962 the U.S. Department of Agriculture sought permission to place a special fee on cotton textile imports to help support domestic producers. Japan and other producers threatened to purchase raw cotton elsewhere and also complained about the negative impact on their respective economies. Six weeks later *U.S. News* reported that "politics or no politics, something drastic had to be done about the large-scale dumping of Hong Kong cotton textiles on the U.S. market." But, as *U.S. News* also noted, such action "could be serious for the British colony, burdened by millions of refugees from Red China." At the same time, American negotiators achieved success at the international conference on textile trade that Kennedy had requested the prior year. *The New York Times* reported that "all nineteen members of the Cotton Textiles Committee of the General Agreement on Tariffs and Trade are expected to join an international accord for regulating trade in cotton goods."[5]

---

[4] *U.S. News & World Report,* "Business Around the World," May 22, 1961, pp. 113-114; *The New York Times,* "Trim in Exports of Textiles Seen," June 28, 1961, p. 43; *U.S. News & World Report,* "Business Around the World," July 3, 1961, p. 78; *The New York Times,* Japan's Textile Exporting Men Criticize New Accord With U.S., September 11, 1961, p. 35; "Japanese Textile Men Press Ikeda on Quota," September 7, 1961, p. 49; "Hong Kong Scores U.S. Cotton Plan," December 14, 1961, p. 69.

[5] *The New York Times,* "Cotton Proposal Draws Protest," February 18, 1961, p. F1; *U.S. News & World Report,* "Business Around the World," February 26, 1962, p.

In succeeding years, the apparent best efforts of U.S. negotiators yielded little practical benefit to the United States. *The New York Times* reported on anger in the Japanese textile sector: "To judge by the Japanese newspapers, the real big news situation in the world these days is not the nuclear test ban treaty, nor Cuba, nor Chinese-Soviet relations, nor any of the other issues of war and peace." Yet only a month later, in late March 1963, *Time* reported on "the plight of the U.S. textile industry." Cotton manufacturers complained that, to support raw cotton producers, the U.S. government subsidized the price of raw cotton internationally and thus gave competitors a price advantage of 8 cents per pound [cotton cost 32 cents per pound for domestic producers] in addition to advantages of lower wages. In July *The New York Times* reported on the annual review of The Association of Cotton Textile Merchants who attacked the rising rate of cotton textile imports. Six months later cotton manufacturers still sought relief against Asian producers. The U.S. government recognized that industrial revolutions and economic expansions began in textile manufacturing, and wanted to encourage this transition in Asian economies.[6]

In the next several years, the State Department was able to announce a series of agreements on cotton textile imports. These agreements as much reflected the move of Asian economies into man-made rather than natural fiber products not covered in these pacts and more generally other export fields as serious breakthroughs in long-term negotiations. In late September 1963, the U.S. and Hong Kong governments announced agreement that would limit cotton exports from the Crown Colony. By January 1965, the U.S. Government was supporting the successful Long-Term Cotton Textile Arrangement which helped equalize markets for cotton exports to help protect domestic American manufacturers; still Stanley Nehmer of the State Department noted that, "over 70 countries export cotton textiles to the United States. The United States is a market open and free from unilateral import quotas." In September 1966, the U.S. and Hong Kong governments renewed the cotton textile agreement again

---

106; *Time,* "King Cotton's Ransom," March 16, 1962, www.time.com/archive; *U.S. News & World Report,* "Business Around the World," April 2, 1962, pp. 87-88; *The New York Times,* "19 Nation Support Expected for Pact on Textile Imports," September 13, 1962, p. 64; "19 Nations Prepare to Sign Cotton Pact," September 27, 1962, p. 73.

[6] *The New York Times,* "U.S. Textile Curb Agitates Japan," February 23, 1963, p. 9; *Time,* "Textile Troubles," March 29, 1963, www.time.com/archive; *The New York Times,* "Rising Rate of Cotton Imports Assailed by Textile Merchants," July 11, 1963, p. 11; *U.S. News & World Report,* "Business Around the World," September 9, 1963, pp. 89-90.

limiting exports from Hong Kong to the United States. The next month, the U.S. and Singapore governments reached an agreement limiting exports from the city-state. There were more agreements, including extension of an international cotton textile pact in 1967.[7]

President Kennedy proposed a solution that seemed largely a continuation of Eisenhower Administration policies. In a message to the Congress on the U.S. balance of payments and gold outflow situation, he called for strengthening the U.S. economy, better promoting U.S. exports, limitations on the value of goods US tourists could bring home duty-free from abroad, and encouraging America's allies to purchase more American weapons for their respective militaries. Kennedy followed up telling Treasury Secretary Douglas Dillon "to undertake coordinating responsibility" and "to report to me periodically on the progress achieved" on the balance of payments problem. Thereafter State, Treasury, Commerce and Defense met regularly to discuss ways to reduce such expenditures as foreign aid and military assistance to minimize the impact on the balance of payments deficit." Eighteen months later, Secretary Dillon wrote the President that the plan "consist[s] of measures to curtail the outflow of dollars stemming from the activities of government itself, and measures to increase our export receipts."[8]

Business Week was not impressed with Kennedy's message to Congress, reporting that "the program contains only a few new measures, all of a limited nature" and that "many of Kennedy's recommendations continue actions that former President Eisenhower set into motion." Henry Hazlitt writing in *Newsweek* told readers that "the basic cause is inflation"

---

[7] *The New York Times,* "Rise in Cotton Textile Imports is slowed by Long-term Pact," May 1, 1964, p. 52; *Department of State Bulletin,* "U.S. and Hong Kong Announce Cotton Textile Agreement," October 12, 1964, p. 517; "Record of U.S. Participation During Second Year of Long-Term Cotton Textile Arrangement," January 11, 1965, pp. 49-50; *The New York Times,* "U.S. Amends Pact on Cotton Textiles Sent From Japan," January 15, 1966, p. 37; *Time,* "King Cotton," March 5, 1965, www.time.com/archive; *Department of State Bulletin,* "United States and Hong Kong Sign Cotton Textiles Agreement," September 26, 1966, p. 467; "U.S. and Singapore Reach Cotton Textiles Understanding," October 3, 1966, p. 509; *The New York Times,* "World Cotton Pact Extended Three Years," March 23, 1967, p. 47; "U.S. and Philippines Reach Accord on Textiles Import," July 4, 1967, p. 41.

[8] *The New York Times,* "Text of President's Message to Congress," February 7, 1961, p. 16; Department of State, *Foreign Relations of the United States, 1961-1963, Volume IX, Foreign Economic Policy,* Washington, DC, Government Printing Office, 1995, Document 2, Editorial Note; see also Documents 6, 7, 8, 9, 14, 15; Document 18, Dillon to the President, October 9, 1962.

and that "nine-tenths of the economic proposals that Mr. Kennedy has made in his first few weeks of office would increase the inflation." Harvard University Economics Professor Gottfried Haberler wrote in *The New York Times* that "the President's message on the balance of payments is a moderate document which in the main continues the policies proposed or started by the preceding administration." *U.S. News* argued that "the South, long vital to the Democratic Party, is increasingly protectionist. Many unions, strong supporters of Kennedy, are demanding tariffs, import quotas." In other words, the weekly news magazine warned readers not to expect dramatic proposals in the near future.[9]

The U.S. government sought to gain control of the balance of payments deficit issue. In addition to the continuing, State Department-led, Cabinet-level coordinating group, senior officials approached friendly governments for assistance. American and British officials, who faced their own severe economic challenges, met in mid-February 1961 about financial matters. Secretary Dillon told his British counterparts that "there was a good chance the US could approach equilibrium with respect to the basic deficit in three to four years." The two allies discussed Germany's trade surplus and efforts "for expansion of German equipment purchases in the U.S." Two months later German Chancellor Konrad Adenauer met with Kennedy in Washington, DC. Kennedy stated "his great concern about the outflow of gold," and that US troops abroad and our foreign aid were primary causes. He did not want to reduce foreign assistance which he viewed as critical in the larger East-West battle in the Third World, so he wanted to discuss the costs of stationing 300,000+ US troops in West Germany to resist possible Warsaw Pact aggression. In mid-September Dillon sent a message to Kennedy through the U.S. embassy in Vienna that he had "reached understanding with other major industrial countries that group of us would commit ourselves to lend additional resources to IMF [International Monetary Fund] to deal with balance of payments pressures." The IMF needed until early January 1962 to finalize all the details and announce the agreement officially.[10]

Several months later a somewhat revised plan garnered new praise and continuing criticism. *Business Week* reversed course somewhat and stated that "the salient points of the Administration's new and flexible battle plan to defend the dollar and strengthen the international monetary network of

---

[9] *Business Week,* "How the New Dollar Moves Add Up," February 11, 1961, p. 27; *Newsweek,* "Saving the Dollar," February 27, 1961, p. 82; *The New York Times,* "Towards Payments Balance," February 12, 1961, p. E8; *U.S. News & World Report,* "Business Around the World," February 20, 1961, p. 98.

[10] *FRUS, 1961-1963, Vol. IX,* pp. 109-110, 115, 128, 134.

the free world were beginning to emerge this week." These plans included bolstering short term interest rates to attract expatriate dollars home, and involving those industrialized economies with balance of payments surpluses to help alleviate speculative runs on the currencies of economies with a deficit. Henry Hazlitt described several parts of the plan as "extremely ill-advised and dangerous." He believed the administration should "halt the inflation," and "stop expanding the supply of money and credit" by "balancing the budget." He returned to his theme two weeks later. He reiterated his "least harmful solution of the dollar problem" and again called every one of the alternatives "inadvisable and dangerous." He claimed that if the Kennedy administration followed through, including abandoning the legal goal reserve, "our people and nation could be ruined as a consequence."[11]

By winter 1961 it appeared the focus had changed to increasing world trade through lowered tariff barriers. In mid-March, Secretary Rusk wrote Kennedy that to "seek the fullest possible measure of tariff reduction by foreign countries to help correct the balance of payments deficit," the administration did not have the legal authority. He indicated the need for new, broader legislation. In May, parties to the General Agreement on Trade and Tariffs announced a November 1961 meeting to consider "tariffs as a hindrance to free trade, elimination of tariff and non-tariff protection in agriculture, and lowering barriers to international trade for less-developed countries." In September Rusk wrote Kennedy recounting challenges for U.S. negotiators and again asking Kennedy "to enlarge the bargaining authority of our negotiators." There was disagreement how to proceed. Kennedy assistant Avery Petersen believed the U.S. government should continue to seek relief on a country-by-country and even industry-by-industry basis. Undersecretary of State George Ball disagreed, writing Kennedy urging him "to give up the item-by-item tariff negotiating approach of the past and negotiate for a major across-the-board reduction in our import restrictions and those from the European Economic Community."[12]

The media followed the situation with great interest. *Newsweek* highlighted a speech by Undersecretary Ball in which he recommended "the president should be freed of Congressional restraints and given authority to negotiate new trade agreements 'across-the-board' rather than [the current] product-by-product." Should such lowering of tariffs "create

---

[11] *Business Week,* "Strategy for Defending the Dollar," May 6, 1961, pp. 34-35, *Newsweek,* "Gold and the Dollar," June 5, 1961, p. 82; "The Dollar Problem," June 19, 1961, p. 82.

[12] *FRUS, 1961-1963, Vol. IX,* pp. 455, 477, 492, 494.

a temporary idling of productive facilities," the government should have fiscal ability to ameliorate the distress in an industry or a region of the country. A few weeks later, *Newsweek* claimed that the "results [of the free trade debate] could cement or cleave the Atlantic alliance, confound or contribute to Communist expansion, make or break industries in Düsseldorf and Hong Kong, in Chicago and Atlanta." It quoted President Kennedy requesting a "new and bold" trade policy" as "extraordinary in economic history as NATO was unprecedented in military history." While the administration's plans excited the news magazine, *Newsweek* also detailed the opposition, noting how various industries were already protesting plans they had not yet seen. *U.S. News* discussed the details, including "across-the-board cuts of 50 percent in the tariffs on most industrial products" and the "power to add to the free list" – goods with no import duties. *U.S. News* warned that "these and other aspects of the new tariff policy will meet with very serious opposition in the Congress and among various industries." Even *Newsweek's* Henry Hazlitt strongly supported the emerging program: "the President deserves the fullest support in his advocacy of greater freedom of trade." "Free trade maximizes the economies and efficiencies of world production."[13]

Despite the excitement and concern over the administration's proposals, the problems in America's payments, gold, and trade balances continued into 1962. In mid-March Secretary Dillon wrote Kennedy predicting improvement in the balance of payments situation. He stated "our situation was much improved over 1960," and noted areas where government officials were working to ameliorate overseas spending. In July, the Cabinet Committee on the Balance of Payments reported to Kennedy claiming improvement "for the first half of 1962 the overall deficit in our balance of payments." The report called it "a very substantial improvement over 1961 and 1960." But, by October 1962, Dillon was reporting new initiatives "to curtail the outflow of dollars" and "increase our export receipts." Carl Kaysen, deputy special assistant for national security affairs, wrote Kennedy in January 1963 that "it is most unlikely that we can achieve the goal of balance in our international accounts by the end of 1963."[14]

The media reported the administration's plans and the response from domestic groups concerned about changes in tariff policy. *Business Week*

---

[13] *Newsweek,* "For the U.S. – Free Trade with Europe?", November 13, 1961, p. 75; "Trade and Tariffs: 'A Devil of a Fight'" December 18 1961, pp. 82-84; *U.S. News & World Report,* "Business Around the World," December 4, 1961, p. 104; *Newsweek,* "Remove Trade Barriers," December 25, 1961, p. 65.

[14] *FRUS, 1961-1963, Vol. IX,* pp. 15-16, 31-32, 43.

reported that "lobbyists open fire, with emphasis on the grassroots, and politicians start log-rolling. By merely sketching in the trade terms he sought, Kennedy left them a wide opening." The business weekly noted that "to proponents of freer trade, it's a national issue, but the practical politicians among them know that, when it comes to a vote in Congress, it comes down to how industries are affected in specific states and Congressional districts." *U.S. News* cited foreign criticism of the US steel industry's decision to boost steel prices. It quoted *Le Figaro*: it is "placing the U.S. economy on the classical inflationary spiral." Britain's *Manchester Guardian* noted the price increase forced the administration into "a cruel dilemma," "either to halt the economic expansion" or "to consider whether a deliberate devaluation of the dollar may not be the lesser evil." *Business Week* proclaimed a "new and tougher battle when Europe's and Japan's up-to-the-minute sheet mills get set to invade the U.S. market." Moreover, inflation in the US economy was sending US investment dollars overseas, worrying the US Treasury. *Time* described a meeting between President Kennedy and Roger Blough, the President of U.S. Steel Corporation. The US gold supply continued to shrink, and speculators believed either the "U.S. might be forced to devalue the dollar." Previous piecemeal actions had not worked, and measures to stop the gold drain could adversely affect America's balance of payments deficit, reverse America's balance of trade surplus, or slow the sluggish American economy.[15]

Hopes of early summer for improvement in the balance of payments deficit were dashed by winter 1962. *The New York Times* editorialized in July that "real progress is being made toward curbing the deficit in our balance of payments." It quoted Treasury Undersecretary Robert Roosa who reported a serious drop in the FY 1962 deficit. *Time* also quoted Roosa and reported that "the administration has taken several measures to solve the problem, with some strong help from U.S. business." The mood changed by mid-November. *The New York Times* quoted Per Jacobsson, managing director of the International Monetary Fund, that "the world cared more that the United States balances its international payments than that it balance its budget." But Jacobsson "acknowledged it is not easy to pursue policies of domestic expansion and international balance at the same time." *Time* stated that, "acknowledging that it had been

---

[15] *Business Week,* "Coming to grips on trade," February 3, 1962, pp. 24-25; *U.S. News & World Report,* "Business Around the World," April 23, 1962, p. 107; "Business Around the World," April 30, 1962, p. 91; *Business Week,* "Steel arms for hotter import fight," June 30, 1962, p. 73; *Time,* "The Solid Gold Dilemma," June 22, 1962; "The Gold Drain," June 29, 1962, both www.time.com/archive.

overoptimistic, the Commerce Department reported that the U.S. overseas deficit widened in this year's third quarter." It cited the old Brooklyn Dodgers lament: "wait till next year." *The New York Times* wrote similarly, that "persistent deficit endangers U.S. position in world money market," and that "faster growth [of the U.S. economy] would tend to increase the payments deficit."[16]

There was little discernible improvement in 1963 despite the efforts of the Kennedy administration. In late February 1963 Kennedy sent National Security Action Memorandum to key Cabinet leaders that "the deficit in our balance of payments and the problems associated with it continue to be major problems which influence national security policy along a broad front." He then directed this group to find solutions. Two weeks later Kennedy wrote the Cabinet Committee on the Balance of Payments that "it appears we can no longer look forward to achieving a balance in our international accounts in the next year." He asked for their "survey of additional possibilities" to "deal with this persistent problem." John Kenneth Galbraith wrote Kennedy in late August that "the heart of the matter is that for everyone concerned with the balance of payments problem, it is subordinate to other concerns." While Galbraith proposed dramatic action, Kennedy continued to work within the confines of the existing structure.[17]

Again, the media reported the discouraging situation. As first quarter results came in, *The New York Times* reported that "payments deficit still [is] a problem." The newspaper quoted Secretary of the Treasury Douglas Dillon who attributed the balance of payments deficit to heavy foreign borrowing in U.S. money markets. *Newsweek* reminded readers that "last year Kennedy predicted that the deficit would be wiped out by the end of this year. This is no longer expected." *U.S. News* reported "the future of the American merchant marine is coming into question again." It noted that "the steady deterioration of America's role in world shipping has taken place during a period when U.S. overseas trade has been rising." Of course, foreign shippers of goods to and from American ports added to the trade deficit. It also noted "the mutual nature of the dollar problem . . . a strong dollar is good for all. A weak dollar would be disastrous for the free

[16] *The New York Times,* "Strengthening the Dollar," July 16, 1962, p. 21; "U.S. urged to end payments deficit," September 16, 1962, p. 35.*Time,* Fashionable Worry," July 20, 1962; "Elusive Balance," November 16, 1962, www.time.com/archive; *The New York Times,* "Uneasy Days for Dollar," December 24, 1962, p. 13. See also *Time,* "Competition Goes Global," December 28, 1962, www.time.com/archive.

[17] *FRUS, 1961-1963, Vol. IX,* pp. 47-48, 49-50, 77-86.

world." At the same time, *U.S. News* reported that "U.S. exporters have a hard time trying to widen their markets abroad." For the past seven years, "U.S. exporters lost much ground competitively" and "U.S. exports of cars, trucks, tractors, steel-mill products, tires, textiles, [and] household appliances fell off between 1956 and 1962."[18]

America's international economic situation sufficiently worsened to result in another presidential message to Congress on trade. After citing examples of success, the president wrote that "continued confidence at home and cooperation abroad require further administrative and legislative inroads into the hardcore of our continuing deficit." Kennedy then proposed to assist expansion of exports, to encourage foreign tourism to America, to control federal expenditures abroad, to better control capital flows, and to deal with the shrinking gold supply and threats to the dollar. Eileen Shanahan explained the causes and results of the gold outflow and balance of payments deficit. She also noted that "there is nothing that Congress or anyone else can do – except complain." *The New York Times* concluded that the Kennedy program "has had mixed results." *The Times* described an interesting scene: "with disturbing frequency, a hydraulic lift truck stops before the compartment of the U.S. Treasury in a sub-basement vault of the New York Federal Reserve Bank. Bank employees open the safe's doors and begin loading a ton of 28-pound gold bars onto the vehicle's pallet." The truck moved to the aisles storing gold of other countries, and America's gold supply shrank. *Newsweek* reminded readers that although "most Americans had long before forgotten and filed the problem, the balance-of-payments deficit has only persisted, but it has progressed to the point where business and government officials are increasingly alarmed." *U.S. News* reported "blunt talk about the problems of the dollar abroad has just come from two Treasury officials." Treasury Secretary Douglas Dillon and Undersecretary Roosa promised "the U.S. is going to play the role of honest debtor – to exercise the discipline needed to reduce international deficits." But promises of more of the same did not impress international bankers and several days later the Administration proposed stronger actions. They included higher interest rates on short-term borrowing, indirect controls on longer-term exports of U.S. money, and a readiness to borrow from the International Monetary Fund, which

---

[18] *The New York Times,* April 26, 1963, p. 55; *Newsweek,* "The Periscope," February 4, 1963, p. 65; *U.S. News & World Report,* "Will American Ships be Forced off the Seas?", April 22, 1963, pp. 75-76; "Business Around the World," May 27, 1963, p. 79; June 10, 1963, pp. 101-102.

ironically "the U.S. originally helped to set up at Bretton Woods in 1944 to bail out poorer foreign countries."[19]

Kennedy's message could do little to improve the situation, and the twin problems continued into and throughout the years of the Johnson Administration. In mid-August *The New York Times* reported "like a block of ice in the sun, the nation's gold stock continues to melt down slowly but steadily." *The Times* editorialized that "the battle of the dollar has taken a sharp turn for the worse." *The Times'* financial correspondent, Edwin Dale, wrote that "of all the problems faced by the United States Government, none is more frustrating and baffling than the chronic deficit in American transactions with the rest of the world, called the balance of payments." *Time* wrote about "the continued gold drain," and noted the "growing deficit in the U.S.'s international balance of payments" "became one of the sorest of all subjects." *The New York Times* noted the contradiction: "the deficit in the United States international payments has influenced every domestic policy decision made to date by the Kennedy Administration – and some foreign affairs and military decisions, too. Yet, very few Americans have been aware of the effect of the balance of payments on their daily lives." When foreign economic leaders gathered in Washington, DC in October 1963, the value of the dollar and thus the status of America's international economic position was a key topic on the formal and informal agendas. In the aftermath of the Kennedy assassination, *The New York Times* noted that "President Johnson still faces some important decisions in the battle to eliminate the chronic deficit in the nation's balance of payments."[20]

---

[19] *The New York Times,* "The Text of Kennedy's Message Proposing a Plan to Cut Balance of Payments Deficit," July 19, 1963, p. 30; "Chronic Gold Outflow: Its Causes and Effects," July 21, 1963, p. 113; "Dollar Trouble," July 21, 1963, p. 109; *Newsweek,* "Balance of Payments: The Worry of the West," July 22, 1963, p. 71; *U.S. News & World Report,* "Danger to the Dollar – What Treasury Wants to do about it," July 22, 1963, p. 81; *Time,* "Waging the Gold War," July 26, 1963, www.time.com/archive; *Newsweek,* "Balance of Payments: Good as Gold," July 29, 1963, p. 59.

[20] *The New York Times,* "Continuing Gold Drain," August 19, 1963, p. 47; "Battle of the Dollar," August 26, 1963, p. 24; "Balance of Payments Problem – What it Means," September 15, 1963, p. 194; *Time,* "The Continued Gold Drain," September 13, 1963, www.time.com/archive; *The New York Times,* "U.S. Foreign Payments; Persistent Deficit Worries Officials; Public is Unconcerned," September 30, 1963, p. 51; *Newsweek,* "Facing Up to the Fiscal Facts of Life," October 14, 1963, p. 100; *U.S. News & World Report,* "A New Look at the Dollar," October 14, 1963, pp. 53-54; *The New York Times,* "Johnson and the Dollar," December 2, 1963, p. 73.

The news reports described the discouraging situation. *U.S. News* told readers that the "dollar's problems will remain as corrosive as ever" and "implications of some of these basic trends are rather chilling." "Competitively, the U.S. is having a hard time in world trade, especially in manufactured items." The next week, the news magazine warned that "President Johnson's willingness to give foreigners 'competitive access' to our market can be expected to stir up double trouble." Again, a month later *U.S. News* noted "U.S. manufactures are no longer having an easy time competitively on world markets" while "shares [of world trade] of Western Europe and Japan are expanding." In early Spring the dollar gained strength seemingly reflecting an improving U.S. balance of trade. Dillon wrote Johnson in late April that the United States had "an overall unadjusted surplus of just over $200 million for the first quarter," but "our weekly figures show us once more running a fairly substantial deficit in April." A month later, the Cabinet Committee on Balance of Payments wrote Johnson that the deficit will continue in 1964, "on the high side of the safe margin of tolerance," though a "substantial improvement over 1963," and that "we must continue to push all parts of our overall program to eliminate the deficit." In October 1964, Dillon wrote Johnson again that "our national balance of payments program has produced striking results," although "the job is not yet complete" and "a gap still remains." In December Dillon, Ball, and National Security Advisor McGeorge Bundy wrote Johnson to accept the report of the Task force on Foreign Economic Policy, to "continue present efforts to reduce tariffs," "resist all attempts to impose non-tariff restrictions on trade," "encourage easy access to our markets for imports from less-developed countries," "encourage trade with the Soviet Union and Eastern Europe," and "continue present policies for dealing with our balance of payments problem." But in October *The New York Times,* gently chided both presidential candidates [Johnson and Arizona Senator Barry Goldwater] for keeping "the deficit in the balance of payments the forgotten economic issue in this year's campaign."[21]

For the next four years, the challenges remained. In January 1965, Secretary Dillon wrote President Johnson that the deficit is "well above

---

[21] *U.S. News & World Report,* "Business Around the World," January 13, 1964, p. 79; January 20 1964, p. 78; February 10 1964, p. 70; Department of State, *Foreign Relations of the United States, 1964-1968, Volume VIII, International Monetary and Trade Policy,* Washington, DC, Government Printing Office, 1998, pp. 7-8, 11, 32-33, 63-66; *The New York Times,* "Impact in U.S.: Trade Balance Improves; the Prospect of Inflation Causes Concern," March 22, 1964, p. E3; "Dollar Gains Strength," April 10, 1964, p. 49; "The Issue: Balance of Payments," October 17, 1964, p. 28; *FRUS, 1964-1968, Vol. VIII,* pp. 4-5.

the $2 billion target we had established," and "the fourth quarter deficit was particularly large." Others, including the Chairman of the Council of Economic Advisors, Gardner Ackley, wanted to go farther. *The New York Times* reported both the U.S. Treasury and the Federal Reserve Board "are deeply concerned" over the continuing balance of payments deficit. The Cabinet Committee on Balance of Payments in early February 1965 sent Johnson a long report with many suggestions to deal with the worsening deficit. Once again, Dr. Ackley wanted even stronger proposals to meet the challenge. Two weeks later Johnson sent a message to Congress and set forth the usual measures to close the gap. *The New York Times* reported surprisingly support by the "heads of big companies and big banks" to the President's proposals. Acting Treasury Secretary Frederick Deming wrote Johnson of the "calm and generally favorable reaction in this country." But, in mid-August, new Treasury Secretary Henry Fowler noted "several factors that might put the third quarter balance of payments into deficit." Chief U.S. trade negotiator William Roth [he succeeded Herter] added "probably no progress in the Kennedy tariff negotiations round until after the German and possibly the French elections." Additional meetings of the Cabinet Committee on Balance of payments made clear the difficulty of dealing with the challenge.[22]

In 1966, the problem worsened. *The New York Times* reported the U.S. government was cutting "the chronic payments deficit" at the cost of "a retreat from the objective of a freer and healthier world economy." But four months later the newspaper reported a drop in US exports and a rise in imports, in part, due to the increasing costs and dislocations of the Vietnam War. Secretary Fowler wrote President Johnson in mid-May that "the balance of payments picture continues to be disturbing." By year's end *The Times* noted that the "drop in trade surplus worries U.S." and the "dollar problem seen persisting."[23]

---

[22] *The New York Times,* "President Facing Conflict of Ideas on Dollar Drain," January 31, 1965, p. 1; "Text of President Johnson's Message to Congress on the U.S. Balance of Payments," February 11, 1965, p. 56; "Johnson Moves to Check Outflow of Gold and Dollars," February 14, 1965, p. E4; *Department of State Bulletin,* "Economic Report of the President," February 22, 1965, pp. 254-255; *FRUS, 1964-1968, Vol. VIII,* pp. 73-76, 77-78; 85-96; 98-100, 112-113, 179, 183, 194-199.

[23] *The New York Times,* "Perils of a Dollar Wall," January 19 1966, p. 53; "Balance of Trade Reduced in April," May 25, 1966, p.87; "Drop in Trade Surplus Worries, U.S.," October 30, 1966; p. F1; "Dollar Problem Seen Persisting," November 14, 1966, p. 41; *FRUS, 1964-1968, Vol. VIII,* p. 269.

In January 1967, *The Times* editorialized about "the persistent deficit," and claimed that "the United States appears to be no nearer a solution for eliminating them than it was when they began." It reported that "the deficit in the United States international payments worsened somewhat in the fourth quarter of last year." By November, it asked "can the dollar be defended," given the chronic payments deficit? It stated that "the consequences are so serious that most knowledgeable people refuse even to discuss what action might be taken afterward." And by year's end it reported payments deficit "worsened significantly in the current quarter."[24]

In early January 1968 Johnson sent yet another message to Congress calling for both temporary and long-term measures to reduce the balance of payments deficit and ease the pressure on the dollar and gold reserves. *The New York Times* headlined the "fight for the dollar is on, and the end is not in sight." Johnson decided "priority had to be given to the defense of the dollar and its international value" over "the liberties of United States citizens" and "the well-being and national security of many foreign countries." *Newsweek* titled its report "The buck stops here," and called it "a tough new program to whittle down the chronic U.S. payments deficit." Famed economist Paul Samuelson said "at last it has come – direct controls on international transactions." *Time* went further, titling its report "at the point of panic." It stated that "the country's continuing balance of payments deficit, its constantly out-of-balance domestic budget and its rising outflow of money to finance the war in Viet Nam are basically responsible for global concern about the soundness of the dollar." It reported on meetings of government bankers at home and abroad to prop up the dollar, moderate the gold markets, and preserve the existing system which America's international trade and payments status threatened to bring down. In the immediate aftermath of the message, Rostow reported, "market – quiet again yesterday and today," "gold pool made no sales yesterday; took in $4 million today, dollar and sterling quiet." By mid-May *Time* was asking "can the U.S. still compete?" It stated that "in one industry after another, U.S. manufacturers are finding their markets at home and abroad besieged by aggressive foreign firms." This "inability to compete" helped account for a shrinking of the U.S. trade surplus, likely causing "renewed peril for the free world's monetary and trade system." It

---

[24] *The New York Times,* "The Persistent Deficit," January 25, 1967, p. 42; "Deficit Worsens in U.S. Payments," January 27, 1967, p. 33; "In the U.S., the Question Is: Can the Dollar be Defended?", November 26, 1967, p. E3; "Payments Deficit Worsens for U.S.," December 20, 1967, p. 1; "Text of President's Statement on Balance of Payments Problem and Steps to Meet It."

concluded "chances of improvement seem slim." By year's end 1968 *Time* reported that "the long-strong trade surplus has shriveled."[25]

The increasing U.S. involvement in the fighting in Southeast Asia made plans for ameliorating the balance of payments challenge more difficult. For John Kennedy, sensing that he was failing to meet the Communist challenge in Cuba, Berlin, and Laos, Vietnam became the place to meet the challenge of Communist aggression and encourage allies in the region and neutrals around the world that America would fulfill its commitments. Nonetheless, the American commitment remained relatively small. It concentrated on building Saigon's military, political, and economic capacity. Despite this effort, the Battle of Ap Bac in January 1963 appeared to represent a turning point, where America military advisors sent trained government troops and regional militia into battle against Vice Cong guerrilla units operating near Saigon and South Vietnamese armed forces failed miserably. They outnumbered the guerrillas about 4-to-1 and yet lost the battle. It indicated a failure of leadership and perhaps a sign that Saigon could not resist Hanoi's strategy of subversion and selected violence.[26]

---

[25] *The New York Times,* January 2, 1968, p. 15; "Fight for the Dollar is On, and the End is Not in Sight," January 8, 1968, p. 49; *Time,* "Staunching the Flood," January 12, 1968, www.time.com/archive; *Newsweek,* "The Buck Stops Here," January 15, 1968, p. 64; "Paul A. Samuelson on Defending the Dollar," January 15, 1968, p. 69; *Department of State Bulletin,* "Economic Report of the President," February 26, 1968, pp. 279-281; *Time,* "At the Point of Panic," March 22, 1968, www.time.com/archive; *Newsweek,* "Gold: The Trouble with Money," March 25, 1968, pp. 69-70; *The New York Times,* "Money, Money Everywhere – What's the Problem," March 31, 1968, pp. SM32-SM36; *FRUS, 1964-1968, Vol. VIII,* p. 491; *Time,* "Can the U.S. Still Compete," May 10, 1968; "The Impact of Imports," November 15, 1968; *The New York Times,* "Massive Economic Problems Confront the Next President," November 6, 1968, pp. 53-54; *Time,* "Trade: Dangerous Drift for the U.S.," December 13, 1968, www.time.com/archive.

[26] On the fighting in Vietnam, see Larry H. Addington, *America's War in Vietnam,* Bloomington, Indiana University Press, 2000; Bruce Palmer, *The 25 year war: America's Military Role in Vietnam,* Lexington, University of Kentucky, 1984; George C. Herring, *America's Longest War: The United States and Vietnam, 1950-1975,* Boston, McGraw-Hill, 2002; Walter L. Hixson, Editor, *Military Aspects of the Vietnam Conflict,* New York, Garland Publishing, 2000; Harry G. Summers, *On Strategy: A Critical Analysis of the Vietnam War,* Novato, CA, Presidio Press, 1982; Edward F. Murphy, *Semper Fi Vietnam: from Da Nang to the DMZ,* Novato, CA, Presidio Press, 1997; Karnow, Stanley, *Vietnam: A History,* New York, Viking Press, 1983; David L. Anderson, *The Vietnam War,* New York, Palgrave Macmillan, 2005; Anthony O. Edmonds, *The War in Vietnam,* Westport, CT,

From Ap Bac until the Ia Drang Valley campaign in fall 1965 both sides sought to expand logistics, determine the intentions of their opponents, and devise their best strategy. Hanoi continued to build capacity, improving the Ho Chi Minh Trail, securing its control over the strategic Plain of Jars in Laos, and developing the port of Sihanoukville in Cambodia. At the same time, Viet Cong guerrillas continued their campaign of sabotage and selective assassination in the countryside with the result that, by 1965, Saigon was losing a battalion a week and American advisors feared a Communist attack through the Central Highlands would sever the South in half. Meanwhile, the South Vietnamese government lurched from the rule of Ngo Diem Dinh and his family, and, after his assassination on November 1, 1963, to a seemingly ever changing alignment of senior military officers no more capable of resisting Hanoi than Diem. The United States engaged in a several part initiative, including overseeing OPLAN 34A, a counter subversion plan whereby South Vietnamese commandos infiltrated the coastline of North Vietnam to commit acts of economic and military sabotage, using such neutral agents as Canadian diplomat Blair Seaborn to convince North Vietnam of America's determination to defend its South Vietnamese ally, offers of economic abundance, including a proposed Mekong Valley Authority modeled after Franklin Roosevelt's Tennessee Valley Authority which transformed much of America's southeast, and building the logistical capacity for a larger American war effort.

From the Battle of the Ia Drang Valley to the Communist Tet offensive beginning in late January 1968, the United States tried to win the Vietnam conflict. Army General William Westmoreland settled upon a strategy of attrition, to kill, capture, seriously wound or cause to desert more enemy soldiers than Hanoi could rationally replace. He could not invade North Vietnam and there were severe limitations on bombing over the north both to avoid Chinese intervention as occurred in the Korean War; he also chose not to draw a line from the seventeenth parallel along the coast westward through Laos to the Thai border which some strategists suggested. Westmoreland's strategy was fraught with difficulty. It conceded the strategic initiative to the North Vietnamese and Viet Cong – the decision whether to fight – in exchange for tactical mobility symbolized by combat helicopters leapfrogging troops to distant battlefields. It caused US forces to establish large base areas and only send small parts of the seven army divisions eventually stationed in Vietnam

---

Greenwood Press, 1998; William S. Turley, *The Second Indochina War,* Boulder, CO, Westview Press, 1986.

into the jungles and highlands to locate, fix, and destroy the enemy. It was expensive because hundreds of thousands of soldiers yielded only tens of thousands of combat troops, yet required vast installations, storage, supplies, and support. The Communist Tet offensive, a near-total military failure, unexpectedly resulted in a dramatic victory in turning American public opinion against the faraway conflict. Thereafter, when Richard Nixon became president, the U.S. government would seek to use its strategic approach to the Soviet and Chinese governments to contain North Vietnam and allow it to withdraw militarily from Vietnam.

The Vietnam War contributed significantly to the balance of payments problem. From a low of several hundred advisors in South Vietnam at the start of the Kennedy presidency to a peak of some 750,000 Americans on the ground in South Vietnam, on air bases in surrounding countries, or at sea in various naval task forces operating in the region all required a wide range of supplies. Food, fuel, equipment, and rent for some bases all sent U.S. dollars abroad. Demands for supplies for the war effort created openings in the domestic civilian economy for imports. Servicemen frequently became tourists spending earnings on refreshments, entertainment, and souvenirs also transferring U.S. dollars into local economies.

By mid-1965, the Vietnam War was costing $1 billion in terms of the balance of payments. *The New York Times* reported that "the moderate increase in the war effort in Vietnam announced today by President Johnson will impose no noticeable strain on the national economy, high economic officials said today." In fact, "most economists in and out of Washington regard the Vietnam buildup as providing the spur the economy needs to keep in high gear." But Francis Bator wrote Lyndon Johnson in mid-November that Treasury Secretary Henry Fowler wanted Johnson to agree to have "the government dramatize the balance of payments program *as part of the total effort connected with the Viet Nam war* [italics in original document]." Fowler wanted to tell the press that "we are in a serious shooting war, and that our voluntary program to bring the balance of payments under control reflects the kind of national effort that is required from all parties." Bator, interestingly, agreed with what he described as Johnson's "policy of being very careful not to over-dramatize the Viet Nam war." Robert Solomon has written that "the immediate impact on the balance of payments was superficially favorable," but there was "a sharp fall-off in the U.S. balance of trade" thereafter.[27]

---

[27] *The New York Times,* "Economic Impact is Called Slight," July 29, 1965, p. 1; "Dissent on Expansion," August 18, 1965, p. 43; *FRUS, 1964-1968, Vol. VIII,* p.

The situation worsened in 1966. In mid-February, the State Department sent a circular telegram describing a press conference on the 1965 balance of payments and prospects for 1966. The telegram noted the "main imponderables are rising balance of payments costs in Southeast Asia and direct impact of Viet Nam on domestic economy and trade." The telegram further noted "U.S. cannot be certain that 'present measures as they currently operate will lead us to that goal [balance] if foreign exchange costs of Viet Nam rise sharply over increases presently projected.'" About the same time the National Industrial Conference board sponsored a financial conference where the majority of economists feared a rise in "inflationary pressures," and if prices rose in America reflecting the increased demand the war caused, it would help imports seize a larger share of the domestic U.S. market. A month later the Cabinet Committee on Balance of Payments considered the rising cost of the Vietnam War. McNamara stated that "DOD expenditures abroad were now estimated at about $350 million higher for 1966 than contemplated last November." Shifting purchases back to the United States could result in "a 125% increase in price." Fowler told the group that "DOD expenditures in Southeast Asia were over a billion dollars higher than in 1961." In late April Secretary Fowler wrote President Johnson that "[a] our trade balance is deteriorating both due to high activity here and the indirect costs of Vietnam and [b] the direct foreign exchange costs of Vietnam are rising." Again, this time in May, Fowler wrote Johnson that "the balance of payments picture continues to be disturbing." He drew especial attention to "the governmental dollar outflows now increasing substantially because of the superimposition of new Southeast Asia costs on the cost of our other commitments throughout the world." Worse, "there were indications from the Department of Defense in late January that the balance-of-payment costs in Southeast Asia were running at or beyond the high end of the range forecast in November exercise." Fowler had few good alternatives, which included "live with a substantial deficit for the duration of the Vietnam conflict," "reduce the deficit by cutting back U.S. commitments overseas," or "reduce the deficit by introducing new economic and balance of payments measures at home." Several days another State Department circular telegram to "certain posts" noted "direct and indirect US expenditures associated with Viet Nam military operation and support thereof are exerting adverse impact on US balance of payments." The telegram gave a sense of the impact of the increasing costs associated with

---

225; Robert Solomon, *The international monetary system, 1945-1981,* New York, Harper & Row, 1982, pp. 102, 104 and 100-109, *passim.*

America's involvement in Vietnam: "Europeans should not expect US to continue carrying financial burden these responsibilities with Viet Nam costs as they now appear and simultaneously to fulfill demands of finance ministers and central bank governors with respect to balance of payments equilibrium." At a press conference a few days Secretary Fowler said that "in terms of over-all results U.S. had 'been little more than holding our own' since mid-1965 beginning with large buildup in direct and indirect costs of military and aid operations in SE Asia." *Business Week* reported "Vietnam is pushing the U.S. balance-of-payments deficit deeper, and officials hold out little hope for help." Moreover, *Business Week* drew attention to the impact on the balance-of-trade: "many of the soaring imports, officials note, are directly related to the war effort, as defense contractors pull in more foreign raw materials – especially metals – for war production." Two weeks later, *Business Week* reported that the "administration sees outflow of dollars for Vietnam as chief factor in worsening of U.S. trade balance." By August, *The New York Times* could still report that "the war has had distinct effects on the economy and on the people and businesses that make it up, but the effects have been far less than in any other war in modern times." But in October *Time* noted that "the cost of Viet Nam may seem small in relation to the overall economy," but "the Viet Nam war is an added burden on a substantially full-employment, full-production economy."[28]

The situation worsened in 1967 and 1968. In January, *The New York Times* quoted Defense Secretary McNamara testifying before Congress who stated that "the Vietnam war will add more than $1 billion to the United States balance-of-payments problem this fiscal year." Frederick Deming in May 1967 wrote that European government and banking leaders understood that the Vietnam conflict was hampering the U.S. government's ability to reach equilibrium in the balance of payments. *Newsweek* stated "the war has been the most important single factor in the U.S. economy for nearly two years." Further, "because of the war, the U.S. dollar and international monetary system are vulnerable to speculative attacks." Walt Rostow, in writing Johnson about the reaction to Johnson's

[28] *FRUS, 1964-1968, Vol. VIII,* pp. 239; *The New York Times,* "Economists Debate Impact of Vietnam War," February 18, 1966, p. 45; *FRUS, 1964-1968, Vol. VIII,* 244-245,255-256, 269-275, 284, 285-287; *The New York Times,* "War Seen Erasing U.S. Payment Goal," May 19, 1966, p. 65; *Business Week,* "Dollars are draining faster," May 7, 1966, p. 28-29; "War costs blunt drive on payments deficit," My 21, 1966, pp. 50-51; *The New York Times,* "War's Impact: Economy Hardly Hurt," August 8, 1966, p. 1; *Time,* "Pressures of Viet Nam," October 7, 1966, www.time.com/archive.

congressional message of early January 1968 about the balance of payments deficit, noted that Italian "Foreign Minister Fanfani in effect told Italian press that deficit and program linked to Vietnam." He also noted the European press reported "the Vietnam war was a main cause of the U.S. deficit." Soon thereafter "a spokesman for an organization of antiwar business executives attributed the gold-buying rush today to world reaction to the expanded United States role in the Vietnam War." *Time* reported that "the country's continuing balance of payments deficit, its constantly out-of-balance domestic budget and its rising outflow of money to finance the war in Viet Nam are basically responsible for global concern about the soundness of the dollar."[29]

Ultimately, the cost of the Vietnam War on the U.S. balance of payments deficit exceeded $4 billion annually, dooming administration efforts to reduce that deficit. In the November 1968 issue of *The Review of Economics and Statistics,* Leonard Dudley and Peter Passell tried to determine the war's impact. They measured "direct overseas expenditures, the import content in domestically produced war materials, and the indirect impact on United States exports due to export diversion and price increases." They believed these three measures more accurately reflected the real impact of the war on the balance of payments. They found that in 1967, the Vietnam War cost $4 billion against the balance of payments and that "the United States would have been in international payments surplus in 1967 in the absence of Vietnam War expenditures." In their analysis, they did not discuss nor measure the impact of servicemen spending as "tourists" during 'rest-and-recreation" leaves in the region or, for example, the steady stream of high-quality, reasonably-priced stereo equipment from such Japanese firms as Pioneer, Panasonic, TEAC, and Sony flowing from post exchanges back to stateside addresses.[30]

America's worsening balance of payments situation and increased spending on the Vietnam War affected the ability of the U.S. government but not its commitment to improve the economies of East Asian countries. The language of commitment remained relatively constant during the Kennedy-Johnson years more reflecting the consistent view that American

---

[29] *The New York Times,* "McNamara cites war," January 27, 1967, p. 37; *Newsweek,* "The Economy: Seesaw," July 10, 1967, pp. 65-66; *FRUS, 1964-1968, Vol. VIII,* Document 284, pp. 284; *The New York Times,* "Antiwar Executives Say Vietnam Policy Causes Gold Crisis," March 16, 1968, p. 49; *Time,* "At the Point of Panic," March 22, 1968, www.time.com/archive.

[30] Leonard Dudley and Peter Passell, "The War in Vietnam and the United States Balance of Payments, *The Review of Economics and Statistics, Vol. 50, No. 4, November 1968,* pp. 437-442.

policymakers had of the nations of East Asia rather than the reality of politics, economics, and society in the region. In 1961, Isaiah Frank, Director of International Financial and Development Affairs, stated America's goal: "we are all simply trying to develop policies that will encourage the most efficient use of the resources that are presently or potentially available to our countries." However, Frank noted "the primary responsibility must be theirs [the developing countries]," but his government had "done so much in recent years to promote the flow of American capital into the less developed countries." Six months later Walter McConaughy noted the goal of East Asians: "freedom from grinding poverty, freedom from ignorance and illiteracy, freedom from disease, freedom from hunger." He warned against "the Communist system of life under coercion." At year's end, Deputy Undersecretary U. Alexis Johnson drew attention to the failure of the Soviet model of economic development as evidenced by the disaster of the Great Leap Forward in China; he stated "one of the most serious problems confronting the raw material and food producing countries of Asia is the abrupt shifts and gyrations in the prices of the one or two commodities which are of controlling importance in their economies." Two weeks later Undersecretary George Ball drew attention to "the provision of markets for the less developed countries." He noted "the production of cotton textiles" as a classic example and insisted that developed countries consider the challenge of providing access to markets by reduction or elimination of national obstacles in the form of tariffs, quotas, or the other familiar paraphernalia of trade restriction." A week later Alexis Johnson returned to his earlier themes. He told a meeting of the Institute of World Affairs that "the most significant development of the 1960s will be the emergence of the nations of Asia with all of their potential." He warned of the "economic and financial poverty of the starkest sort, poverty of trained personnel, poverty of experience, poverty of administrative ability, poverty of even basic literacy." He noted the gap had narrowed in a few nations "notably Japan, the Republic of China, Thailand, and Malaya." He stated the United States must "give such cooperation and support as we can to the orderly social, economic, and political development of the emerging nations." Johnson reiterated the same themes in August, calling Asia "an area of problems – stubborn, intractable problems" but also "a land of hope and opportunity." He reiterated the full range of U.S. economic assistance to countries in Asia.[31]

[31] *Department of State Bulletin,* March 27, 1961, pp. 461-462; October 16, 1961, pp. 634-635; December 18, 1961, pp. 1011-1013; January 1, 1962, p. 5; January 8, 1962, pp. 53-59; August 20, 1962, pp. 279-283.

The next year Assistant Secretary Roger Hilsman noted America's commitment "to the defense of independent nations" of East Asia and "to contribute as we are able to the prosperity and development of nations which request our assistance." The next year Assistant Secretary William Bundy repeated the familiar comments and commitment, stating that "in most of the countries of free Asia there has been a notable degree of improvement in what economists call 'human resources'." ""Within the last fifteen years there have been some remarkable success stories – Japan, the Republic of China, and, despite some remaining weaknesses, the Republic of Korea, the Philippines, [and] Thailand." He praised examples of economic cooperation, and, of course, pledged continuing American support for Asian development.[32]

In February 1965, despite America's persistent balance of payments deficit, dollar weaknesses, and gold outflows, Undersecretary Averell Harriman said the United States had "inescapable responsibilities that go with power and the opportunities that it opens up." He noted "our economy 'feeds' the economies of so many other nations – they cannot be prosperous and strong if we are not." He claimed that "economic nationalism is as much of an anachronism for the United States today as it was at the end of World War II." He praised the Kennedy Round negotiations, and he reiterated earlier government statements that the developed countries must "give these [the developing countries] reasonable access to our markets, enable them to expand their export earnings and pay more of their own way toward modernization." Developing countries "also will require steady progress toward a trading world progressively free of restrictions and toward an international monetary system that encourages the flow of capital among all nations." In April 1966 President Johnson made more concrete America's commitment announcing ratification of the charter for the Asian Development Bank. He called the act "an economic Magna Carta for the diverse lands of Asia." Three months later Vice President Hubert Humphrey noted some achievements: "Consider South Korea, where exports have increased by 500 percent in the past 3 years. Consider Taiwan, which has been transformed from an aid-receiving to an aid-growth higher than even that of Japan. Consider Malaysia and Thailand, where ambitious development plans are being launched. Yes, consider Indonesia, where new leaders are determined to see that potentially rich country resume a responsible place in the world community." Much as Humphrey, U. Alexis Johnson again

[32] *Department of State Bulletin,* September 9, 1963, pp. 386-392; October 19, 1964, pp. 534-537.

took credit for economic advances in East Asia: "most of us would list Japan as the brightest of all." "Equally encouraging has been what could now be called a 'takeoff' of South Korea." "The economic record of Taiwan has also been notable." He praised founding of the Asian Development Bank and increasing economic cooperation among the free nations of East Asia.[33]

In February 1967, Undersecretary Bundy again praised advances. "The Japanese economic success story is well known." "In nearby Korea you can see the beginning of what could turn quite rapidly into a smaller scale but dramatic success story." "On Taiwan, the Republic of China has had a sustained growth rate averaging percent annually over the past 3 years." "In Singapore, Malaysia, and Thailand, we find extremely rapid economic growth." "With our help, that of the World Bank, and we hope others, [Philippine President] Marcos is working on the key problems of his country – smuggling, land reform, agricultural productivity." After the failure of the communist coup in Indonesia, "we may hope to see an increasing realization of Indonesia's great economic potential." In May 1967 William Bundy favorably described economic progress in East Asia. "In Japan with substantial United States economic help until the mid-fifties, spectacular economic advances took place." South Korea "beginning in the early 1960s took hold of its affairs, carried through a genuine democratic election, and began to make real economic progress." Taiwan "carried out sound and efficient policies" "which made possible the reduction and in 1965 the elimination of U.S. assistance programs." He had similar though more reserved comments about the Philippines, Thailand, Malaysia, and Singapore. Again, in July 1968, Bundy spoke publicly about economic progress in East Asia. He stated that "the economic, social, and political development of East Asia over the last 23 years has been at an extraordinary pace." "The economic progress of East Asia has been striking in recent years." Economic progress "of the less developed nations of East Asia, during the period from 1961 to 1966 showed an annual per capita economic growth rate of 2.3 percent per year" [more if one subtracts Indonesia under Sukarno]. More importantly, Bundy noted that "the figure is far higher than what was achieved in Latin America and South Asia in the same period." He praised "assistance we give in social and economic development." On the eve of the presidential election, Secretary Rusk spoke of economic progress in East Asia: "Japan's real gross national product has increased nearly sevenfold since

[33] *Department of State Bulletin,* February 22, 1965, pp. 245-249; April 4, 1966, pp. 521-522; July 4, 1966, pp. 2-6; October 24, 1966, pp. 639-641.

1950." "Per capita income in the Republic of China on Taiwan has doubled in 10 years." "Korea's GNP has increased an average of 9 percent annually during the last five years, and its exports are up from $18 million ten years ago to more than $400 million today." "Thailand's annual growth has averaged more than 7 percent in the last 10 years." "Singapore and Malaysia have moved ahead at a fast clip, and they enjoy the highest per capita income in East Asia, after Japan."[34]

Kennedy believed the solution lay in expanding trade by reducing barriers. "Trade policy," as Robert Pastor has written, "was third on John F. Kennedy's list of economic priorities when he took office." He dealt first with the domestic economic recession and then the balance of payments problem, and in August 1961 he considered trade liberalization. In late 1961, Kennedy approached Congress for legislation to liberalize America's trading system and thus to force its trading partners to liberalize their respective systems. George Ball sent a long circular telegram to "certain diplomatic missions" in late January 1962. He informed key senior diplomats that "new trade bill sent [to] Congress by President [on] January 25 represents [a] watershed in US foreign economic policy." It "is intended to give [the] U.S. the means to take fullest part in building [an] economically strong and progressive free world." The "legislation placed before Congress would give [the] President far-reaching and flexible authority [to] further reduce US tariffs beyond anything previously authorized in trade." It would "open prospects for mutual reduction and elimination [of] tariffs between [the] two largest economic units in [the] world, the U.S. and the European Common market." After describing the legislation with its "four separate authorities for reducing tariffs," Ball concluded that "it is of [the] utmost importance that other countries responds positively to [this] new initiative of [the] President."[35]

---

[34] *Department of State Bulletin,* February 27, 1967, pp. 323-327; May 22, 1967, pp. 791-792; July 1, 1968, pp. 16-21; November 4, 1968, pp. 461-462.

[35] Robert A. Pastor, *Congress and the politics of U.S. foreign economic policy, 1929-1976,* Berkeley, University of California Press, 1980, p. 105, and Chapter 4, Trade Expansion or Contraction, *passim; FRUS, 1961-1963, Vol. IX,* pp. 512, 516. For a first-rate discussion of trade policy, see Thomas Zeiler, *American Trade and Power in the 1960s,* New York, Columbia University Press, 1992; Zeiler concentrates on trade policy, although, to be sure, there were other reasons discussed in this chapter helping explain the erosion of American economic hegemony. See also Raymond Vernon, "A Trade Policy for the 1960s," *Foreign Affairs, April 1961, Vol. 39, No. 3,* pp. 458-470; William Diebold, Jr., "Trade Policies since World War II," *Current History, June 1962,* pp. 356-361; Jacob Viner, "Economic Foreign Policy on the New Frontier," *Foreign Affairs, July*

Again, the media closely followed the situation with its various twists and turns. In the same article, *Time* reported on Undersecretary Ball's remarks to the business meeting in New York City and on the meeting of American and Japanese Cabinet secretaries in the shadow of Mt. Fuji to discuss economic issues. Ball "urged across-the-board tariff cuts" while the discussants in Japan "came increasingly to realize that there could be mutual profit in liberalizing their economic attitudes toward each other." The next week *Time* quoted Kennedy: "my judgment is that the time to begin is now." Kennedy focused on trade with Europe: "we have to begin to realize how important the Common Market is going to present us with major economic challenges and, I hope, opportunities." Kennedy wanted to lower America's tariffs to press its trading partners to lower theirs. *Business Week* reported that "within 18 months, if the Administration has its way, the U.S. will have a drastically liberalized trade policy – one that would put it in position to bargain down the common tariff that will surround the enlarged European Common Market now developing across the Atlantic." *Business Week* further reported that "the President's determined fight for freer trade policies will have an effect on all other issues next year." Kennedy and his advisors believed that lower tariff barriers and freer trade were essential ingredients of their plan to expand the American economy without ramping up inflation and create new jobs as the oldest members of the "baby boom" generation would begin to enter the work force.[36]

The battle for trade legislation continued into 1962. *U.S. News* informed readers about Kennedy's Trade Expansion Act of 1962. Kennedy wanted "general authority to reduce existing tariffs by 50 percent in reciprocal negotiations." He also wanted a "special authority, to be used in negotiating with the EEC [European Economic Community], to reduce or eliminate all tariffs on those groups of products where the United States and the EEC together account for 80 percent or more of world trade in a representative period." Joseph Coppock, Director of the Foreign Economic

---

1961, Vol. 39, No. 4, pp. 560-577; Alfred C. Neal, "New Economic Policies for the West," *Foreign Affairs, January 1961, Vol. 39, No. 2,* pp. 247-258. See also Robert E. Baldwin and Anne O. Krueger, *The structure and evolution of recent U.S. trade policy,* Chicago, IL, University of Chicago Press, 1984, Chapter 1: The Changing Nature of U.S. Trade Policy since World War II, *passim* and Stephen D. Cohen, *Fundamentals of U.S. foreign trade policy: economics, politics, laws, and issues,* Boulder, CO, Westview Press, Inc., 1996, pp. 34-38.

[36] *Time,* "The Big Push," November 10, 1961; "Urgent Aim," November 17, 1961, www.time.com/archive; *Business Week,* "New Trade Policy Coming?", November 11, 1961, pp. 27-28; "Kennedy's big gamble," December 16, 1961, pp. 23-24.

Advisory Staff in the State Department, told an audience that the United States "must provide the leadership." "We do these things because they are necessary for our national security, to thwart the expansion of Soviet-Communist power." Coppock noted that in addition to the two provisions noted above, "the numerous small countries of the world must have markets in which to sell their specialized wares if they are to improve their economic lot." Two weeks later, Coppock added another reason to support the trade legislation: "our foreign trade is inevitably a part of our foreign political relations." He stated that "if Congress gives the President the authority to negotiate for lower trade barriers, the United States will be able to take the lead, commensurate with its power, in strengthening the economic bonds among members of the North Atlantic Treaty Organization and in promoting the economic development of the other free countries." Coppock did not mention America's balance of payments deficit or the gold/dollar challenge.[37]

The media closely followed the legislation as it worked its way through both houses of Congress. *The New York Times* editorialized about Kennedy's "eloquently stated message," agreeing that "the United States can only expect rapid economic growth and improved productivity if producers have to face competition." *Newsweek* recounted a Kennedy meeting with the sixty Democratic Senators and the case he made "for his bold, new program of freer trade." The news magazine reported that Kennedy "has convinced many reluctant businessmen that the danger he sees is real – that such a program is the only way to meet the challenge of the Common Market, check the gold outflow, and speed economic growth." But *Newsweek* also asked if "freer trade: salvation or a coffin nail," and quoted representatives in various industries reacting to "the 378 pages of tables, footnotes, and small print." *Business Week* described the House Ways & Means Committee opening hearing on the trade debate, and questions from Republican members who wondered "what is in the

---

[37] *U.S. News & World Report,* "What the President wants to do about Tariffs and Trade," February 5, 1962, p. 55; *Department of State Bulletin,* "The President's Trade Expansion Program and U.S. National Security," June 11, 1962, pp. 956-957; "Trade Policy Choices Facing the United States," June 25, 1962, pp. 1027, 1029. Interestingly, in an issue devoted to "Foreign Policy of the Kennedy Administration" [January 1962] and another on "United States Trade Policy, 1962," [February 1962], *Current History* did not deal with foreign policy or trade relations with Southeast or East Asia. For a detailed discussion of the act, its passage through the Congress, and its reception by European leaders, see Edward S. Kaplan, *American trade policy, 1923-1995,* Westport, CT, Greenwood Press, 1996, Chapter 4: "The Trade Expansion Act and the Kennedy Round," pp. 65-88.

bill to guarantee that we get what we pay for in tariff reductions." Congressman John Byrnes [R-Wisc.], according to *Business Week,* "was reflecting a view of many congressmen that the U.S. is naïve and overly generous in its international trade negotiations." The business weekly also commented on "the scores of lobbyists" in the hearing room. *U.S. News* reported "the big tariff battle of 1962 is opening." *Newsweek* stated that "the nation has been vehemently choosing up sides since Mr. Kennedy sent his legislation to Congress eight weeks ago." *The New York Times* reported the House's approval of the bill, and opined the "vote should speed passage of the trade bill through the Senate without altering its form."[38]

The New York Times largely was correct, and on October 11, 1962, Congress granted President Kennedy historic authority for five years to negotiate significant, broad tariff reductions. The clock was ticking, and Kennedy and his successor, Lyndon Johnson, raced that clock to secure agreement with major trading partners. A week after securing passage, Kennedy "proposed an international conference of ministers next year to seek ways to cut down obstacles to world trade." Kennedy said "I would like to take full advantage of the authority which the Trade Expansion Act confers upon me." In the meantime, "members of the European Economic Community will debate and probably decide on their first response to the new United States Trade Expansion Act within the next three months," and so there was a pause through the holiday season.[39]

Kennedy moved quickly to organize for the difficult negotiations abroad and dealing with industry and union leaders at home. On March 4, he wrote key Cabinet secretaries that, "while the Secretary of State has the primary responsibility for the conduct of foreign policy . . . Governor [Christian] Herter is charged with conducting the trade negotiations and related trade matters." Kennedy told Cabinet leaders that Undersecretary George Ball will "be the point of coordination for all important statements

---

[38] *The New York Times,* "America's Historic Choice," January 26, 1962, p. 30; *Newsweek,* How to Succeed in Business: Down Go Tariffs – Up Goes Trade," January 29, 1962, p. 64-65; "Tariffs: 'This May Hurt, But . . .," February 5,1962, p. 61; "Freer Trade: Salvation or a Coffin Nail," March 19, 1962, p. 87; *Business Week,* "Chips are down in fight over trade," March 17, 1962, pp. 47-48; *U.S. News & World Report,* "Business Around the World," March 19, 1962, p. 105; *Newsweek,* "The White House First Team Fights the Hot Tariff Battle," March 26, 1962, p. 74; *The New York Times,* "Bipartisan Victory," June 30, 1962, p. 18.

[39] *The New York Times,* "President Urges a World Parley to ease Tariffs," October 1962, p 1; "Action Foreseen on U.S. Trade Act," October 26, 1962, p. 143; "Common Market Scans Trade Act," October 31, 1962, p. 67.

and actions bearing on relations with Europe." A few days later Ball wrote Kennedy setting out short- and long-term objectives as well as basic strategy in this fourteen month period before the formal Kennedy Round talks commenced. Two months later Carl Kaysen wrote Kennedy to refine the strategy, agreeing that "we need to increase our already large trade surplus further in order to meet our military and tourist outlays." Kaysen wrote however "it may not be helpful to our negotiating position to emphasize these truths." He did not want to "suggest that we are in a weak position" or that "we are seeking more from Europe in the trade negotiations than we are willing to give." He wanted to emphasize the economic benefits to Europe, the U.S. and the "rest of the world" from "successful trade negotiations." Kaysen hit the proverbial nail on the head. The Free World still depended on the United States largely for its defense, but had enjoyed fifteen years of the United States also paying for that defense [including using the U.S. economy to drive allied economic reconstruction and expansion]. Changing this construct would prove challenging.[40]

Before the talks began, there would be difficulties. Governor Herter wrote Jean Rey of the European Economic Community that President Kennedy believed "it is difficult for the United States Government to commit itself to broad-scale negotiations and set the machinery of the Trade Expansion Act in motion without having agreement with the EED regarding the general basis upon which the reduction of tariffs is to take place." French ambassador Hervé Alphand told Rusk that "the atmosphere surrounding the forthcoming tariff negotiations was a matter of concern." He claimed "the U.S. formula was too rigid." While the U.S. Trade Expansion Act was "important and beneficial," "other countries had not been consulted." Happily in mid-May 1963 "U.S. and EEC representatives compromised on their disagreement on the rules that should govern tariff reductions for the Kennedy Round GATT negotiations scheduled to begin May 4, 1964." British and American diplomats discussed strategy in October, and the "British thought the clouds looked very ominous from France." When Lyndon Johnson succeeded John Kennedy, American diplomats and trade negotiators were still working to smooth matters before the negotiations formally began.[41]

The Kennedy and thereafter the Johnson administrations pressed for, negotiated, wheedled and urged action on the so-called Kennedy Round of tariff reductions to replace the existing General Agreement on Tariffs and Trade. Kennedy asked for the tariff talks to begin in 1964, a delay of some

---

[40] *FRUS, 1961-1963, Vol. IX,* pp. 569-570, 582-584, 598-599.

[41] *FRUS, 1961-1963, Vol. IX,* pp. 603-604, 621, 628-629, 640-2.

fourteen months after he secured Congressional approval of the Trade Expansion Act. *U.S. News* predicted that "bitter trade battles will rage back and forth across the Atlantic for months, probably years to come." It noted that "obstacles to freeing trade are more visible now." The news magazine told readers that European governments "regard the U.S. with suspicion on trade matters" and concluded that "protectionism is here to stay on both sides of the Atlantic." Within weeks it seemed the prediction had come true. *The New York Times* described "a clash of two different philosophies of tariff reduction" between America and the European Common Market and that "this clash is only one of the problems besetting the negotiations." Europeans believed initial U.S. proposals "would help United States exports more than United States reductions would help foreign exports." By May, *The New York Times* reported that a "crisis looms in negotiations with [the] Common Market at GATT talks in Geneva." By November, *The Times* hoped GATT negotiators would resist rising protectionism, foreign traders expressed "grave doubts" about success in the talks, and *The Economist* told readers that "in case the Kennedy round of tariff negotiations fails, Britain should have some other initiative at the ready" – all signs of the difficulty in this lead-up to formal Kennedy Round talks.[42]

There were immediate problems in 1964. Christian Herter wrote Agriculture Secretary Orville Freeman and Undersecretary of State George Ball that "it will become increasingly difficult but important to recognize the full range of agricultural interests and avoid oversimplification in seeking solutions." "The agriculture phase of the trade negotiations is going to be difficult and complex." *The New York Times* reported in February that, "as the May opening of the 'Kennedy round' of trade talks draws closer, prospects for the trade expansion negotiations in Geneva seem to be getting dimmer." Great Britain disagreed on many issues with continental European nations. *The Economist* [and also *The New York* Times] reported that French President Charles de Gaulle wanted to protect

---

[42] *U.S. News & World Report,* "Business Around the World," February 4, 1963, pp. 91-92; *The New York Times,* "Clash on Tariffs mars trade talk," April 8, 1963, p. 77; "Meeting to Consider 3-Sided Program," April 17, 1963, p. 55; "French add snap to tariff cutting," May 1, 1963, p. 3; *Newsweek,* "GATT and the Kennedy Round," May 20, 1963, pp. 79-80; *The New York Times,* "U.S. Faces Split with Trade Bloc over Tariff Cuts," May 20, 1963, p. 1; "Resisting Protectionism," November 9, 1963, p. 19; "Rules on Tariffs Snag Trade Talk," December 2, 1963, p. 73; "Foreign Traders Doubt Success of Kennedy Tariff Negotiations," November 21,1963, p. 70; *The Economist,* November 23, 1963, "Wanted: An Alternative Trade Policy," p. 743.

French farmers in advance of the talks and that American negotiators were already in "retreat but not rout" three months before the talks formally opened. *Time* described the issue: "will the Common Market develop into a closed corporation under French leadership, or a free-trading force?" *The New York Times* editorialized that "there is scant prospect of reaching agreement on a constructive program." It noted that "far too many countries will seek to transform the conference into a propaganda platform to air their grievances and to make demands that will only provoke conflicts instead of resolving them." Several weeks later *The Times* reported that "a significant gap still separates the United States and the European Common Market on the troublesome question of tariff disparities n the forthcoming Kennedy Round of tariff negotiations." Some experts recommended the United States "should not push too hard on the agricultural question" given European concerns. *The New York Times* agreed: "agriculture seems certain to be the critical issue in the forthcoming 'Kennedy Round.'" American negotiators worried more generally about the length of the "exceptions" lists from "linear tariff negotiations." Long lists of exceptions by America's allies would make it all the more difficult to deny such exceptions to American agricultural commodity groups, textile manufacturers, steel producers, etc. Meanwhile, the Japanese government hoped "the Kennedy Round talks may result in a reduction of some of the non-tariff barriers that are hampering expansion of Japan's export trade in many parts of the world."[43]

The Kennedy Round finally opened in Geneva. *The New York Times* admitted that "the United States and the Common Market are not yet ready for detailed bargaining." *Business Week* stated that "from the start of this GATT session – commonly called the Kennedy Round – the U.S. seemed to be getting nowhere." *Time* reported "the air was heavy with torpor and reluctance." It quoted GATT executive secretary Eric Wyndham White: "this is disappointing, and it would be foolish to pretend otherwise." *Time* concluded that "at least no nation is deluding itself that the negotiations

[43] *FRUS, 1964-1968, Vol. VIII,* p. 615; *The New York Times,* "Prospects Poor for Trade Talks," February 2, 1964, p. F1; *The Economist,* "Kennedy Round: More Conditions," February 8, 1964; "Kennedy Round: Retreat but not Rout," February 29, 1964; *Time,* "Toward the Kennedy Round," March 6, 1964, www.time.com/archive; *The New York Times,* "Preparing for the Kennedy Round," March 7, 1964, p. 22; "Shaping World Trade," March 23, 1964, p. 28; "Tariff Disparity Remains an Issue," April 16, 1964, p. 51; "Easier U.S. Policy urged for Talks," April 20, 1964, p. 45; "The Kennedy Round," April 21, 1966, p. 36; *FRUS, 1964-1968, Vol. VIII,* p. 631, 696-698; *The New York Times,* "Japan Optimistic on Trade Talks," May 3, 1964, p. F3.

will be anything but long and arduous." *Newsweek* was less negative, instead stating success "depends on what the delegates decide in these key areas," including the percentage tariff cut, how to deal with agricultural issues, the exceptions lists, and resolving non-tariff barriers.[44]

It would take months for the two sides to present their complete positions. Still, *Time* noted some progress, including the narrowing of the "once-angry issue of tariff disparities." Participating nations soon agreed to "general guidelines" which however "did not advance the negotiations in any substantial way." Six months later the U.S. government conceded to talk about tariffs on industrial products without complementary talks on agricultural commodities, which the European Economic Community accepted. *The New York Times* predicted "the odds are against a successful outcome" and stated that, "even now, the preliminary sparring is not over." Secretary of State Dean Rusk and other American officials sought to pressure European allies to engage in serious negotiations, and stated that "we expect that the negotiations in both industry and agriculture will go hand in hand." *Time* criticized the "top-secret lists of sensitive and important products" that each nation wanted exempted from the tariff bargaining. It noted for months the talks "have quietly been going nowhere." *Newsweek* was encouraged by the lists, because "the step was taken at all." *The New York Times* said the Kennedy Round "moves to crucial stage," and that "with the speed of an Alpine glacier, the Kennedy Round was moving." By year's end *The New York Times* reported that key negotiators believed the talks would succeed by early 1966, and that "the three major road blocks that loomed so forbiddingly a few months ago no longer are reasons for despair."[45]

There was little more progress in 1965. *The New York Times* reported that "despite recurrent waves of pessimism, the Kennedy round made

---

[44] *The New York Times,* "The Kennedy Round Opens," May 4, 1964, p. 28; "43 Nations adopt Tariff Formula," May 7, 1964, p. 49; *Business Week,* "The broadest trade talks – and slowest," May 9, 1964, pp. 30-31; *Newsweek,* "First Round of the 'Kennedy Round,'", May 11, 1967, pp. 78-81; "A Disappointing Start," May 15, 1964, www.time.com/archive.

[45] *Time,* "Concession on Trade," November 5, 1964, p. 44; "Common Market approves Accord on Kennedy Round," November 15, 1964, p. 1; Opening the Kennedy Round," November 16, 1964, p. 30; "National Foreign Trade Convention is Opened Here," November 17, 1964, p. 57; *Time,* "A Question of Exceptions," November 20, 1964; "Tribute to Perseverance," November 27, 1964, www.time.com/archive; *Newsweek,* "Tariffs: Smoothing a Rough Road," November 30, 1964, pp. 82-83; *The New York Times,* "Kennedy Round Moves to Crucial Stage," November 22, 1964, p. E4; "Kennedy Round of Tariff Talks to be Concluded Early in 1966," December 21, 1964, p. 49.

some progress and reports of its death proved highly premature." The newspaper believed more progress was made in trade-liberalizing than in trade-restriction, and concluded "in 1964 the Kennedy round got off the ground." Herter wrote Johnson in mid-January that "we have reached a critical stage in the Kennedy Round." "Unless clear steps are taken to get the agriculture phases of the negotiations under way promptly there is a grave risk that the opportunity to achieve significant liberalization of agricultural trade will be seriously compromised." Johnson responded that "I approve the negotiating strategy" Herter proposed. Two months later *The Times* reported progress, noting "the long deadlock in agriculture has finally been broken." While the newspaper made clear that the fact of having the talks "does not mean that a successful outcome is guaranteed," it believed this raised the likelihood of "meaningful bargaining." Several weeks later, *The Times* reported some backsliding and that some of the confidential, "exceptions" lists – especially from Common Market countries – were "overly large." It quoted chief U.S. trade negotiator, Christian A. Herter, who "predicted that at least another year of secret bargaining is in store before agreement is reached." By July, *The Times* reported that the negotiations went into summer recess "in an atmosphere of uncertainty." France was boycotting the Common Market's attempt to formulate a joint agricultural policy. Orville Freeman expressed concern about "the growing protectionism in the EEC." Herter wrote Johnson that "we have come to another critical point in the Kennedy Round negotiations." He proposed temporary tabling U.S. agriculture proposals or else risk "the clear danger of the collapse of the entire Kennedy Round." [Johnson agreed to table the agriculture proposals on September 16.] By September *The Times* criticized the Johnson Administration's insistence on jointly liberalizing agricultural and industrial trade, noting "the important thing now is to keep the talks going." The next month Michael Blumenthal announced that "the continuing stalemate within the Common Market threatened the outcome of the worldwide effort to liberalize trade." "Time is running out," he said, since the Trade Expansion Act would expire on June 30, 1967. Assistant Secretary of State Anthony Solomon stated publicly that "preparations for the Kennedy Round have been long and difficult" and "there has been a setback in the timetable that we did not anticipate." He recognized the Kennedy Round might grind to a "halt."[46]

---

[46] *The New York Times,* "Despite Moments of Pessimism, Kennedy Round makes Gains," January 11, 1965, p. 50; *FRUS, 1964-1968, Vol. VIII,* pp. 699, 701; *The New York Times,* "Progress in the Kennedy Round," March 21, 1965, p. E10; "New Phase Near in Kennedy Round," April 7, 1965, p. 59; "Peek at the Kennedy

Throughout 1966 the deadline to conclude a treaty weighed on participants in the Kennedy Round talks. As the new year began, Common Market nations remained unable to resolve their internal differences about tariffs and preferences and thus to develop a common position for the talks. Common Market representatives requested at least a four month delay before the Kennedy Round reconvened. Eric Wyndham White, Director-General of GATT, made his report to the GATT Trade Negotiations Committee and stated "unhappily . . . it is somewhat difficult even to apply a similar degree of cautious professional optimism." He was "disturbed at the lack of progress in the negotiations" and he "felt that time is beginning to run out." In particular, he stated in "the negotiations on agriculture, the picture is frankly one inviting complete depression." *The New York Times* editorialized that "time is running out on the Kennedy Round of negotiations to liberalize world trade." In addition to the Common Market deadlock that "effectively stalled bargaining during the last half of 1965," other nations established new restrictions and preferences to favor their home products. *The Times* feared "the negotiations will deteriorate into a bitter and sterile competition to maintain protectionist barriers." In mid-April U.S. trade officials warned that "success or failure of the Kennedy Round of tariff negotiations will be told in the coming weeks rather than months." They worried about "the long European summer vacation" which made progress difficult. The situation was so difficult that William Roth, Deputy Special Trade Representative, stated that "European rumors that the United States may have lost its enthusiasm for these important trade negotiations are wide of the mark." Roth noted that "there are no practical alternatives if global trade expansion is to be achieved." Six weeks later *The New York Times* editorialized that "the pall of gloom that has enveloped the 'Kennedy Round' of trade negotiations is lifting." *The Times* noted that "these optimistic assessments run counter to widely aired notions that the 'Kennedy Round' is either dead or dying." A month later, a senior GATT official stated the negotiations were "really on the road." While admitting "that many difficulties remained," Deputy Secretary Finn Gundelach stated that "the determination to bring the Kennedy Round to a successful conclusion was shown by the talks to be manifestly present in all quarters." U.S. trade negotiators reported in mid-July "a tone of prudent

---

Round," May 22, 1965, p. 30; GATT Parley Ends for the Summer," July 24, 1965, p 33; *FRUS, 1964-1968, Vol. VIII,* pp. 737, 738, 746; *The New York Times,* "Pause in the Kennedy Round," September 24, 1965, p. 4; "Kennedy Round Periled," October 29, 1965, p. 69; *Department of State Bulletin,* "Challenges Facing United States Trade Policy," November 15, 1965, p. 787-9.

optimism" at the recent GATT meeting. "The general feeling of the participants was that it will be possible to complete successful negotiations on time." Soon thereafter, reporters noted "an unusual glow of goodwill" and that "the Americans are more relaxed and optimistic." But *Time* reported that "since the first meeting in May 1963, Kennedy Round negotiations have moved mostly in circles." Agriculture remained an issue, as well as chemicals, aluminum, and steel. But in early winter *The New York Times* editorialized that the Kennedy Round continues "to lag seriously behind schedule." "From the start," *The Times* continued, "the Kennedy Round has not lived up to expectations." *Business Week* quoted "a veteran trade official" who said "the trouble with the Kennedy Round is that it was launched in 1962 in a mood of U.S.-European togetherness. Now, it has to be wound up in a growing climate of economic nationalism."[47]

The bellwether year of 1967 began as conflicted as prior years. *The New York Times* quoted GATT Director General Eric Wyndham White who said "a good basis for a substantial tariff disarmament existed." Yet several days later *The Times* quoted Congressman Thomas Curtis, a member of the U.S. delegation, that "he is no longer optimistic about the outcome because of 'the lack of forward momentum.'" Similarly George Ball wrote Lyndon Johnson that "I am deeply concerned that the world trading community appears to be drifting into regional blocs and discriminatory arrangements which, if unchecked, would have serious political and economic consequences for the United States." In addition, Ball proposed to "offer the poor countries of the world a 'head start' in such a move – the benefits of tariff reduction would be given to them immediately while reductions among industrialized countries are phased over a longer period. Ball did note "there is the problem, of course, of possible injury to U.S. industry and labor arising from increased imports

---

[47] *The New York Times,* "Delay is Sought in Kennedy Round," January 12, 1966, p. 38; "Kennedy Round Timetable," March 5, 1966, p. 19; "Time is seen running short for Kennedy Round in Geneva," April 19, 1966, p. 61; *Department of State Bulletin,* "The Johnson Trade Policy," May 30, 1966, pp. 856-857; *FRUS, 1964-1968, Vol. VIII,* pp. 820-823; *The New York Times,* "'Kennedy Round' Comes Alive," June 4, 1966, p. 22; "Trade Talks take optimistic turn," July 9, 1966, p. 33; *Fortune,* "The Kennedy Round: Down the Homestretch," pp. 67-68, August 1966; *Time,* "A Will to Agree," September 232, 1966," www.time.com/archive; *FRUS, 1964-1968, Vol. VIII,* pp. 833-835; The *New York Times,* "Good Will found at Tariff Talks," October 3, 1966, p. 90; *FRUS, 1964-1968, Vol. VIII,* 834-845, *passim; The New York Times,* "Test for the Kennedy Round," November 29, 1966, p. 42; *Business Week,* "Tariff cutters get set for big push in Geneva," December 10, 1966, pp. 42-43.

from low-wage countries." Johnson asked Rusk to put together a small group to "examine these ideas further." Rusk reported in February 1967 "unanimous agreement both on the need for a new United States trade policy and on broad outlines of the policy itself" along the lines of the Ball memo of August 1966. Soon thereafter the U.S. government announced it set a deadline of March 26 for conclusion of the Kennedy Round talks.[48]

By April the talks had come down to the wire. *The New York Times* editorialized that "the heat is on the negotiators." *Business Week* warned readers that "after four years of leisurely haggling, the Kennedy Round of trade negotiations has a firm – and probably frantic – timetable." Francis Bator reported to Johnson in mid-April that "we will be facing the crunch in the trade negotiations during the next 2-3 weeks." Bator noted "your entire trade policy is at stake." *The New York Times* reported that the deadline and the need to reach agreement on agriculture threatened to scuttle the talks. Roth wrote Johnson the next month that "we are presently in the final, critical stage of the Kennedy Round" and noted the "most important negotiating problems we face." A week later Bator wrote Johnson "it now appears that the negotiations will end Sunday night [i.e., May 14] – win or lose." Again Bator wrote Johnson at midnight on May 15 that "our negotiators came up with a package late last night – after several days of round-the-clock bargaining." The "overall bargain is a good one for the United States and a good one for the world." State Department staffer Thomas Enders wrote Rusk the next day that "Bill Roth has brought off a handsome deal in Geneva." *Time* reported "after for years of continuous and suspenseful bargaining, 53 non-Communist countries struggled to the verge of an agreement that should result in the biggest bundle of tariff cuts in history." *Newsweek* concluded "the Kennedy round was the Free World's sixth assault on tariff walls since World War II – and by far the most successful." While the agreement did not result in a full 50% reduction in all economic sectors, the chief U.S. negotiator commented that "we've come a long way from Smoot-Hawley," referring to the seriously protectionist U.S. trade legislation of the early 1930s. Still, *Business Week* drew attention to weaknesses in the tariff treaty, including "critical areas of chemicals, steel, aluminum, and textiles." While, economist Milton Friedman editorialized that "the sweeping reductions in tariffs achieved in the Kennedy round" "need a

---

[48] *The New York Times,* "Progress Predicted in Kennedy Round," January 8, 1967, p.15; "Key to the Kennedy Round," January 20, 1967, p. 36; *FRUS, 1964-1968, Vol. VIII,* pp. 846-849, 874-876; *The New York Times,* "U.S. Sets March Deadline on Talks to Reduce Tariffs," February 15, 1967, p. 1, 58; "President Confers on Kennedy Round," February 23, 1967, p. 51, 53.

reduction in non-tariff barriers to trade." Months later, in late November, Johnson transmitted the multilateral trade agreement concluding the Kennedy Round of negotiations with a special message to Congress.[49]

Securing agreement did not lead immediately to the easing of tariff and non-tariff barriers sought by American negotiators. In January 1968, *Time* reported that "a wide assortment of other trade barriers loomed as high as ever. These are non-tariff gimmicks designed to impede the inflow of foreign goods." *The New Republic* criticized Congress, claiming "it seems bent on wrecking the Kennedy Round: no fewer than 90 senators are acting as sponsors of one or more bills that propose to slap import quota limits on foreign goods that range from steel to textiles, from zinc to mink." It also reported "the House has already passed a bill calling on the President to halt imports from 'low-wage countries'; the vote was 340 to 29." The next week *The New Republic* editorialized that "the US is going to get a fairly bad deal out of the Kennedy Round." It concluded that "viewed from the perspective of history, it would be a tragedy if this, the most ambitious effort ever made to reduce tariffs by the hundreds, were to founder on the emerging insistence of the United States on no longer being a 'sucker'." President Johnson expressed his disapproval: "non-tariff barriers pose a continued threat to the growth of world trade and our competitive position." Ten months later the Commerce Department reported that for the first time since 1893 the United States ran trade deficits. *Time* reported that "the current problem lies primarily in the growing U.S. appetite for foreign products." This left the Johnson Administration "a difficult dilemma." "If the U.S. substantially reduces the comparatively free access other countries enjoy to the world's largest

---

[49] *The New York Times,* "Kennedy Round Countdown," March 14, 1967, p. 46; "Preparing the Johnson Round," March 26, 1967, p. 154; *Business Week,* "Kennedy Round turns into a cliff-hanger," March 18, 1967, pp. 162-163; *Newsweek,* "Tariffs: End in Sight," March 20, 1967, p. 92; *FRUS, 1964-1968, Vol. VIII,* pp. 888-889, 906, 919-920, 934-935, 936-937, 969-970; *The New York Times,* "Tensions Mount in Kennedy Round," April 24, 1967, p. 47; "Gloom Deepens at Trade Talks," April 29, 1967, p. 39; "Outlook Brighter in Kennedy Round," May 8, 1967, p. 63-64; "Accord in Kennedy Round Appears Almost Certain," May 13, 1967, pp. 45-47; "Kennedy Round Succeeds; 50 Nations to Cut Tariffs, Liberalizing World Trade," May 16, 1967, p. 1; "Success in the Kennedy Round," May 17, 1967, p. 46; *Time,* "Toward Agreement," May 19, 1967, www.time.com/archive; *The New York Times,* "Kennedy Round: What It Will Mean for U.S.," May 21, 1967, p. E3; *Newsweek,* "The Kennedy Round: Success," May 29, 1967, pp. 80-82; *Business Week,* "Where tariffs go down," July 1, 1967, p. 18; *The New York Times,* "After the Kennedy Round," July 4, 1967, p 13; *Newsweek,* "Milton Friedman on the Kennedy Round," July 17, 1967, p. 80.

market, it risks a prosperity-wrecking shrinkage in world trade." *Time* worried about "a return to protectionism" because "two dozen U.S. industries are pressing for higher tariffs or import quotas on everything from shoes to glass, from steel to electronic components." [50]

A combination of factors constrained American foreign and foreign economic policy towards the non-communist nations of East Asia. On the one hand there was the Cold War confrontation with the Soviet Union and the challenge that the People's Republic of China posed. On the other, there were the very real economic challenges the United States faced in its balance of payments and balance of trade. Finally, American policymakers, perhaps not unnaturally, did not recognize these nations in East Asia as the stable polities and strengthening economies that they were. This issue of perceptions provided the background to the America's combined diplomacy with individual nations in the region, the subject of succeeding chapters.

As discussed in the opening chapter, senior American policymakers and their advisors focused on the superpower confrontation. They believed that the Soviet Union represented a threat to the established world order, and Soviet leaders regularly tested American resolve. John Kennedy felt somewhat besieged by Nikita Khrushchev, and after Kennedy died and Khrushchev was deposed, Lyndon Johnson largely continued Kennedy's policies while seeking a series of breakthroughs to develop a Soviet-American dialogue, contain nuclear proliferation, create a Sino-American dialogue, and generally improve the quality of life abroad as he was committed to improving it at home.

Soviet purposefulness and the widespread perception of Chinese aggression faced relatively new and/or weak governments in the region. These governments expected the United States to create a shield behind which they could develop, secure the allegiance of their peoples, and cooperate with their neighbors. Successive presidents and their advisors believed this required a strong military stand in the region, hence the flawed policies and strategies of American foreign policy in Laos and thereafter Vietnam.

---

[50] *Time,* "Non-Tariff Tricks," January 12, 1968; "The Impact of Imports," November 15, 1968; "Trade: Dangerous Drift for the U.S.," December 13, 1968, www.time.com/archive; *Business Week,* "Fighting to keep the trade walls," October 14, 1967, p. 36-37; *The New Republic,* "Trade Warriors," November 11, 1967, pp. 5; "Who Gets What from the 'Kennedy Round,'" November 18, 1967, pp. 15-16.

America's military muscle, the basis of the system resisting the supposed Soviet threat, rested on a weakening economic foundation. The balance of payments deficit reflected an economy that was less competitive internationally. Both Kennedy and Johnson tried to strengthen America's international economic position with little success. In addition to a series of halfway measures, Kennedy secure passage of the Trade Expansion Act of 1962 and Johnson achieved the required tariff cuts from GATT members as the five year window was about to expire.

But, the increasing involvement in Vietnam exacerbated America's international economic challenges. And these constraints made the twin conduct of foreign policy and foreign economic policy much more difficult.

CHAPTER THREE

THE UNITED STATES AND JAPAN

In 1960, Prime Minister Ikeda Hayato committed Japan to doubling its Gross National Product during the decade – an annual growth rate of 7.2%. His announcement on December 27, 1960 focused on investments in science and technology, subsidizing loans to industries with the best prospects for expansion, and greatly expanding international trade. Surprisingly, while many contemporary observers viewed the plan as overly aggressive, Japan achieved its goal in just seven years for an average growth rate of 10.2%.[1]

The Ministry of International Trade and Industry, known by its acronym, MITI, occupied a central position in Japan's economic game planning and foreign policy deliberations. It targeted such industries as shipbuilding and steel and then oil refining, chemical fertilizers, plastics, petrochemicals, machine tools, electronic goods, and synthetic fibers as nylon to help Japan move from its prewar orientation as a producer of light industrial goods to a serious global contender in heavy industry. MITI spurred Matsushita and SONY in electrical appliances for the home, and Japanese exports in televisions, audio equipment, vacuum cleaners, and videocassette recorders helped drive American and European manufacturers out of business. *Time* had reported that "addicted to quality, SONY has done as much as any company to demolish the cheap and imitative image of Japanese goods." In the 1960s, MITI believed automobiles was a fertile ground for economic growth. It supported import barriers, and as the decade ended it supported exporting of Japanese cars, although Japanese car manufacturers gained an international reputation in the 1970s as the oil shocks following the 1973 Arab-Israeli War caused consumers to view well-made, reliable, high mileage Japanese compact cars with greater favor. The numbers help illustrate the coordinated nature of Japanese industrial planning. In 1960, Japan produced 481,551 cars and exported 38,809; in 1965, it produced 1,875,614 cars and exported 194,168; in 1970, it produced 5,289,157 and exported 1,086,776. The domestic market

[1] "Japan lifts its targets," *Business Week,* June 17, 1961, p. 131-134.

grew 11-fold and exports increased 25-fold. Japan's success caused many foreign observers to call the phenomenon "Japan, Inc."[2]

There were many factors behind Japan's success. Japanese families saved a high proportion of their income in low interest postal savings accounts providing an inexpensive source of capital for economic expansion. In addition, most Japanese agreed on the need to sacrifice to promote economic growth, and as many Japanese moved from the countryside [in 1950, nearly one half of Japan's labor force worked in agriculture] to teeming cities, they accepted the lack of goods and services considered typical in western industrialized countries. While the American occupation had dismantled Japan's large, family-controlled, banking and industrial conglomerates, the *zaibatsu,* Japan enjoyed remarkable cooperation between various government ministries, the ruling Liberal-Democratic Party, and large industrial concerns. Finally, based on theories of Edward Deming, Japanese companies efficiently produced vast quantities of reasonably priced, reliable goods which consumers in Japan and across the globe welcomed into home and business. Production moved from goods heavily dependent on expensive raw materials to goods – e.g., cars, requiring fewer imports.

Japan also benefited from its relationship with the United States. America protected Japan with a nuclear umbrella and U.S. naval, air, and ground forces augmented Japan's Self Defense Forces. As important as America's military shield was the access that Japan enjoyed to the American market. Japan's neighbors did not have enough goods Japan wanted to buy and lacked cash reserves to consume significant amounts of Japanese exports. Latin America and Africa, while important for the future, also did not have sufficiently robust economies to absorb much imports. Europe had trade barriers that made imports expensive and thus uncompetitive. That left the United States, which accepted the obligation to grant Japan [and other East Asian nations] access even if such access resulted in weakening of American industries and pain for American workers.

The results astounded the world throughout the decade, although, to be sure, there were momentary ups and downs. In April 1961, Walt Rostow provided George Ball with an analysis of the Japanese economy and noted that "Japan has not actually been treated by advanced Western European nations as a completely equal partner" and less developed countries lack

---

[2] *Time,* "Small Wonder," July 12, 1963, http://www.time.com/time/magazine/article/0,9171,940333,00.html; Michael A. Cusumano, *The Japanese Automobile Industry: Technology and Management at Nissan and Toyota,* Cambridge, MA, Harvard University Press, 1985, pp. 3-4.

the foreign exchange reserves to soak up Japanese exports. Still, he predicted continued high growth for the next several years. In June, *U.S. News* reported that "Japan's boom is moving so fast the Ikeda Government is getting nervous." Soon thereafter, Prime Minister Ikeda made an official visit to Washington, DC, and as *Time* reported, "Ikeda addressed the House of Representatives and flew on to New York, where, in polite phrases, he issued a clear warning: U.S. restrictions against Japanese products can hurt the Japanese economy—and that economy is vital to Far East stability." Ikeda painted a picture of a Japan whose economy was still recovering from wartime, yet the Japanese economy was powerful, adaptive, and entrepreneurial. *Time* reported on the success of Honda producing motorcycles for export, which dominated European motorcycle races. "Honda in 1960 produced 750,000 machines—20% of total world output—and made pre-tax profits of $14.2 million on sales of $136.5 million. This year's racing successes have obliged Honda to increase production to 85,000 machines a month [or 1,020,000 – an annual increase of 36%]." Three months later *Time* reported that "last week Japan's growth rate was still clipping along at over 13%—and the Japanese economy was suffering from too much boom" but Ikeda "stoutly denied that the mounting balance-of-payments deficit poses any real threat to Japan's economic health." Still, both *U.S. News* and *The New York Times* reported on the possible overheating of the Japanese economy. *U.S. News*, for example, stated that "Japan is suffering from too much prosperity" while *The Times* cited others who feared Japan's "economy is shooting up too high and too quickly."[3]

In 1962, for example, *Newsweek* reported that "for ten years Japan has ridden the crest of a boom that has been at once the marvel and envy of Asia." "Today the Japanese economy is running into trouble." *U.S. News* agreed, stating that "clouds gathered quite suddenly over Japan during 1961." The cause: there was "an enormous drain on Japan's gold and foreign-exchange reserves." Japan accompanied its foreign borrowing with an overriding commitment to quality and reliability in its products. *Business Week* reported on a government laboratory that tested for quality,

[3] JFK Library, NSF, Box 123, Japan, General, 3-4/61, Rostow to Ball, April 13, 1961; "Business Around the World," *U.S. News & World Report,* June 19, 1961, p. 106; "For Those At Home," June 30, 1961; "Precision on Wheels," August 2, 1961; "The Overheated Boom," September 8, 1961; *Time,* www.time.com/archive; "Business Around the World," *U.S. News & World Report,* September 11, 1961, p. 92, "Japanese Boom Causing Alarm," *The New York Times,* September 17, 1961, p. F1; "Business Around the World," *U.S. News & World Report,* November 13, 1961, p. 131.

and helped industry improved its products. In September, *Business Week* reported on Japan's steel boom that soon would make the country the number three producer behind the United States and the Soviet Union and in front of West Germany and Great Britain. By October, *U.S. News & World Report* headlined that "seldom, if ever, has the world seen the like of Japan's rampaging prosperity." While the news magazine could not explain the factors behind Japan's success, it reported that "foreign economists and businessmen call Japan's postwar surge one of which Japanese are beginning to wonder how much more trade the U.S. can absorb."[4]

Japanese economic growth continued throughout the decade and continued to attract the attention of American news media. In January 1963, *Newsweek* reported on Japan's commanding lead in large shipbuilding. It noted that "Japanese yards produced more than 2 million gross tons of ships in 1962 to lead other nations for the seventh straight year." An efficient shipbuilding industry provided real advantages for an export-driven economic expansion. But, *The Economist* contrasted Japan "arranging for a $305 million standby credit from the International Monetary Fund" with Japan intending to continue its economic expansion. *The New York Times* noted that Japan's economy was enjoying more moderate and more sustainable growth which *The Times* called "a transition to adulthood." *U.S. News & World Report* told readers that "Japan at this time is showing the United States and Western Europe the way towards a possible solution of the problem of costly traffic bottlenecks . . . de luxe trains that streak between major cities at speeds as high as 160 miles per hour." *The New York Times* reported economic growth and the rise of a consumer economy: "Riding a wave of economic growth and industrial modernization, Japan has entered the era of mass consumer spending." *The Economist* ended 1963 noting "Japan's spectacular growth rate, averaging about 9 percent annually for the past three years." *Business Week* agreed that "the Japanese, for the first time, are enjoying a taste of affluence" and believed that such consumerism might help American exports. *Time* proclaimed Japan "the new number 3 in steel." *The New York Times* editorialized that this continuing and

---

[4] "Japan's Boom Turns into a High-Level Stall," *Newsweek,* January 8, 1962, p. 30; "Business Around the World," *U.S. News & World Report,* February 5, 1962, p. 81; "Japan's newest quest for quality," *Business Week,* July 2, 1962, p. 98; "Sparking steel boom in Japan," *Business Week,* September 29, 1962, pp. 113-114; "In the New Japan: Biggest Boom of All," *U.S. News & World Report,* October 22, 1965, pp. 72, 74; "Japan: Overheated economy simmers down," *Business Week,* November 3, 1962, p. 84.

dramatic economic growth meant that Japan is ready "to re-establish itself as a great power in the Far East."[5]

Japan's economic performance received praise from the Western industrial powers. *The Economist* published a glowing analysis of Japan headlined "The Economist reconsiders Japan." By December 1964, *Business Week* wondered "can Japan maintain the pace?" It stated that "after 10 years of the most rapid growth rate in the world, the economy shows hints of strain. But there's no sign of that in the confident drive of industry." *Time* noted the contrast: "Japan can boast of more economic superlatives than ever." Achievements included constructing 40% of the free world's merchant ships, being No. 1 in making motorcycles, sewing machines, watches, clocks, transistor radios, cameras, and binoculars. Yet the Japanese had become so complacent about economic success that "anything less than new superlatives distresses them." In April 1965, *Newsweek* used the president of Fuji Iron and Steel Company, Shigeo Nagano, to note that "in recent months the thunder of Japan's 'economic miracle' has been increasingly muffled under a deadening weight of debt." A month later *U.S. News & World Report* added to the doom and gloom: "Japan's economic miracle appears to be in real trouble." The real culprit: "have the Japanese lived too long on borrowed money and borrowed time?" *U.S. News* reported in July that "the Japanese economy appears plagued by overexpansion, crippling interest charges, overemployment." *The New York Times* noted that despite a recession "Japan achieved the world's highest economic growth rate."[6]

---

[5] "Japan: Doko-san and Me," *Newsweek,* January 7, 1963, p. 44; "Japan: Brake and Accelerator," *The Economist,* March 14, 1963, p. 1024; "Japan Advancing with Discretion after Long Boom," *The New York Times,* April 5, 1963, p. 66; "Rapid Transit: Japan Shows Way," *U.S. News & World Report,* June 3, 1963, p. 86; "Japan: Holding the Lead," *The Economist,* December 28, 1963, p. 1356; "Japanese Survey a Rising Economy," *The New York Times,* March 22, 1964, p. 12; "Consumer's day dawns in land of rising sun," *Business Week,* March 21, 1964, p. 129; "The New No. 3 in Steel," *Time,* July 17, 1964, www.time.com/archive; "Resurgent Japan," *The New York Times,* August 3, 1964, p. 24; "Japan's Economy Praised by West," *The New York Times,* August 31, 1964, p. 37.

[6] "Year of the Open Door," *The Economist,* November 28, 1964, pp. 993-1018; "Can Japan maintain the pace," *Business Week,* December 19, 1964, p. 71; "Bumps in a Boom," *Time,* February 26, 1965, www.time.com/archive; "Japan: A Danger of Dominoes," *Newsweek,* April 26, 1965, p. 80; "As Japan's 'Miracle' Begins to Fade," *U.S. News & World Report,* May 24, 1965, pp. 113-114; "Japan: Reflationary Rescue," *The Economist,* June 26, 1965, p. 1546; "Business Around the World," *U.S. News & World Report,* July 19, 965, p. 93; "In Japan, It's a

After a year of government action, the economy boomed again in 1967 and 1968. In 1966, the government in Tokyo helped inflate the economy and made credit easier to prop up the banking sector. In 1967, Toshiba, considered the "GE of Japan" by *Business Week*, revived after several poor years. The business weekly reported "signs of soaring boom are beginning to appear in the Japanese economy again – after a slowdown in 1965-66." It further noted that Japan's vast steel industry could not satisfy domestic demand, and "the Japanese auto industry also is booming." *The New York Times* reported in late May that "the flourishing Japanese economy has been expanding to such a degree that the Government has cautioned against "overheating." By Summer 1967, *The Economist* reported that "Japan's authorities have managed to push their country's economy from recession to full scale upswing with an ease and balance that must leave virtually all of their western tutors gasping." *The New York Times* somewhat ironically reported in January 1968 that "Japanese growth slows to a gallop." Two months later *U.S. News & World Report* cautioned that "Japan seems to be heading for trouble. Trade is running in the red. Profits are down. Bankruptcies up." Yet, in summer, *The Economist* wrote that "Japan can congratulate itself on having chalked up the smoothest and most painless correction yet of a bad balance of payments situation." Meanwhile, *The New York Times* reported that "the remarkable Japanese economy is growing so fast that even the Government has a hard time keeping track of it" and a few weeks later headlined "Japan's Economy in a Major Boom." *Business Week* reported that Japan "expects to become the world's No. 3 industrial power this year." *The Economist* found that Japan's economic boom also caused a surplus in its balance of payments and helped ease the debt load of major commercial banks. *The New York Times* looked back at 1968 and stated on "Growth in Japan: The Soaring Sun has eclipsed West Germany."[7]

Money Problem," *U.S. News & World Report,* July 26, 1965, p. 80; "Japan's Growth World's Highest," August 11, 1965, p. 44; "An End to Pessimism," *Time,* October 8, 1965, www.time.com/archive.

[7] "New spark at the 'GE of Japan,'" *Business Week,* February 11, 1967, p. 123; "International Outlook," *Business Week,* March 4, 1967,.p. 143; "Industry Speeds Growth in Japan," *The New York Times,* May 28, 1967, p. F15; "Japan: New economies, old success," *The Economist,* August 12, 1967, p. 595; "Business Around the World," *U.S. News & World Report,* October 2, 1967, p. 72; "Japanese Growth Slows to a Gallop," *The New York Times,* January 19, 1968, p. 51; "Business Around the World," *U.S. News & World Report,* March 11, 1968, p. 71; "Tokyo's balancing trick," *The Economist,* August 12, 1968, p. 60; "Japan's Economy: "High is Up," *The New York Times,* August 28, 1968, p. 67; "Japan's Economy in a Major Boom," *The New York Times,* September 9, 1968; "Japan

While Japan's domestic market absorbed the majority of this dramatic increase in manufacturing, export sales provided a comfortable profit margin for many businesses and Japanese and foreigners alike focused on Japan's drive for markets worldwide. In April 1961, *Time* reported on Japan's largest advertising firm, Dentsu Advertising, Ltd., and its drive to secure accounts outside Japan. *U.S. News* asked rhetorically "what keeps Japan's boom going?" It responded "aggressive export ideas, for one thing," and noted that "Japan's camera manufacturers are going after the consumer market in Germany, once the world's top producer of cameras." South Africa sufficiently wanted Japanese capital that it offered to classify Japanese as "white" under its strict apartheid regulations, but Japan declined fearing a greater loss of trade with other African and with Asian nations. *U.S. News* claimed that "neither Britain nor the Common Market has been at all happy with the flood of Japanese goods appearing in Europe." Apparently, Japanese saw themselves as "a kind of pariah among major industrial nations."[8]

As the Japanese economy boomed in the early 1960s, so did interest in Japan's exporting success. *Time* compared Japan seeking "with guns" to impose its Greater East Asian Co-Prosperity Sphere in the 1940s and the current "briefcase brigades of Japanese businessmen" "swarming over Asia." *The Economist* drew attention to Japan's balance of payments which had "improved steadily throughout 1962," and "the surplus subsequently increased steadily." *The New York Times* reported that "Japan's export trade staged a roaring comeback last year, and its prospects are as good or better for 1963." *Time* explained that Japan had become "shipbuilder to the world" because its shipyards "can turnout ships in about one-third less time than their competitors." *The Economist* drew attention to Japanese businessmen who "are busy chalking up one economic victory after another in Asia and Africa." By February 1966, *The Economist* reported "common market charges that Japanese goods are flooding the African market." *The Economist* also informed readers that "Japan in recent years has turned its trading glance increasingly towards South America both as a source of raw materials, particularly cotton and

---

rides unscheduled boom," *Business Week,* October 12, 1968, p. 56; "Japan: Someone else has a surplus," November 23, 1968, p. 91; "Growth in Japan: The Soaring Sun Has Eclipsed West Germany," *The New York Times,* January 17, 1969, p. C65.

[8] "The View from Fuji," *Time,* April 7, 1961, www.time.com/archive; "Business Around the World," *U.S. News & World Report,* July 24, 1961, p. 82; "Business Around the World," *U.S. News & World Report,* July 31, 1961, p. 76; "Business Around the World," *U.S. News & World Report,* August 27, 1962, p. 89.

iron ore, and as a market for its exports of capital goods." Japan's Minister of International Trade and Industry, Hajime Fukuda, predicted both an "era of evenly paced economic growth" and a "steady rise in Japanese exports." By December 1965, *Business Week* reported on the success of Japanese cameras in Germany: "after decades of loyalty from professional photographers, the German camera's place at the top is being challenged by a more versatile newcomer from Japan." Japan's success at obtaining raw materials and selling finished goods abroad drew attention from *Time* which wrote that "from Soviet Russia to Sumatra and across the broad Pacific to South America, Japanese businessmen smilingly signed agreements last week that will guarantee them industrial raw materials for years to come." *The Economist* in early 1968 praised Japan for increasing its trade surplus "in spite of the British devaluation and American balance of payments measures."[9]

Inevitably, Japan's protectionism at home and fearsome commitment to exports led to friction with neighbors and trading partners. This certainly was the case with U.S.-Japanese relations. Japanese officials regularly claimed the need to protect industries at home, while demonstrating little concern, save for political niceties, for the damage done in American communities when Japanese imports led to factory closings. The commitment to containing the People's Republic of China, the consequent need for an economically success Japan, and a willingness to sacrifice a measure of prosperity at home for Cold War goals all constrained American diplomats.

Friction arose initially with textile exports. *U.S. News* wrote in early 1961 that "textile imports from Japan were again very high last year. U.S. cotton manufacturers aren't happy at the trend." Jacob Potofsky, president of the Amalgamated Clothing Workers of America, "threatened two weeks ago to have the members refuse to work on clothing or fabrics made in

---

[9] "Briefcase Brigades," *Time,* February 8, 1963, www.time.com/archive; "Japan: Recovery Course," *The Economist,* April 4, 1963, p. 80; "Japan's Energetic Export Drive Shows No Sign of Losing Speed," *The New York Times,* July 14, 1963, p. 83; "Shipbuilder to the World," *Time,* January 3, 1964, www.time.com/archive; [see also "Why It's 'Made in Japan' on Big Ships," *U.S. News & World Report,* September 19, 1966, pp. 92-93;] "Honourable Salesmen," *The Economist,* March 7, 1964, p. 883; "Japan: An Import Subsidy," *The Economist,* February 5, 1966, p. 541; "Japanese South American Trade," *The Economist,* May 30, 1964, p. 1013; "Steady Expansion is Forecast as Exports Increase in Japan," *The Economist,* June 30, 1964, p. 41; "Nikon crowds into Leica's picture," *Business Week,* December 11, 1965, p. 49; "New Co-Prosperity Sphere," *Time,* February 25, 1966; "Japan: Strengthening Exports," March 9, 1968, p. 73.

Japan." Minoru Takita, president of the Japan Trade Union Congress, met with President Kennedy to protest this boycott. He noted that "great danger lay in the fact that the boycott might expand and do great damage to our relationships." In August 1961, the new Kennedy Administration and the Japanese government opened talks on cotton textile quotas. While U.S. representatives wanted to limit Japanese exports, Japanese negotiators insisted on similar limitations on exports from other Asian countries, complicating discussions. Happily, by mid-September negotiators agreed on a 7-8% increase compared to the 30% growth the Japanese had wanted. Of course, in time, such quotas caused Japan to look to other industries to increase exports.[10]

It moved into transistors, small electrical products and even steel. *U.S. News* reported in early 1961 that "imports of electronic transistors – mostly from Japan – have become so massive that domestic producers have asked Washington to limit importation in the interests of national defense." Japanese imports threatened American jobs and *Business Week* quoted the president of an International Brotherhood of Electrical Workers local union that "they will work on any American-made parts, union or nonunion, but will not install Japanese or other foreign-made parts." In late 1962 American steel manufacturers increased "complaints of dumping of Japanese steel on U.S. market," and to preserve their position, Japanese steelmakers "will rein in their export drive to quiet fears of giant U.S. steelmakers." In January 1963, Japanese makers of vinyl and sponge-rubber footwear as well as tape recorders worried about higher American tariffs. In August 1963 *Business Week* noted "Japan has the largest sewing machine industry in the world," and that "only Singer Co. now stands in the way of Japan's complete domination of the U.S. sewing machine market." In Fall 1966, *Business Week* reported Yamaha of Japan moving from exporting motorcycles into pianos and skis to America. In Spring

---

[10] "Business Around the World," *U.S. News & World Report,* January 16, 1961, p. 66; JFK Library, NSF, Box 123, Japan, General, 3-4/61, "Trade: United States and Japan," March 3, 1961; "'Made-in-Japan' Dilemma," *The New York Times,* June 12, 1960, p. 208; "U.S. and Japan open textile trade talk," *The New York Times,* August 23, 1961, p. 47; "International Outlook," *Business Week,* August 26, 1961, p. 70; "Business Around the World," *U.S. News & World Report,* September 25, 1961, p. 115. Companies involved in U.S.-Japanese trade held an opposite view; the United States-Japan Trade Council wrote Kennedy to argue that the U.S. can hardly expand its exports "by adopting restrictive quota barriers against imports or similar protectionist devices which would invite retaliation," JFK Library, President's Office Files-Countries, Box 120, Japan, General 1961, Press release of May 1, 1961.

1968, Secretary of Agriculture Orville Freeman attacked Japanese restrictions on food imports from the United States, citing such products as soybeans, citrus, meat, dairy products, and processed fruits and vegetables. *U.S. News* warned readers that "the resurrection of Japan's giant industrial combines is creating new and potent rivals for the biggest and best producers in the U.S. and Europe." By Fall 1968, *The New York Times* noted "the United States and Japan appear to be headed for a clash over economic policies that could seriously damage their relations." *The Times* further noted that "as the Japanese economy has grown in power and demonstrated its ability to compete with the United States in world markets, differences over economy policy have created friction." Several days later *The Times* reported that "an ever-widening circle of American industry is demanding retaliation against the Japanese and protection for themselves." As the Johnson Administration drew to a close, *The Journal of Commerce* noted "American and Japanese businessmen may be heading for a serious showdown over Japan's investment limitations and the tendency in the United States toward a revival of protectionist policies."[11]

American negotiators sought Japanese help with America's balance of payments deficit, with opening their home markets, and with using some of Japan's surplus to assist economic development elsewhere in East Asia. Eugene Braderman of the Commerce Department asked Japan to reduce barriers to U.S. exports, a demand repeated many times in coming years. Interestingly, Japan feared that initial proposals for Kennedy Round tariff reductions might adversely affect Japanese trade.[12]

---

[11] "Business Around the World," *U.S. News & World Report,* January 16, 1961, p. 66; "In Labor," *Business Week,* January 21,, 1961, p. 98; "Business Around the World," *U.S. News & World Report,* November 1, 1961, p. 96; "Business Around the World," *U.S. News & World Report,* January 21, 1963, p. 101; "Japan sews up a market," *Business Week,* August 3, 1963, p. 76; "Yamaha's potpourri finds a market," *Business Week,* October 1, 1966, p. 82; "Can stew supplant sukiyaki," *Business Week,* April 6, 1968, pp. 58-59; "Japan's curbs on U.S. food imports assailed," *The Washington Post,* April 6, 1968, as copied in LBJ Library, Papers of Henry H. Fowler, Box 39, Cabinet Mtgs: Japan; "Business Around the World," *U.S. News & World Report,* .April 22, 1968, p. 75; "Japan's giants: challenge for U.S.," *U.S. News & World Report,* May 27, 1968, p. 89; "U.S. ties with Japan face growing strain as economic conflicts multiply," October 8, 1968, p. 9; Japan: Trouble over U.S. trade," *The New York Times,* October 20, 1968, p. E9; "U.S.-Japan showdown feared," *The Journal of Commerce,* November 5, 1968, photocopy in LBJ Library, Henry Fowler Papers, Box 39, Cabinet Mtgs: Japan.

[12] "Japan Urged to Speed Removal of Barriers to U.S. Products," *The New York Times,* October 7, 1960, p. 49; "U.S. trade moves worrying Japan," *The New York Times,* May 6, 1962, p. 173.

In mid-June 1961 Prime Minister Ikeda made an official visit to Washington, DC. Secretary Rusk prepared President Kennedy: "Ikeda's visit provides an opportunity to set the pattern for our relations with Japan during your Administration." He proposed a joint Cabinet-level committee on economics and trade, and noted "it would counteract the Japanese impression that their economic interests are overshadowed in U.S. policy determination" by other factors. While official conversations with President Kennedy and Secretary Rusk covered the range of international "hot topics," international economics and U.S.-Japanese economic relations figured prominently. Ikeda and Foreign Minister Zentaro Kosaka discussed the balance of payments issue with Rusk and Treasury Secretary Douglas Dillon who provided background on the U.S. challenge. Washington welcomed Tokyo's help when the U.S. economy recovered from its mild recession, for imports most likely would increase, and thus the balance of payments might worsen. Rusk continued on the topic of trade liberalization, especially Washington's hope for more liberalized trading rules with respect to American companies doing business in Japan. Ikeda responded that "there is considerable opposition to liberalization from certain segments of Japan industry" but "Japan now plans virtually full liberalization by 1963." After Rusk expressed his appreciation, Undersecretary George "Ball commented that, as the Prime Minister recognized, Japan had a greater number of quantitative restrictions on imports than any major trading country." Pleasant talk did not result in effective government action.[13]

Cabinet-level talks took place with great correctness and pomp but with few demonstrable outcomes. A State Department position paper noted the conundrum: for Japan, "international transactions constitute the vital element in its economy." Further, "Japanese concern is enhanced by fears that other countries would follow any U.S. retreat from a liberal trade policy." *Time* described a meeting of Japanese and American Cabinet members at a resort in the shadow of Japan's famed Mt. Fuji. Secretary of State Dean Rusk and others called the talks "frank" and "informative," but "promised to support efforts to reduce or eliminate trade barriers against

[13] JFK Library, NSF Country Files, Box 123A, Japan, General, 6/61, Rusk to Kennedy, June 9, 1961; see also Box 125, Japan, Subjects, Ikeda Visit, 6/61, Briefing Book, Substantive, "Visit of PM Ikeda, Scope Paper," June 16, 1961; U.S. Department of State, *Foreign Relations of the United States, 1961-1963, Volume XII, China, Korea, Japan,* Washington, DC, GPO, 1996, Document 331, Memorandum of Conversation, "United States and Japanese Balance of Payments Problems," June 20, 1961; Document 332, Memorandum of Conversation, "Liberalization of Trade and Payments," June 20, 1961.

Japanese goods in Western markets." *Business Week* was less positive: "Japanese officials felt disappointment over our failure to promise easing of trade restrictions, though U.S. Cabinet members came away fairly satisfied with meeting." Cabinet members met again in December 1962, and "the Japanese made blunt demands that the United States reduce its trade and aid restrictions," but American delegates only offered "explanations." In turn, "the Americans gently chided the Japanese for trade curbs that prevent many U.S. products from competing in the Japanese market," including cars, tractors, heavy power units, large computers, aircraft, and color film. By Spring 1963 Japan was rejecting the proposed 50% reductions in tariff rates of the Kennedy Round talks and claimed it "still needed tariff protection for many of its industries."[14]

The change from the Kennedy to the Johnson Administration produced little change in trade negotiations between Tokyo and Washington. At first, "some top officials in Tokyo fear[ed] a conservative shift in U.S. economic policy that would bring greater protectionism." Although much of the world marveled at Japan's economic success, the Japanese government believed "it vital to protect certain weak sectors" – and thus the dynamic tension that continued throughout the Johnson presidency. In late June 1964 U.S. and Japanese cabinet officials met without reaching agreement on individual or joint economic measures to resolve issues between the two governments. In January 1965, William Bundy wrote Rusk to discuss Japanese-American economic issues in advance of Prime Minister Sato's visit. Interestingly, U.S. negotiators achieved little progress in the areas he listed, including cooperative defense arrangements, aid to developing countries, liberalization of trade and investment, and Kennedy Round negotiations. At the same time, Bundy stated that "the Japanese fear that the U.S. is shifting to a protectionist trade policy," an interesting view in light of the very Kennedy Round discussions the U.S. government pushed. In early 1965 *Business Week* reported that "protectionist-minded Tokyo is relaxing restrictions on 'invading' foreign companies – but joint ventures are still the only possible entry." In Summer 1965, *The New York Times* reported "the United States and Japan

---

[14] JFK Library, NSF, Box 253, Conf, Tokyo-11/61, US-Japan Economic Committee, Talking Papers & Position Papers, October 13, 1961; "Japan and World Trade," *The New York Times,* November 2, 1961, p. 36. "The Big Push," *Time,* November 10, 1961, www.time.com/archive; "U.S.-Japan talks miss the mark," *Business Week,* November 11, 1961, p. 79; "Frankness governs U.S.-Japan trade talks," *The New York Times,* December 7, 1962, p. 59; "Business Around the World," *U.S. News & World Report,* December 17, 1962, p. 94; "International Outlook," *Business Week,* April 20, 1963, p. 156.

began a three-day meeting today to discuss the trading frictions that have arisen." American government efforts to rein in the balance of payments deficit hurt the Japanese economy, and added to the stress at the talks. The next summer Cabinet ministers gathered again and affirmed "new bonds of friendship despite persistent differences on political and economic questions." Japanese negotiators "defended retention of a long list of import restrictions" claiming they were "necessary for the health of struggling small-scale local industry." As the meeting ended, Secretary of Commerce John Connor expressed "concern because liberalization actions by Japan on imports since 1964 have been few." He also "criticized the treatment of American investors in Japan." Finally, Connor noted "Japan had reached industrial maturity and the policies that served her well during the reconstruction period are no longer acceptable nor applicable to Japan's situation today as a major industrial power."[15]

Ultimately, the government in Washington lacked the levers the government in Tokyo possessed, and that involved the Cold War in East Asia. The key was the role of the People's Republic of China in policy deliberations. As American analysts recognized the depth of the Sino-Soviet split, it seemed to unshackle Beijing's most aggressive instincts. In turn, this required a stronger American commitment to containment, and that necessitated allies in the region that could resist Communist aggression and the appeal of communism for the mass of their peoples. The government in Tokyo, much as other governments in the region, recognized that it possessed levers to resist American government entreaties about Japanese exports and closed markets at home; it simply had to talk about the Cold War and play the so-called China card.

The government in Tokyo wanted to improve diplomatic and expand trade relations with nations in the region. In September 1963, for example, Prime Minister Ikeda toured the Philippines, Australia, New Zealand, and Indonesia. American diplomats reported on Ikeda's progress. The American embassy in Manila reported that Ikeda proposed a five nation summit meeting "to foster regional cooperation on their respective

---

[15] "International Outlook," *Business Week,* November 30, 1963, p. 84; "A tariff dilemma confronts Tokyo," *The New York Times,* January 13, 1964, p. 40; *FRUS, 1961-1963, Vol. XXII,* Document 7, "Editorial Note;" NARA, RG 59, CFPF, Box 23275, POL 7 Visits, Mtgs, Japan, 1/1/65, Bundy to Rusk, January 6, 1965; "Japan puts out small welcome mat," *Business Week,* February 27, 1965, p. 116; "U.S. and Japan Begin Meetings on Disagreements Over Trade," *The New York Times,* July 13, 1965, p. 43; "U.S. and Japan Reaffirm Amity as Parley ends," *The New York Times,* July 7, 1966, p. 3; "U.S. Chides Japan on Trading Policy," *The New York Times,* July 9, 1966, p. 33.

economic and cultural affairs." The embassy in Canberra reported Ikeda had "a successful four-day official visit," and that Australian officials were delighted with "Ikeda's remarks in Sydney that by 1970 Japan would triple its purchases from Australia." An embassy summary noted "Australian-Japanese trade relations constituted the most repeated single theme during Japanese Prime Minister Hayato Ikeda's four day official visit to Australia." In fact, *The Sydney Morning Herald* "published a 20 page lift-out supplement on the Japanese economy and on Australian-Japanese relations." The embassy in Wellington reported "the visit of Prime Minister Ikeda was a public relations success." "Trade and Malaysia [discussed in a later chapter] dominated press interest in the Japanese Prime Minister's visit." The embassy reported quoted Ikeda's official remarks that "the expanding prosperity of New Zealand and Japan depends on the extent to which such prosperity is shared by their neighbors." During each visit Ikeda downplayed the idea of a Pacific/Asian common market, likely favoring a more complicated system for Japanese business and government officials to exploit.[16]

Increased trade led logically to an expanding international role. Washington wanted Tokyo to take a larger role in regional economic development to balance America's military effort in Vietnam and in East Asian defense. When Ikeda's successor, Eisaku Sato met with Dean Rusk during an official visit in January 1965, Rusk stated that "he was pleased with the increasing role Japan is playing in the world, a rightful role to which Japan's accomplishments entitle it. Sato responded that "Japan hoped to play a larger and even more useful role." However, "some concern exists in Japan," he noted, "that it might over-extend itself."[17]

The key became increased Japanese economic assistance in the region and support for the Asian Development Bank. Sato raised the issue during his January 1965 luncheon meeting with Rusk. He stated that Japan was "conducting studies on the practical aspects of formation of an Asian Development Bank." "He did not think that overt American participation would be desirable," but he asked about American interest to which Rusk

---

[16] NARA, RG 59, CFPF, Box 3956, Pol 7, Visits/Mtgs, JAP, 2/1/63, Amembassy Tokyo to State, No. 924, September 21, 1963; same folder, Amembassy Manila to State, #469, September 26, 1963; same folder, Amembassy Canberra to State, #A-280, October 4, 1963; same folder, Amembassy Canberra to State, #A 304, October 11, 1963; same folder, Amembassy Wellington to State, #A-233, October 10, 1963.

[17] NARA, RG 59, CFPF, Box 2383, Pol-PolAff&Rel, Japan-US, 1/1/65, "U.S.-Japan Relations and Related World Problems," January 13, 1965.

replied he "welcomed the idea of an Asian Development Bank." Sato quickly wrote Johnson after his speech at Johns Hopkins University to praise it, and Johnson in turn wrote that "your endorsement of my proposal that Free World nations begin now to build a foundation for a durable peace in Southeast Asia through a large-scale cooperative development program is also most welcome." At the same time, embassy officials reported that the Japanese Foreign Office "is studying plans for establishment [of a] 'Southeast Asia Development Organization' as part of GOJ policy of 'active cooperation' with President Johnson's $1 billion development program." In July Rusk wrote Johnson about his meeting with Japanese Cabinet officials. Rusk noted that "during Eugene Black's recent trip, Japanese officials indicated [a] readiness to give leadership in forming the Southeast Asia Development Bank" that Sato had raised six months earlier and that Johnson had promoted in his famous Johns Hopkins University speech in early April 1965. Johnson was so committed to this Asian Development Bank as the driving force for a general economic development program for the region that he accepted a recommendation from Treasury Secretary Henry Fowler and others that "the United States pick up the shortfall [about $100 million] in the capitalization of the ADB." On November 26, Johnson announced the official founding of the Asian Development Bank with headquarters in Manila. In his statement, he noted that "the problems of Asia are of an order and a diversity requiring the widest possible participation in their solution by the economically developed nations. The next month, Vice President Humphrey had to report that during his visit to Japan, Prime Minister "Sato expressed his country's disappointment that Manila rather than Tokyo was the headquarters for the Asian Development Bank, but hoped that the Bank's president would be Japanese." On a more positive note, Humphrey noted that "Sato is deeply interested in hosting Southeast Asia Ministerial Conference on Economic Development about April even possibly including Indonesia and Cambodia. I strongly urged Japanese leadership in this regional economic development effort, even if discussions had to be bilateral."[18]

[18] NARA, RG 59, CFPF, Box 2383, Pol-PolAff&Rel, Japan-US, 1/1/65, "U.S.-Japan Relations and Related World Problems," January 13, 1965; Box 1899, Pol 1, Asia SE-US, 4/1/65, Read to Bundy, April 20, 1965; same folder, Tokyo to SecState, #3361, April 21, 1965; same folder, State to Amembassy Tokyo, #2699, April 21, 1965; *FRUS, 1964-1968, Vol. XXIX,* Document 53, Rusk to Johnson, July 13, 1965; Document 66, Humphrey to Johnson, December 31, 1965; NARA, RG 59, Policy Planning Staff, Box 312, Subject and Country File, 1965-1969, Asia, 1965, Fowler to Johnson, November 18, 1965; same folder, Black to

Japanese-American cooperation helped make the Asian Development Bank a reality. Each government provided $200 million of the bank's initial $1 billion capitalization; governments in the region donated generously, while France, the People's Republic of China, and the Soviet Union all declined the invitation to contribute. *The New York Times* reported the bank "represents a significant new experiment in international finance." *Time* reported the successful conclusion of the negotiations: "28 nations sent delegates" to Bangkok. "All of them came to Bangkok last week to set up a $1 billion Asian Development Bank to help lift Asia from its morass of poverty." *Time* also reported in mid-December that "meeting in Manila, 160 delegates from 26 nations put the finishing touches on the long-needed Asian Development Bank launched in October in Bangkok." "The bank is not only Asia's first common banking venture, but one of the very few joint ventures of any kind brought to fruition in Asian history." American delegates read a message from President Johnson: "Your initiative has captured the imagination of us all." A Japanese Finance Ministry official, Takeshi Watanabe, served as the bank's first president; his selection demonstrated Japan's key role in the ADB and in the future economic development of the region. In July 1968, *Time* was more measured about the ADB. It noted the ADB "has sought to prove its own stability in an area of economic turmoil." It "has made only one loan." The bank was concentrating on "getting to know its far-flung customers – and vice versa."[19]

The next year State Department officials noted "while we do not want to appear to be pressuring the Japanese on SEA development, we consider it timely to explore discreetly with them the possibilities of their – and our – taking further actions or initiatives, particularly in areas where Japan's taking the leadership and primary responsibility would be of mutual benefit to our two countries." The State Department was particularly interested in an Asian Agricultural Development Fund. The following November Henry Owen wrote Rusk that "the U.S. should encourage Asians to take the lead in inaugurating an Asian Development Program, a unified and concentrated attack on the problems of development in Asia." He envisioned a dynamic initiative that would capture the imagination of people in the region. In September 1967 as America became increasingly

---

Johnson, November 19, 1965; same folder, "Statement by the President, November 26, 1965.

[19] *Time,* "A Lift out of the Morass," October 29, 1965; *Time,* "A New Temple," December 10, 1965; *The New York Times,* "Asia's New Bank," November 26, 1966, p. 34; *NYT,* "Tokyo Expects Aide to Head Asian Bank," January 15, 1966, p. 7; *Time,* "Self-Help with Outside Help," July 19, 1968, www.*time*.com/archive.

consumed by the Vietnam War, the embassy in Tokyo reported that "prospects for significant expansion of GOJ economic assistance during Prime Minister Sato's tenure in office are dimmed by Sato's unwillingness to assert his political authority over the bureaucrats of the Finance Ministry." The embassy reported a luncheon conversation with Bunroku Yoshino that "Sato's fine words about $100 million of economic assistance to the Southeast Asian countries he is visiting in September-October are being vitiated by his continuing refusal to back up the Foreign Ministry vis-à-vis the Finance Ministry." At about the same time, Rusk wrote Johnson on the eve of his talks with Japanese Cabinet members that "we want Japan as a partner in Asia, but as partner sharing the political and economic burdens of regional responsibility." Rusk saw this, in part, as "redressing the imbalance in our balance of payments."[20]

Sato took a series of trips in late summer and early fall 1967 to visit virtually every country in the region. He gave contradictory signals on Japan's willingness to provide desired economic assistance. Sato began in Malaysia after Japan provided a loan to support Malaysia's economic development plan and had signed an agreement settling the "blood debt" dispute going back to the Second World War. But, on the issue of purchasing Malaysian rubber, Japanese diplomats said "GOJ could not make any commitments since [the] government itself did not purchase rubber" and "Japanese synthetic rubber production was increasing." Sato then visited Singapore and the resulting communiqué "reflected emphasis on economic rather than politico-military activity." Yet Singapore Prime Minister Lee Kuan Yew commented that "I think it is unrealistic to believe that a thrusting nation like Japan will, you know, forever be penitent for its misdemeanors in the last war and just produce transistors and scooters and little cars for the rest of Southeast Asia." Lee likely untactfully said what many Asian leaders were thinking and feared. Sato's visit to Thailand produced positive results: Thai leaders wanted to "reduce the imbalance in trade with Japan [through greater purchases by Japan of Thai primary products). "Sato pointed out that since Japan's trade was largely private and the GOJ does relatively little direct purchasing, a firm GOJ commitment to increase imports could not be given." Interestingly, the next month the embassy in Manila reported on Sato's visit to the Asian Development Bank, in which he told ADB officials that "the ADB was born out of long-cherished aspiration of Asian nations." "Japan is prepared

[20] NARA, RG 59, CFPF, Box 2383, Pol, Japan-US, 1/1/66, State to Amembassy Canberra, #1191, June 28, 1966; NARA, RG 59, PPS, Subject and Country File, 1965-1968, Box 312, Asia, 1966, Owen to the Secretary, November 7, 1966; *FRUS, 1964-1968, Vol. XXIX,* Document 96, Rusk to Johnson, September 4, 1967.

to give its fullest cooperation for the sound future development of the bank." Yet several days later the embassy in Djakarta reported Sato told Indonesian leader Suharto that "Japan would do what it could but coupled this with lengthy explanation of Japanese balance of payments problem." Japanese Deputy Vice Minister Haruki Mori told embassy officers that Sato's trip to Southeast Asia was "designed to show Japanese now view that area as important and affording it separate treatment" and "to discuss bilateral questions between GOJ and his hosts – largely economic in nature."[21]

Tokyo granted aid only to promote Japanese exports and Japanese economic development, which engendered some resentment in countries that still remembered Japan's wartime occupation experience. American officials continued to urge Japan to take a leading role, but generally speaking Japanese leaders only promised aid that supported Japanese economic diplomacy. In May 1967 U.S. officials met with their Japanese counterparts at Shimoda to discuss "regional cooperation efforts," and left with promises. Several weeks later the State Department wrote the American embassy in Tokyo that "we would like to continue dialogue with GOJ on further steps re Asian regional cooperation," but urged the embassy to make "clear that any suggestions we have are response to GOJ initiative, and further action up to GOJ." The issue came up when Foreign Minister Takeo Miki visited Washington in September 1967. Rusk began saying that "the United States appreciated the leadership taken by Japan in the area of regional economic assistance as well as Japanese economic aid to such institutions as the Asian Development Bank." In response Miki "hoped the United States would bear in mind the relative capabilities of Japan and the United States to extend economic aid." Several days after returning to Tokyo Miki addressed the Asia Research Council and stated that Japan "will cooperate for the solving of poverty in Asia. It will play the role of a bridge so that the Pacific Ocean will become a sea linking together the East and the West." The disagreement on the appropriate contributions of the United States and Japan remained until the end of the

[21] NARA, RG 59, Box 2245, Pol 12, Japan, 1/1/67, Amembassy Tokyo to State, No. 338, September 12, 1967; Box 2243, POL 7, Japan, 8/1/67, Amembassy Kuala Lumpur to State, #2798, September 26, 1967 and #2802, September 27, 1967; same folder, Amembassy Singapore to State, #1281, September 27, 1967 and #1288, September 30, 1967; same box, POL 7, Japan, 10-1-67, Amembassy Bangkok to State, A-370, October 6, 1967; same folder, Amembassy Manila to State, #3753, October 24, 1967; same folder, Amembassy Tokyo to State, #6703, October 4, 1967; same folder, Amembassy Djakarta to State, #3975, October 13, 1967.

Johnson presidency. In June 1968 the American embassy in Tokyo sent an analysis of U.S.-Japanese relations to the State Department. It recognized that "U.S. leverage for exertion of influence [was] waning and perhaps aid to SEA [was] coming into competition with China trade for available credit."[22]

It is interesting to review major intelligence estimates of Japan and of Japanese-American relations. In the early 1960s, there was little recognition of Japanese-American economic tensions; by the late 1960s, such tensions gained great prominence in these analyses. That is, the intelligence studies less predicted the future, e.g., foretelling the explosive growth of the Japanese economy and the challenge it would pose for the United States, than explained that which had recently taken or was taking place. In February 1960, National Intelligence Estimate 41-60 noted "the economic outlook for Japan is good, assuming continued high levels of foreign trade, particularly with the US," and "continued access to the US market." Interesting, the NIE predicted that "a prolonged economic recession would probably create strong pressures within Japan for expanded relations with the Bloc, particularly Communist China." A year later a new NIE noted Japan was "economically vigorous and prosperous. Its gross national product has increased at an average annual rate of 9 percent over the past decade . . . its standard of living is by far the highest in Asia." However, "because the Japanese economy is so dependent on foreign trade," "Japan will remain extremely sensitive to foreign market conditions and the actions of foreign governments, especially the US, as about one-third of Japan's total trade is with the US."[23]

Sometime in early 1962, the State Department issued a new "guidelines paper" titled "Guidelines of U.S. Policy and Operations Toward Japan." It viewed "Japan as our principal ally in East Asia, our second largest world trading partner, the host for important forward U.S. military facilities, and a source of technical skill and capital contributing to the economic development of South and Southeast Asia. Japan offers the prospect of development as an increasingly important political, economic

[22] NARA, RG 59, CFPF, Box 2250, POL 1, Japan-US, 1/1/67, Amembassy Tokyo to State, #8564, May 26, 1967; same folder, State to Amembassy Tokyo, #207405, June 2, 1967; Box 2249, PolAff&Rel, Japan-US, 1/1/67, "Regional Economic Assistance," September 14, 1967; Box 2246, Pol 15-1, Japan, 1/1/68, #A-2017, State outgoing telegram, September 13, 1968; Box 2249, PolAff&Rel, Japan-US, 1/1/68, Amembassy Tokyo to State, #8931, June 5, 1968.

[23] *FRUS, 1961-1963, Vol. XII,* Document 354, Department of State Guidelines Paper, undated [although the copy in the JFK Library is dated "March 1962," NSF, Box 124, Japan, 3/17-31/62].

and, possibly, military counterweight to the rising power of Communist China." To keep Japan firmly in the US alliance, the guidelines indicated that "U.S. and European economic and trade policies must be responsive to Japanese marketing needs." The State Department document further recommended that "resisting pressures to establish U.S. import restrictions, or to 'negotiate' Japanese 'voluntary' export quotas, except where absolutely essential; when Japanese export quotas to the U.S. are unavoidable they should be negotiated on a multilateral basis." The document had similar recommendations for the U.S. balance of payments issue and other matters – not to press Japan if the outcome might injure the Japanese economy.[24]

A few months later, a new NIE, 41-63, noted that "Japan's economy continues too grow vigorously." But, "it is heavily dependent on foreign trade and is exceptionally vulnerable to threats to its export markets." The NIE stated "Japan is deficient in nearly all the basic natural resources needed to keep the economy running," thus Japan will need to export sufficient "to pay for vital and increasing imports of sources of energy, raw materials, and food." The NIE believed that "further removal by Japan of restrictions on imports should increase US sales to Japan." Yet "a number of crucial problems will plague Japan-US trade relations and may create sensitive political issues as well." In June 1964, the State Department issued "The Future of Japan," and it clearly recognized the dilemma of a strong Japanese economy needing to take advantage of the U.S. economy: "It is difficult to see how Japan's minimum economic goals can be attained unless Japan is afforded opportunity to expand its sales on the U.S. market." "This will require firm "Executive Branch" resistance of American industry demands for curtailment of Japanese exports." "It is only less important that, when the U.S. must act contrary to Japanese trading interests, time and effort must be taken to put the best possible face on the action through diplomatic and other means to minimize the adverse reaction in Japan." In November 1964, William Bundy wrote Undersecretary of State George Ball that "the accumulation of a number of irritating problems between the U.S. and Japan has had an abrasive effect on the fundamentally sound and mutual beneficial relations between our two countries." Domestic pressure on U.S. economic policy "underscores the growing Japanese belief that the U.S. is shifting to a protectionist trade policy." Moreover, "each U.S. action seems to be taken in isolation without regard for its consistency with our other important

[24] *FRUS, 1961-1963, Vol. XII,* Document 354, Department of State Guidelines Paper, undated.

requests or for the over-all partnership relationship between the two countries."[25]

But such growth was not completely convincing. A month later U.S. Ambassador to Japan, Edwin Reischauer wrote Secretary Rusk that the U.S. seeks "the development of Japan as a major power center in Asia acting in concert with U.S. and Free World objectives." He continued that "there are discordant notes, however, both within and outside of our bilateral economic relationship, and, with the growth of Japan's power, our direct leverage on troublesome issues has lessened." Furthermore, "our influence on Japan in trading with Communist China, as also in its trade with Cuba, is limited." Finally, he concluded that "in our bilateral affairs frictions exist partly because our relationship is intimate and huge, but also because we are giving insufficient recognition to the fact Japan now has wide-ranging legitimate interests to protect, for example, in civil aviation and high-seas fishing." A month later Bundy wrote Rusk that "during Prime Minister Sato's visit we should be prepared to state the U.S. Government's position on a number of important economic problems of common concern to the U.S. and Japan." He also suggested seeking "to eliminate needless difficulties in current U.S.-Japanese economic relations." When Sato met with President Lyndon Johnson, Johnson began noting "he heard a lot about trade problems between our two countries." Sato in turn said that, "in his view, the major problem is to sustain the prosperity of the United States." Six months later Rusk prepared Johnson to meet with Japanese Cabinet officials. Rusk warned the President that "the Japanese are putting on record their dissatisfaction with various protectionist features in the handling of our economy." At the same time, "we have expressed sharp dissatisfaction with Japan's treatment of Americans desiring to make direct investment in Japan, reviewed with them their protectionist policies and discussed the wisdom of Japan's showing some restraint in hitting the American market too hard in narrow vulnerable sectors." Perhaps disingenuously, Rusk concluded that "our give and take on these matters has been constructive." Reischauer wrote Rusk once again to express his concern over U.S. pressure on economic issues. He stated the key issues, including keeping Japan's industrial potential in the western camp and its bases available for defense in the

---

[25] NARA, RG 59, CFPF, Box 3956, POL 2-3, JAP Politic & Economic, Rpts, 2-1-63, "Political-Economic Assessment – May 1963, June 17, 1963; "Japan's Problems and Prospects, NIE 41-63, October 9, 1963; www.foia.cia.gov/browse; *FRUS, 1961-1963, Vol. XXII,* p. 674; *FRUS, 1964-1968, Vol. XXIX,* Document 15, Department of State Policy Paper: The Future of Japan, June 26, 1964; Document 33, Bundy to Ball, November 9, 1964.

region, and Japan taking a "growing role in the economic development" of Asian countries. He recommended taking "whatever steps we can to lessen present friction with Japan" and working to "minimize our irritants in our relations."[26]

In November 1965 a new NIE concluded that "economic conflicts between Japan and the US will remain." The NIE mentioned the "current slowdown," government measures to stimulate the economy, and predicted – in retrospect very inaccurately – that "resolution of such basic problems of the overstretched economy . . . will require additional years of governmental effort." The NIE noted a conundrum for Japan. It was highly dependent on exports to the United States which typically brought out protectionist sentiment, and, although they resented it, Japanese businessmen accepted "voluntary" restrictions on certain exports. The NIE concluded the "economics" section that "Japan's importance as a market for US exports and as a logistical base gives Japan substantial leverage of its own." In July 7, 1966, Rusk met with Prime Minister Sato in Japan; the American secretary of state took the lead. He indicated that "bilateral relations were generally in good shape." But he noted that "Japan has a favorable trade balance with the U.S. of about $300 million a year" and gained another $300 to $350 million from "American military expenditures in Japan." He also noted that "Japanese sales to the U.S. were rising faster than American sales to Japan." Interestingly, the State Department minutes did not indicate Sato's response.

In September another joint Cabinet meeting followed Rusk's July meeting in Tokyo. Treasury Secretary Henry Fowler wrote Johnson to stress "that we pursue the balance of payments objectives with Japan independently and separately." These included increased Japanese purchases of U.S. military goods and "sharing the non-military economic burdens in Asia." Rusk soon followed Fowler in providing advice to Johnson, agreeing in many ways with Fowler. Rusk indicated that "we want Japan as a partner in Asia, but as partner sharing the political and economic burdens of regional responsibility." Thomas Hughes, Director of State's Intelligence and Research office, wrote Rusk in mid-October 1967 about Japan's role in Asia. Hughes noted that "Japan is becoming increasingly conscious that it has an important international role to play, commensurate with its strong economic position, powerful industrial

---

[26] *FRUS, 1964-1968, Vol. XXIX,* Document 35, "Politico-Economic Assessment: Japan, as of December 1, 1964," December 4, 1964; Document 39, Bundy to Rusk, January 6, 1965; Document 41, "Current U.S.-Japanese and World Problems," January 12, 1965; Document 53, Rusk to Johnson, July 13, 1965; Document 55, Reischauer to Rusk, July 14, 1965.

potential, advanced science and technology, wide-ranging commerce, strategic location, and large, highly educated population. Inhibitions toward becoming involved on the world stage are receding."[27]

Prime Minister Sato returned in mid-November 1967, and the State Department's Executive Secretary Benjamin Read wrote Walt Rostow that "Sato's visit takes place at a time when United States-Japan relations are at a high point." Read also noted that "Sato also comes to Washington holding strong domestic political cards and with his economy booming." Read then asked Rostow to consider asking President Johnson to seek greater Japanese contributions to East Asian economic development programs and efforts for a "significant reduction in our bilateral balance of payments deficit, which results in part from increased military-related expenditures in Japan during the Vietnam conflict." Fowler once again wrote Johnson on November 11, only two days before the start of Sato's visit to emphasize action on the balance of payments deficit. "I believe it is of major importance to the overall U.S. balance of payments program that you obtain the Prime Minister's approval." When Sato met with Johnson he noted that "he understood the U.S. hoped Japan would help out in the balance of payments problem by providing $500 million." He responded that "$300 million was possible." Rusk responded that "the American people were becoming more restive and unwilling to carry burdens by themselves," and he emphasized an increased Japanese contribution to demonstrate that "Japan was truly participating in the defense of the free world."[28]

The next NIE was more than two years later, in the weeks before the Communist Tet Offensive in Vietnam, and predicted "high rates of economic growth likely through the early 1970s." It noted "many external variables which could significantly affect our estimates," including "strong protectionist trends in US trade policy" and "worldwide constriction of

---

[27] NIE, 41-60, "Probable Developments in Japan," February 9, 1960, www.foia.cia/gov/browse_docs; LBJ Library, National Security Files, NIE, Box 6, 41j Japan, NIE 41-61, "Prospects for Japan," 7 February 1961; LBJL, NSF, NIE, Box 6, 41j Japan, NIE 41-63, "Japan's Problems and Prospects," 9 October 1963; LBJL, NSF NIE, Box 6, 41j Japan, NIE 41-65, "Japan," 26 November 1965; *FRUS, 1964-1968, Vol. XXIX,* Document 75, "U.S.-Japan Bilateral Relations, July 7, 1966.

[28] *FRUS, 1964-1968, Vol. XXIX,* Document 95, Fowler to Johnson, August 31, 1967; Document 96, Rusk to Johnson, September 4, 1967; Document 98, Read to Rostow, October 13, 1967; NARA, RG 59, CFPF, Box 1853, PolAff&Rel, Asia SE-A, 1967, Hughes to Rusk, October 20, 1967; *FRUS, 1964-1968, Vol. XXIX,* Document 103, Fowler to Johnson, November 11, 1967; Document 104, Memorandum of Conversation, November 14, 1967.

markets." In early June 1968, David Osborn in the Embassy in Japan wrote the State Department about U.S.-Japanese relations. He noted challenges, including "the Arab-Israeli War, balance of payments difficulties, [and] 'protectionism' scare." He worried that Japanese leaders had concerns about "the extent to which Japan can continue to count on us to carry its ball as well as our own." He also discussed the impact of the North Korean seizure of the *USS Pueblo* and the Communist Tet Offensive in Vietnam. He believed that "it is quite possible that Japan is moving toward a serious reappraisal of our relationship." He did believe that counterbalancing any change in policy was that "over the years Japan also has become habituated to receiving special favors in the economic field."[29]

Economic weaknesses affected U.S. leverage and there were other issues to be sure. These included such bilateral issues as civil aviation routes, North Pacific fisheries, the return of the Bonin Islands [Iwo Jima] and the Ryukyus [including Okinawa].

The status of the Ryukyus and Okinawa was a serious sticking point. Japanese wanted return of the islands, while native Okinawans wanted independence from Japan and the United States. The American military focused on the important role that military facilities played in America's defensive position in eastern Asia and, as the Vietnam war expanded, in the increasing American involvement in that Southeast Asian conflict. Prime Minister Ikeda raised it during his visit in June 1961. Previously Japanese Foreign Minister Kosaka Zentaro had asked Secretary of State Dean Rusk about flying the Japanese flag over government buildings on New Year's Day, and Ikeda expanded it to include major holidays. Kennedy demurred, indicating he needed to consult with Secretary of Defense Robert McNamara. Ikeda stated "he had no intention of seeking restoration to Japan of civil administration over the Islands or interfering in any way with U.S. administration." Ikeda noted the relative poverty of the islands raised the issue of restoration of Japanese control. Kennedy promised to take steps to raise the living standards of Ryukyuans to those of Japanese on the main islands. In August Kennedy told Rusk and McNamara he intended to fulfill his promise. He called for a task force to make recommendations for change in U.S. policies and practices. By February 1962 the task force had submitted its report, and the Kennedy Administration determined there would be no public release. Generally,

---

[29] LBJL, NSF, NIE, Box 6, 41j Japan, NIE 41-68, "Main Trends in Japan's External Relations," 11 January 1968; *FRUS, 1964-1968, Vol. XXIX,* Document 123, Reischauer to Rusk, June 5, 1968.

the task force report called for increased U.S. and Japanese economic aid, determined efforts to minimize friction between servicemen and the local population, but continued U.S. control.[30]

Thereafter, the State and Defense Departments disagreed over the Ryukyus with State wanting to ease tensions with Tokyo and with Defense wanting to maintain valued facilities. On October 4, 1962, the President signed Public Law 87-746, which raised the annual authorization ceiling on U.S. economic aid to the Ryukyus from $6 to $12 million," which was about half of the requested amount. In late December, Assistant Secretary Averell Harriman wrote Secretary Rusk to request approval of Japanese economic aid to the Ryukyus, even though it might raise uncomfortable issues about the status of the islands. Subsequently, Rusk convinced McNamara that they "should not get into argument with GOJ over $400,000 but should accept $5.1 million aid offer." Japanese aid notwithstanding, Kennedy and the Joint Chiefs of Staff agreed "on the continued strategic essentiality of Okinawa to the U.S. military posture in the Pacific." In early November 1963, the Tokyo embassy prepared a briefing paper for U.S. members of the U.S.-Japan Committee on Trade and Economic Affairs, although the Kennedy assassination postponed this meeting scheduled for November 25-27, 1963. The embassy warned that "as nationalism revives in Japan, Okinawa can, unless wisely handled, become cause of serious trouble between US and Japan even if Japan continues to have a conservative government." It recalled "the new policy announced by President Kennedy on March 19, 1962 constitutes an effort to meet this challenge." It continued that "for the past year, the US and Japanese Governments have been engaged in negotiations, in accordance with the Presidential statement of March 19, 1962, to implement a cooperative relationship in providing assistance to promote the welfare of the inhabitants of the Ryukyu Islands and their economic development."[31]

---

[30] For a first-rate overview of the ultimate return of both island chains, see Nicolas Evan Sarantakes, "Continuity through Change: The Return of Okinawa and Iwo Jima, 1967-1972," *The Journal of American-East Asian Relations, Vol. 3, No. 1, Spring 1994,* pp. 35-53; *FRUS, 1961-1963, Vol. XXII,* Document 338, "Memorandum of Conversation, June 21, 1961; Document 340, National Security Action Memorandum No 68, August 11, 1961; Document 350, State to US Embassy in Tokyo, February 8, 1962; Document 355, Harriman to Johnson, April 6, 1962; Document 357, Editorial Note.

[31] *FRUS, 1961-1963, Vol. XXII,* Document 367, Harriman to Rusk, December 28, 1962; Document 370, Editorial Note; Document 379, Briefing Paper, November 1, 1963.

After Johnson succeeded Kennedy, the issues remained the same. Increasing numbers of Japanese wanted a return of Japanese control over Okinawa; the U.S. State Department wanted to limit tensions; and the Defense Department wanted to retain its military bases on Okinawa. At a daily White House staff meeting in early May 1964, staffers discussed continuing problems with the military administration on Okinawa, but could not agree on a recommendation to Johnson. At a meeting of State and Defense Department officials, Undersecretary U. Alexis Johnson said that "in the Ryukyus we have to walk a narrow line between paternalistic protection of the Ryukyuans from their own mistakes and a policy of autonomy for the Ryukyuans. This is a hard job and there are no clear answers as to how it can best be accomplished." Johnson continued that "the High Commissioner is confronted with the dilemma of reconciling the political desires of the Ryukyuans and the Japanese with the military requirements of our mission there. By mid-August, James Thomson wrote McGeorge Bundy that "Okinawa remains a simmering and potentially dangerous issue in terms of U.S. relations with Japan. The Japanese Left embarrasses the Government, and the Government presses the U.S.; public feeling is temporarily quiescent but can easily become enflamed. The political situation in Okinawa itself is unstable. We are also vulnerable, to a lesser degree, to the trouble-making possibilities of the Ryukyu issue in the United Nations." Two months later, Thomson wrote Robert Komer "The key issue at the moment is the mounting pressure for popular election of the Okinawan Chief Executive."[32]

In December, Rusk visited with Foreign Minister Shiina Etsusaburo in New York for the UN session. Shiina raised the issue of Okinawa and told Rusk that "we should jointly consider what steps U.S. and Japan can take together to (1) promote development of islands; (2) promote public welfare; (3) enlarge self-government to degree possible." Rusk responded that, given the war in Vietnam, there could be no discussions about island governance. When Sato Eisaku became Prime Minister, he made return of Okinawa a key issue, but the island was too essential for the American war in Vietnam and he had to settle for return of the Bonin Islands, including Iwo Jima. At a meeting in January 1965, Sato told Johnson that "that Japan fully agreed with the United States on the importance and necessity of the U.S. military installations on Okinawa to peace in the Far East." But Sato told Johnson that "the nearly one million Ryukyuans and 95 million

---

[32] *FRUS, 1964-1968, Vol. XXIX,* Document 13, Memorandum for the Record, May 6, 1964; Document 14, "U.S. Policy toward the Ryukyu Islands," June 4, 1964; Document 23, Thomson to Bundy, August 21, 1964; Document 32, Thomson to Komer, October 29, 1964.

Japanese ardently aspire to the return of administrative authority over the islands to Japan."[33]

As America expanded the air war over North Vietnam, Sato expressed concern about the use of B-52s based on Okinawa. Undersecretary Ball wrote Defense Secretary McNamara with his concerns about making U.S. bases on Okinawa part of the expanding Vietnam conflict. "Recurrent use of the Okinawa bases, as a practical political matter, will seriously heighten pressures in Japan on the issue of Okinawa generally, and indeed will significantly affect the whole atmosphere of our relations with Japan in every sphere." Sato's visit to Okinawa added to the tensions. Bundy wrote Johnson in May 1966 that Japanese-American relations were good, but "Okinawa is a different matter." "We have about six months," he told the president, "to frame a careful and forward-looking policy." Two months later Ambassador Reischauer wrote Rusk about his meeting with Sato to assess Japanese-American relations. Sato told Reischauer that Soviet officials responded to his efforts to regain the Kurile Islands seized by Soviet forces in the closing days of the Second World War with a comment that it was the same situation as U.S. forces on Okinawa.[34]

For the remainder of the Johnson presidency, there was little movement concerning Okinawa. Japan wanted to secure its return, but Okinawa was too central for the Vietnam War. In late August 1967, the National Security Council considered reversion of the Ryukyu and Bonin island groups. Johnson framed the discussion. He wanted to decide the American position on Japan's continuing desire to regain the two island groups, on securing Japanese cooperation on the balance of payment challenge, and increasing Japanese economic aid in the region all before the visits of the Japanese foreign minister in September and the prime minister in November. During the discussion, Johnson "said he wanted to know in all of this—on bases and the Ryukyus—what was in it for the United States. He said we always seem to think of what is necessary or good for others." Participants agreed to seek Japanese economic aid while not conceding much on Okinawa. Rostow wrote Johnson on the eve of the

---

[33] *FRUS, 1964-1968, Vol. XXIX,* Document 42, Memorandum of Conversation, January 12, 1965.

[34] *FRUS, 1964-1968, Vol. XXIX,* Document 56, Embassy Tokyo to State Department, July 30, 1965; Document 59, Embassy Tokyo to State, August 25, 1965; "Okinawa: Troubled Keystone," *Newsweek, August 30, 1965,* pp. 35-36; *FRUS, 1964-1968, Vol. XXIX,* Document 68, Bundy to Johnson, May 23, 1966. See Document 87, Memorandum of Conversation, July 10, 1967; Document 91, Action Memorandum from William Bundy to Rusk, August 7, 1967, especially "TAB A."

Sato visit that "a major subject during Prime Minister Sato's visit in mid-November will be the future status of the Ryukyu and Bonin Islands," but, he added "Sato does not want a fight with us on this issue." Thomas Hughes, Director of the State Department's Office of Intelligence and Research, wrote Rusk that "attention to the reversion question is at a high pitch in Japan and Okinawa, pending" Sato's visit to Washington. Hughes warned that "Sato has staked a large measure of his political prestige on his handling of the reversion issues, and his future position will be significantly affected by the outcome of the negotiations." During his visit, Sato told Rusk that he wanted to move quickly from discussion of the issue to framing the communiqué since he was more concerned with Japanese domestic opinion than with American forces operating from Okinawa. Rusk agreed "that the two governments are closer to agreement on the Ryukyus than public opinion in both countries, but both governments must deal with their differing public opinions."[35]

The Johnson administration approved reversion the Bonin Islands as substitutes of a sort for the Ryukyu Islands. Other than lumping the status of the Bonin Islands with the Ryukyus in broad policy documents, the Kennedy administration did not spend much time on the status of the Bonin Islands. In late June 1964, Fukuda Tokuyasu, Director-General of the Japan Defense Agency, met with Secretary McNamara, and as part of a discussion of Okinawa, Fukuda raised the status of the Bonins. He noted the Soviet Union permitted Japanese to visit family gravesites in the Kurile Islands and asked for similar consideration in the Bonins. During his visit to Japan in early December 1964, Rusk met with Foreign Minister Shiina who asked, much as Fukuda about permitting Japanese to visit the graves of relatives and Rusk indicated he would speak with McNamara, which was the same response that McNamara had given Fukuda! Rusk proposed to McNamara that U.S. authorities permit a limited number of visits. Rusk then recommended to Johnson that he inform Sato during Sato's visit that "On the *Bonin* Islands, we accept in principle a *Bonin graves visit* (for the former inhabitants who now live in Japan)," a

[35] *FRUS, 1964-1968, Vol. XXIX,* Document 99, Rostow to Johnson, October 27, 1967; LBJ Library, NSF Country File, Box 253 (2 of 2), Visit of PM Sato (1 of 2), 11/14-15/1967, Hughes to Rusk, November 1, 1967; *FRUS, 1964-1968, Vol. XXIX,* Document 105, Memorandum of Conversation, November 15, 1967. See Hong N. Kim, "The Sato Government and the Okinawa Problem," *World Affairs, Vol. 134, No. 3, Winter 1971,* pp. 220-233 and Paul M.A. Linebarger, "America's Okinawa Policy," *World Affairs, Vol. 126, No. 2, Summer 1963,* pp. 85-91.

concession which Sato accepted during his official visit. [Italics in original][36]

When Rusk traveled to Japan, Foreign Minister Shiina asked about permitting several hundred of the former 7,000 inhabitants of the islands to return. Rusk promised to review the request when he returned to Washington. In late June 1967, the Joint Chiefs wrote Secretary McNamara about the "Military Utility of the Bonins." The Joint Chiefs found that "these islands represent an important strategic asset which should be retained by the United States." The Chiefs further noted that "Strategically, these islands are important as a backup for US bases in Japan, the Ryukyus, and the Philippines." Ambassador U. Alexis Johnson disagreed, and wrote the State Department in August that "The Japanese are well aware of the marginal importance of the Bonins in our defense structure and the sooner we are able to agree to reversion the more we establish a credible rationale for our position on the Okinawan bases." Despite the Joint Chiefs' concern, a State Department planning paper proposed that "we consider that retention of these islands has little military justification. The U.S. does not now maintain any major regional installations on these islands and we have no current plans for any new facilities." It further stated that even "if it is decided not to negotiate on the Ryukyus, we should agree to a prior return of the Bonins in an effort to try to stem, for a time, pressures for reversion of the Ryukyus."[37]

In October 1967, Benjamin Read wrote Walt Rostow about planning for Sato's impending visit. The key goal was to retain Japan as a partner in national security matters and much as America conceded economic issues, Read enclosed a memorandum from James Walker who proposed that "we will need to work out a formula for tidying over the difficult territorial issues. The Japanese apparently recognize that we are not now in a position to make any firm commitment on reversion of the Ryukyus, but they want a "step forward"—the terms of which are still to be worked out. The Japanese would, however, like a commitment on the early return of the Bonins, an issue still to be resolved within our Government." Rostow forwarded a State Department review to President Johnson in which Rusk proposed making "a commitment to enter into early negotiations for the

[36] *FRUS, 1964-1968, Vol. XXIX,* Document 16, Memorandum of Conversation, June 30, 1964; Document 36, Rusk to State Department, December 5, 1964; Document 40, Bundy to Johnson, Tab A, January 11, 1965.

[37] *FRUS, 1964-1968, Vol. XXIX,* Document 73, Memorandum of Conversation, July 7, 1966; Document 86, Memorandum from JCS to McNamara, June 29, 1967; Document 90, Tokyo to State Department, August 1, 1967; Document 91, Action Memorandum from Bundy to Rusk, August 7, 1967.

return of the Bonin Islands (permitting, however, United States retention of the whole island of Iwo Jima as a military base); and, b) Interim measures relating to the Ryukyu Islands which would not commit us to return these islands." The resulting communiqué stated that "The President and Prime Minister also reviewed the status of the Bonin Islands and agreed that the mutual security interests of Japan and the United States could be accommodated within the arrangements for the return of administration of these islands to the GOJ." Several months later, Nobuhiko Ushiba, Japan's Foreign Affairs Vice Minister, called on Rusk and "expressed appreciation on behalf of the Japanese government for the return of the Bonin Islands."[38]

Washington also sought a Republic of Korea-Government of Japan rapprochement, support for the U.S. military effort in Vietnam, for America's policy of isolating the People's Republic of China as part of the larger Cold War effort, and having Japan use some of its economic gains to benefit Asia, including support for the Asian Development Bank.

Japanese-Korean relations demonstrated a profound difference of opinion between Tokyo, Seoul, and Washington. While the full discussion will occur in the next chapter, the Japanese government believed that, by the 1960s, Japan had sufficiently apologized for guilt over its occupation of Korea from 1905 to 1945. It engaged in relations based on diplomatic equality and free trade. However, the Korean government insisted upon continuing Japanese economic assistance to stimulate the troubled Korean economy and to atone for Japan's brutal reign over the peninsula.

The war in Vietnam demonstrated a division in Japanese opinion. The government, and thus the ruling Liberal Democratic Party, largely supported the American effort in Vietnam. There was obvious benefit for the Japanese economy and Japan relied on America's nuclear and military umbrella in East Asia. Many Japanese had doubts. News reports of the Vietnam War reminded too many Japanese of their troubling experience in China during the Second World War. Others had concerns about American nuclear-powered ships and American nuclear weapons, again reminding Japanese of the atomic bombing of Hiroshima and Nagasaki in the closing days of the Second World War. During the visit of Prime Minister Ikeda to

---

[38] *FRUS, 1964-1968, Vol. XXIX,* Document 98, Read to Rostow, October 13, 1967. The Joint Chiefs continued to disagree, seeking to retain Iwo Jima and Chichi Jima; see Document 100, Rostow to Johnson, November 3, 1967. *FRUS, 1964-1968, Vol. XXIX,* Document 100, Tab B, "Draft Language for Sato Communiqué on the Bonin Islands;" Document 118, Bundy to Rusk, March 23, 1968; NARA, RG 59, CFPF, Box 2249, PolAff&Rel, Japan-US, 1/1/68, "U.S.-Japan Relations," June 6, 1968.

Washington in June 1961 Japanese Foreign Minister Kosaka and Secretary Rusk discussed port calls by Nautilus-class nuclear-powered submarines. Rusk recognized "the sensitivity of this issue to Japan" and asked if "the visit of nuclear-powered submarines would create much of a problem for Japan." Kosaka responded that "The public still tends to relate anything atomic to nuclear weapons and thereby to the possibility of involvement in a nuclear war. The Japanese Government would therefore like to give further study to this problem before agreeing to the visits of nuclear-powered submarines" and Rusk agreed. Five months later Rusk visited Ikeda as part of the joint Cabinet economic talks. "Ikeda showed great misgivings about introducing US combat forces in[to Vietnam]." The previously cited "Guidelines Paper" also noted that "The Japanese people are haunted by the fear of involvement in another nuclear war ." Despite ongoing discussions, Washington and Tokyo did not reach agreement on entry of nuclear-powered submarines into Japanese ports until 1964. Six weeks before the Gulf of Tonkin incident, McNamara met with Fukuda Tokuyasu, Director-General of Japan's Defense Agency, and discussed the situation in Vietnam. Fukuda responded to a McNamara question about a Viet Cong takeover "that it would be like the chessman on a board falling over (the Domino theory), and the repercussions would be felt in Thailand, Indonesia, and in other countries in that area." Fukuda added that an American defeat in South Vietnam "would strengthen the left wing elements in Japan, who would probably protest US military bases in Japan and the Japanese-US Mutual Security Treaty." Also, "Japan would lose trading opportunities in SEA [Southeast Asia].""[39]

As Sato became prime minister, the United States was expanding the war in Vietnam. In January 1965, McGeorge Bundy provided President Johnson with a policy analysis from James Thomson who wrote that Sato "supports our efforts to keep Vietnam free but is deeply worried about the outcome." After a Viet Cong mortar attack on an American helicopter base at Pleiku in Vietnam's Central Highlands, the United States responded initially with a limited – "Operation Flaming Dart" – and later with a sustained – "Operation Rolling Thunder" – bombing campaign over North Vietnam. Ambassador Reischauer soon wrote William Bundy that "not since the crisis over the U.S.-Japan security treaty in 1960 has any issue so

---

[39] *FRUS, 1961-1963, Vol. XXII,* Document 334, Memorandum of Conversation, June 21, 1961; Document 347, Rusk to State, November 4, 1961; Document 354, Department of State Guidelines Paper, Undated; Document 378, Memorandum of Conversation, August 5, 1963; *FRUS, 1964-1968, Vol. XXIX,* Document 16, Memorandum of Conversation, June 30, 1964; Document 22, Embassy in Japan to State, August 20, 1964.

seriously affected the climate of Japanese-American relations as the bombing of North Vietnam." Reischauer made clear that "public opinion has been overwhelmingly critical." A month later Reischauer recounted a conversation with Prime Minister Sato in which he asked for Sato's "personal evaluation of how Japanese public reaction to expanded Vietnam war has affected the various aspects of U.S.-Japanese relationship." Sato responded that "he was disturbed over strength of reaction of left and intellectual community to Vietnam." However in July Sato passed word to the U.S. embassy that, while he would not question America's flying B-52 bombers from Okinawa to bomb North Vietnam, he "expressed his deep personal concern re the adverse impact this action will have in Japan." The embassy worried that opposition parties would expand such public dissatisfaction into more general rejection of the LDP. Sato was deeply concerned about the impact of the Vietnam conflict on Japan, and he began working behind the scenes for a negotiated settlement, trying to approach both Saigon and Hanoi without notable success.[40]

In its annual policy assessment in May 1966, the Tokyo embassy wrote that "in spite of the shock which the Vietnam conflict gave to Japanese public emotions and the efforts of the organized left in Japan to exploit this, U.S.-Japan relations retain their essential closeness and stability." The next year, the embassy had better news. "The Cultural Revolution and antics of the Red Guards in mainland China struck at some of the assumptions about Communist China," and Vietnam hostilities "dropped noticeably in prominence as an irritant in US-Japan relations." Several years and hundreds of thousands of American troops in South Vietnam later, Secretary of Defense McNamara called on Prime Minister Sato and in discussing Vietnam Sato stated that "he found everywhere realization and appreciation of U.S. sacrifices to safeguard freedom." Two months later the Communist Tet offensive forever altered the situation in Vietnam. Nonetheless, Ambassador U. Alexis Johnson met with Japanese Foreign Minister Takeo Miki in August 1968 for a free-ranging discussion. Miki stated "flatly that Japan did want any settlement that would result in a communist SVN." He also "laid strong emphasis upon acceptance of basic

[40] *FRUS, 1964-1968, Vol. XXIX,* Document 40, Bundy to Johnson, January 11, 1965; Document 46, Embassy Tokyo to State, May 19, 1965; Document 50, Reischauer to Bundy, June 15, 1965; Document 56, Embassy Japan to State, July 30, 1965; Document 61, Editorial Note.

relationship with the US, quote there is no one else to whom Japan could turn unquote."[41]

In the last months of the Johnson administration, the embassy in Tokyo offered its views on relations with Japan. It suggested that events of the past year may have "unsettled" the Japanese government; these events included the Arab-Israeli War in June 1967, the Communist Tet offensive, the increasing tension between Czechoslovakia and the Soviet Union, the Cultural Revolution in China, and America's worsening balance of payments challenge. The review noted that "the major factor that has in the past kept the floor under periodic ups and downs in US-Japan relations is a fairly stable conception on the part of the Japanese leadership and most influential Japanese of the U.S. world position and the importance of that position to themselves." In addition to international events, the race riots and antiwar protests in American cities shook Japanese confidence in the U.S. government. But embassy staffers could not predict the impact of these negative factors. The embassy also obtained and sent to the State Department a Japanese foreign ministry summary of "Japan-US relations." "The pattern of past Japan-U.S. relations shows a movement between poles of closeness and apartness." "For post-war Japan, the relationship with the United States has been at the heart of everything: survival, reform and recovery, security and development, and now, resurgence and reassertment." "The relationship has been extremely close and for Japan, supremely profitable." "Nevertheless, this policy and relationship is coming under increasingly critical reappraisal." "One aspect is the change in the U.S. image because of Viet Nam, violence and race relations, the end of nuclear, space and monetary supremacy, as well as general awareness of a trend toward 'multipolarization.'" "There is also the rise in Japanese self-esteem commensurate with economic power."[42]

The U.S. government could claim credit for a largely successful policy. *U.S. News* headlined "Amazing Success Story in Asia." It noted that "there's a cheerful side to the unfolding story of modern Asia . . . in Japan,

---

[41] NARA, RG 59, CFPF, Box 2384, Pol 1, Japan-US, 1-1-66, "U.S. Policy Assessment – Japan, 1965," May 2, 1966; NARA, RG 59, CFPF, Box 2250, Pol 1, Japan-US, 1/1/67, "US Policy Assessment – Japan, 1966," April 17, 1967; *FRUS, 1964-1968, Vol. XXIX,* Document 104, Memorandum of Conversation, November 14, 1967; LBJ Library, NSF Country File, Box 252, Japan, Cables (1 of 2), Vol. VII, 10/67-12/68, Amembassy Tokyo to State #2042, August 21, 1968.

[42] LBJ Library, NSF Country File, Box 252, Japan, Memos (1 of 3), Vol. VII, 10/67-12/68, American Embassy to Secretary of State, June 5, 1968; NARA, RG 59, CFPF, Box 2250, Pol 1, Japan-US, 1/1/67, "Japan-US Relations – Present Patterns and the Next Decade," 27 December 1968.

South Korea and other nations aided by U.S., prosperity is spreading." "The stamp of Japanese power is seen everywhere in Asia – and other Asians want the same success for themselves." "To American diplomats, these problems are annoying but not explosive. These diplomats are satisfied that Japan – because of its new affluence and power – is obliged to stand with the United States and the free world in order to protect its own interests." In mid-December 1968 Alexis Johnson sent Dean Rusk a summary of his "first substantive meeting with Foreign Minister [Kichi] Aichi today" "during which we have very frank and very production discussion" on the full-range of topics in Japanese-American relations. Interestingly, Aichi's statements were little different from his predecessor in 1961. He wanted "to base Japanese foreign policy on the relationship with the U.S." and he recognized "that [the] security relationship with the U.S. is very much in Japan's benefit." Aichi recognized the need to make progress on outstanding issues in trade and hoped to approach the new Nixon administration soon.[43]

Modern scholars have written extensively about U.S.-Japanese relations. James Matray noted that Japanese Foreign Minister Ohira Masayoshi [appointed in 1962] "developed a plan to expand exports as a means to boost economic growth, which required maintaining close commercial ties with the United States." But "the Vietnam War, that under [Prime Minister] Sato transformed the U.S. military presence in Japan into an incendiary issue." Sato defended the U.S. war effort, and that led to political unrest at home. Bert Edström noted similarities in Prime Ministers Ikeda and Sato: "For Ikeda as new prime minister, it was important to restore the relationship with the United States," so he "played down contentious issues, adopted a 'low posture' and concentrated on economic growth." Sato "stressed the US-Japan security treaty as the guarantee of Japan's security." Marc Gallicchio agreed with Edström about Sato's interest in regaining Okinawa and noted that "Johnson salved Sato's disappointment over Okinawa by agreeing to return the sparsely populated Bonin Islands to Japanese control." He further argued that "mounting Japanese pressure for the return of Okinawa, escalation in Vietnam, the gold drain, and a growing trade imbalance signaled the end of the era of benign neglect in U.S.-Japan relations." William Nester wrote that "there were few significant economic issues" in Japanese-American relations, and that "America's economic power remained dynamic and

[43] "Amazing Success Story in Asia," *U.S. News & World Report,* March 11, 1968, pp. 48, 50; LBJ Library, NSF Country File, Box 252, Japan, Memos (1 of 3), Vol. VII, 10/67-12/68, Amembassy Tokyo to SecState, #3750, December 11, 1968.

unchallenged." Thus, "presidents and their foreign policy staff concentrated on managing crises and wars." Given this primacy of traditional diplomatic concerns, Nester found that "American economic policy toward Japan involved providing Japanese exporters access to American, Southeast Asian, and global markets, and tolerating Tokyo's web of import and investment barriers." He claimed that "American policymakers acted consistently on the belief that beefing up Japan geoeconomically was vital to strengthening American geopolitical interests throughout the Far East. And they were largely right. Even more interestingly, he wrote that "The Johnson administration viewed Japan's surging economic power without trepidation." "Johnson and Rusk became concerned not that Tokyo continued to maintain huge trade and investment barriers and dump its goods in the United States and elsewhere, but that Japanese firms were merely selling in Southeast Asia and not trying to develop the region." "Like other administrations, Johnson's sought but failed to achieve a larger Japanese defense role." Timothy Maga wrote about Kennedy's commitment to free trade: "Kennedy lashed out at protectionism in general." He quoted Kennedy: "'a return to protectionism is not a solution. Such a course could result in retaliation abroad with serious consequences for U.S. exports and our trade balance.'" Michael Schaller found that "even as Japan's economic growth surged during the 1960s, American views of its ally's vulnerability remained fairly constant." In contrast to Maga and some others, Schaller also wrote that "shortly after taking office in January 1961, President John F. Kennedy told aides that among his greatest fears were the threat of nuclear war and America's growing balance of payments problem." In contrast to Nester, he also wrote that "Kennedy was the first modern president forced to adopt an economic strategy for an America in relative economic decline." Later, after Johnson succeeded Kennedy and U. Alexis Johnson followed Edwin Reischauer as Ambassador to Japan, Schaller noted that Ambassador "Johnson believed that while Japan initially needed a protected market to speed recovery, its booming export market and growing trade surplus with the United States meant the time had come for Tokyo to change its economic policy." Perhaps most critically, Schaller wrote that "Kennedy and Johnson's determination to secure Tokyo's nominal support for the Vietnam War obscured their understanding of Japan's economic transformation and the implications it held for the United States." Glenn Hook and colleagues set out the conundrum for Japanese and American officials. "The pattern of Japan's trade relations with the world is characterized by a heavy reliance on the US market for the export of finished products." "Export dependence on the US was 27 percent in 1960 and 31 percent in 1970 [of a greater total].” If the government in Washington continued to insist on limiting Japanese trade with Communist countries, if the European nations maintained various non-tariff barriers to Japanese goods, and until the underdeveloped free nations of Asia could absorb more Japanese exports, the government in Tokyo could only grow the Japanese economy by exporting ever greater quantities of goods to the United States. Walter LaFeber focused on the economic relationship and its impact on Japanese-American relations. “Ikeda’s economic scheme succeeded astoundingly, but, at the same time, slowly ate away at the ties between Japan and the United States.” “The Japanese began to demand what they called ‘equal partnership,’ by which they seemed to mean more economic access while America bore the responsibility for maintaining Asian security.” While LaFeber focused on the Vietnam conflict, he also noted that “as the war accelerated, so did three disagreements between the Americans and Japanese: the return of Okinawa, trade with China, and the removal of U.S. discriminations against imports from Japan while Japanese discriminations against U.S. exports (and capital) remained in place.” Roger Buckley found U.S.-Japanese relations to be unsatisfactory and apportioned blame rather equally. He wrote that once Reischauer began as U.S. ambassador to Japan, “the subject of Japan rapidly lost any priority with the new Kennedy administration.” He was disappointed with the handling of “Japanese security relations with the United States and the degree of economic support between the two nations.” He faulted “Japanese authorities [who] gave little ground during the decade” in trade and investment.” He found interesting that Japan “preferred to recall the humiliations of the Meiji era when the Western merchant and banker had a hammerlock on a vulnerable and underdeveloped state” even when “Japan possessed the third largest economy in the world.” On the other hand, “What was largely absent in the 1960s was any very effective American sanction against Japanese trade. The crude message that without the vital trade link with the United States the entire pro-American foundation of Japanese external relations might crumble was usually sufficient to prevent display of overt American displeasure.” Hideo Kanemitsu chose to concentrate on the changing eras in Japanese-American relations. He noted the Kennedy and early Johnson years “as one of patron-protégé relations, in which the United States gave unilateral support and protection as a powerful patron of Japan” and that “throughout this period Japan was almost totally dependent upon the United States for both exports and imports." By 1965, "Japan had a surplus in its merchandise trade balance for the first time since the end of World War II."[44]

As the Johnson Administration was drawing to a close, administration officials began putting together lists of President Johnson's major foreign policy accomplishments. Officials noted that "economic success stories in the Pacific area are numerous and impressive." "Japan has achieved one of the highest growth rates in the world not only in terms of GNP but in terms of its international trade, which jumped from $7.7 billion in 1960 to $17 billion in 1966. Trade with the U.S. jumped from $2.6 billion to $5.6 billion during this period." Officials also noted the U.S.-Japan partnership and the successful meetings Johnson held with Prime Minister Sato. "As a consequence of these meetings, Japan today plays a more positive role, especially in the economic sphere, in our common endeavor to assist the free nations of Asia in their aspirations for economic growth, political stability and security." [45]

---

[44] James I. Matray, *Japan's Emergence as a Global Power,* Westport, CT, Greenwood Press, 2001, pp. 51, 52; Bert Edström, *Japan's Evolving Foreign Policy Doctrine: from Yoshida to Miyazawa,* New York, St. Martin's Press, Inc., 1999, pp. 53, 56, 59; Marc Gallicchio, "Occupation, Dominion, and Alliance: Japan in American Security Policy, 1945-1969," in Akira Iriye and Robert A. Wampler, Editors, *Partnership: The United States and Japan, 1951-2001,* New York, Kodansha International, 2001, pp. 127, 128; William R. Nester, *Power across the Pacific: a diplomatic history of American relations with Japan,* New York, New York University Press, 1996, pp. 263, 264, 265, 287; Timothy P. Maga, *John F. Kennedy and the New Pacific Community, 1961-1963,* Houndmills, Basingstoke, Hampshire, England, The MacMillan Press, Ltd., 1990, p. 89; Michael Schaller, "Altered States: the United States and Japan During the 1960s," in Diane B. Kunz, Editor, *The diplomacy of the crucial decade: American foreign relations during the 1960s,* New York, Columbia University Press, 1994, pp. 256, 261, 263, 279 and *Altered states: the United States and Japan since the occupation,* New York, Oxford University Press, 1997; Glenn D. Hook, Julie Gibson, Christopher W. Hughes and Hugo Dobson, *Japan's international relations: politics, economics and security,* New York, Routledge, 2001, p. 106; Walter LaFeber, *The clash: a history of U.S.-Japanese relations,* New York, W.W. Norton & Company, Inc., 1997, pp. 326, 333, 339; Roger Buckley, *US-Japan alliance diplomacy, 1945-1990,* New York, Cambridge University Press, 1992, pp. 99, 103, 111, 112; Hideo Kanemitsu, "U.S.-Japan Trade Relations, 1955-1982," in Akira Iriye and Warren I. Cohen, *The United States and Japan in the postwar world,* Lexington, The University Press of Kentucky, 1989, pp. 145, 146.

[45] LBJ Library, NSF Subject File, Box 19, Report of Accomplishments during LBJ [3 of 4], "Major Accomplishments in East Asia and the Pacific Since 1961," 6c, p. 5; same box, Foreign Affairs Data Sheets 12/63-6/68, Read to Rostow, "Significant turning Points in International Relations," March 10, 1968, 4c, p. 1.

Despite America's overwhelming military power, the government in Washington held a relatively weak bargaining hand in negotiating with Tokyo. An economically vibrant Japan firmly in the Western camp was a basic tenet of American foreign policy since the onset of the Cold War. As John Kennedy became president he beheld a dangerous world, and an aggressive Communist bloc threatening the world. He also believed that friendly governments in Eastern Asia were relatively weak and required continuing American support. When Lyndon Johnson succeeded Kennedy as president, the Japanese economy was booming, but Japanese leaders clamed the expansion was more fragile than it appeared, and Johnson and Rusk acquiesced because, again, given the cost of containing China, increased rather dramatically with the Vietnam war, the cost of permitting Japan some advantage in the economic relationship appeared a wise investment.

Japan pressed its economic advantage as far as it could. Japanese government and business leaders recognized that their country's economy needed continued access to the U.S. economy. Economies in East Asia were too small and underdeveloped to absorb a great deal of Japanese exports, although they were sources of raw materials. The Communist world frequently wanted favorable financing or barter arrangements the Japanese would rather avoid, and European countries maintained various barriers against imported goods. The government in Tokyo recognized the way that Washington viewed Japan in the Cold War and containment of China, and claimed that it needed various concessions on trade to serve as a buttress of American foreign policy in the region.

The U.S. conceded a great deal in the economic/trade sphere to retain Japan as an anchor in maintaining the containment of China in East Asia. At first, the Kennedy and later Johnson Administrations permitted imports of Japanese [and other country] textiles which resulted in the closing of American factories and loss of jobs for American workers. Then Japan moved into consumer electronics – radios, televisions, and stereo equipment were notable examples – and other value added items - cameras. Finally, as the decade ended, Japanese automobile manufacturers were beginning to export more and more cars to the United States. As a consequence, the balance of payments deficit – reflecting the costs of American forces stationed in Japan and Vietnam war-related spending in Japan – soon became a balance of trade deficit as America produced far fewer goods it exported to Japan than the seemingly endless stream of Japanese goods arriving in American ports and spreading across the country.

Finally, by August 1971, the situation had become intolerable and Richard Nixon announced the so-called Nixon shocks to protect America's international economic position, but those shocks and the oil embargo and crude oil price increase following the Arab-Israeli War of October 1973 all appeared to have little enduring impact on the Japanese economic juggernaut. After Nixon became president, the long-standing balance of payments deficit became an increasingly serious balance of trade deficit. As a result, the U.S. government printed more and more dollars which it sent abroad to pay for purchases of various goods and services, and then more and more gold moved from the U.S. Treasury to gold speculators abroad. Fearing great damage to the U.S. international economic position, Richard Nixon announced on August 15, 1971 that the United States would no longer exchange dollars for gold, a step on the road to floating rather than fixed currency rates. He also announced a 10% surcharge on all imports, which hit Japan harder than most countries. Finally, he also announced 90 day wage and price controls but this merely pent up demand for later rather than deal directly with troubling domestic inflation.

CHAPTER FOUR

THE LITTLE TIGERS ROAR: THE REPUBLICS OF KOREA AND CHINA

In 1961 South Korea and Taiwan seemed two sides of a similar coin. Both governments fixated on their respective opponents – North Korea and the People's Republic; they used the threat of invasion to avoid hard economic decisions and strengthening political ties to the general population. Each received significant U.S. assistance and neither seemed poised for great change.

In fits and starts, both governments strengthened their economies while remaining strong U.S. allies. A military coup in Korea brought Park Chung-hee to power and he reduced corruption and improved government efficiency; economic growth followed. At the same time, Jiang Jieshi concentrated on Mao's communist regime but his economic advisors made dramatic progress towards moving Taiwan off U.S. economic assistance and laid the groundwork for another Asian economic powerhouse.

By December 1968, the situations for South Korea and Taiwan had changed dramatically. They no longer feared invasion, and the United States government no longer had to provide foreign aid.

The Republic of Korea faced very real challenges at the beginning of the Kennedy Administration. Syngman Rhee's fifteen years in power had hindered Korean political and economic development; fear of a renewed North Korean invasion resulted in too much emphasis on defense and military spending; and the Korean people could not set aside justifiable attitudes toward their former occupiers to recognize the need for a formal accommodation with Japan.

North Korea remained antagonistic, and heavily armed. The government in Seoul worried about a new invasion and, more immediately, the regular efforts of Pyongyang to infiltrate guerrillas into the South to attack Republic of Korea and American units and to seek to foment rebellion. Seoul viewed Beijing as a supporter of Pyongyang and worried about Chinese support for Pyongyang's activities.

Syngman Rhee, longtime strongman, had finally ceded power, but the political system was weak. A Special National Intelligence Estimate of March 1961 concluded that "the April anniversary of the fall of Syngman Rhee will be marked by demonstrations and, probably, some acts of violence." Ominously it further noted that "the ROK will continue to be plagued by formidable economic and political problems, and the long-term outlook for the ROK is bleak." The government party held a bare majority in the House of Representatives, and a younger faction in Prime Minister Chang Myon's own Democratic Party found his leadership "not sufficiently imaginative or vigorous." More troubling, "the Communists have increased their efforts to subvert the ROK." A military coup on May 16, 1961 added to the challenge of building a polity committed to the Republic of Korea.[1]

The real worry was the South Korean economy. *The New York Times* wrote that "South Korea's wobbly economy was pictured this week as the principal security problem of allied armed forces defending the country against the Communists in the north." It quoted General Carter B. Magruder that "people are impatient for an improvement in their standard of living." The March 1961 SNIE reported "mounting signs of frustration and resentment directed at the government and, increasingly, at the US, over the slow pace of reform and progress in South Korea." Similarly, "corruption continues to be a major problem for the government." Economic challenges had several causes: "the weak and uncertain state of an economy poor in natural resources and diverted from the major problems of reconstruction by the requirements of one of the largest military establishments in proportion to population in the world." [2]

The government was committed to making necessary changes but seemed unable to make progress. It promised to reduce corruption, strengthen the economy, and thus have the efficiency and capacity to remain alert to North Korean aggression and subversion. But, in the first year after replacing the long, aged, and inefficient regime of Syngman Rhee, the government of Prime Minister Chang Myon made little progress. Hugh Farley of the International Cooperation Administration in March 1961 wrote Kennedy aide Walt Rostow about three major challenges

---

[1] Director, Central Intelligence, Special National Intelligence Estimate Number 42-61, "Short-Range Outlook in the Republic of Korea," 21 March 1961, www.foia.cia.gov, pp. 3, 4.

[2] *The New York Times,* February 9, 1961, p. 8; Director, Central Intelligence, Special National Intelligence Estimate Number 42-61, "Short-Range Outlook in the Republic of Korea," 21 March 1961, www.foia.cia.gov, pp. 3, 4, 5.

facing the government: "The extent and depth of graft, corruption and fraud in the major institutions of Korean society today and the consequent lack of confidence on the part of Koreans, high and low, in these institutions, in themselves, in their own future, and--because of the absence of a U.S. posture on integrity--an increasing loss of confidence in the U.S.;" "The dangerously deteriorating direction of the dynamics of the situation in South Korea, particularly over the next several months;" and "The indecisive and inadequate leadership of the USOM in Korea, its critical role at this time, and the lack of a rapport between the USOM and the decision-makers in the ROK Government." Robert Komer agreed with Farley: "Look at the basic problems of the ROK: (a) a poor country with few resources and skills; (b) saddled with staggering task of supporting a far larger military establishment than it really able to (or than is needed); (c) corruption feeding on inexperience in democratic government; and (d) a rising nationalism and expectancy frustrated by what the ROKs increasingly believe is US disinclination to accord them full equality, push for unification, or change overwhelming military emphasis in ROK." Komer concluded "underlying ills and needs are economic." He then proposed an ambitious program clearly beyond the capacity of the government. Rostow then wrote Kennedy, indicating that "the underlying fact is that all hands agree the situation in Korea is not good; and American policy in Korea requires a fresh look." In early April, Secretary of State Dean Rusk wrote Ambassador Walter McConaughy, about to return to Washington, DC as Assistant Secretary of State for Far Eastern Affairs, that one great problem awaiting him was the "very dubious future free Korea so long as ROK lacks forceful leadership, exhibits serious weakness in moral fiber, and permits graft and corruption on scale equaling if not excelling that during moral nadir of Rhee regime."[3]

A military junta overthrew the elected civilian government. On May 16, 1961, a group of army officers led by Park Chung-hee seized control. American officials in Korea quickly informed the government in Washington; only 3,600 officers and men produced the coup. *The New York Times* reported the junta "seems to be in general control throughout South Korea," and "the United States must now accept a *fait accompli*." *The Times* characterized junta leaders as "dedicated to cleaning up

[3] Department of State, Foreign Relations of the United States, 1961-1963, Volume XXIII, Northeast Asia, Washington, DC, GPO, 199X, Document 202, Farley to Rostow, March 6, 1961; Document 203, Komer to Rostow, March 15, 1961; Document 204, Rostow to Kennedy, March 15, 1961; Document 207, Rusk to McConaughy, April 1, 1961.

corruption and operating a more efficient government than the shaky, faction-ridden regime that has been replaced." *U.S. News & World Report* stated "tremendous stakes for U.S. are involved in the military take-over in Korea." It warned "more uncertainty ahead, not only for South Korea's economic and political future, but for the whole balance of military power in Asia."[4]

American diplomats had many concerns. A new SNIE, 42-2-61, noted "the coup group will probably inject a new sense of drive and discipline into the ROK Government's economic and administrative efforts, and may make some headway, especially in curbing corruption." But the intelligence analysis believed the problems were so great that the military junta will have great difficulties "because of their inexperience and a probably reluctance to accept outside advice." *U.S. News & World Report* noted one change: "American diplomats, generals and economic experts have lost a great deal of their power to tell the South Korean Government what to do and how to behave in conducting its affairs." The junta that seized power "wanted to restore Korea's self-respect." Two months later, US intelligence analysts wrote that "the military junta now ruling the Republic of Korea [is] tough, nationalistic, and ambitious." "The ROK's new ruling group intends to bring a new order and discipline into Korean life and to initiate major economic development effort." While it wants "close relations" with the United States, "it intends to run Korean affairs its own way." The junta resented "initial US opposition to the takeover." As a result, "the junta will be less responsive to US advice in political matters, and almost certainly intends to go about the tasks of reform and political control in its own way." [5]

Soon after the coup, President Park traveled to Washington to meet President Kennedy. *U.S. News & World Report* interviewed Park before he left Seoul. Park said that "there must be better utilization of American aid," and he noted that "we have to constantly maintain sufficient military power to counter Communist threats." In turn, Deputy National Security Advisor Walt Rostow provided briefing materials to President Kennedy,

---

[4] *The New York Times,* "The Future in South Korea," May 19, 1961, p. 30; *U.S. News & World Report,* "Korea: 'Reformers' Out and Army in," May 29, 1961, p. 48.

[5] Director, Central Intelligence, Special National Intelligence Estimate Number 42-2-61, *U.S. News & World Report,* "U.S. Choice in Korea: Accept less Power, or Pull Out," June 19, 1961, pp. 49-50; DCI, "Short-Term Prospects in South Korea," 31 May 1961, www.foia.cia.gov, p. 3; DCI, SNIE No. 42-3-61, "The Current Regime in the Republic of Korea, 18 July 1961, www.foia.cia.gov, pp. 3, 5.

noting goals for the meeting, including "increase of Chairman Park's prestige," "demonstration of United States understanding of Korean problems," and impress Park "with power and capacity of United States." While the U.S. government worried about the junta's dissolving of the legislature, curbs on freedom of the press, and jailing of some 40,000 political prisoners, *Time* reported that "with Communist pressure mounting in Asia, the U.S. badly needs a stable government in South Korea." Kennedy was impressed with Park's commitment to hold elections and a constitutional referendum in 1963 and to improve relations with Japan. Other administration officials promised the aid Park needed to reform the economy.[6]

Six months after the military coup, the situation seemed to stabilize. While North Korea remained a threat, "the greatest threat to South Korea, at least in the near term, comes from within South Korea." The South Korean economy remained the major concern, and "US will probably succeed in preventing economic collapse." Economic difficulties imperiled the political system, and if matters did not "improve significantly," North Korea might increase its influence over the peninsula. *Time* reported Park was "making an unprecedented effort to clean out his country's age-old corruption and laxness." Still the government in Washington worried that political unrest was frustrating South Korea's economy growth. The junta tried to reform Korean life, to introduce a measure of austerity, and to create funds for investing in industry. Another half year later, the situation remained unclear. "The economic outlook is grim but not hopeless." "The Communist powers will continue their attempts to destroy the independence of South Korea by various forms of political warfare and subversion." Five months later American intelligence analysts remained concerned. "The junta currently has little popular support. Blatantly rigged elections or further economic deterioration could cause riots and demonstrations." "ROK-US relations will continue to be difficult over the next few months." And, of great concern for American experts, "it is doubtful that the issue of ROK-Japanese relations will soon be resolved." "While the military danger from the North continues to exist, the Communist threat to South Korea remains primarily political, psychological, and

[6] *U.S. News & World Report,* "After a Revolution: Where South Korea Stands Now," November 20, 1961, pp. 112-113; *Time,* "Help for Korea," November 24, 1961, www.time.com/time/magazine/article/0,9171,828834.00.html; John F. Kennedy Library, President's Office Files, Box 121, Korea, Security, 1961-1963, Rostow to Kennedy, November 13, 1961; JFK Library, POF, Box 121, Korea, Security Briefing Book, Park Visit, 11/61, "Chairman Park's Visit: Scope Paper."

subversive in nature."[7]

In 1963, there were clear signs of progress, while much remained to be done. In April the American embassy in Seoul reported "the Korean people could look backward on a year of economic fluctuations and forward to a period of economic uncertainty and political turbulence." "The political crisis contributed to a general feeling of uneasiness that was manifested economically in hoarding, speculation, and an upward thrust of prices." Compared to earlier years, "the economic situation is not critical" and "there is a good possibility of achieving a reasonable stabilization of the economy." About the same time, *The New York Times* reported that "there are growing worries among financial experts that South Korea will face serious economic difficulties and a threat of inflation next summer." "Economic problems, in fact, have posed the chief stumbling block to the military government's progress to social reforms." By September, the issues seemed typical of developing economies: "to stabilize supplies and prices of rice and other grains and contain inflationary pressures; to halt the foreign exchange outflow; [and] to assure orderly transition to a government having the support of the Korean people." Soon thereafter, *The Times* editorialized that "the South Korean economy remains in deep trouble. The main difficulty is ever-worsening inflation."[8]

By Spring 1965, President Park claimed he had largely achieved the goals that precipitated the coup four years earlier. In mid-December 1964, *The New York Times* reported that "United States officials here believe South Korea is on the way to becoming self-supporting." "South Korea's improved economic prospects are in striking contrast to the prevailing opinion a few years ago." On the eve of another visit to Washington, *Time* reported in May that Korea was "moving toward economic takeoff, the

---

[7] DCI, NIE No. 14.2/42-61, "The Outlook for Korea," 7 September 1961, www.foia.cia.gov, p. 5; *Time,* "The New Life," November 3, 1961, www.time.com/time/archive; *The New York Times,* "Political Unrest holds back economy in Korea," January 9, 1962, p. 69; DCI, SNIE No. 42-62, "The Outlook for South Korea," 4 April 1962;LBJ Library, NSF, NIE, Box 6, 42, S Korea, p. 2; DCI, SNIE No. 42-2-62, "Short Term Outlook for South Korea," 7 September 1962, www.foia.cia.gov, p. 5-6, 11.

[8] NARA, RG 59, CFPF, Box 4037, POL 2-3, Politics-Econ Rpts, 2/1/63, AmEmbassy Seoul to State, A796, April 1, 1963; *The New York Times,* "Fiscal Deficits and Rising Prices Foreshadow Korea Crises," April 5, 1963, p. 82; NARA, RG 59, CFPF, Box 4037, POL 2-3, Politics-Econ Rpts, 2/1/63, Amembassy Seoul to State A-195, 3 September 1963; *The New York Times,* "Korea's Economy hurt by Inflation," October 6, 1963, p. 8.

scars of war [were] nearly healed, and a viable (if still somewhat fragile) democracy [was] emerging." *U.S. News & World Report* struck a discordant note: "If the U.S. and Japanese programs can be meshed, there is hope that South Korea will be able to stand on its own feet. If the programs fail, the resulting political and economic shambles could easily propel South Korea towards a deal with the Communist North."[9]

While the Johnson Administration supported Park and his reform efforts, there was some frustration with these official visits. In mid-June 1964, US Ambassador Samuel Berger cabled Rusk that "I let the prime minister know of my displeasure that his planning for Washington trip had been carried so far without any indication from USG that visit in near future would be acceptable." Berger added that "I am aware that U.S. Government could not comply with most of prime minister's specific requests." When Korean officials continued to press this visit, Berger replied to the accompanying aid request with "it would be difficult to justify in terms of need and that there is no prospect for such funds becoming available." Rusk cabled Berger that "we are as strongly opposed to visit of Prime Minister as you are. Koreans propose such 'lobbying' expeditions at least every year" "in connection with aid appropriations." "We recently have successfully resisted such visits." Ambassador Brown wrote Rusk of a proposed visit by Korean Foreign Minister Yi: "political counselor threw cold water on Yi's idea of calling on president and questioned him closely on purpose of visit to Washington at this time." Nonetheless, the State Department approved a ten minute visit with President Johnson on March 17, 1965. McGeorge Bundy prepared Johnson noting Yi's role in negotiating the Korea-Japan settlement and U.S. efforts to secure more Korean combat troops for Vietnam.[10]

In many ways, the state of ROK-Japan relations seemed indicative of the challenges the junta faced. American officials viewed an accommodation

---

[9] *The New York Times,* "U.S. and Seoul Officials see South Korea moving toward self-support," December 11, 1964, p. 2; *Time,* "The Striking Parallel," May 21, 1965, www.time.com/time/magazine/article/0,9171,901694,00.html; *U.S. News & World Report,* "Korea after 12 years: saved from reds, but still in trouble," May 31, 1965, p. 48.

[10] NARA, RG 59, CFPF, Box 2401, Pol 7, Visits, Mtgs, KOR S, 1/1/64, Seoul to Secstate, #1696, June 20, 1964; same folder, Seoul to Secstate, #1701, June 22, 1964; State to Amembassy Seoul, #223, September 10, 1964; Box 2402, Pol 7, KOR S, 1/1/65-2/27/65, Seoul to SecState, #703, February 3, 1965; same box, Pol 7, Visits, Mtgs, KOR S, 3-1-65, Memorandum for McGeorge Bundy, March 17, 1965.

as critical to Korea's economic development and national security. As he was leaving to become an Assistant Secretary of State, U.S. Ambassador Walter McConaughy wrote Secretary Rusk that "Japan, longtime and natural trading partner of ROK, offers great possibilities for developmental aid to Korea—at least in form of long-term investment loans—and for furnishing technological assistance which Korea eminently requires." Soon after the military junta took power, Robert Johnson of the National Security Council wrote McGeorge Bundy that "the new Korean regime seems, on present evidence, much more anti-Japanese than its immediate predecessor. Therefore, though we believe that ROK-Japanese rapprochement is of great economic importance to Korea, State is not optimistic that Japanese investment in, or economic aid to, Korea is an immediate prospect." In the immediate aftermath of the coup, the National Security Council discussed the report of the task force on Korea, and agreed that "The improvement of Japanese-ROK relations should be discussed with the Japanese Prime Minister during his visit to Washington." A week later, President Kennedy discussed a Korea-Japan rapprochement with Japanese Prime Minister Ikeda during his visit. Ikeda told Kennedy that "the Koreans are difficult to deal with, being exclusive and self-willed ." He also noted his government's concern for the military coup, and the lack of civilian government, using it as an excuse for inaction on a Korean-Japanese accord. Kennedy stated his hope for an accord, but agreed that "this is difficult due to the nationalistic flavor of the coup group and the popular dislike in Japan for militaristic regimes." Two months later, the continuing nationalism – meaning, in part, anti-Japanese – view of the military junta concerned American officials. They also concluded that Seoul wanted outstanding issues, including reparations for 35 years of Japanese control of Korea, resolved before committing to meaningful negotiations.[11]

As President Park and the junta strengthened their control, there was little progress towards a Korea-Japan agreement. In November 1961, Secretary Rusk called on Park. Rusk recounted the conversation with Ikeda, and remarked that both Park and Ikeda faced domestic opposition in reaching a settlement, but he nevertheless urged them to negotiate.

[11] *FRUS, 1961-1963, XXIII,*, Document 210, McConaughy to Rusk, April 11, 1961; Document 225, "The Task Force Report on Korea," June 6, 1961 and Document 227, "The Task Force Report on Korea," June 13, 1961; Document 230, Record of National Security Council Action No. 2430, June 13, 1961; Document 232, Memorandum of Conversation, June 20, 1961; Document 242, "Progress Report," August 24, 1961.

Meeting again a week later during Park's visit to Washington, DC, Park agreed with Rusk that "it was necessary to normalize relations between the two countries to assure peace and security for the Far East" A month later, Ambassador Samuel Berger wrote Rusk to reflect on Park's visit, and concluded that "without a normalization of Korean-Japanese relations, I can see little hope for the economic future of South Korea ." The situation changed little the following year. Averell Harriman wrote Rusk from Tokyo in March 1962 that "An expression of your concern over the apparent new impasse in the ROK/Japanese negotiations would be highly desirable at this point" Harriman noted South Korea's animosity dated back to 1951, while Ikeda's economic doubling plan led to a short term balance of payments deficit so he wanted to avoid new foreign commitments. Two months later President Kennedy asked Rusk about measures to resolve the impasse, and Rusk responded that "the principal obstacle to a settlement at present is the gap between unrealistically high Korean claims against Japan, arising out of the Japanese occupation, and unrealistically low Japanese counter-offers." Rusk concluded that the United States had few levers to manipulate. The accompanying formal analysis began with a statement that "Prospects for early normalization of relations between the Republic of Korea and Japan are not bright." [12]

There still was little progress toward a settlement throughout the remainder of 1962 and into 1963. Averell Harriman expressed "concern about the Korean-Japanese negotiations" to Korean ambassador, Il-Kwon Chung. U.S. diplomats feared the early stages of Japan's phenomenal economic boom might provide Tokyo with the strength to avoid continuing negotiations. Michael Forrestal of the National Security Council staff wrote Harriman that "that if we don't get this settlement agreed to very shortly, the occasion may pass away for the foreseeable future." Forrestal commented that "I cannot estimate whether the President's personal leverage will have much effect in this area ." The embassy in Seoul, however, reported Korean assurances that "Chairman Park was determined to bring negotiations to successful conclusion before he retires." A month later, Seoul reported that the Korean Foreign Office "renewed efforts [to] formulate [a] compromise proposal on fisheries question for presentation to Japanese." On July 5, the Korean government

[12] *FRUS, 1961-1963, Vol. XXIII,* Document 245, Memorandum of Conversation, November 5, 1961; Document 246, Memorandum of Conversation, November 14, 1961; Document 249, Berger to Rusk, December 15, 1961; Document 252, Harriman to Rusk, March 18, 1962; Document 260, Rusk to Kennedy, May 17, 1962; Document 261, "Korean-Japanese Relations," May 17, 1962.

did, indeed, transmit the new proposals to Tokyo. When the new Korean ambassador presented his credentials to President Kennedy in June, Kennedy stated "we continue to be interested in the negotiations between Japan and the ROK. We believe that a settlement between Japan and Korea is most important. The extra resources which Korea will obtain by means of the settlement will be very useful in Korean economic development."[13]

The fisheries dispute was a key to a successful resolution. The Tokyo embassy reported that "talks between Foreign Ministers Kim and Ohira ended July 30 with little concrete accomplished." "Talks concerned fisheries question exclusively." In November Foreign Minister Yong Shik Kim told Rusk that "the fishery issue remained unsettled." [14]

There was seemingly little progress in 1964. Ambassador Edwin Reischauer in Tokyo wrote Rusk in January that "We feel now is more favorable time for settlement than we shall see again before 1965 at earliest." Reischauer believed that otherwise the 1964 Tokyo Olympics would absorb Japan's undivided attention. However, Reischauer noted "we see little we can do at Tokyo end to speed settlement." While Japanese leaders recognized Washington's continuing interest in a settlement, they remained unwilling to concede more than their original position. A few weeks later Robert Komer wrote the obvious to President Johnson: "It would mean a flow of over a half billion dollars into the Korean economy, which would greatly reduce the burden on us over time." Moreover, "a ROK/Jap settlement would be a nice foreign policy plus in 1964." Rusk then traveled to Tokyo and asked Japanese Foreign Minister Masayoshi Ohira about the status of the negotiations, Ohira indicated the major remaining issue was an agreement on fisheries and the width of the exclusion zone and he awaited action by President Park. Over the next several months, American diplomats tried to find a formula to

---

[13] NARA, RG 59, CFPF, Box 3964, Pol-PolAff&Rel, Korea-A, Memorandum of Conversation, February 8, 1963; *FRUS, 1961-1963, Vol. XXIII,* Document 288, Forrestal to Harriman, February 12, 1963; NARA, RG 59, CFPF, Box 3958, Pol-PolAff&Rel, Japan-US, 2/1/63; same folder, Seoul to SecState, #840, April 30, 1963; same folder, Tokyo to SecState, #101, July 10, 1963; *FRUS, 1961-1963, Vol. XXIII,* Document 309, Memorandum of Conversation, June 17, 1963.

[14] NARA, RG 59, CFPF, Box 3958, Pol-PolAff&Rel, Japan-US, 2/1/63, Tokyo to SecState, #364, August 1, 1963; same folder, Seoul to SecState, #156, August 7, 1963 for a discussion whether Korea should insist on a 12-mile limit on fisheries; Box 3964, Pol-PolAff&Rel, Korea-A, Memorandum of Conversation, November 19, 1963.

overcome remaining Japanese and Korean objections to a treaty. In March and April Korean and Japanese Cabinet members met to resolve the remaining issues without success. Student demonstrations affected Seoul's ability to negotiate. Rusk sent a long cable suggesting Seoul "place primary emphasis on broad economic, political and security advantages of settlement for Korea," and suggested talking points. In April 1964, *Newsweek* described efforts of college students in Seoul to disrupt Korea-Japan talks then underway in Tokyo. Students believed that "the Korean bargainers seemed to be assuming a 'low posture' before the people who ruled Korea – not always gently – for 35 years before the end of World War II." They found Japan's offer of $300 million in reparations to be "insulting." *The Economist* reported the negotiations were "in the doldrums." "The argument has centered on fishery arrangements. The Koreans fear the technical superiority of the Japanese fishing fleets. Japan is offering technical aid in this field." Finally, "General Park's government desperately needs capital to get South Korean development plans off the ground and has apparently staked its future on a settlement with Japan as a means of doing so." In addition, some Koreans feared Japanese economic power and an agreement turning Korea into an economic colony of Japan fewer than twenty years after independence.[15]

Once again Washington sought to move the discussions forward between Seoul and Tokyo. In May, Undersecretary George Ball wrote Ambassador Berger that "Department believes that in this crucial period of ROK-Japanese negotiations careful consideration should again be given to possibility of US initiative which might help to drive agreement over the top." In reviewing the history of the negotiations, Ball concluded that "serious obstacles to full and final agreement nevertheless lie on Korean

[15] Department of State, *Foreign Relations of the United States, 1964-1968, Volume XXIX,* Washington, GPO, 1999, Document 332, Reischauer to Rusk, January 3, 1964; Document 334, Komer to Johnson, January 23, 1964; Document 335, Memorandum of Conversation, January 26, 1964. On the efforts to find common ground and secure agreement, see Document 336, Rusk to Berger, February 14, 1964; 337, Berger to Rusk, February 17, 1964, and Document 338, Memorandum of Conversation, February 29, 1964 for examples of continuing American planning and discussions with Japanese and Korean leaders on a settlement; NARA, RG 59, CFPF, Box 2380, PolAff&Rel, Japan-KOR S, 4-1-64, State to Seoul, #901, April 4, 1964; *FRUS, 1964-1968, Vol. XXIX,* Document 339, Editorial Note; *Newsweek,* "Korea: 'Stop Japan,'" April 6, 1964, p. 38; *The Economist,* "Japan and South Korea: Pride or Cash," July 11, 1964, p. 147; NARA, RG 59, CFPF, Box 2380, PolAff&Rel, Japan-KOR S, 9-1-64, Seoul to SecState, #250, September 17, 1964.

side." A week later, Komer wrote National Security Advisor McGeorge Bundy that the "top priority in NE Asia today is *ROK/Jap settlement*." Komer succinctly stated the issue: "We're still spending over *$300 million* a year on 20 million ROKs, with no end really in sight. So we've got to find someone to share the long-term burden, and it's logically the Japs." Nonetheless, as spring became summer, there was little progress. In early September with the Olympics passed, American diplomats once again sought to move Tokyo and Seoul to agreement. Reischauer wrote Rusk that "Japanese are ready to continue negotiations with Koreans at any time Koreans feel able to negotiate." Ambassador Berger wrote William Bundy from Seoul that "there are indications that the Koreans will seek to gain maximum concessions from Japan in connection with remaining differences and there may be some retreat from previous positions." Reischauer soon reported that Foreign Minister Shiina agreed that "this was time for Japan to show maximum magnanimity." But Shiina further stated that "deep fears of Japanese economic domination sometimes made magnanimous gestures suspect in Korean eyes, and since many Koreans are more interested in profit to themselves or their groups than in benefit to Korea, Japanese economic concessions became embroiled in domestic Korean politics." When new premier Eisaku Sato came to Washington in January 1965, he told Rusk that "his Government found the domestic political situation in the Republic of Korea hard to understand."[16]

Eventually, after much posturing and hard negotiating, Seoul and Tokyo were able to reach an accommodation and thus helping to buttress that part of America's so-called Bamboo Curtain in East Asia. In February 1965, James Thomson shared good news with McGeorge Bundy: "We have just had word that both sides have initialed a draft treaty that includes: (1) the establishment of embassies and an exchange of ambassadors at once; (2) Japanese recognition of Korea's status; and (3) agreement that all ancient treaties (i.e. 1905, etc.) between the two countries have already been abrogated." Soon thereafter, Rusk expressed America's appreciation to Korean Foreign Minister Tong Won Lee: "Initialing of the Basic Relations Treaty had been a very important step." Rusk "hoped that Korea and Japan were close to a final settlement." Lee in turn responded that "recently there had been very satisfactory

---

[16] *FRUS, 1964-1968, Vol. XXIX,* Document 341, Ball to Berger, May 12, 1964; Document 342, Komer to McGeorge Bundy, May 19, 1964; Document 349, Reischauer to Rusk, September 8, 1964; Document 350, Berger to William Bundy, October 23, 1964; Document 352, Rusk to Berger, November 11, 1964; Document 353, Reischauer to Rusk, November 21, 1964; .

developments." A trade agreement in March 1965 preceded establishment of diplomatic relations. *The Economist* reported the successful negotiating of a diplomatic treaty, although, to be sure, the respective national parliaments had to approve. "On April 3rd, after protracted negotiations," negotiators initialed the agreements. *U.S. News & World Report* informed readers that "for U.S., if the treaty works out as expected, it means Japan will take over much of the job of getting the South Korean economy on its feet." When President Park visited Washington, DC in May, President Johnson congratulated him "on the progress of Korean negotiations with Japan." *Time* reported on the formal signing in Prime Minister Eisaku Sato's official residence: beaming officials signed, toasted each other with French champagne, and listened to Handel's Toll for the Brave." Nonetheless, South Koreans had ambivalent feelings toward their island neighbor. Some believed the Park government had conceded too much on fisheries. The news of the treaty signing sent thousands of students into Seoul's streets, charging that President Park "had sold out to the Japanese on such vital matters as fishing rights." The government responded with force to regain control. Finally, on December 11, 1965, the media reported that Japan ratified the treaty although the Socialist, Communist, and Buddhist parties all boycotted the session. That led to exchange of documents the following month. In February 1967 the American Embassy in Tokyo sent an analysis of the year since ratification. "The Embassy's overall impression is that, in the year since the restoration of formal diplomatic relations, there has been a significant broadening and deepening of private and unofficial contact and understanding between the two countries." In December George Denney of Intelligence and Research wrote Rusk that both Tokyo and Seoul "continue to bend their efforts toward the maintenance of this relatively amicable relationship." [17]

With the accord in place, Seoul, Washington and Tokyo could turn to

---

[17] *FRUS, 1964-1968, Vol. XXIX,* Document 357, Thomson to Bundy, February 20, 1965; Document 358, Memorandum of Conversation, March 15, 1965; *The New York Times,* "Japan and Korea Initial Trade Pact," March 27, 1965, p. 4; *The Economist,* "Japan and Korea: Together at Last," April 10, 1965, p. 169; *FRUS, 1964-1968, Vol. XXIX,* Document 363, Editorial Note; Document 365, Editorial Note; *U.S. News & World Report,* "Worldgram," July 5, 1965, p. 47; *Time,* "A Treaty for Tomorrow," July 2, 1965, www.time.com/time/magazine/article/0,9171,833841,00.html; *Newsweek,* "Korea: School Days," September 6, 1965, p. 30; *The New York Times,* "Japanese ratify South Korea pact," December 11, 1965, p. 33; *FRUS, 1964-1968, Vol. XXIX,* Document 369, Embassy in Japan to State, February 14, 1967.

the Korean economy. In January 1964, Edward Doherty forwarded the embassy's views on Korea; he wrote that "the most urgent domestic problem" "is the easing of short-run economic strains and establishment of a foundation for long-term economic growth." "Economic stabilization is an immediate and crucial necessity." "Rising prices are stirring resentment among labor and in the military." The next month President Park set an example: he closed five of his six presidential villas, and ordered government officials to stop driving cars, commute by bus or bicycle, reduce liquor intake, and "cut restaurant side dishes to a maximum of three." He wanted a "nationwide bout of belt tightening" to help counter South Korea's "shaky" economy. During an official visit to Washington, Korean Prime Minister told State Department officials that "the first task for the Government of Korea was to achieve a self-supporting economy." Then, "the economy must be modernized to satisfy the aspirations of younger and better educated generations and to keep them from turning to communism." Thus the government wanted to "expand exports so that economic growth will not be at the expense of economic liability."[18]

Improvements became visible in 1965. In January, a National Intelligence Estimate on "The Korean Problem" was discouraging: "lasting stability is not likely unless further progress is made in improving a weak and imbalanced economy, heavily dependent on large-scale US assistance and burdened with serious problems of unemployment and a population growing at nearly three percent per year." Several months later, in its annual "politico-economic assessment," the U.S. Embassy reported "economic and political conditions have improved." "The economy has registered some significant breakthroughs." Moreover, "the government appeared to be carrying through forcefully on the agreed stabilization goals." Interestingly, "growth of the economy is sufficiently marked to permit continued reductions in the levels of grant aid." When Foreign Minister Yi visited Washington in March 1965, Rusk told him that he was "much encouraged by the Republic of Korea's expanding exports." William Bundy informed Rusk in mid-September that "we are aiming at an annual 6% increase in GNP, through emphasis on financial stability, rationalization of other economic policies, and improved economic planning; and through continued but diminishing U.S. economic assistance."

---

[18] NARA, RG 59, CFPF, AmEmbassy Seoul to State, A-483, January 8, 1964; *Time,* "The Simple Life," February 7, 1964, www.time.com/time/archive; NARA, RG 59, CFPF, Box 2399, Pol 2, Gen Rpts & Status, KOR S, 1/1/64, Memorandum of Conversation, September 14, 1964.

In late 1965, *The New York Times* reported that "South Korea is pushing an ambitious program to expand exports so that the country, now largely dependent on American aid, can become self-supporting over the next five years. Stress is being placed on light industry products, mainly for the United States market." *The Times* further noted the dramatic increase in exports to the United States and the expected increase to Japan given restoration of full diplomatic relations.[19]

Within several years, Korea's economy became an example to emulate. In February 1966, *Newsweek* described an all-too typical scene: "in the mountain-rimmed capital of Seoul, where 3.5 million of South Korea's 28 million people live, the roar of the bulldozer is omnipresent and the sidewalks are piled high with construction materials." The news weekly ascribed the turn of fortunes to quality but inexpensive labor, Japanese long-term loans, and U.S. Vietnam War-related spending. The U.S. embassy reported similarly good news. "Korea's economy enjoyed continued rapid growth." "Exports for the quarter increased by 54% and for the year by 47%." The embassy noted "the Korean Government's drive to boost exports as a major means of attaining a self-supporting economy." Though, to be sure, "Vietnam has also become an important market for Korean goods." In a follow-up report two weeks later, the embassy wrote "our economic assistance to the ROK has begun unmistakably to pay off in the form of steady growth in GNP and exports." *Business Week* reported that "Korea is using its cheap and plentiful labor force to make low-priced products that can be exported around the world." "Exports have risen five-fold." On the eve of President Johnson's visit to Asia, *U.S. News & World Report* gushed that "South Korea, short of resources and with too many people, is setting an impressive example for other Asian countries." "South Korea is moving boldly into the twentieth century, is taking its place as one of the leaders of 'New Asia.'" When Johnson visited South Korea in early November 1966, "a revitalized South Korea greets the

---

[19] NARA, RG 59, CFPF, Box 2401, Pol 2-4, Gen Rpts, KOR S, 1/1/65, AmEmbassy Seoul to State, A-295, December 18, 1964; Lyndon Baines Johnson Library, NSF, NIE, Box 6, 42, South Korea, NIE 42/14.2-65, "The Korean Problem," 22 January 1965; NARA, RG 59, CFPF, Box 2399, Pol 2, Gen Rpts & Status, KOR S, 1/1/65, "Current Korean Problems," March 15, 1965; NARA, RG 59, PPS, Subject and Country Files, 1945-1969, Box 305, Korea, 1968, Bundy to Rusk, "National Policy Paper for the Republic of Korea," September 15, 1965; *The New York Times,* "Exports pushed by South Korea," November 14, 1965, p. F15; LBJL, NSF, Files of Edward K. Hamilton, Box , 1965 – Non-Committee on Foreign Aid (1 of 2), "Korea," 12-22-65.

president," *The New York Times* reported. "With a growth of confidence, the South Koreans discovered new capabilities in themselves. Among these was the Korean excellence in producing tiny parts for many electronic devices."[20]

By 1967, the Korean economy was gaining strength, and, in part, because of U.S. Vietnam War-related spending, achieved significant surpluses. *Time* reported in March 1967 that "South Korea can take credit for some remarkable gains in the difficult task of nation-building." "South Korea is constructing a political and economic base that is the envy of its Asian friends." As President Park began Korea's second five year economic expansion plan, "Korea is pulsing with activity" – reflecting Vietnam War-related needs of the U.S. military. The next month *Time* followed up that "South Korea, with some 50,000 U.S. troops still stationed there to guard the northern border, has achieved a relatively stable government, and its economy is slowly improving." January 1968 that "South Korea ran up a payments surplus of some $100 million last year, partly by exporting such military items as jungle boots, uniforms and galvanized steel for troops fighting in Viet Nam." Indeed, "one result is spreading prosperity – including even traffic jams – in Korean cities." Indeed, in May 1968, "government figures confirm[ed] unofficial assurances that the South Korean economy is still expanding at a rate that one expert called phenomenal."[21]

With the economy strengthened, the polity more mature, and its relations with its neighbors more secure, the government in Seoul proposed an alliance among free nations in Asia. Ambassador Brown

---

[20] *Newsweek,* "South Korea: Ready for Take-off," February 7, 1966, p. 36; NARA, RG 59, CFPF, Box 2401, Pol 2-4, Gen Rpts, KOR-S, 1/1/66, Amembassy Seoul to State, A-401, Quarterly Economic Summary – Republic of Korea, April 14, 1966; Box 2400, Pol 2, Gen Rpts & Status, KOR S, 9/22/66, AmEmbassy Seoul to State, A-418, "U.S. Policy Assessment," April 28, 1966; *Business Week,* "Koreans build a peacetime economy," May 7, 1966, p. 171; *U.S. News & World Report,* "South Korea 'Takes off' – an Asian success story," October 31, 1966, p. 42; *The New York Times,* "A revitalized South Korea greets the President,: November 1, 1966, p. 8.

[21] *Time,* "Hope in the Hermit Kingdom," March 10, 1967, www.time.com/time/magazine/article/0,9171,836734,00.html; *Time,* "The News-Mostly Good-Beyond Viet Nam," April 7, 1967, www.time.com/time/magazine/article/0,9171,843504.00.html; *Time,* "Where the Surpluses Are," January 5, 1968, www.time,com/time/magazine/article/0,9171,712096,00.html; *The New York Times,* "The Economic Boom is Continuing in South Korea," May 12, 1968, p. 18.

cabled details of the Korean initiative, and that Korean Foreign Minister Yi Tong-Won noted "the changing situation in Southeast Asia has increased need for promotion of friendship and cooperation of free nations in areas." Washington responded, at least initially, without enthusiasm. Dean Rusk telegrammed Seoul and copied American embassies in the region that, "with regard to the Far East Foreign Ministers' Conference proposed by Yi Tong-won, we have misgivings." These included "the vague purposes," the ability of Korean officials to organize an effective conference, and concern that many governments will decline the invitation. Rusk urged the embassy to counsel Yi to secure agreement quietly. Two weeks later, the embassy in Taipei noted that Jiang was seeking support for the gathering. The embassy in Bangkok reported in mid-October that "the Thai Government had not yet made a decision to attend." But apparently Seoul already received Bangkok's acceptance. The Manila embassy reported that the Philippine government had not yet reached a decision. Meanwhile, the Tokyo embassy reported that the Korean ambassador asked Japanese Foreign Minister Shiina, and that Shiina was "non-committal."[22]

In mid-November 1964, the State Department informed various embassies it was "considering offering to assist Korean efforts to organize Far Eastern Foreign Ministers' Conference." "Our purpose," the telegram noted, "would be to strengthen ties among invited countries." Several weeks later, George Ball continued "we believe conference could usefully engage in general discussion of Far Eastern problems." Further, "fruitful" topics included "security against the Communist military threat;" "insurgency and counter-insurgency;" "economic development;" and

---

[22] NARA, RG 59, CFPF, Box 2401, Pol 7, Visits, Mtgs, KOR S, 1/1/64, Seoul to Secstate, #197, September 1, 1964; same folder, State Department to Seoul 196, September 13, 1964; same folder, Seoul to State, A-274, September 25, 1964. The airgram referred to Jiang's long support of an Asian equivalent to NATO; same box, Pol 7, Visits, Mtgs, KOR S, 9/1/64, Taipei to State, 284, October 3, 1964; same folder, Bangkok to State, A-280, October 12, 1964; same folder, Manila to State, A-352, November 6, 1964; same folder, Tokyo to State, 1730, November 14, 1964. Jiang had raised the issue in 1961, proposing "a formal and permanent defense organization" "involving the United States, the GRC, the ROK, the GVN, Thailand, and the Philippines." American embassies were negative, noting "such arrangement should cause serious political repercussions in some Far Eastern countries," see JFK Library, NSF, Box 22A, China, General, 12/1/61-12/15/61, Memorandum for Mr. McGeorge Bundy, December 4, 1961. For the pact's origins, see Charles M. Dobbs, "The Pact That Never Was: The Pacific Pact of 1949," *The Journal of Northeast Asian Studies*, Winter 1985.

"expansion of regional collaboration in diplomatic, economic, and perhaps other spheres." Ball followed a week later with "if governments ask for US attitude on proposed FonMins' meeting, you should say we believe conference could play a useful role." About that time, James Weir of the New Zealand Embassy called on Robert Fearey in the State Department; Weir indicated Wellington "saw little value in such a conference." Fearey asked that Weir's government "take no negative step now, and would reserve its decision until [they] had time to consult again." Alan Renouf, Minister of the Australian Embassy, asked Marshall Green, a Deputy Assistant State Department Secretary about the conference. Green responded that "the U.S. was interested in helping the conference along and was glad to hear, indirectly, that Australia would attend." Green noted the conference would help the ROK and GRC "break their feeling of isolation by bringing them into closer contact with their Free Asian neighbors." Renouf responded that Australia would participate. About the same time, Ball wrote the embassy in Kuala Lumpur that, if the Malaysian government so inquires, diplomats should respond it "can serve useful purposes."[23]

There was little significant movement in 1965. In April, Robert Aylward in the Taipei Embassy informed the State Department that Taiwanese officials "expect the Far East Foreign Ministers' Conference to be held in Seoul in July or August, but that virtually no progress has been made on arrangements for the conference since the time of the Bangkok preparatory meeting." Three months later the embassy in Taipei reported Taiwanese officials believed the successful conclusion of the Korean-Japan rapprochement discussions would permit the proposed Far East Foreign Ministers' Conference to take place. By late August, American diplomats were reporting confusion over the Korean-sponsored conference on security and the Japanese-sponsored meeting that eventually led to the Asian Development Bank, discussed in the previous chapter. In October, Taipei reported Nationalist Chinese irritation "by the repeated and optimistic predictions by Korean officials that a Seoul conference was imminent."[24]

---

[23] NARA, RG 59, CFPF, Box 2401, Pol 7, Visits, Mtgs, KOR S, 9/1/64, State to Seoul, 434, November 18, 1964; same folder, State to Seoul, 485, December 4, 1964; same folder, State to Seoul, 497, December 10, 1964; same folder, "ROK Proposed Foreign Ministers' Conference," December 4, 1964; same folder, "Far Eastern Foreign Ministers' Conference," December 21, 1964; same folder, State to Kuala Lumpur, 515, December 18, 1964.

[24] 24 NARA, RG 59, CFPF, Box 2401, Pol 7, Visits, Mtgs, KOR S, 3-1-65,

Korean efforts achieved success in 1966. Korean Foreign Minister Yi Tong-Won indicated a likely June meeting date. Japanese Prime Minister Sato agreed to such a date in Seoul, and Japan's presence would cause virtually every nation in the region to attend. Australia informed the State Department of its likely participation as a result of Japan's acceptance. After President Park visited Taiwan, American observers again reported that "the Chinese found the Koreans more optimistic than themselves about the long-discussed Far East Foreign Ministers' Conference." New Zealand diplomats expressed concern that Korea was not inviting Singapore. Regardless, participating foreign ministers met in Bangkok in mid-April to plan for the actual meeting in Seoul, June 14-18, 1966. The U.S. embassy in Manila gained a copy of the agenda for the June meeting, and focused on its agreement to consider "political field of cooperation," "security field of cooperation," "economic, trade and technical fields of cooperation," and "social and cultural fields of cooperation" although some participating nations were uncomfortable with discussions of security and others believed the discussions in Tokyo that led to the Asian Development Bank sufficed for economic issues. The foreign ministers had moved far beyond their disappointment with SEATO and with the nature of French and British involvement in that organization to consider an organization designed to foster the development of the region. [25]

The Ministerial meeting for Asian and Pacific Cooperation (ASPAC) took place as planned in Seoul in mid-June. The State Department informed key embassies that "the conference is attracting considerably more interest than was apparent a few months ago." Rusk clearly stated that "we continue to regard conference as an Asian initiative in which US

Bangkok to State, A-686, March 15, 1965; same folder, Taipei to State, A-850, April 28, 1965; same box, 6-1-65, Taipei to State, A-55, July 21, 1965; same folder, State to Seoul, 214, August 29, 1965; same folder, Taipei to State, A-301, October 8, 1965.

[25] NARA, RG 59, CFPF, Box 2402, Pol 7, KOR-S, 1/1/66, Amembassy Seoul to SecState, #782, January 26, 1966; same folder, State to Seoul, #778, January 27, 1966; same folder, Amembassy Taipei to State, A-636, February 11, 1966; same folder, Amembassy Taipei to State, A-683, February 26, 1966; same box, Pol 7, KOR-S, 2/28/66, Amembassy Bangkok to State, A-736, March 13, 1966; same folder, Memorandum of Conversation, March 23, 1966; same folder, Amembassy Bangkok to Secstate, #2209, April 18, 1966; same folder, Amembassy Seoul to SecState, #1174, April 19, 1966. same folder, Amembassy Bangkok to Secstate, #2229, April 20, 1966; same folder, Amembassy Bangkok to Secstate, #2236, April 20, 1966; same folder, Amembassy Manila to State, A-892, April 25, 1966; same folder, State to Canberra, Kuala Lumpur and Saigon, May 18, 1966.

should remain in the background," "for we welcome growing sense of regional identity among Pacific area nations." *The New York Times* reported "ASPAC is Born," and informed readers that "a new, wholly Asian and Pacific organization devoted to regional cooperation in economic and cultural fields has promising possibilities." Echoing Secretary Rusk, *The Times* noted "the United States has every reason to wish them luck and to stand gracefully aside." *The Times* further noted that, "while there was a disposition to avoid the abusive language of the cold war in the communiqué, private expressions left no doubt that the nine nations had come together to turn back the Marxist challenge in Asia." Rusk gave a fairly neutral, yet supportive public reaction – "we welcome the constructive and forward looking initiatives taken by the conference," but carefully warned the U.S. embassy in Seoul that "we wish to avoid giving any impression that Seoul conference was arranged in response to US bidding or designed to serve purely US interests." However, Rusk noted his "great admiration for ROK diplomacy which has produced major step forward in developing regional cooperation among non-Communist nations." [26]

By this point, America was supporting the dominoes through its involvement in Vietnam. Governments in the region needed time to strengthen their economies and earn the allegiance of their peoples; they informed Washington that absent an American stand in Vietnam their countries could fall under Chinese influence if not outright control. In return, American diplomats sought visible signs of support – especially the commitment of combat troops – from those governments.

Korea provided help in the form of several divisions of troops. "In early March 1964 former Korean Prime Minister Kim Hyon-chol informed Ambassador Berger that the Republic of Korea might be willing to provide

---

[26] NARA, RG 59, CFPF, Box 2042, Pol 7, KORS, 6/1/66, State circular telegram, #2446, June 11, 1966; *The New York Times,* "ASPAC is Born," June 16, 1966, p. 46; NARA, RG 59, CFPF, Box 2042, Pol 7, KORS, 6/1/66, Amembassy Seoul to Secstate, #1457, June 16, 1966; same folder, Amembassy Seoul to Secstate, #1465, June 16, 1966; *The New York Times,* "New Asian Council Supports Saigon," June 17, 1966, p. 8; NARA, RG 59, CFPF, Box 2042, Pol 7, KORS, 6/1/66, State to Seoul, #1365, June 17, 1966; same folder, State to Seoul, #1370, June 18, 1966; same folder, Amembassy Seoul to Secstate, #1472, June 18, 1966. See also *The New York Times,* "Asians Inch Toward a Regional Defense System," June 20, 1966, p. 2; *Newsweek,* "Asia: Optimism out of Seoul," June 27, 1966, pp. 45-46; *Time,* "A New Alliance, and More Help for Viet Nam," June 24, 1966, www.time.com/time/magazine/article/0,9171,835789,00.html.

3 or 4,000 troops to assist the United States and South Vietnam 'in carrying war to North Vietnam.'" Two months later, the State Department wrote key embassies that Johnson and Rusk were convinced "that it is important for more nations of the Free World to 'show their flags' in Viet Nam " in order to create a unified stand against communism in Southeast Asia." Seoul quickly responded that it would consider a field hospital unit and signal corps support. In December, Ambassador Winthrop Brown met with President Park to relay President Johnson's request particularly for East Asian countries "to broaden and deepen the basis of international support" for Vietnam. At that point, Johnson sought "engineer or construction units, transport pilots, LSTs, medical or service units." Pak responded that "the ROK Government was willing to send combat troops to Vietnam ... two combat divisions if necessary."[27]

Negotiations were long and difficult, and the issues quite significant. Fundamentally, the government in Washington paid for South Korean troops to fight in Vietnam because they cost less than U.S. troops and their participation in the Vietnam conflict allowed the U.S. military to retain the tens of thousands of American troops in South Korea as a "trip wire" against North Korean aggression. The debate in the Korean National Assembly and the January 26, 1965 vote reflected concern "that the dispatch of more troops would leave South Korea vulnerable to North Korean subversion." In return, the U.S. government agreed to "an unvouchered cash grant" to Korean troops and "assuming all costs" for Korean troops already in Vietnam. In March, a Special National Intelligence Estimate concluded that "the introduction of one ROK combat division into South Vietnam for static defense purposes would provoke Communist China, North Korea, or North Vietnam overtly to invade South Korea or South Vietnam." The SNIE believed "the Communists" might fear the division "portended a substantial further buildup of foreign forces." However, "it is possible that North Korean technicians or anti-aircraft personnel might be brought in." Most important, "the introduction of a ROK division would add one more complication to an already difficult situation for Moscow." "The USSR might agree to North Vietnamese requests for greater or speedier assistance." The Seoul Embassy wrote the State Department that the Korean government would need legislative approval to commit a combat division, and that might be difficult to gain. North Korea was a more immediate threat than North

[27] *FRUS, 1964-1968, Vol. XXIX,* 1999, Document 5; Editorial Note; Document 28, Memorandum of Conversation, December 19, 1964.

Vietnam, and this debate would take place alongside discussions to normalize relations with Japan. The "ROKG would expect all expenses of the operation to be borne by US" and "would expect its active role in Vietnam to be reflected in US economic aid levels in Korea." The embassy counseled caution.[28]

President Park's visit to Washington in May 1965 helped move the discussions along. Rusk helped prepare Johnson for the meeting. Ambassadors Henry Cabot Lodge, Jr. and Winthrop Brown had only discussed a regimental combat team [4,000 soldiers] with President Park, although Rusk indicated the U.S. government wanted to expanded the request "at a later phase" to a full combat division. James Thomson of the National Security Council Staff recommended that Johnson delay pushing Park for more combat forces in Vietnam until "Park overcomes the acute problems he currently faces in pushing through a Japan-Korea settlement." When Johnson asked Park "if he could send one division" to Vietnam, Park responded "the Korean Government would have to study that matter." He was concerned about possible North Korean aggression. The following month, Saigon asked Seoul "to send a division combat troops to RVN and asked that such troops be sent as soon as possible." Park found the timing, given the Korea-Japan settlement, "embarrassing," and Brown assured the Korean president that Saigon acted without consulting first with Washington. Brown wrote Rusk that "if Korea provides a combat division for RVN this will add a new dimension to our relationship," and Korea "will be in actual combat in one of the most active areas of RVN against Communist forces." But "Korea does not have to do this" and "it does involve Korea in some additional risk." Brown suggested increased "US offshore procurement from Korea" to help close the deal. Brown recognized "that this course will add something to our dollar outflow. But the amount pales into insignificance in comparison with the cost of sending a US division to RVN instead of a ROK division." In December Brown spoke with President Park seeking "his reaction to the possibility of the contribution of further Korean division by July and a brigade by October." Park responded that "he would have to consider [the issue] very carefully." Brown reported that "I got the impression that the President felt this was going to be a very sticky problem for him." A week later Brown reported that Korean Prime Minister Chong Il-kwon told him "ROK

[28] *FRUS, 1964-1968, Vol. XXIX,* Document 32, Editorial Note; Document 35, SNIE 10-4-65, March 19, 1965; Document 37, Embassy Seoul to State, March 30, 1965.

should send additional troops we had requested but that US help would be required in handling problems with political opposition and press that would arise when request became public knowledge." In mid-January, Brown wrote the State Department that the U.S. request for an additional division of troops "came as a shock" to President Park. Brown noted that Park "never expected to be confronted with another request so soon." Park was concerned for "the security of ROK" and not to impose an economic burden. At month's end, Assistant Secretary John McNaughton wrote Defense Secretary Robert McNamara with Seoul's extensive list of items it wanted to agree to another division to Vietnam. McNaughton recommended McNamara authorize the items. Bundy wrote Johnson about the requested "sweeteners." Bundy noted "the loan commitment is $5 million higher than we would probably make in normal course, but is much cheaper than any of the items on the long list the Koreans requested." Johnson approved. *The Economist* noted "the South Koreans were thinking of sending even more troops until bargaining broke down over the Americans' refusal to meet their conditions." A key issue: "a great slice of profit has already come its way in the form of trade and civilian employment." Seoul wanted more: "highest priority" for Korea as a supplier of war materials the United States is buying for use in Vietnam. "On February 28, 1966, the Korean Government publicly announced its decision to provide one regiment and one division to Vietnam." On March 20, 1966, the Korean National Assembly approved the resolution enabling Korea to dispatch additional troops to Vietnam.[29]

Although South Korea made a significant contribution of troops, the struggle in Vietnam made Washington consider seeking more. In mid-October 1966, in response to a question, Brown cabled the State Department that "I can think of no surer way to destroy the good effects of

[29] *FRUS, 1964-1968, Vol. XXIX,* Document 46, Rusk to Johnson, May 17, 1965; Document 47, Thomson to Johnson, May 17, 1965; Document 48, Memorandum of Conversation, May 17, 1965; Document 55, Brown to State, June 14, 1965; Document 57, Brown to Rusk, July 10, 1965; Document 62, Brown to Bundy, December 16, 1965; Document 63, Brown to State, December 22, 1965; Document 70, Brown to State, January 15, 1966; Document 75, McNaughton to McNamara, January 27, 1966; *The Economist,* "Korea and Vietnam: Fighting tiger for rent," February 19, 1966, p. 701; *FRUS, 1964-1968, Vol. XXIX,* Document 78, Bundy to Johnson, February 3, 1966; Document 81, Editorial Note; Document 85, Editorial Note. For an example of the pride many Koreans felt at their nation's participation in the Vietnam conflict, see Joungwon A. Kin, "Korean Participation in the Vietnam War," *World Affairs, Vol. 29, No. 1, Apr/May/June 1966,* pp. 28-35.

President Johnson's visit here than for us to raise the subject of more Korean forces for SVN either during his visit here or in Manila." Brown called it "high-level arm-twisting." William Jorden on Walt Rostow's National Security Council staff agreed, and "advocated against pushing 'the Koreans too hard.'" *The Economist* reported that "Korean planners are hoping that the new export of manpower and increased trade will push that figure [earnings from the Vietnam War] to more than $200 million." In late February the Korean Prime Minister, Il Kwon Chung, told Brown that Seoul agreed to reinforce its current marine brigade in Vietnam with another "provided that it could be equipped and supported by U.S." American officials kept pushing for additional troop units, and on September 4, 1967, Park told Brown's successor, William Porter, that he would comply with Johnson's request for additional troops. Yet Washington asked for more in November 1967. On November 30, Rusk wrote Porter that "highest levels now wish to pursue additional ROK troop contribution with maximum urgency." A week later Porter wrote Rusk that Park agreed to provide a light division. The next month, Hanoi launched the Tet Offensive and two months later Johnson announced he would seek peace in Vietnam, and thus the troops requests ended.[30]

Korea's experience in Vietnam had very real consequences for the former Hermit Kingdom. Han Hong-gu has written that "under Park Chung Hee, [Korea] sent the second largest number of troops to the war after the U.S. A total of 320,000 Korean soldiers, paratroopers and, marines fought in Vietnam between 1964 and 1971. For South Korea, the

---

[30] *FRUS, 1964-1968, Vol. XXIX,* Document 93, Brown to State, October 19, 1966; Document 101, Brown to State, November 22, 1966; *The Economist,* "Korea and Vietnam: Hired Hands," January 21, 1967, p. 217; *FRUS, 1964-1968, Vol. XXIX,* Document 108, Brown to State, February 22, 1967; Document 126, Editorial Note; *Time,* "Hope in the ; *FRUS, 1964-1968, Vol. XXIX* ,Document 134, Porter to State, November 25, 1967; Hermit Kingdom," March 10, 1967, http://www.time.com/time/magazine/article/0,9171,836734,00.html; *FRUS, 1964-1968, Vol. XXIX* ,Document 134, Porter to State, November 25, 1967; Document 136, Rusk to Porter, November 30, 1967; Document 137, Porter to Rusk, December 6, 1967.

Document 136, Rusk to Porter, November 30, 1967; Document 137, Porter to Rusk, December 6, 1967.

Hermit Kingdom," March 10, 1967, http://www.time.com/time/magazine/article/0,9171,836734,00.html; *FRUS, 1964-1968, Vol. XXIX* ,Document 134, Porter to State, November 25, 1967; Document 136, Rusk to Porter, November 30, 1967; Document 137, Porter to Rusk, December 6, 1967.

economic gains were very generous as the U.S. footed all the bills for it. The revenues from soldiers' paychecks and procurements and contracts with the U.S. made up about 40% of South Korea's foreign exchange earnings during the intervention."[31]

Perhaps because North Korea was simultaneously assisting North Vietnam, there remained tensions along the 38th parallel. In September 1967, a new SNIE concluded "we believe that the recent, more vigorous activities of North Korea against the South have several motivations: to create new pressures on the Park government; to tie down large ROK forces; to strengthen the Communist clandestine apparatus in the South; and to be in a position to exploit any new and major disruption in the ROK. The timing of these tactics has been strongly influenced by the Vietnamese War, for example by such factors as the absence of 50,000 ROK troops in South Vietnam." Further, "the North Koreans will almost certainly continue their campaign of military harassment in the DMZ," and "North Korea will also continue attempts to infiltrate guerrilla-type teams into rear areas of South Korea."[32]

The tensions came to a head with a failed assassination attempt in January 1968. On January 17, 1968, 31 North Korean Army officers disguised as South Korean soldiers crossed the Demilitarized Zone and four days later reached the presidential palace, the Blue House. Before they could launch their suicide attack, a policeman questioned them, they drew weapons, and in the end 30 died and South Korean troops captured the survivor who provided details. In 1967, North Korea caused some 120 incidents, and there was fear that the North Koreans were planning an attack across the DMZ by 1970. Kim suffered a propaganda loss by the failed assassination attempt.[33]

The North Korean seizure of the *USS Pueblo* several days later added to the tension. On January 23, 1968, North Korean gunboats seized a US Navy intelligence ship, the *Pueblo,* in international waters off North Korea's east coast. A North Korean sub chaser neared the *Pueblo* which responded by raising the US flag, and the North Korean ship ordered the

---

[31] Han-Hong-gu, "Did we forget the past," Hankyoreh, April 17, 2003, http://www.zmag.org/content/print_article.cfm?itemID=3482&sectionID=1.

[32] Special National Intelligence Estimate, No. 14.2-67, "North Korean Intentions and Capabilities with Respect to South Korea," 21 September 1967, www.foia.cia.gov/browse.

[33] Mitchell Lerner, "A Dangerous Miscalculation: New Evidence from Communist Bloc Archives about North Korea and the Crises of 1968," *Journal of Cold War Studies, Vol. 6, No. 1, Winter 2004,* pp. 3-21.

Pueblo to "stand down." North Korean sailors soon blindfolded the Americans, alleging beating them with AK-47 rifles. Once the ship moved clearly into North Korean waters, high-ranking North Korean officials boarded the ship. The *Pueblo* moved to the port of Wonsan, and North Korean troops transported the crew to two different POW camps perhaps fearing a US rescue attempt. After they were released, the crew reported their captors had starved and beaten them regularly. Kim may have seized the *Pueblo* to distract attention from his effort to assassinate South Korean President Park Chung-hee several days earlier. An update to SNIE 14.2-67 noted "events since last September tend to confirm the conclusions of NIE 14.2-67, that North Korean activities will include a campaign of military harassment in the DMZ area, continued attempts to infiltrate guerrilla teams, and the dispatch of terrorist and sabotage missions. The raid on the Blue House represents the most dramatic and flagrant manifestation of the campaign begun in late 1966 to disrupt political order in South Korea." North Korean handling of the *Pueblo* crisis reflects an intention to heighten tensions and exploit US preoccupations with Vietnam." "These developments have hardened Seoul's attitude and increased the likelihood of a major ROK reaction to North Korean harassments." In mid-May a new SNIE concluded "Pyongyang might be tempted to go well beyond incidents in the DMZ." "Hence, in the short term, the principal danger is that of miscalculation."[34]

Headlines blared the shock of the seizure, and uncertainty about its causes and purposes. *The New York Times* told readers that "North Korea seizes navy ship, holds 83 on board as U.S. spies; [USS] *Enterprise* is ordered to area; 4 crewmen hurt." That same day another story stated "Perplexing Questions; Explanations for the Failure to Prevent Capture of Pueblo may await Inquiry." *Newsweek* titled it "Prometheus Bound," *U.S. News & World Report* headlined "Now a Bigger War Threat in Asia?"

---

[34] The best, most-detailed, and recent account is Mitchell B. Lerner, *The Pueblo Incident: A Spy Ship and the Failure of American Foreign Policy,* Lawrence, University of Kansas Press, 2002; see also Daniel V. Gallery, *The Pueblo Incident,* Garden City, NY, Doubleday & Co., 1970; Ed Brandt, *The Last Voyage of the USS Pueblo,* New York, W.W. Norton & Co., 1969; and Commander Lloyd M. Bucher with Mark Rascovich, *Bucher: My Story,* Garden City, NY, Doubleday & Co., 1970. See *The New York Times,* January 24, 1968, "North Korea Seizes Navy Ship," p. 1; CIA, "Memorandum to Holders of NIE 14.2.-67," 23 February 1968, www.foia.cia.gov/browse; CIA, SNIE, 14.2-68, "The Likelihood of Major Hostilities in Korea," 16 May 1968, www.foia.cia/gov/browse.

while *Time* called it "The Impotence of Power."[35]

Of course, the government in Washington sought return of the crew and the ship, while condemning the government in Pyongyang, but it had few effective levers with Kim Il-sung. The White House released a statement on January 26 in which President Johnson indicated "we are very shortly today taking the question before the Security Council of the United Nations." He also stated that "we have been making other diplomatic efforts as well." The State Department approached the Soviet Union, but, as the media reported, "the Russians, apparently enjoying U.S. embarrassment, announced that the affair had to be settled by the two nations directly involved." President Johnson also wrote Japanese Prime Minister Eisaku Sato that "the assassination mission of the North Koreans against President Pak and the seizure of the *Pueblo* in international waters are the latest actions in a campaign of harassment and violence that is threatening the maintenance of peace in Northeast Asia." "I ask you to consider approaching the Soviet Union" and "to consider what approaches you might make to the North Koreans." Sato responded that "my government has already expressed its concern to the Soviet Union" and "made a request that she should exert her influence for the sake of a peaceful solution of the matter." *Time* reported that "the Soviet Union ordered a powerful 13-vessel squadron into the Sea of Japan as a counterforce to the strong U.S. task force there." Nonetheless, US Ambassador Llewellyn Thompson continued to visit the Soviet Foreign Ministry seeking to obtain "Soviet intercession" to free the *Pueblo* and its crew.[36]

---

[35] *Newsweek,* February 5, 1968, p. 15; *U.S. News & World Report,* February 5, 1968, pp. 23-26; *Time,* February 2, 1968, pp. 11-15. See B.C. Koh, "The Pueblo Incident in Perspective," *Asian Survey, Vol. 9, No. 4, April 1969,* pp. 264-280; Bernd Schaefer, "North Korean 'Adventurism' and China's Long Shadow, 1966-1972," Working Paper #44, 2004, and Sergey S. Radchenko, "The Soviet Union and the North Korean Seizure of the USS Pueblo: Evidence from Russian Archives," Working Paper #47, 2005, both Cold War International History Project, Woodrow Wilson International Center for Scholars, Washington, DC and Roy U.T. Kim, "Sino-North Korean Relations," *Asian Survey, Vol. 8, No. 8, August 1968,* pp. 708-722 all of which argue that Pyongyang's action not only surprised Beijing and Moscow but caused considerable consternation since they could not predict Washington's response.

[36] *U.S. News & World Report,* February 5, 1968, p. 26; *Newsweek,* February 12, 1968, pp. 33-34, "Pueblo Crisis: Impossible Choice?"; NARA, RG 59, CFPF, Box 2279, Pol 15-1, KOR S, 1/1/68, State to Amembassy Tokyo, #46, January 25, 1968; same folder, State to Amembassy Tokyo, #46, February 2, 1968; *Time,*

In the aftermath of the attempted assassination of Park Chung-hee and the seizure of the *Pueblo* American news media returned again to the more general North Korean threat. Thirteen months earlier, *Newsweek* wrote that "armed bands of North Korean infiltrators have crossed the armistice line by night to ambush U.N. patrols." It quoted American officials who believed that "the North Koreans have every intention of stepping up the rate of infiltration and ambush." Perhaps the improving South Korean economy and Park's efforts to create a more effective political system frustrated North Korean analysis on a collapse in the south. Again in July *Newsweek* reported that "perhaps precisely because of these impressive strides, North Korea never allows Seoul to forget that there is only a shaky truce along the 38th parallel. Pyongyang has accelerated the infiltration of guerrillas across the Demilitarized Zone." Then, on January 22, 1968, *U.S. News & World Report* asked if readers could "remember Korean negotiations?" It used the failed history of the Panmunjom talks to downplay any similar peace talks in Vietnam, noting that "in countless ways the solemn promises given by North Korea and Red China at Panmunjom have been repeatedly broken." "The Communists deny everything, concede nothing, seeking only peace on their terms: the handing over of all South Korea."[37]

The reporting turned more negative after the *Pueblo's* capture. *Time* reported that "dramatic and dangerous as it was, the seizure of the U.S.S. Pueblo was only the latest and loudest thunderbolt from a long-gathering storm of North Korean belligerence." *Time* claimed that Kim "set up subversion and terrorist schools in North Korea, where some 2,400 commandos are now being trained to infiltrate the South to start a guerrilla war." *The Economist* reported on North Korea's attempt to establish a guerrilla movement in the south, a la North Vietnam and South Vietnam. Jack Anderson in *The Washington Post* quoted President Park as charging that "the U.S. policy of turning the other cheek was responsible for North Korea's boldness." "Every time we have been struck by North Korea,"

February 16, 1968, p. 21, "Still Dangling"; *The New York Times,* January 25, 1968, "North Korea and Russia Rebuff U.S. Efforts to Free Seized Ship," p. 1; January 26, 1968, "Rusk is Insistent on Ship's Release," p. 7; *The New York Times,* January 29, 1968, p. 30; January 26, 1968, "Soviet's Rebuff on Ship Linked to Fragile Ties to North Korea," p. 8 and "Tass Sees U.S. 'Provocation," p. 8; January 27, 1968, "U.S. Again Requests Soviet Intercession," p. 1.

[37] *Newsweek,* "Korea: Creating a Crisis," February 27, 1967, p. 45; *Newsweek,* "South Korea: A Growing Girl's Problem," July 31, 1967, p. 32; *U.S. News & World Report,* "Remember Korean Negotiations," January 22, 1968, p. 33.

Anderson wrote, "we have done nothing." A month later, *U.S. News* claimed South Korean leaders worried about America's commitment to defend their nation. The combined effect of the *Pueblo,* the Tet offensive in Vietnam, and the strengthening of the antiwar movement in the United States combined to frustrate the government in Seoul who claimed "scores of Communist training bases" and even "springboard bases" from which to send guerrillas across the parallel. That same week *Newsweek* contrasted the Johnson Administration's careful diplomacy to keep the *Pueblo* Incident from sparking a new Korean War with the unintended result that Johnson "had, all unintentionally, shaken the U.S.-South Korean alliance to its foundations." It reiterated the same concerns three weeks later: "South Koreans, in fact, are already dismayed by what they consider the 'soft' U.S. response to the seizure of the Pueblo." Seoul worried that Washington would "apologize" to secure release of the ship's crew, and that would have a damaging affect on South Korean morale. In late April *Newsweek* reported additional North Korean infiltration attempts. In late November *The Economist* reported that "the past two years have seen a sharp increase in tension along the demilitarized zone and more than 900 incidents have been reported. North Korean saboteurs armed with grenade-launchers and Russian sub-machine guns try to get through to the south and even more frequently try to reach home after completing their missions there."[38]

In 1961, Taiwan seemed as troubled as South Korea. Jiang Jieshi and 2 million Chinese refugees uneasily sat atop 8 million native Taiwanese. Jiang remained committed to regaining all of China, and this preoccupation overwhelmed his interest in economic development, building popular support for his regime, or creating a true Taiwanese society. He counted on the U.S. government to maintain his regime, prop up his economy, and supply his military, and he continued to regard himself as a world leader,

[38] *Time,* "A New Belligerence," February 2, 1968, www.time.com/time/archive; *The Economist,* "Towards a happy life in the bosom of Marshal Kim," February 3, 1968, p. 20; see also *The Economist,* "South Korea: Fire in their bellies," February 10, 1068, p. 26; NARA, RG 59, CFPF, State to Amembassy Seoul, February 121, 1968; *U.S. News & World Report,* "If Reds open up a 'Second Front' in Korea," February 26, 1968, pp. 31-32; *Newsweek,* "The U.S. Tightrope in Korea," February 26, 1968, p. 36; *Newsweek,* "Korea: Invitation to Abasement," March 18, 1968, p. 66; *Newsweek,* "South Korea: The Courage to Talk Back," April 29, 1968, pp. 16-17; *The Economist,* "Korea: Nobody here but us chickens," November 30, 1968, p. 28.

the last of the Allies, Roosevelt, Churchill, and Stalin.

Jiang Jieshi seemed determined to "recover" the mainland. Mao Zedong and the government in Beijing disrupted Chinese life in the 1950s and then in the 1960s with a series of campaigns that extended China's time of sorrow. Repression after the "100 Flowers Movement," the organization of communes and production "units" in the countryside, and the "Great Leap Forward" resulted in fear, famine, and famine-induced disease for many millions of Chinese on the mainland. To Jiang, this presented an opportunity to undo the outcome of the Chinese Civil War. George McGhee in the State Department wrote Dean Rusk in June 1961 "the principal problems between the United States and the GRC stemmed from its over-riding objective of reestablishing its rule over all of China." He "concluded that the United States could not expect that the GRC leadership would soon abandon its ambition to return to the mainland." A National Intelligence Estimate agreed that "the GRC's principal objective will continue to be to regain control of the mainland. The GRC leaders believe that now is a good time to agitate the question of taking probing actions against the mainland in order to capitalize on the economic distress and other sources of discontent there." In early August Nationalist Chinese Vice President Ch'en Ch'eng told Kennedy that "as a result of his work in Youth organizations on the China mainland many years ago, there were 30,000 potential agents on the China mainland who were loyal to him. They were lying low for the time being but would respond when the time came for action." Drumright wrote Rusk about Jiang's 1962 New Year message and emphasized "Jiang's plainly expressed feeling that mainland rebellion or uprising is imminent" and Jiang's "direct call to mainland people to rise against tyranny and his pledge of help once mainland people take action." Rusk replied within days that "department recognizes sensitivity whole mainland recovery issue for President Jiang." Rusk concluded that "GRC must be left in no doubt concerning its obligation to obtain US concurrence in any offensive military action against mainland." McGeorge Bundy wrote Ray Cline in Taipei to discourage Jiang and then, several days later, he met with Chinese Ambassador Ting-fu Tsiang and "I took the occasion to raise with him the matter of GRC plans to return to the mainland" and "I indicated that our own intelligence did not give us much hope that the time was ripe for any such operations. I also reiterated our belief that our discussions and relations on this question should be governed by the exchange of notes of December 1954 between Dulles and Yeh." Ralph Clough reported in mid-month on a meeting with Jiang: "we discussed at length his strategy for return to mainland." Jiang "expressed confidence President Kennedy was sympathetic with his objectives and would do nothing to deter or prevent him from acting." Several days later, the *Taipei China News* reported that "Taipei is reported today to be urging Washington to study the advisability of the question of liberating the China mainland in light of unprecedented famine and popular discontent." Several days later Chiang Ching-kuo, Jiang's son, met with Roger Hilsman and "said that indications on the mainland were never more favorable than this year," and that "the Chinese Government did not desire any open U.S. involvement or participation; all they wanted was our airplanes and our 'tacit' agreement."[39]

A Special National Intelligence Estimate concluded that Beijing's "control apparatus is still intact and effective. Present indications are that the regime will continue to be able to isolate and repress any likely internal challenge to its authority. Even if GRC special forces teams could be successfully established on the mainland, they would almost certainly be destroyed in a short time. Very few people, and no significant military units, would be likely to join the GRC forces in the absence of clear military success--which we believe would be impossible without large-scale US support." In late March 1962, President Kennedy used a press conference "to discourage any belief that the United States would support the Chinese Nationalist Government in an effort to put forces on the Communist mainland." Hilsman wrote Averell Harriman that "the GRC has apparently concluded that the US Government is temporizing on the question of support for GRC moves," and thus "the GRC is proceeding somewhat independently to ready itself to return to the mainland should an opportunity occur." He meant the GRC increased expenditures for the bloated military with obvious negative impact on the Taiwanese economy. Jiang believed the worsening Sino-Soviet split and "the economic troubles

---

[39] JFK Library, NSF, Box 21A, China, General, 1/20/61-2/19/61, "Red China's Food Crisis," January 1961; *FRUS, 1961-1963,* Document 30, McGhee to Rusk, June 15; 1961; Document 31, NIE 43-61, June 20, 1961; Document 46, Memorandum of Conversation, August 1. 1961; JFKL, NSF, Box 23, China, General, "Return to the Mainland," 1/1/62-5/6/62, Drumright to Rusk, January 11, 1962; same folder, Rusk to Drumright, January 17, 1962; same folder, Komer to Bundy, January 29, 1962, in which Komer argued "before fobbing Chiang off, let's at least consider his case," and Komer made a proposal for "a major landing in South China;" *FRUS, 1961-1963, Vol. XXII,* Document 89, Bundy to Cline, March 6, 1962; Document 92, Clough to State Department, March 15, 1962; JFKL, President's Office Files, Countries, China, General, 1962, Taipei China News, March 17 or 18, 1962; JFKL, Roger Hilsman Papers, Countries, Box 1, China, Planning on Mainland Ops, 3/62.

besetting the Chinese Communist regime" combined to make the time propitious for a return. Six months later, the government in Taipei stated "it was determined to carry out an armed return to the mainland 'no matter what people in foreign countries may think.'" Taiwan Premier Chen Cheng said the "rebellion would sweep the mainland after the landings 'just as naturally as water flows downward.'" A.M. Rosenthal provided a lengthy report on Jiang the next month, and noted that for Jiang, a "return to the Chinese mainland, from which the Communists drove him, may exist only in a dream. But this dream rules Taiwan." Rosenthal wrote that "nobody, not even Jiang and the few around him, believes that the Nationalists themselves have the military capability to retake the mainland." But they believed "the Chinese mainland would be swept by rebellion," and hence they needed to be ready.[40]

Taiwan continued to supply remnants of Nationalist Armies occupying parts of northern Burma. As the Chinese Civil War drew to a close, some armies retreated across the border into Burma and apparently they were crossing into Laos giving the People's Republic an excuse to intervene in Laos. During a long discussion on February 3, Secretary Rusk told Nationalist Chinese Ambassador George Yeh that he thought Jiang agreed not to supply these irregulars anymore, and Yeh claimed Taiwan only airdropped medical supplies. Rusk stressed that "the irregulars were not under discipline and were not an effective fighting force. They simply opened up, by their presence in the area, possibilities of counter-pressures from the Communists." Rusk followed up on February 21 with a memo to the US Embassy in Taiwan to "please see President Jiang at earliest practicable moment and impress upon him utmost seriousness USGov regarding KMT irregulars in Burma and Laos." Rusk added "It is imperative that GRC make immediate arrangements to evacuate all KMT personnel who are willing to return to Formosa, especially those who were transported into area with GRC assistance during past three years." Jiang called the US ambassador, Everett Drumright, to his residence. Jiang "believed at time no harm was being done to US interests. Moreover, attempts at that time to evacuate irregulars would have affected fighting

---

[40] *FRUS, 1961-1963, Vol. XXII,* Document 95, SNIE 13-3-62, "Probable Consequences of Chinese Nationalist Military Operations on the Chinese Mainland;" March 28, 1962; *The New York Times,* "Kennedy is Wary on Taiwan Appeal," March 30, 1962, p. 30; JFKL, NSF, Box 23, China, General, "Return to the Mainland," 1/1/62-5/6/62; *NYT,* "Taipei, seeking to still doubts, again pledges Mainland return," September 19, 1962; *NYT,* "Chiang, at 75, waits in his final fortress," October 28, 1962, p. 221-222.

spirit and morale of forces. In view of these factors, President said he felt at time he could do or say nothing regarding evacuation."[41]

As the Cultural Revolution worked its way across China, Jiang raised the issue of a return to the mainland. On January 11, 1967, *The New York Times* reported that "the State Department noted that President Chiang Kai-shek was bound by a pledge not to launch an invasion of the Communist controlled mainland, or indeed undertake any military action except in self-defense, without prior approval of the United States." The department was responding to news reports from Taipei that Jiang "was eager to take advantage of the current political chaos on the mainland." Two weeks later, despite the department's cold water, Jiang announced that "the Peking regime is on the brink of total collapse," and Vice President C.K.Yen told a crowd that "now is the opportunity for our counterattack." *Time* told readers that "Chiang stands ready for any eventuality. The country's 600,000-man army is well trained and well equipped." Two weeks later *The New York Times* wrote that "the turmoil in Communist China has inspired new feelings of optimism in the Chinese Nationalist Government about the prospects of its return to the mainland." Samson Shen, Deputy Minister of Foreign Affairs stated "the likelihood of our going back is better now than at any time since we came to Taiwan 17 years ago." Nationalist officials made clear they were simply ready for action as Mao's regime continues to disintegrate.[42]

Jiang also regularly sought assurances of U.S. support, which Washington carefully provided. George McGhee asked Rusk to approve a statement that the U.S. "would be willing to support Taiwan, but not the GRC's mainland ambitions. It is a principal thesis of this paper that continued pursuit of those ambitions would endanger both the GRC's base on Taiwan and the U.S. itself." Jiang interpreted such caution as America turning to Beijing. Drumright wrote Rusk in mid-March that "f For first time since I came to Taiwan three years ago, I sense a feeling among high

---

[41] *FRUS, 1961-1963, Vol. XXII,* Document 3, Memorandum of Conversation, February 3, 1961; JFKL, NSF, Box 21A, China, Genera, 2/20-61-2/28/61, Stoessel to Dungan providing background information on "Chinese irregulars" for the president's review; *FRUS, 1961-1963, Vol. XXII,* Document 5, Rusk to Drumright, February 22, 1961; Document 7, Drumwright to Rusk, February 25, 1961.

[42] *The New York Times,* "U.S. quashes hopes for China invasion," January 11, 1967, p. 3; *NYT,* "Taipei sees victory on mainland soon," January 24, 1967, p. 5; *Time,* "Ready & Waiting," January 27, 1967, www.time.com/time/archive; *NYT,* "Turmoil in China raising hopes for return among Nationalists," February 15, 1967, p. 10.

GRC authorities that USG is looking for some way out of China impasse at their expense." President Kennedy wrote Jiang to reiterate US support: "I assure you, Mr. President, that my Government will faithfully adhere to its commitments under the Mutual Defense Treaty between our countries."[43]

French recognition of the People's Republic of China in 1964 increased Jiang's fear of a U.S. "deal" with Beijing. In February 1964, France formally recognized the government in Beijing as the *de facto* and *de jure* ruler of the mainland. *The New York Times* explained that "France Seeking a Larger Role in Asia," and provided a map showing France's goals in Asia, including "replacement of U.S. influence." Several days later, French Consul General André Saint-Mleux in Hong Kong said that Paris had informed its diplomats that "the Chinese Communists can be wooed with overall advantages to the West" and he implied that "France was, in fact, paving the way for America's relations with China."[44]

---

[43] *FRUS, 1961-1963, Vol. XXII,* Document 12, McGhee to Rusk, March 10, 1961; Document 15, Drumwright to Rusk, March 20, 1961; Document 21, Kennedy to Jiang, April 17, 1961.

[44] Department of State, *Foreign Relations of the United States, 1964-1968, Volume XXX, China,* http://www.state.gov/www/about_state/history/vol_xxx/01_10.html, Document 1, Telegram from the Department of State to the Embassy in France, January 15, 1964; NARA, RG 59, CFPF, Box 2014, POL 16, CHICOM Recognition, Department of State Circular Telegram, January 17, 1964. See Document 4, Circular Telegram from the Department of State to the Embassy in France, January 18, 1964, for the department's explanation to key embassies of Alphand's visit and the French government's position; see also RG 59, CFPF, Box 2013, Independence/Recognition-CHICOM, 2-1-64, "Circular Telegram 1352," January 23,1964; *New York Times,* January 19, 1964, p. 4. Interestingly, President Kennedy's response to questions at a November 14, 1963 press conference on his statement "concerning conditions under which the US might consider trade with mainland China" worried Taiwan newspapers which believed that "trade could be equated with recognition," National Archives and Records Administration, Records of the Department of State, RG 59, Central Foreign Policy Files, Box 3863, POL CHICOM-US, "Reaction to President Kennedy's November 14 Press Conference," November 22, 1963; NARA, RG 59, CFPF, Box 2013, POL 16, Independence/Recognition CHICOM, 2-1-64, "French Consul General's Observations About French Recognition of Communist China," January 24, 1964; see also same folder, State Department circular telegram 1410 February 1, 1964, and Paris 3792, February 7, 1964; and French diplomats found "the United States reaction to France's recognition as "much too highly charged emotionally," NARA, RG 59, CFPF, Box 2013, POL 16, Independence/Recognition, CHICOM, 2-11-64, "Knowledgeable French Diplomat Comments on Recognition of

The so-called Chinese recognition issue arose every year at the UN General Assembly session. Jiang studied U.S. pronouncements for hints of change in U.S. policy towards the governments in Beijing and Taipei. American diplomats met regularly among themselves and with their Chinese Nationalist opposites to plan for these sessions, to coordinate diplomacy with key foreign governments, especially with newly independent regimes in Africa.

The French decision seemingly brought the issue to the forefront. *The New York Times* reported that French recognition of Beijing made it "more difficult for the Generalissimo [Jiang] to press on Taiwanese the fading dream of a 'return to the mainland.'" A month later, despite French recognition of Beijing, *The Times* reported that "Premier C.K. Yen pledges the further build-up of military and economic strength for the perennially imminent attack on the Communist-ruled China mainland." "Jiang and his subordinates profess to believe that discontent is so rife in Communist China that a Nationalist landing in force on the mainland would detonate an anti-Communist uprising in conjunction with which they could sweep to power." Few outside observers agreed.[45]

American diplomats had been studying the nation's policy on the China question, but found few good alternatives. A small group of State Department China experts, including Roger Hilsman, Assistant Secretary for Far Eastern Affairs, James C. Thomson, Jr., Special Assistant in that bureau, Lindsey Grant of Mainland China Affairs, and Allen S. Whiting, Director of the Office of Research for Far Eastern Affairs, believed it time for a more realistic policy towards China. They drafted and Hilsman delivered on December 13, 1963 at the Commonwealth Club in San Francisco, California, a speech suggesting a new policy freed of the emotion of the past yet firm, flexible, and dispassionate expecting Chinese concessions before the U.S. government would respond in kind. Hilsman followed the outline suggested by Walt W. Rostow in his "Basic National Security Policy" and stated his belief that Beijing, like Moscow, might be willing to make concessions and engage in realistic diplomacy to reduce tensions and thereby help it improve the quality of life for its people. That is, Hilsman was suggesting the U.S. government deal with China as it

---

Communist China, February 13, 1964. Interestingly, months later, *The New York Times* headlined "France Disappointed at Relations with Red China," having expected recognition to lead to substantive talks on East-West issues in Asia, September 27, 1964, p. 9.

[45] *The New York Times,* "Pressures mount on Nationalist China," February 16, 1964, p. E5; *NYT,* "Chiang still dreams his dream," march 22, 1964, p. SM18.

dealt with the Soviet Union, and he was silent about the status and fate of the regime on Taiwan.[46]

While Hilsman generally restated long-standing American policy towards Beijing, there were some issues. He did not clear the speech ahead of time with Secretary Rusk, and the tone of his remarks did differ from previous high level statements on Sino-American relations. He implicitly accepted the reality of Communist rule of the mainland, thus undercutting the entire, highly flawed, goal of "unleashing Jiang," and he left the door open "to the possibility of change", that is, if Beijing moderated its behavior, there could be a thawing in Sino-American relations. To be sure, Hilsman was tough on Beijing, calling it "the torchbearer of a rigid totalitarian ideology that threatens all its neighbors," and "wedded to a fundamentalist form of communism which emphasizes violent revolution, even if it threatens the physical ruin of the civilized world." The consulate in Hong Kong echoed Hilsman's view of China. "Peiping has not altered its fundamental stance toward the U.S. . . .[and] Peiping's leaders were acting as though the East Wind were prevailing over the West." It concluded that "though the challenge will be great, it is by no means unmanageable if the U.S. remains flexible in tactics and firm in principle."[47]

Nonetheless, the international reaction was prompt. George Ball sent a circular telegram to US embassies noting that Hilsman's speech "does not represent any new policy . . . rather, it is public presentation of assessment and thinking for some time within Department." He concluded that the new administration was continuing the policies of the Kennedy Administration within respect to the competing regimes in Beijing and Taipei. The Nationalist Chinese sought reassurances that American policy was not changing. Tsai Wei Ping of the Foreign Ministry in Taipei

[46] Charles J. Pellegrin, "United States Military and Diplomatic Relations with the Republic of China in the Era of the Vietnam War, 1961-1969," unpublished Ph.D. dissertation, Mississippi State University, 2005; Roger Hilsman, "United States Policy Toward Communist China," *Department of State Bulletin,* 50, January 6, 1964, p. 12; to sample media opinion on Hilsman's remarks, see *The New York Times,* December 14, 1963, p. 1, 2. Nearly a year later, and out of the State Department, Hilsman called talks with China on arms control, noting "the time has come," but also "he voiced doubt that recognition of Communist China, North Korea, or North Vietnam would be of any benefit," *The New York Times,* November 19, 1964, p. 4.

[47] LBJ Library, Papers of William P. Bundy, Box 1, Chptr 10, 12-16, "Chapter 16: East Asia in the Fall of 1964," p. 16-13.

protested that while his government understood Hilsman was not breaking new ground, "both foreign and domestic press treatment has been such that general readers, especially in Afro-Asian world, might be led to conclude that speech did point to new China policy." Tsai concluded that his government ordered its ambassador in Washington to seek a public statement noting no change in US policy. Ambassador Tsiang Ting-fu followed up with a "frank talk" with Hilsman and other Department officials. He indicated that his government was "puzzled and disappointed by it" while the Legislative Yuan was "highly critical" and the media in Taipei was "angry." Hilsman stated "it was important to explain to the public the differences between our Soviet policy and our Communist China policy," especially because "we signed a test ban treaty with the Soviet Union and substantial sales of wheat are being given consideration. These developments may lead some Americans to expect better relations with Peiping." But Tsiang was absolutely convinced that the American diplomat was seeking to move – however gradually – US foreign policy, and that belief aroused great fear in the Nationalist government.[48]

Rusk was particularly adamant against changing policy, and on September 5, he sent a telegram to all American diplomat posts [save for the Soviet bloc] that "I trust you will do all in your power to ensure that countries now recognizing the GRC will continue this policy and that those not r[e]p[ea]t not now recognizing Peiping will not rpt not move closer to Communist China. It is clear that the Chinese communists are mounting a subtle, persistent offensive, particularly in Africa, with a view to improving their international position at the expense of the GRC." The State Department followed this circular telegram with a "National Policy Paper" on U.S. policy towards the Republic of China. It stated "we should continue to oppose the admission of the Chinese Communists to the UN . . . our main task will be to dampen down the repercussions of the recent French recognition of Peiping."[49]

---

[48] NARA, RG 59, CFPF, Box 3863, POL CHICOM-US, "Circular to All Diplomatic Posts," December 14, 1963; same folder, Taipei to Sec State 490, December 17, 1963; see NARA, RG 59, CFPF, Box 3863, POL CHICOM-US, 8-1-63, "Mr. Hilsman's Speech to the Commonwealth Club," December 20, 1963, and State Department to Amembassy Taipei, #520, December 20, 1963, for a summary of the meeting and the department's information to interested embassies. See also same folder, "*China News* editorial on Hilsman's speech," December 21, 1963: "the government owes the people an explanation on this foremost issue in view of Kennedy's and Hilsman's recent unfortunate remarks."

[49] NARA, RG 59, CFPF, Box 2012, POL 16 Independence/Recognition, CHICOM,

Meanwhile, after France granted recognition, attention turned to Africa. By the early 1960s, the majority of African nations had gained their independence. In the 1950s, Libya, Egypt, the Sudan, Morocco, Tunisia, and Ghana became independent, and in 1960 Mauritania, Mali, Burkina Faso, Cote d'Ivoire, Senegal, Gabon, Cameroon, Nigeria, Congo, Central African Republic, Democratic Republic of the Congo, Benin, Togo, Madagascar, and Somalia, and in 1961 Sierra Leone and Tanzania, and in 1962 and 1963 Algeria, Uganda, Rwanda, Burundi, and Kenya joined them as independent nations.

As independent countries, they soon joined the United Nations and became prime targets in the competition for votes on the Chinese recognition question. Until the Great Proletarian Cultural Revolution overwhelmed the People's Republic, it was not clear who was winning this contest for influence. In late 1964, the State Department concluded of 35 independent countries in Africa, 19 recognized only the Republic of China, 14 recognized the People's Republic, and 2 recognized neither. By mid-April, the Central Intelligence Agency reported that "in the UN itself, the Chinese representation situation is currently too fluid for a close estimate of the vote in this fall's General Assembly session. The "we-they" dichotomy of the Cold War concerned some African governments. Ambassador Leon Ndenzako of Burundi called on State's G. Mennen Williams to note that his government's recognition of the PRC "was merely an expression of Burundi's policy of non-alignment" and he hoped it "would not alter in any way the friendly relations between Burundi and the United States." Kenyan officials told embassy officers in Nairobi that "U.S. China Policy is Wrong" and "the U.S. is not being realistic," which caused the officers to comment that "this is an indication of how Kenya may vote in the U.N. on the China problem."[50]

4-1-64, State Department Circular Telegram 446; *FRUS, 1964-1968, Volume XXX,* Document #48, "National Policy Paper," September 11, 1964. George Kennan did call for a review of China policy, see *The New York Times Magazine,* November 22, 1964, pp. 27, et. al., but he still accepted the general need to contain Beijing. In 1966, the Johnson Administration again reviewed China policy and predictably pleased neither Taipei nor Beijing; see Charles M. Dobbs, *Triangles, Symbols, and Constraints,* Chapter 5, pp. 34-39.

[50] NARA, RG 59, CFPF, Box 2035, POL 16, Independence/Recognition, CHINAT, 1-1-64, State Outgoing Telegram #586, January 16, 1964; Lyndon Baines Johnson Library, NSF Country Files, Box 237, China Cables, Vol. I (2 of), OCI No. 1117/64, "Nationalist China's position in the UN, 16 April 1964; NARA, RG 59, CFPF, Box 2035, POL 16, Independence/Recognition, CHINAT, 1-1-64,

The U.S. Government also provided quiet support via "Operation Vanguard." Since the 1950s the Republic of China began Operation Vanguard to extend technical assistance "to ensure that the GRC would continue to retain majority support for its seat in the UN." An interim report in late February 1965 noted, "from its inception, the USG [U.S. Government] has supported Operation Vanguard but has not been publicly identified with the project." *The New York Times* did report that "Chinese spur food for Africans," and noted that "teams from Taiwan assist new nations to provide more" and have resulted in "increasing demand for Nationalist Chinese farm teams."[51]

State Circular Telegram #1293, January 18, 1964. For an example, see same folder, Amembassy Accra to State, January 17, 1964, reporting on Zhou's talks with Ghanaian leaders and NARA, RG 59, CFPF, Box 2013, POL 16, Independence/Recognition, CHICOM, Hong Kong 1523, February 24, 1964, for a report in the mainland press of the establishment of relations with Congo, "hailed by Chinese Communist media as further indication of Peiping's successful diplomacy." NARA, RG 59, CFPF, Box 2013, POL 16, Independence/Recognition, CHICOM, "Burundi's Recognition of Communist China," February 24, 1964; NARA, RG 59, CFPF, Box 2032, POLAFF&REL CHINAT, 1-1-66, Ambassador Jerauld Wright to Roger Hilsman, March 10, 1964; NARA, RG 59, CFPF, Box 2013, POL 16, Independence/Recognition, CHICOM, Paris 4264, March 11, 1964; NARA, RG 59, CFPF, Box 2019, POL 1, Gen Policy/Background, CHICOM-US, 1-1-64, "Extension of Comments by Murumbi on Trip to USSR and China"; see also NARA, RG 59, CFPF, Box 2019, POL POLAFF&REL, CHICOM-US, 7-1-64, "Kenyan Views on Communist China, US Policy, and Soviet-Chicom Dispute." In Mali, a Soviet diplomat told Bayard King, the American Chargé, the Chinese were succeeding by proclaiming their revolutionary ardor against "American imperialism," while the Soviet Union was working towards détente, NARA, RG 59, CFPF, Box 2871, POL, US-USSR, 5-30-64, "Conversation with Soviet Second Secretary." See also NARA RG 59, CFPF, Box 2033, POL 7 VISITS-MISSIONS-CHINAT, 1-1-64, "Chinese Week in Lome," August 18, 1964, discussing the impact of Vice Minister Yang Hsi-nan of Taiwan's visit to Togo, and Box 2035, POL 16, Independence/Recognition CHINAT, 1-1-64, of report of September 12, 1964 reporting on continued deterioration of Senegal-Taiwan relations.

[51] NARA, RG 59, CFPF, Box 2037, POL-POLAFF&REL CHINAT-A, "Operation Vanguard," February 26, 1965; NARA, RG 59, CFPF, Box 2012, Independence/Recognition, CHICOM, 4-1-64, "GRC Concern About Growing Chinese Communist Influence in Africa," October 1, 1964; NARA, RG 59, CFPF, Box 2041, POL 17 Diplo&Consular Representation, CHINAT-US, 1-1-64, "Ambassador Tsiang's Call on You—Talking Points," October 30, 1964; NARA, RG 59, CFPF, Box 2033, POL 7 Visits-Missions CHINAT, 1-1-64, "Vice Minister

Perhaps Beijing's miscues helped more than Taipei's efforts to win friends through economic and technical assistance. As 1964 turned into 1965, it did seem that Beijing was coming closer to winning the vote in the United Nations, based on the votes of African delegations. But, the logical outcome was to be postponed for many years, unbeknownst to US diplomats. Within a year the Great Proletarian Cultural Revolution began extracting its great price on Chinese foreign policy. Beijing's support for radicals threatening existing regimes in Africa, the reduction of its aid program, and the withdrawal of its diplomats along with the world's shock at the anarchy, violence, and destruction of the Cultural Revolution combined to undo Beijing's gains and postpone resolution of China's UN seat for many years.

Again in 1966 the question of China's seat in the United Nations arose once again. Assistant Secretary Joseph Sisco wrote Rusk in late April 1966 that "we could alter our strategy in order to help place the onus for Chinese Communist exclusion on them." Sisco suggested a "two-Chinas" policy, believing that Beijing would reject it, a General Assembly Study Committee to "buy us another year," taking the issue to the International Court of Justice, a rather remote possibility, and largely retaining the present strategy which was losing support every year in the General Assembly. Rusk in turn wrote Johnson about the "need for new tactics on Chinese representation." He indicated that he believed the traditional U.S. position of recognizing the government in Taipei as the government of all of China would likely fail, and that some change was needed; he recommended discussing alternative strategies with Jiang. Rostow, in transmitting the memo, noted that the recommendation was "something of a landmark since it recommends to you that we begin to shift off our present policy toward Communist China in the UN, starting with talks in Taipei." Rostow suggested that Johnson speak with President Eisenhower since, as he reminded Johnson, Eisenhower had "warned President Kennedy that this [recognition of the People's Republic] was the only issue in foreign policy where he might take out after him." He also noted a need to speak first with Jiang to avoid blindsiding him. Interestingly, President Johnson met with George Ball, Goldberg, William Bundy and Rostow for a discussion of China policy on May 24, 1966 but, there is no

---

Yang's Visit to Africa," December 31, 1964; and NARA, RG 59, CFPF, Box 2034, POL 15-7, Head of State Exec Branch, CHINAT, 1-1-65, "Departmental Discussions of GRC-Africa Relations with Yang Ksi-k'un, GRC Vice Foreign Minister, December 31, 1964 and January 6, 1965," February 11, 1965; *New York Times,* April 1`3, 1964, pp. 41, 43.

record of that discussion.[52]

Jiang remained a stumbling block. The American embassy in Taipei suggested that Rusk raise the issue of "two Chinas" when he visited the Nationalist capital. The American ambassador, Walter McConaughy, told Jiang that "past ChiRep tactics might not serve in upcoming GA." Jiang replied that "any sort of 'two Chinas' resolution, if passed and accepted . . . would compel GRC promptly to withdraw from UN." When Rusk, Bundy, and McConaughy met with Jiang, Foreign Minister Wei Tao-ming, and several other officials, Wei presented a detailed analysis that the ChiRep question in the UNGA in 1966 more favored Taipei than it did in 1965; that is, there was no need for the U.S. government to consider a change in policy on recognition of China or even a change in tactics. Wei noted the success of the Republic of China's diplomacy in Africa and a series of challenges that the People's Republic faced in winning over more African countries. Rusk told Wei he had doubts. However, Jiang would not budge, and Rusk did not push too hard.[53]

In the end, the American position prevailed in the vote on Chinese recognition in the United Nations General Assembly. Alfred Jenkins in writing Rostow presaged the coming vote. He noted that "prior to Red Guard excesses and Lin Biao's redeclaration of global "People's War," majority U.S. opinion . . . seemed to hold that effort should be made to bring Communist China into the world community." He further noted "the effects of recent Peking extravagances on sentiment for a UN invitation is not yet known, and could go either way." As the excesses of the Cultural Revolution shocked more and more governments, the trend was running against Beijing. Ten days later the State Department informed key American embassies and consulates that the U.S. government would not change its position in the coming UN vote, it would oppose an Albanian resolution substituting Beijing for Taipei in the UN.[54] Two months later

[52] *FRUS, 1964-1968, Vol. XXX,* Document 143, Sisco to Rusk, April 27, 1966; Document 144, Goldberg to Johnson, April 28, 1966; Document 148, Bundy to Rusk, May 13, 1966; Document 149, Rusk to Johnson, May 14, 1966; Document 150, Rostow to Johnson, May 17, 1966; Document 151, Goldberg to Rusk and Johnson, Nay 17, 1966. See Document 154, Editorial Note, for the tantalizing hint. Document 156, Harriman to Moyers, June 3, 1966.

[53] *FRUS, 1964-1968, Vol. XXX,* Document 157, Embassy in Taipei to State, June 15, 1966; Document 162, Embassy in Taipei to State, July 1, 1966; Document 173, Embassy in Taipei to State, July 5, 1966.

[54] *FRUS, 1964-1968, Vol. XXX,* Document 179, Jenkins to Rostow, September 6, 1966; Document 185, Circular Telegram from Department of State, September 16,

the Department reported success. "Today's votes on Chinese representation were even better than we had anticipated." Deputy Assistant Secretary of State Popper wrote Rusk that "the important question resolution was carried 66-48-7 as opposed to last year's vote of 56-49-11. The Albanian resolution was defeated 46-57-17, in contrast to last year's tie vote of 47-47-20." [55]

The vote in 1966 delayed the inevitable international acceptance of the People's Republic. Thomas Hovet, Jr. in July 1966 stated that "there is every likelihood that the PRC may be seated in the UN within the next one, two, or three years." His report, "Chinese Representation in the United Nations," supported Bundy's view that "the situation was not very promising." The US Embassy in Taipei was similarly concerned, stating "the United Nations situation holds obvious dangers after last year's disappointingly close vote on the Chinese Representation question, despite some GRC diplomatic successes in the intervening year." The vote on November 29 was 57 to 46 to sustain the US position; it would have taken a two-thirds majority to reverse it. Apparently several African delegations changed their vote from the previous year, perhaps reflecting the problems facing Chinese diplomacy caught up in the political correctness of the Cultural Revolution.[56]

1966.

[55] *FRUS, 1964-1968, Vol. XXX,* Document 220, Popper to Rusk, November 29, 1966.

[56] LBJ Library, NSF Country File, Box 243, China (A) (2 of 2), Vol. XIII, 7-12/68, "Chinese Representation in the United Nations," 14 July 1966; NARA, RG 59, CFPF, Box 2040, POL, POLAFF&REL, CHINAT-US, 1/1/64 (2 of 3), "GRC Views on Chinese Representation," March 23, 1966; same files, Box 2032, POL-2, CHINAT, "Annual Politico-Economic Assessment," June 4, 1966; same files, Box 2035, POL 16, Independence, Recognition, CHINAT, 1/1/64, AmEmbassy Blantyre, July 11, 1966; same files, Box 2041, POL, POLAFF&REL, CHINAT-US, 1/1/64, "Upper Volta China Policy and GRC Assistance," November 28, 1965; Box 2012, POL 16, Independence, Recognition, CHICOM, 1-1-65, "Subject: CHIREP," November 10, 1966; same folder, State to Amembassy Taipei, #91450, November 25, 1966; same files, Box 2006, POL, CHICOM (3 of 3), 1966, "Communist China and the Far East," April 11, 1966; same files, Box 2041, POL 17, Diplo&Consular Representation, CHINAT-US, 1/1/64, "Japan's Reaction to Hearings on China", April 7, 1966; same files, Box 2008, POL 2-1, CHICOM, 5/1/66, Chinese Communist Joint Weeka No. 48, December 1, 1966. On the final vote, see *The New York Times,* December 4, 1966, P. E4, "The China Debate Is Over – For This Year" and Department of State *Bulletin,* December 19, 1966, "Move to Change Representation of China in U.N. Again Rejected by the

The issue of China and the United Nations arose once again in 1967. In early April, Rostow asked President Johnson to approve renegotiating the Public Law 480 Agreement with Taiwan that funded Operation Vanguard. He noted that the resulting technical assistance to increase food production in 23 mostly African nations helped the GRC to "impede Peking's efforts to gain political and economic footholds in Africa, boost GRC prestige and strengthen its position in the UN and with other nations; and provide a good example of success for our own foreign aid programs by dramatizing Taiwan's progress." In separate memoranda, the Departments of Agriculture and State supported the request. Support for Taiwan in the United Nations did not preclude consideration of improving relations with China, and it was a delicate path to follow. The State Department advised Johnson on a meeting Nationalist Vice President Yen Chia-kan that "we seek to reassure the Republic of China that the U.S. long-term objective of seeking conditions for a reconciliation with Communist China detracts in no way from our support of the Republic of China." It continued that "we will use our efforts and influence to support the Republic of China's seat in the United Nations." Several days later the department reported to the embassy in Taipei that the visit "was highly successful from every standpoint." As the Cultural Revolution affected Beijing's diplomacy and Operation Vanguard supported Taipei's efforts, Thomas Hughes reported to Secretary Rusk in mid-August that 62 nations had diplomatic relations with Taiwan, 47 with the PRC, and 18 had no relations with either Chinese government. State Department officials continued to follow Taiwan's efforts to best China in the battle for African votes. American officials believed the situation had turned, at least momentarily, and the National Security Council minutes for September 13, 1967 noted that "developments on the mainland continue to work in our favor on this issue which should be manageable this year."[57]

General Assembly," pp. 926-929.

[57] NARA, RG 59, PPS Subject & Country Files, 1965-1969, China 1968, Box 302, "Public Law 480 Agreement with the Republic of China; Operation Vanguard," April 7, 1967; LBJ Library, NSF Country Files, Box 241, China, Memos, Vol. IX (2 of 2), "PL-480 Agreement with the Republic of China," April 8, 1967; Department of State *Bulletin,* May 1, 1967, "China, the United Nations, and the United States," pp. 689-695; RG 59, CFPF, Box 1983, POL 7, CHINAT, 1-1-67, Memorandum for the President, May 5, 1967; same folder, State Outgoing Telegram to Taipei, #192977, May 12, 1967; same folder, State Outgoing Telegram to Taipei, #195150, May 16, 1967; LBJ Library, NSF Country File, Box 241, China, Cables, Vol. IX, 3-6/67, Taipei to SecState, June 9, 1967; CFPF, Box

With the waning of the Cultural Revolution, governments began reconsidering the status of the People's Republic and the United Nations. The new Italian Foreign Minister, Pietro Nenni, informed embassy officials that "the Italian government has decided to proceed with the recognition of Communist China" and this would affect Italy's vote on Chinese representation in the United Nations for the next session. Canada took the lead in rethinking its position relative to China and Taiwan, forcing US diplomats to return to old arguments and tactics, less effective with the passing years. Secretary William Rogers met with Canadian Ambassador Albert Ritchie and indicated American "concern" about Canada's move toward recognition. Belgium released a statement that it "has always maintained that the isolation of Communist China was unhealthy and dangerous" and that the government "was disposed to recognize the government of Peking." The Japanese government wanted a two-China formula, a move away from its once staunch support for America's isolation of Beijing. The issue was so serious that the State Department sent a telegram to key embassies outlining the meeting with the Canadian Ambassador and the current status of the Chinese recognition issue.[58]

This preoccupation and the accompanying military spending had negatively affected economic development for many years. Then, as the government in Taipei began focusing on economic development, a rather

---

1984, POL 17, CHINAT, 1-1-63 and Box 1968, POL 17, CHICOM, 1-1-67, Hughes to Secretary of State, August 11, 1967; same files, Box 1983, POL 7, CHINAT, 6-1-67, "Conversation with the Chinese Ambassador," August 18, 1967; same folder, Amembassy Cotonou to SecState, #875, August 24, 1967; LBJ Library, Papers of Bromley K. Smith, Box 31, 575th NSC Mtg., September 13, 1967; CFPF, Box 1983, POL 7, CHINAT, 6-1-67, "View of GRC Vice Foreign Minister Yang on African Visit," 13 October 1967; same folder, "Views on GRC Vice Premier's Visit to Canada," November 11, 1967.

[58] NARA, RG 59, CFPF, Box 1966, POL 16, CHICOM, 1-1-67, Amembassy Rome to SecState, #9272, December 24, 1968; same folder, Amembassy Tokyo to SecState, #3934, December 27, 1968; same folder, Amembassy Rome to SecState, #9289, December 27, 1968; same files, Box 1967, POL 16, CHICOM, 1-1-69, Amembassy Ottawa to SecState, #4243, January 29, 1969; same folder, Amembassy Brussels to SecState, #7936, January 30, 1969; same folder, Amembassy Rome to SecState, #9615, January 31, 1969; same folder, Amembassy Seoul to SecState, #4689, January 31, 1969; same box, 2-1-69, Memorandum of Conversation, February 6, 1969; same folder, Amembassy Tokyo to SecState, #4613, February 6, 1969; same folder, State Outgoing Telegram, #19748, February 7, 1969; *Department of State Bulletin,* December 9, 1968, pp. 609-611.

amazing story unfolded. Taiwan became one of the "Little Tigers," along with South Korea – a great economic success.

For some years, Taiwan had paid lip service to economic development. In early April 1960 the government announced it was preparing "to live without United States economic aid by the end of 1964." Plans rather optimistically "envisage[d] 36 per cent increases by 1964 in both national production and national income, with an 18.6 per cent increase in average individual income." The goal was a great propaganda victory compared to the economic situation on the mainland. Much as Japan and Korea, Taiwan tied economic development to expanding trade, with "special interest given to newly independent countries in Africa, where the Nationalists believe they can sell textile products." In mid-August 1961, K.T. Li of the Chinese Council for United States Aid met with Walt Rostow to discuss Taiwan's economic development, and they both agreed that Taiwan was in "the take-off stage" and "on its way to self-sustaining growth." The real challenge was sufficient growth "to enable [the] GRC to carry exceptionally heavy defense burden as well as to support rapidly growing population." U.S. officials had little success in convincing the government in Taipei to reduce military expenditures to ease pressure on the economy. In April 1962 the State Department cabled the embassy that "department agrees imperative induce GRC curb military spending but recognizes appeals to GRC economic officials of limited effect." Moreover, Rusk stated the Chargé d'Affaires should tell Taiwan's vice president for economic development that the "U.S. Government [is] deeply concerned over threat to economic stability of Taiwan posed by alarming increase in military expenditures now taking place and proposed. Such spending cannot in our view be justified on ground of military necessity. While we appreciate GRC desire to be prepared for eventual return to mainland, our best intelligence convinces us that Chinese Communist security controls have not yet deteriorated to point where attacks could have any hope of success." Ralph Clough responded several days later that the vice president responded "it was essential for GRC to prepare for action against mainland. Even though US and GRC views of mainland might differ, it was always right to prepare."[59]

[59] *The New York Times,* "End of aid by '65 is Taiwan's goal," April 3, 1960; *NYT,* "Taiwan to study trade," January 30, 1961, p. 5; JFKL, NSF, Box 22, China, General, 8/24/01-8/31/01, "Taiwan's Economic Development," August 15, 1961; JFKL, NSF, Box 25, China, Cables, 10/16-12/31/61, Taipei to SecState, #433, November 16, 1961; same box, China, Cables, 1/62-4/62, Battle to Smith and attachment, April 28, 1962; same box, China, Cables, 5/62, Taipei to SecState,

In 1962, the Taiwanese economy began to boom. American officials feared the rapid growth concealed the economy's capacity to meet all the demands it faced; for example, Taiwanese ate more meat and rice than any other peoples in Asia, so that Taiwan had moved from a rice-exporting to net rice-importing nation. Castro's takeover in Cuba and turn to communism opened the American market for sugar exports, and Taiwan gained entry for an additional 29,000 tons of sugar. By the following March, *Time* reported "Formosa's economic effort is succeeding." American officials told the Taiwanese media that "within a few years, Taiwan will be in a position to maintain a viable economy without special economic assistance from the U.S. Government." Taiwan's GNP was increasing 7.7% annually, and industrial production increased 11%. *Business Week* told readers that "the other China is steadily building its economy behind the protective guns of the U.S. Seventh Fleet." "In some ways," *Business Week* reported, "Taiwan today is like Japan several generations ago." By July *The New York Times* noted "an 18-day tour of the island offered visual evidence of a thriving rural economy." American economic experts believed that "Taiwan's industrial future lay in taking over the lucrative export market in cheap consumer items that is now being abandoned by Japan."[60]

In 1964, the Taiwanese economy boomed. *The New York Times* listed power, port development and tourism as three key sectors. Exports reached record levels in 1963. By late May the United States announced "it would

---

#766, May 2, 1962. There was continued discussion throughout May but Taiwan made its military expenditures and calculated Washington would not permit its economy to fail; see JFKL, NSF, Box 25, China, Cables, 5/62, Memorandum of Conversation, May 3, 1962; same folder, Clough to Rusk, May 4, 1962; same folder, Taipei to SecState, #837, May 18, 1962; same folder, Taipei to SecState, #869, May 22, 1962; same folder, Taipei to SecState, #885, May 25, 1962. The disagreement continued until the year's end, when Taipei concluded the Communist regime on the mainland would not soon collapse, and turned somewhat from emphasizing military expenditures to economic development; see JFKL, NSF, Box 25A, China, Cables, 9/5/62-10/15/62, Taipei to SecState, #478, October 14, 1962; same folder, Memorandum of Conversation, October 14, 1962; same folder, Taipei to State, A-236, October 15, 1962.

[60] *The New York Times,* "Taiwan economy a worry to U.S.," April 1, 1962, p. 4; *NYT,* "Taiwan sugar deal set," April 21, 1962; *Time,* "Formosa: Success Story," March 8, 1963, www.time.com/time/magazine/archive/0,9171,896624,00.html; *NYT,* "Taiwan expands but rate slows," April 5, 1963, p. 66; *Business Week,* "The other China builds up," July 13, 1963, pp. 120-122; *NYT,* "A mixed economy grows in Taiwan," July 15, 1963, p. 2.

discontinue economic aid to Nationalist China in June 1965." *U.S. News & World Report* called Taiwan "an economic and agricultural beehive." "Formosa is riding the crest of a boom that may continue for years." "Exports are booming and the Government has rich reserves of foreign exchange." The news weekly contrasted the success of Taiwan with "Red China wallowing in economic troubles." By December, *The New York Times* noted that "the concept of creating a prosperous society on Taiwan" was replacing "the dream of a counterattack against the Communist-held mainland."[61]

The economic boom continued into 1965. The U.S. Agency for International Development was so impressed with Taiwan's boom, it decided to spend $25,000 to publicize Taiwan's success and America's role to other developing countries. Taiwan was diversifying from a dependence on agriculture and cotton textile exports, and invested in electrical manufacturing. Taiwan's low labor costs and high productivity attracted foreign investors. Finally, on June 30, the United States ended economic assistance to the Republic of China – "graduation day," according to *The New York Times. Time* reported that "Formosa today boasts the Orient's second highest standard of living (after Japan)."[62]

For the remainder of the decade, the good news continued. *The New York Times* contrasted declining diplomatic influence with increasing economic power and prestige. In January 1967 *The New York Times* reported that Taiwan's "foreign trade passes $1 billion mark and is still growing fast." *Time* noted that "Taiwan has become a model for Asian economic development." GNP had risen annually at 8.2% since 1952; foreign reserves, per capita income, and industrial production all continued to rise. In January 1968, *The New York Times* said economists had difficulty explaining Taiwan's prolonged economic growth. Taiwan was among "the fastest growing economies in the world." *Time* praised

---

[61] *The New York Times,* "Taiwan economy makes wide gains," January 13, 1964, p. 48; *NYT,* "U.S. economic help for Taiwan to end," May 29, 1964, p. 8; *U.S. News & World Report,,* "The China that is really thriving," August 3, 1964, p. 52; *The New York Times,* "Taiwan shifting emphasis from war to prosperity," December 21, 1964, p.1, 16.

[62] *The New York Times,* "U.S. to publicize effects of aid on boom in Taiwan," January 13, 1965, p. 3; *NYT,* "Taiwan is buoyed by U.S. aid plan," January 18, 1965, p. 45; *NYT,* "Foreign investors are attracted to Taiwan," June 9, 1965, p. 65; *NYT,* U.S. economic aid to Taiwan ended; 'graduation' hailed," July 1, 1965, p. 1; *NYT,* "Taiwan's economic rise," July 1, 1965, p. 2; *Time,* "On their own," July 2, 1965, www.time.com/time/magazine/article/0,9171,833842,00.html.

Taiwan's carefully programmed economy" compared to too many developing nations "which try to move from agrarianism to industrialization in one unrealistic step."[63]

Taiwan had issues in dealing with Japan, though they differed from those of South Korea. The issue in South Korean-Japanese relations was the 35-year Japanese occupation of the peninsula, and what was the extent of Japan's guilt. Taiwan worried that Japan would extend recognition to the People's Republic to gain trade advantages. *The New York Times* reported in September 1963 that the Japanese embassy in Taipei received anonymous threats "if Japan continued to trade with Communist China." Several months later the Japanese government noted that Taipei was worried that Japan was "leaning more openly toward the 'Two Chinas policy,'" which Taipei rejected. As tensions continued, Tokyo stated clearly that "Japan intended to maintain economic relations with Communist China while continuing diplomatic recognition of the Chinese Nationalist regime." Interestingly, this policy also did not please the People's Republic which charged Japan with a "policy of hostility," and "accused Japan of designs to reoccupy the island of Taiwan." As Sino-Japanese economic relations expanded, some predicted Japan would move from recognizing Taiwan to recognizing the People's Republic as the rightful "government" of China. Interestingly, in 1968, *The New York Times* reported that "Japan is steadily improving her top-rank position among world nations in the economic life of Nationalist China." While Japan enjoyed a significant trade surplus, "Nationalist officials are mindful of the fact that the larger economic stake built up by the Japanese here the less inclined they will be to make concessions in order to develop their trade with Communist China."[64]

---

[63] *The New York Times,* "Taiwan's economic role grows as diplomatic prestige shrinks," March 25, 1966, p. 6; *NYT,* "Foreign trade passes $1 billion mark and is still growing fast," January 20, 1967, p. 49; *Time,* "The Model," May 12, 1967, www.time.com/time/magazine/article/0,9171,843770,00.html; *NYT,* "The boom is even bigger in Taiwan," January 19, 1968, p. 54; *Time,* "A step at a time," February 232, 1968, www.time.com/time/magazine/article/0,9171,837979,00.html.

[64] *The New York Times,* "Attacks on Japan growing in Taipei," September 23, 1963, p. 3; *NYT,* "Links to Chinese worrying Japan," December 8, 1963, p. 16; *NYT,* "Japan reaffirms tie to Taiwan but will keep up China trade," March 8, 1964, p. 24; *NYT,* "Peking attacks Tokyo 'hostility,'" December 9, 1964, p. 3; *NYT,* "China denounces Japan on Taiwan," December 13, 1964, p. 31; *NYT,* "U.S. expert on Asia says Japan will shift to China recognition," March 4, 1966, p. 6; *NYT,* "Japan expanding leading role in economic ties with Taiwan," October 21,

Much as Korea, Taiwan offered to assist US efforts in Vietnam. Jiang wanted to interpret the Vietnam fighting as part of a larger effort to contain the People's Republic in which Taiwan was at the center. Unlike Korea, Washington declined, wanting to keep the decades-old Chinese civil war out of the Vietnam conflict.

To complicate the situation, Jiang Jieshi tried to involve Nationalist China in the Vietnam conflict. In May 1965 the semi-official Taiwan media discussed an invasion of China's Hainan Island, near Vietnam, to be a first step in the liberation of the mainland and to support US operations in Indochina; of course, US diplomats provided no support for these trial balloons. In August, Jiang passed along a message that "the Chinese Communists and their Vietnamese allies are about to engage the U.S. in a long ground war of attrition which we cannot hope to win; Jiang stands ready to provide troops to Vietnam; but most important, he urges that now is the time for an amphibious Chinese Nationalist landing on the South China coast to cut Peking's supply lines to Vietnam and begin the reconquest of the mainland." Again in September, Jiang's son, Jiang Xingguo met with Secretary of Defense Robert McNamara and noted that President Jiang had asked "how the GRC can help the US in Vietnam." McNamara punted, noting that Vietnam valued GRC economic and technical aid but that "the war will be ultimately won or lost by how well the government takes care of its people."[65]

Still, from the beginnings of the expanded U.S. involvement, the Pentagon used Taiwan as both a staging area and a site for R&R for units assigned to the Vietnam theater of operations. On January 11, 1966, *The New York Times* headlined "U.S. Expands Taiwan Air Base For a Key

---

1968, p. 69.

[65] Department of State, *Foreign Relations of the United States, Volume XXX, China,* Washington, DC, GPO, 1998, Document 86, US Embassy Taipei to Department of State, May 18, 1965; Document 95, "Ray Cline's Talks with Chiang Kai-shek," August 5, 1965; Document 104, Memorandum of Conversation, September 22, 1965. Jiang Xingguo tried again with State Department officials the next day with no greater success; see Document 106, Memorandum of Conversation, September 23,1965. Again in November President Jiang tried to link landings on the Chinese mainland with the US effort in Vietnam, to no avail: see Document 110, GRC Proposal for Landings on Mainland China, November 16, 1965. To be sure, there were some in the US government who wanted to accept Jiang's offer of troops; see Document 113, "Chinese Nationalist Military Forces vis-à-vis Vietnam," December 6, 1965, in which Ray Cline, the CIA Deputy Director, called attention to "the half-million OR SO Chinese Nationalist ground forces supported by qualitatively good though small air forces and naval forces."

Role in Vietnam War." Republic of China officials viewed American military use of Taiwan as an opening to greater involvement in the Vietnam conflict, and initially proposed to produce small arms ammunition the United States used but did not manufacture.[66]

Jiang renewed his call for a Pacific Pact, seeking to expand the Vietnam conflict into an anti-People's Republic pact of surrounding nations backed by American military might. As American use of Taiwan increased, State Department officials worried Jiang would tie government approval of these U.S. facilities to American support for a Taiwanese attack on the mainland, especially as the People's Republic descended into the hell of the Cultural Revolution. Jiang submitted proposals for an attack from Taiwan aimed at south China coastal provinces thereby "surrounding" North Vietnam. Rusk counseled and other American officials followed a policy of simply not replying to such proposals.[67]

The U.S. government kept Jiang out of Vietnam, recognizing that such involvement would change the entire nature of the conflict. When the Pentagon first considered using Taiwan as a base to support the effort in Vietnam, the State Department expressed concern. Dean Rusk cabled the American Embassy in Taipei that such actions would provoke an obvious reaction from Beijing and complicate Vietnam policy. Jiang complained, stating that it was "essential that a firm and clear-cut policy should be adhered to" to defeat communist in Vietnam; he feared a negotiated peace in Vietnam might threaten prospects of "liberating" the mainland. He claimed in a meeting with Assistant Secretary of State William P. Bundy that only the threat of an invasion by Nationalist forces kept the People's Republic from sending troops to Vietnam. ROC officials devised an invasion plan for the mainland before the U.S. quit Vietnam. When Vice President Hubert Humphrey visited Jiang in Taipei in early January 1966, Jiang "stressed as he has before that we could not expect to match Communist manpower in Asia, and . . . the objective should be to utilize Asian manpower with American logistics support." In December 1966, Jiang was telling Secretary Rusk that he feared the United States would

---

[66] *The New York Times,* January 11, 1966, p. 1; Lyndon Baines Johnson Library, NSF Country Files, Box 239, China Cables Vol. V, George Ball to American Embassy Taiwan, January 11, 1966. See also Charles J. Pellegrin, "United States Diplomatic and Military Relations with the Republic of China in the Era of the Vietnam War, 1961-1969," unpublished doctoral dissertation, Mississippi State University, May 2005.

[67] FRUS, 1964-1968, Vol. XXX, China, Document No. 121, Thomson to McGeorge Bundy, February 3, 1966.

concede Taiwan to the People's Republic in return for peace in Vietnam, claimed Beijing was considering launching ten nuclear bombs at Taiwan, and of course wanted American reassurances.[68]

In summer and fall 1968, key White House aides oversaw a summary process of foreign policy accomplishments during the Johnson presidency. One such draft noted "normalization of relations between Japan and the Republic of Korea." It also drew attention to the "economic growth of the Republic of Korea." "The annual increase in real GNP averaged 9.7 per cent during 1963-1966." "Exports increased 357 per cent (46 per cent per year)." In May 1968, another such summary noted "U.S. commitments in Korea" and "leadership and support for the new Asia – Asian Development Bank and ASPAC" as key parts of "Focusing on Asia," one of ten major foreign policy accomplishments." More specifically, another report focused on accomplishments in Asia and the Pacific, and noted "the Republic of Korea has reached a growth rate in excess of 8% a year, increased exports from $30 million in 1960 to $250 million in 1966. A target figure of $350 million has been set for 1967." This listing also reiterated the formation of ASPAC and the incorporation of the Asian Development Bank. Another compilation contrasted the situation in late 1963, including "much of Asia still dependent on the American dole," including Korea and "tension high among Asian neighbors," including Japan and Korea, and the situation "today," including "old differences healed – Japan/Korea," "steady economic progress in most countries – Korea booming," To what did William Jorden attribute such significant change? "A solid U.S. policy emerged in Asia" – "with the U.S. as a reliable partner."[69]

---

[68] For the earliest incarnation of Jiang's effort to bind the United States to a coalition in East Asia, see Charles M. Dobbs, "The Pact That Never Was: The Pacific Pact of 1949," *The Journal of Northeast Asian Studies*, Winter 1985; LBJ Library, NSF Country Files, Box 239, China Cables, Vol. V, Rusk to American Embassy Taipei, December 7, 1965. Rusk would later change his mind and support use of Taiwan, but he raised the right issue in his earlier cable. *FRUS, 1964-1968, Vol. XXX,* Document 116, January 2, 1966. See Pellegrin, op. cit., "The ROC and Vietnam." See LBJ Library, NSF Country Files, Box 239, China Cables, Vol. VI, CIA Cable, April 16, 1966; *FRUS, 1964-1968, Vol. XXX,* Document 224, Rusk to Department of State, December 10, 1966.

[69] LBJL, NSF Subject File, Box 19, Foreign Affairs Data Sheets, 12/67-6/68, Read to Rostow and attachment, March 10, 1968; same box, Rpt of Accomplishments during LBJ (1 of 4), May 17, 1968; same box, Rpt of Accomplishments during

Similarly, in the closing days of the Johnson administration, the State Department authored a history and concluded it largely achieved success in South Korea. Korea and Japan normalized their relations, which provided Korea with investment capital and industrial expertise and offered Japan a market for its finished goods. In part because of this agreement, Park's commitment to improving the economy, and U.S. spending in Korea for the Vietnam War, the Korean economy expanded. As the economy expanded, the need for outright U.S. economic aid lessened, thus helping America's balance of payments challenge. With a more stable political system, and a booming economy, Korea became more active internationally increasing its diplomatic relations, participating in the Asian Development Bank, and in helping to form ASPAC. The only real negative was the apparent renewal of North Korean aggression with the failed assassination attempt and the seizure of the *USS Pueblo*, both in January 1968.[70]

American diplomats could take equal credit for the Republic of China on Taiwan. In 1961, Taiwan had a struggling economy, in part because Jiang Jieshi was focused almost obsessively on preparing for a return to the mainland. There was a huge gap between the mainland expatriates who fled with Jiang and native Taiwanese, and it seemed that Beijing would replace Taipei formally as the home of the internationally recognized government of China.

Eight years later, matters had improved greatly. The excesses of the Great Proletarian Cultural Revolution had, at least momentarily, halted momentum towards recognizing the People's Republic as "China" in the United Nations; similarly, the Cultural Revolution and fear of Beijing exporting its revolutionary violence made relations with Taipei more palatable to governments in the region. Much as Korea, the Taiwanese economy boomed, in part owing to favorable trade relations with the United States, good economic relations with Japan, and the positive impact of American spending in Taiwan for the Vietnam War. [71]

LBJ (3 of 4), May 17, 1968; LBJL, NSF Subject File, Box 18, Progress in Foreign Policy Since 1964;

[70] LBJL, Administrative History of the Department of State, Box 1, Chapter 7 (East Asia), Sections A-D, F. "Republic of Korea," pp. 1-41, *passim*

[71] LBJL, Administrative History of the Department of State, Volume I, Chapters 7-9, Box 3, Chapter 7: Sections A-D, "D. Republic of China," *passim.*

CHAPTER FIVE

ALLIES NEEDING REASSURANCE: THE PHILIPPINES AND THAILAND

The Philippines and Thailand faced challenges and had concerns similar to South Korea and Thailand. Fifteen years after U.S. colonialism ended, the Philippines had made little progress towards an effective and broad political system; the economy was typical of too many Third World nations, and Philippine leaders seemed more interested in seeking military hardware and in interfering in the internal affairs of neighbors than in expanding the economy and opportunity for all peoples. Bangkok focused on the increasing insurgencies in Laos and South Vietnam and also seemed more fixated on military hardware than economic development.

Similarly, Washington had its issues with Manila and Bangkok as it did with Seoul and Taipei. Corruption, sadly, characterized the Philippine government, and its reach did not extend much past major cities in the northern islands. Similarly, the Thai government focused on the situations in Laos and Vietnam when American officials believed the more important issue was reaching out to villages in the northeast and south along the Malayan border, for those Thais had little connection to and likely little loyalty towards their governments

Although the respective situations seemed difficult in 1961, by 1969, Thailand and, to a lesser extent, the Philippines were on the road to an effective political system and an expanding economy based on trade. Thailand was the greater success story, as successive leaders provided political stability, and the expansion of the American effort in Vietnam pumped the Thai economy. Roads to the frontier to assist military defense also brought Bangkok closer to isolated villages far from the capital; economic development improved the quality of life and thus helped create a sense of loyalty towards the government. The Philippines took longer, but, in time, the government reduced corruption to manageable levels, and the islands enjoyed a significant economic boom.

Corruption in Manila greatly concerned the Kennedy Administration. The government of Carlos Garcia combined corruption with great inefficiency which furthered political instability and economic inequality. As the election neared in summer 1961, the government in Washington noted that Garcia "has, of course, run a very corrupt administration" and that "it is characteristic of Philippine politics." Indeed, government analysts noted that "the Philippine population is very cynical about the subject of corruption in government." Former U.S. Ambassador, Myron Cowen, told State Department officials that, during a meeting with Garcia, he was "brutally frank" and "went into some detail with respect to the graft and corruption in the Garcia Administration." When Garcia asked what steps he should take, Cowen replied he should "go to the IMF [International Monetary Fund] and ask for consultants to be placed in key ministries." Undersecretary of State George Ball wrote the embassy that "department is gravely concerned with graft and corruption in Garcia Administration," and "this rotting of the moral fiber of Philippine public life constitutes a potential threat to [the] best interest[s of the] U.S. and free world in Asia." Ball asked for a reaction to Cowen's suggestions. Several weeks later, Cowen's suggestions to Garcia became more explicit State Department advice to the Embassy after inauguration of a new Philippine government in January.[1]

At the same time, the Filipino Government worried about America's commitment to fighting communism in Laos. When Vice President Lyndon Johnson visited Manila as part of an Asian good–will trip in 1961, Philippine Foreign Secretary Felixberto Serrano commented off-the-record about the "empty and worthless trip" because he could not "extract from Johnson specifics on US position on Laos" and such other matters as the Chinese representation issue and the Nationalist-occupied islands of Quemoy and Matsu off the Chinese mainland. Several months later the complaining about "our failure to stand up to the Communists in Asia," so bothered President Kennedy that he asked National Security Advisor McGeorge Bundy to find out "how many troops the Philippines contributed to the Korean War." After all, "this is a propaganda war against us and we ought to see how we could make that known." Several

---

[1] Department of State, *Foreign Relations of the United States, 1961-1963, Volume XXIII, Southeast Asia,* Washington, GPO, 1994, Document 355, Johnson to Rostow, July 14, 1961, pp. 775-777; Document 356, Memorandum of Conversation, July 28, 1961, pp. 777-778; John F. Kennedy Library, National Security File, Box 152, Philippines, General, 8/61-4/62, Ball to Amembassy Manila, #133, August 4, 1961; *FRUS, 1961-1963, Vol. XXIII,* Document 357, State to Amembassy Manila, August 5, 1961, pp. 778-779.

days later, the State Department reported that President Garcia "declared that even if the U.S. voted for Red China's admission to the UN the Philippines would continue to oppose it." A week after Johnson's visit, Garcia told a reporter he "urged the U.S. to stand firm on the question of Communist expansion in Asia 'before it's too late.'" Garcia stated the U.S. "should put out the fires [Laos and Vietnam] now before they get too large." Garcia also expressed "doubt on the effectiveness of SEATO" and the existing collective security system in the region.[2]

Manila and Washington viewed the Philippine War Damage Act somewhat differently. After the Second World War ended, the U.S. government agreed to pay for damage that the American recapture of the Philippines had caused. The Philippine Rehabilitation Act of 1946 provided $400 million to "assist in the restoration of private property destroyed during World War II in the Philippines." A final accounting called for another payment of $73 million, and the bill was moving, slowly, through the Congress. In early September 1961, the House of Representatives decided to "put the Bill over for consideration during the next session," which State Department officials stated would disappoint the Philippine people.[3]

The following spring the Kennedy Administration tried again to secure passage of the Philippine War Damage Act. In addition to fulfilling a promise, Edward Rice wrote that "payment this year would make an especially significant contribution to the foreign exchange reserves of the new Philippine Administration of President Macapagal." In turn, Macapagal cancelled his state visit, "attributing his decision to Philippine popular and Congressional 'resentment' over the War Damage Bill disapproval. The State Department agreed, and asked President Kennedy for a letter, "as warm and friendly as possible under the circumstances," to assuage Macapagal's feelings. Macapagal gave a strongly negative interview with UPI expressing his frustration, but American diplomats worried that such strong comments would make it more difficult to secure Congressional approval. *U.S. News & World Report* noted "the Filipinos aren't at all happy about U.S. recalcitrance in money matters." It further stated that "the U.S. Congress has recently shown reluctance to complete promised compensation for war-damage claims in the Philippines," and

---

[2] *FRUS, 1961-1963, Vol. XXIII,* Document 350, Amembassy Manila to State, May 18, 1961, pp. 764-5; Document 353, Kennedy to Bundy, July 10, 1961, p. 769; Document 354, Battle to Bundy, July 13, 1961, pp. 769-773.

[3] *FRUS, 1961-1963, Vol. XXIII,* Document 351, Bell to McConaughy, June 9, 1961, pp. 766-7; Document 360, McConaughy to Rusk, September 7, 1961, p. 784; Document 361, Amembassy Manila to State, September 18, 1961, p. 785.

reminded readers that "the Filipinos are military allies of the U.S. and could be very useful in the Laos-Thailand operations." After Macapagal cancelled his visit, Philippine Vice President Emmanuel Pelaez called on Kennedy, who "explained to Mr. Pelaez that he had done everything he could to get it passed." Kennedy attributed the negative vote to having "so much of the money [going] to prosperous corporations" rather than needy individuals. Finally, on August 1, 1962, the House of Representatives passed the bill by 194 to 35 and three weeks later the Senate passed it unanimously providing the full, requested $73 million. Philippine and American officials hailed the vote. Philippine ambassador Emilio Abello stated the vote "will no doubt improve immeasurably the climate of relations between our two countries," while President Kennedy indicated the vote "honor[s] a long-standing moral commitment to the Filipino people." When the Senate approved the request, Kennedy said that "we have taken another step in our valued partnership with the Philippine nation and with its able and vigorous new leader, President Macapagal."[4]

When Diosdado Macapagal succeeded Garcia, relations improved. Macapagal expected a "special US representative at [the] inauguration [on] December 30." Macapagal made such a presence a test of American esteem for his incoming administration. But, as noted above, the long effort to secure Congressional approval of the Philippine War Damage Bill greatly disappointed Macapagal and other Philippine leaders. Still, in January 1962, Macapagal announced the abolition of controls that had been in effect for thirteen years. He stated that "controls have hampered the economic growth of the country and have been a source of graft." Macapagal recognized that "corruption was as much a way of life as poverty in the sprawling, underdeveloped island republic." He fought the idea of "graft and corruption as a fact of life and as a condition for success." By October 1962, *The New York Times* gave him credit for success, "at least in the upper levels of government." He told a press

---

[4] *FRUS, 1961-1963, Vol. XXIII,* Document 366, Rice to Feldman, February 7, 1962, p. 793; Document 368, Amembassy Manila to State, May 10, 1962, p. 368; Document 369, Brubeck to Bundy, May 23, 1962, pp. 797-8; *U.S. News & World Report,* "Business Around the World," May 28, 1962, p. 81; *FRUS, 1961-1963, Vol. XXIII,* Document 371, Memorandum of Conversation, June 8, 1962, pp. 798-9; Document 373, Memorandum of Conversation, June 26, 1962, pp. 803-5; Document 375, Editorial Note, p. 809; *The New York Times,* "House approves bill on Philippine war damage," August 2, 1962, p. 3; *NYT,* "Senate approves Philippine funds," August 25, 1962, p. 1; the issue of the war damage bill continued into 1963, see NARA, RG 59, CFPF, Box 4016, Pol PHIL-A, State to Amembassy Manila, #1129, May 20, 1963.

conference in June that "official relations with the United States had deteriorated." "The Philippine press, which does not hesitate to rake Mr. Macapagal over the coals when it disagrees with him, is almost unanimously behind him." Several weeks later Macapagal told a television audience that "as a result of the action of the United States Congress, the ties between the Philippines and the United States have never been weaker." [5]

Philippine sugar quotas remained an issue, given Manila's need for foreign earnings and Washington's domestic concerns with Hawaiian cane sugar and northern Great Plains beet sugar. In June 1961, Ambassador Carlos Romulo questioned Washington's decision to reduce the Philippine sugar allocation, and several days later the State Department informed the embassy in Manila and Romulo that it had increased the sugar allotment by 150,000 tons. Soon after Macapagal took office, the new Philippine Ambassador, Emilio Abello, and President Kennedy agreed that the Philippines did not produce enough sugar to fulfill its U.S. quota and meet the needs of regional countries; interestingly, since the U.S. government paid a premium, Abello did not want his country to sell to other countries and lose that premium over market price; Kennedy assured him the United States "had no intention of denying the Filipinos the premium price." Philippine sugar interests fought to retain the U.S. import premium. The executive secretary of the Philippine Sugar Association, José E. Romero, told the New York Sugar Club that the Philippine sugar industry could not survive a drop from 4 cents to a pound to the world price of 2 ¾ cents a pound. Romero believed the steady Philippine sugar supply was worth the increased cost to U.S. consumers. When Philippine Vice President Emmanuel Pelaez called on Kennedy in late June, they discussed sugar. Pelaez wanted to expand the U.S. quota, but Kennedy indicated that domestic producers were pressuring Congressional representatives; Kennedy suggested the Philippines sell to Japan to keep Japan from purchasing Cuban sugar which supported the relatively new communist regime of Fidel Castro. When Pelaez indicated his country was "a high cost producer," Kennedy responded he "might consider giving a subsidy to sugar to earn foreign exchange just as the U.S. gave cotton producers."

---

[5] *FRUS, 1961-1963, Vol. XXIII,* Document 362, Amembassy Manila to State, December 9, 1961, pp. 786-7; Document 363, Amembassy to State, December 12, 1961, p. 789; *The New York Times,* "Macapagal eases hostility to U.S.," June 2, 1962, p. 2; *NYT,* "Philippines making strides in battle on graft and poverty," October 15, 1962, p. 3; *NYT,* "Macapagal sees red gains in Asia," June 25, 1962, p. 3.

[On the other hand, Philippine leaders did not have an adequate response to questions about quotas on importation of American tobacco.][6]

Military assistance appropriations were another issue, and reflected as much Filipino worries about Indonesia's foreign policy as concern for Chinese expansion. In February 1963 Macapagal asked for "increased and accelerated" military assistance. State Department analysts noted the request "probably comes as a result of his concern over developments in Indonesia [discussed in the next chapter], and similar to Philippine Defense Secretary Macario Peralta's request earlier in the month. U.S. defense analysts concluded that "this level of assistance is neither justified by any increased threat to the Philippines nor digestible by the country's military establishment as it now stands." State suggested Kennedy reply reaffirming the mutual defense treaty and that Washington was "studying" the request. Three months later, the Joint Chiefs informed McNamara that a new study determined "planned types and levels of MAP equipment to support the armed forces of the Philippines are considered appropriate."[7]

Interestingly, a study team provided "a development program for the Philippines" in late July 1961, and it seemed oblivious of all these issues. The summary noted ""the Philippines have effected a remarkable recovery from the ravages of World War II" and "the Filipinos show competence and sophistication." Curiously, the study team did not comment on the endemic corruption and graft that other State Department communications highlighted, the high cost of some Philippine export crops, especially sugar, trade deficits and lack of foreign capital, and the lack of raw materials to expand industrial production. The team did note the lack of community among Filipinos occupying many islands, and divided into Catholic, Spanish speaking northern islands and Moslem, native speaking southern ones.[8]

---

[6] *FRUS, 1961-1963, Vol. XXIII,* Document 352, "Sugar Quota for the Philippines," June 28, 1961, pp. 767-8; Document 367, "Philippine Sugar," February 20, 1962, pp. 794-5; *The New York Times,* "Philippine sugar growers seek to retain U.S. import premium," March 21, 1962, p. 53; *FRUS, 1961-1963, Vol. XXIII,* Document 373, Pelaez call on the President, June 26, 1962, p. 805; on tobacco importation see JFKL, NSF, Box 152, Philippines, General, 8/61-4/62, "Tobacco," February 20, 1962; same folder, State to Manila, #992, February 22, 1962.

[7] *FRUS, 1961-1963, Vol. XXIII,* Document 379, Brubeck to Bundy, March 20, 1963, pp. 814-5; Document 385, Joint Chiefs of Staff to McNamara, May 29, 1963, p. 823.

[8] JFKL, NSF, Box 152, Philippines, General, 2/61-7/61, "A Development Program for the Philippines," July 31, 1961, pp. V1-V5.

Macapagal quickly strengthened the Philippine economy. Besides battling graft, Macapagal freed the peso of its complex import and exchange controls to open the economy. *The New York Times* editorialized that Macapagal had "justified the hopes for progress." It noted the increase in gross national product, agricultural production, and industrial production. Exports increased, imports decreased, and so foreign reserves rose. Even the wealthy were paying a greater share of their fair taxes. The peso stabilized at 3.90 pesos to the U.S. dollar, far below the feared drop to six pesos. With red tape reduced greatly, businessmen in the Philippines and abroad expanded operations. Foreign trade increased, and Philippine foreign reserves rose more than a third to $140,240,000. State Department analysts were not as uniformly positive. In early April 1963, they noted Macapagal's commitment "to bring about the moral regeneration of the Philippine people and to advance economic development and social reform." They concluded that "graft and venality have been damped down, but there remains much to be done." A follow up assessment a week later had a similar theme – some economic progress but not enough to provide for a rapidly increasing population or to help even the great disparities of wealth. Looking back on 1963, *The New York Times* approved "a ferment for increased productivity [that was] pervading the Philippines" and also applauded a commitment "to put down on paper the country's unwritten policy of attracting foreign investments." [9]

Nonetheless, challenges remained. In the annual assessment, the U.S. embassy in Manila reported that "the government's poor performance in the economic field and the relatively slow rate of economic growth contribute to the feeling of discontent." More specifically, the government "has shown itself to be incapable of implementing the President's Five-Year Socio-Economic Program," it has "largely abandoned organized economic development," it has "made only minimal improvements in the country's infrastructure," and "its land reform program still awaits implementation." It also expected as Macapagal emphasized relations with neighboring countries, he would seek some distance from the United States. *Business Week* reported in September 1964 that "for a year the Philippine Congress has refused to enact President Macapagal's reform program. The confused situation has U.S. investors wondering about their

---

[9] *The New York Times,* "Good record for Philippines," January 15, 1963, p. 6; *NYT,* "Philippines moving ahead in optimistic atmosphere," April 5, 1963, p. 66; NARA, RG 59, CFPF, Box 4014, Pol 1, Philippines, 2/1/63, "Philippines: Political, Economic and Military Problems," April 1, 1963; Box 4015, Pol 2-3, PHIL, 2/1/63, "Politico-Economic Assessment – Philippines," April 10, 1963; *NYT,* "Philippine foreign investments policy takes definite shape," January 13, 1964, p. 49.

future." In October after returning home from a visit to Washington, Macapagal called on Americans to "assist his people to have economic freedom from poverty." Macapagal told an audience at Fordham University in The Bronx that the Philippines were "a show-window of Asian Christianity and American democracy" facing Islamic nations to his south and Communism to the west across the Pacific. [10]

Finally, there were the competing claims to Sabah and Filipino reaction to the merging of several Malay states into a greater Malaysia. While the U.S. government during the time it controlled the Philippines never expressed a claim to this territory on the northern part of the island of Borneo, the Philippine government asserted such rights. In January 1964, Macapagal agreed to meet with Prince Abdul Rahman, Prime Minister of Malaysia, to discuss the situation. While Macapagal would not recognize the combination of Malaya, Singapore, Sarawak, and Sabah as Malaysia, he shared concern with Abdul Rahman about Indonesian leader Sukarno and his support for guerrilla bands in Sabah as well as the southern Philippines. In January, *The New York Times* reported that efforts to resolve the dispute over Sabah "had reached an impasse." Indonesia claimed the merger of former British colonies into Malaysia "constituted a 'neocolonialist' attempt by Britain to 'encircle' Indonesia." The Philippines merely seemed interested in pressing its claim to Sabah. The claims merged with concern about Indonesian encouragement of guerrilla movements in the southern Philippines. The government in Washington was so concerned, that in October 1964, Dean Rusk warned Indonesia that "an attack on the Philippines would be considered an attack on this country." Rusk was responding to Macapagal's expression of "his country's growing concern over Indonesian activities in Southeast Asia." The following March *The Economist* noted how mutual crises with Indonesia and the suspicion of support from the People's Republic of China helped bring Malaysia and the Philippines together.[11]

President Macapagal visited Washington a month before the U.S. presidential election. Four months before traveling to Washington,

---

[10] NARA, RG 59, CFPF, Box 2580, Pol 2-2, Politico-Economic Rpts, PHIL, 1/1/64, "Politico-Economic Assessment," April 17, 1964; *Business Week,* "Stalemate in Manila," September 5, 1964, p. 102; *The New York Times,* "Macapagal asks U.S. help Philippines' fight on poverty," October 10, 1964, p. 2.

[11] *The New York Times,* "Malaysia and Philippines will discuss dispute," January 22, 1964, p. 11; *NYT,* "Rusk reaffirms defense accords with Manila," October 9, 1964, p. 2; *NYT,* "Dispute over Sabah disrupts Asian alliance," January 12, 1965, p. 6; *The Economist,* "Philippines: Suspect your neighbors," March 27, 1965, p. 1377.

Macapagal issued a statement that "the Philippines would consider acting on a request for assistance from the South Vietnamese" – foreshadowing a long effort to send a 2,000 man engineering battalion to Vietnam. The background memo for Johnson noted that Macapagal was both "pro-American" and a "Philippine nationalist." While giving him credit for his support of the U.S. position towards Vietnam, the backgrounder did state that "he has been only moderately successful with his domestic programs, which emphasize economic and social reform." Rusk suggested Macapagal would seek concessions on the sale of U.S. rice, the purchase of Philippine sugar, additional military assistance, and assurances of U.S. determination to resist Communism in East Asia. The next day Rusk wrote Johnson that Macapagal thought the situation in Vietnam was nearing "desperation," and "part of the trouble might be that the American advisers and military units, being 'Westerners and white men,' seemed to the Vietnamese little different from the French and are consequently unable to 'convey a sense of common purpose to them.' He suggested that the 16,000 American soldiers in Viet-Nam be replaced by an equal number of Filipinos and Thais." Rusk recommended that Johnson reiterate his commitment in the region, thank Macapagal for his support, but not give him any encouragement about increasing military assistance. Robert Komer of the National Security Council Staff echoed Rusk's advice.[12]

On October 5, Johnson met Macapagal. After a reception on the South Lawn of the White House, Johnson led Macapagal to his car for a 25-minute parade through downtown Washington, echoing with the applause of lunchtime crowds. The conversation went as expected. Macapagal offered to send support personnel to Vietnam, and Johnson asked that the Philippine leader speak with Secretary McNamara about American financial support. Macapagal indicated the need for rice, and Johnson indicated the U.S. would supply 100,000 tons immediately. With the two big issues quickly decided, the conversation proceeded amicably. The next day Macapagal and McNamara met, and discussed Vietnam and the Philippine defense budget; again, the conversation was friendly and open. Three months later Philippine Secretary of Finance, Rufino Hechanova, and U.S. Assistant Defense Secretary John McNaughton, further discussed a Philippine contingent to Vietnam and what the record called "the Philippine shopping list." McNaughton offered financial support for the

---

[12] *The New York Times,* "National Security Seen Imperiled by Crisis," June 14, 1964, p. E4; Department of State, *Foreign Relations of the United States, Volume XXVI, Indonesia, Malaysia-Singapore, Philippines,* GPO, Washington, DC, 2001, Document 296, Rusk to Johnson, October 2, 1964; Document 298, Rusk to Johnson, October 3, 1964; Document 299, Komer to Johnson, October 4, 1964.

Philippine contingent in Vietnam, but did not agree to seemingly excessive military equipment and assistance requests. Macapagal wrote President Johnson re-stating his support for the American effort in Vietnam, and blaming the "partisan atmosphere" in the Congress, especially the Philippine Senate, for failure to secure approval for the 2,000 man engineering battalion. After promising to try again after the national elections, Macapagal stated that "My conviction that South Vietnam should be supported by freedom-loving peoples from falling to the communists needs no reiteration. I am certain that the Filipino people themselves share and support this policy." Several weeks later, Johnson responded that he appreciated Macapagal's support. Despite the seemingly positive visit, *U.S. News & World Report* told readers that "the warm, easy relationship between the two countries is not what it once was. Tensions and antagonisms have been on the increase lately."[13]

In the end, the Philippine Congress did not enact the necessary legislation to commit the promised 2,000 troops. There were other issues, principally extending the authority of the government in Manila throughout the southern islands; this necessitated orienting the Philippine military toward counter-insurgency and civil action operations and less toward the accumulation of vast amounts of military hardware or sending the best trained forces to Vietnam. Extending the government's authority figured in the Macapagal-McNamara conversation in October 1964 and the Hechanova-McNaughton follow-up conversation in January 1965. In March 1965, the Joint Chiefs of Staff recommended an increase in military assistance for this purpose: At the same time, embassy officials cabled the State Department that Macapagal's re-election prospects were weak, and his ability to work with the Philippine Congress limited; there was little likelihood of gaining approval to send the troops to Vietnam. Johnson continued to press for the Philippine contingent when Ambassador Oscar Ledesma called. In early July McGeorge Bundy wrote Johnson that Macapagal believed the only way he could commit Philippine troops was as "volunteers" paid "under the table" by the CIA, which Bundy considered "messy." Several days later Rusk cabled the embassy in Manila that the matter was dead: "we believe it necessary to recognize that Macapagal will not recertify aid to Viet-Nam bill, and that further efforts by us to persuade him to do so will be unproductive." In response, U.S.

---

[13] *The New York Times,* "President greets Philippine chief," October 6, 1964, p. 16; *FRUS, Vol. XXVI,* Document 300, Memorandum of Conversation, October 5, 1964; Document 301, Memorandum of Conversation, October 6, 1964; Document 303, Memorandum of Conversation, January 21, 1965, *U.S. News & World Report,* "A New Worry for the U.S. – Trouble With An Old Ally," October 12, 1964, p. 77.

Ambassador William Blair visited with Macapagal, and stressed that "Washington was both gravely concerned and disappointed that the Vietnam bill had not been pressed. " Macapagal told Blair he had concluded that "it was best to postpone action until after the elections." [14]

After serving a four year term, Macapagal lost his re-election to Senator Ferdinand Marcos. The campaign remained close into its final weeks, and U.S. analysts feared election "manipulation." A CIA report predicted that "given past experience both sides will undoubtedly engage in widespread manipulation tactics, including vote frauds, subversion of election officials, stuffing of ballot boxes, votes lost through managed counting, etc. In addition, both sides will use every other means at their disposal to improve their own position." Four days before the election William Bundy predicted that if Macapagal won, he would seek approval to commit Philippine troops to Vietnam; if Senator Ferdinand Marcos won, Bundy predicted he would be more of a Philippine nationalist. In either case, Bundy stated the goal remained to same: "forward movement in solving the Philippines' badly neglected internal problems."[15]

As with Macapagal, Marcos promised to help the United States in fighting communism in the Pacific. In the weeks and months after the election, the U.S. government believed Marcos could play a leading role in East Asian political affairs, but was unsure of his policies. A post-election analysis stated that "what Marcos really believes in, what his goals are, and how he proposes to go about achieving them, are largely matters of conjecture." However, "there are those who assert that era of corruption under Garcia will return in magnified form." But "President Macapagal recently observed, as earlier reported, that Marcos was brilliant but unscrupulous, but that great responsibility might sober him." Regardless, "Marcos' first preoccupation must inevitably be with domestic affairs in view of facts that government till may be almost empty, that the stability of peso must be defended, and that severe demands are imposed on administration by rapidly growing population." *The New York Times* reported that "Manila intellectuals and government officials are saying privately, "this may be our last chance." Vice President Hubert Humphrey

---

[14] *FRUS, 1964-1968, Vol. XXVI,* Document 304, Joint Chiefs to McNamara, March 13, 1965; Document 305, Cooper to Bundy, March 29, 1965; Document 306, Bundy and Thomson to Johnson, June 1, 1965; Document 307, Bundy to Johnson, July 7, 1965; Document 308, Rusk to Amembassy Manila, July 7, 1965; Document 309, Blair to Rusk, July 9, 1965; Document 310, Macapagal to Johnson, July 24, 1965; Document 311, Rusk to Amembassy Manila, August 26, 1965.

[15] *FRUS, 1964-1968, Vol. XXVI,* Document 315, "The 1965 Philippine Election," October 27, 1965.

attended Marcos' inauguration, and reported to Johnson and Rusk that "Marcos is strong, confident and competent. Clearly a good bet as a reliable friend of the US and has potential to become strong leader in Asian world." Humphrey followed up several days later that "we need Asians to take the lead in Asian affairs. Best asset to US is strong Asian leader, who is our friend, who understands us, and is prepared to weld Asians together toward objectives that coincide with our aims. Suggest we bet on Ferdinand Marcos of the Philippines as having good potential for this kind of tough, charismatic leadership." [16]

At the same time, the news media focused on tensions in the relationship between the two countries. *The New York Times* worried the relationship was "deteriorating." The *Times* noted the younger generation had no memory of the Second World War or America liberating the Philippines from Japanese oppression. They wanted a new and more equal relationship. Several weeks later *The Times* claimed that "the leading newspapers have carried on a prolonged and inflammatory anti-American campaign." At the same time, "the steady retailing of the anti-American line by radio commentators, who are heard throughout the archipelago, has been far more damaging." *U.S. News & World Report* claimed that Indonesian leader Sukarno was behind the deteriorating relationship. "It was Indonesian money, poured into some sectors of the Philippine press, that created the wave of anti-Americanism." Sukarno took advantage of "sentiment for a Philippine 'national identity' linked with but not dependent on the United States." *U.S. News* in June noted "anti-Americanism is on the rise," and it resulted from "professional 'ultranationalists,'" "the many newspaper columnists and radio commentators who give the Philippine audience a daily fare of anti-American diatribes," "a small group of agitators" taking their cue from Mao Zedong and Sukarno. Richard Butwell, writing in *United Asia,* claimed that many of the tensions developed from the reality that, for Filipinos, "the United States is the most important foreign nation," but they have difficulty accepting that "they are not America's number one ally." As the presidential campaign was drawing to a close, *The New York Times* again noted "in its search for

[16] *FRUS, 1964-1968, Vol. XXVI,* Document 318, Blair to Rusk, November 26, 1965; *The New York Times,* "Marcos termed 'last chance' for democracy in Philippines," November 22, 1965, p. 2; *FRUS, 1964-1968, Vol. XXVI,* Document 320, Smith to Johnson, December 31, 1965; Document 322, Valenti to Johnson, January 4, 1966.

a new Asian identity, the Philippine Republic is drifting away from the United States." [17]

Despite these early hopes, an NIE in February 1966 concluded that the Philippines faced the same challenges that too many other American allies in the region faced. "Though its problems are not critical in the short term, the Philippines confronts many of the same underlying difficulties that beset other states of Southeast Asia--land hunger in the countryside; unemployment in the cities; and a grinding poverty for the overwhelming majority of the people. The situation is aggravated by widespread violence and lawlessness, and by corruption in government. Hopes for change are now focused on the incoming President Marcos, a capable and forceful man. Marcos seems aware of the country's problems, but it is not yet clear how effectively he will cope with them. If he fails to reduce economic discontent and to achieve greater honesty and efficiency in governmental affairs, public disillusionment is likely to grow and political stability could be seriously undermined."[18]

The consequent "National Policy Paper for the Philippines" restated America's purpose in the Philippines. "By almost every criterion for policy development, the Philippines constitutes an area of key interest of the US in Asia. While the Philippines since independence has achieved much, it again faces some very serious problems." "To preserve the Philippines as an independent and democratic nation, friendly to the US and maintaining a foreign and defense policy in general alignment with our own," the National Policy Paper proposed the U.S. government "promote motivated and dynamic Filipino leadership, which is dedicated to serve the Philippine national interest and which is convinced of the abiding interest of the US in the survival of a free and democratic Philippines," "persevere in helping Philippine efforts to achieve self-sustaining economic growth," "work toward a revised and modernized bilateral trade and investment relationship with the Philippines, in which the element of partnership replaces that of outworn special consideration or advantage for either side," "encourage and assist development of

[17] *The New York Times,* "Filipinos looking anew at U.S. ties," January 17, 1965, p. 10; *NYT,* "Why Filipinos demonstrate," January 31, 1965, p. E10; *U.S. News & World Report,* "Meddling by Sukarno – Why Filipinos turn against U.S.," January 11, 1965, p. 59; *USN&WR,* "Now: an old friend turning away from U.S.," June 14, 1965, p. 68;Richard Butwell, "The United States and the Philippines," *United Asia, Vol. 17, No. 4, July-August 1965,* pp. 301-304; *NYT,* "Philippines seeks new identity," November 21, 1965, p. 1.

[18] *FRUS, 1964-1968, Vol. XXVI,* Document 323, NIE 56-66, "Prospect for the Philippines," February 17, 1966.

greater Philippine capabilities for external and especially for internal defense," and "seek to make the presence of our military bases more palatable and secure for the longer term."[19]

It soon became clear that Marcos wanted a tremendous amount of American aid, while Washington was reluctant to be so generous. In late February 1966, Johnson invited Marcos to visit Washington. In early May James Thomson shared his view of the situation with Walt Rostow. "You should know (and at some point the President should know) that the problem of a Marcos visit is becoming more complex." "Marcos is acting more and more like a Philippine President than the tough and far- sighted New Dealer/pragmatist that he appeared to be earlier this year." "In brief, Marcos does not want to come to Washington unless he can return with some highly tangible goodies." Rostow wrote Johnson in mid-May that Marcos wanted clear and substantial "areas of agreement" before coming to Washington, while the State Department believed there remained need for "extensive economic dialogue."[20]

The news media probed the Marcos presidency and the resulting Philippine-United States relationship. *Time* stated "every incoming President of the Philippines has taken office with a vow to clean up the corruption that plagues the nation, and the country's new leader is no exception." It claimed that "Marcos has got off to an impressive early start." A few weeks later, *The New York Times* approvingly reported that Marcos intended to commit Philippine troops to Vietnam. He told his nation that "it is essential that the relentless pressure of Communist aggression in Vietnam be stopped." By April *U.S. News & World Report* believed that "a new government in the Philippines is raising hopes for stronger and friendlier relations between the U.S. and its former possession." It described Marcos as a "young, vigorous and bold." Emmet John Hughes writing in *Newsweek* found Marcos "activist and pragmatic in temper." *The Journal of Commerce* cited Philippine government officials who declared that "high interest levels and a tightening credit squeeze in major world capital markets are retarding the industrial and agricultural growth of the Philippines as well as most other developing nations."[21]

---

[19] *FRUS, 1964-1968, Vol. XXVI,* Document 325, Bundy to Rusk, February 23, 1966.

[20] *FRUS, 1964-1968, Vol. XXVI,* Document 326, State to Amembassy Manila, February 25, 1966; Document 330, Rostow to Johnson, May 11, 1966.

[21] *Time,* "Crusade in Manila," February 4, 1966, www.time.com/time/magazine/article/0,9171,898939,00.html; *The New York Times,* "Philippine President seeks to send troops to Vietnam," February 19, 1966,

The issues all came together during a state visit in mid-September 1966. Several weeks before Marcos' visit, James Thomson wrote Walt Rostow. "Finance Minister Eduardo Romualdez is here to push for more money, in one form or another, as icing for the Marcos State Visit. His appearance coincides with that of at least two other Filipinos in pursuit of the same thing: Ben Romualdez (Marcos' brother-in-law and probable ambassador to the US) who has just arrived to do some high level pushing, and Mapa-&-Melchor, who are key financial advisors." "*The fundamental problem is one of Fil expectations:* Marcos has been led to believe, both by visiting Americans and by his own people, that a) his dynamic potential as a leader and b) his success on aid to Vietnam will assure him a very big pay-off when he comes to Washington. (The figures we have heard tend toward $100 million in economic aid in the coming year, and $500 million over five years.)." "Fact of the matter is that Marcos does have promise, and that he did belatedly deliver on Vietnam aid (and at considerable political cost)--but also that the Fil economy is in dreadful condition and Fil performance has been terrible." Ten days later Donald Ropa of the NSC Staff wrote Rostow that "setting Marcos' state visit continues an established ritual for a Philippine president during his term of office. Its two major elements: Ceremonial reaffirmation of friendship ties developed during the colonial period and second world war; Confirmation of a "special relationship" with the U.S. In return for their loyal support, Phils expect special consideration for their material needs. Every Philippine president feels he must bring home tangible evidence of the benefits of our association." The next day Rostow wrote Johnson about a Philippine technical assistance mission serving as an advance for a Marcos state visit. "It came with inflated expectations of new U.S. bilateral aid for the new Philippine development plan and implied that a worthwhile Marcos State Visit hinged on fulfillment of their expectations." On the eve of Marcos' visit, Johnson decided that, despite Marcos wanting US military assistance out of proportion to the needs and ability of Philippine armed forces to use it effectively, the U.S. would continue to provide reasonable aid, the only addition to support the battalions of Philippine engineers going to Vietnam. William Jorden gave President Johnson alternatives to appeal to Marcos, including proposing a Philippine astronaut, a pilot program for

---

p. 4; *U.S. News & World Report,* "U.S. and Philippines – drawing closer," April 4, 1966, p. 84; *Newsweek,* "Emmet John Hughes on the Philippines and its president," April 25, 1966, pp. 51-52; *The Journal of Commerce,* "World Credit Squeeze is Reported Retarding Philippines Development," October 7, 1966, in Lyndon Baines Johnson Library, Papers of Henry H. Fowler, Box 40, International Countries: Philippine Islands.

typhoon damage control, a regional military defense college, a regional development institute, and two others that Jorden dismissed after fleshing them out. When Marcos visited Washington, Johnson discussed their respective visions for Asia and the role of the Philippines. When discussion turned to specific matters, Johnson was less fulsome, and Marcos returned to Manila without securing guarantees of dramatically increased assistance programs. *The New York Times* reported the U.S. government had announced "'a heavy increase in its economic assistance to that country [Philippines]." *Time Times* quoted government officials that cited U.S. officials who described it as a "sharp upgrading of the priority the United States attaches to its relations with the Philippines." *Time* reported "the nation last week offered a vibrant welcome to an Asian statesman who stands to lose more than an argument if the U.S. reneges on its commitments across the Pacific." *The Economist* reported that Marcos told the Philippines people that his visits to Washington and Tokyo resulted in "a billion dollars in aid from abroad."[22]

The following year the return of the Huks threatened the stability of the Philippines. The Huks had been taking advantage of the Philippines' uneven economic situation, especially in the southern islands, and had regained a measure of power through calculated violence against selected targets. In March 1965, *The New York Times* reported that the Huks "appear to be in their second rising." The Huks "grew from an archaic and oppressive land tenure system, which the Communists have been able to exploit." In mid-April 1967, the CIA concluded that Marcos had showed "little more than good intentions on the domestic front," continuing the economic difficulties that led to peasant support of the Huk movement. The analysis warned that "During the past 20 months, both the strength and the activities of the Huks have shown a marked increase ." "Among

---

[22] *FRUS, 1964-1968, Vol. XXVI,* Document 333, Thomson to Rostow, August 1, 1966; Document 334, Ropa to Rostow, August 11, 1966; Document 335, Rostow to Johnson, August 12, 1966; Document 339, Rostow to Johnson, September 9, 1966; Document 340, Rostow to Ball, September 11, 1966; Document 341, Rostow to Johnson, September 121, 1966 and attachment from Jorden. See Document 343, Rostow to Johnson, September 14, 1966; Document 344, Memorandum for the Record, September 15, 1966; and Document 345, Editorial note for details on the discussions; *The New York Times,* "Americans widen aid to Philippines," September 16, 1966, pp. 1, 3; *Time,* "Formula from the Philippines," September 23, 1968, www.time/com/time/archive; *The Economist,* "The Philippines: Marcos polishes his image," October 22, 1966, p. 358; see also LBJL, Papers of Henry H. Fowler, Box 72, International Classified Material – Countries, Philippine Islands, "Philippines: General Economic Background, undated [likely September 1966].

the peasantry the Huks maintain a "Robin Hood" image of assisting the poor ." Peasant support for the Huks "can be expected to continue as long as local landlords block reform efforts, as corruption by officials diverts funds from development projects, and as legal redress remains slow and one-sided." *The New York Times* agreed that the Huks "is believed to have already achieved working political control of Central Luzon." A month later *The Times* quoted Marcos who said that "the Communist threat in the Philippines was 'as grave now as it was in the early nineteen-fifties.'" Worryingly, in mid-1968, *The New York Times* reported clashes between Christian and Moslem Filipinos that presaged, perhaps, more challenges for the government.[23]

Despite other concerns, the government in Washington was most concerned with expanding the Philippine economy. *The New York Times* reported that "the Philippines economy in the last two months has been eagerly awaiting a financial bonanza represented – in the hopes of President Ferdinand E. Marcos at least – by massive infusions of American aid." But "Marcos and Philippine economic planners are beginning to suspect that neither manna from Washington nor a windfall from Tokyo may materialize." Two months later, *The Times* cited Marcos as "fighting a critical battle to overcome the complex social and economic problems impeding the economic and political development of the republic." The embassy in Manila reported to the State Department in early January that "the manufacturing industry has been employing a smaller proportion of the gainfully employed," "employment is not increasing as fast as the population growth," "unemployment and underemployment is increasing in the Philippines," "consumer prices have been rising much faster than wages," and "communism has grown and consolidated its influence" – certainly not a ringing endorsement of the Marcos administration. Three weeks later the embassy provided an assessment of Marcos' first year in office. "The progress of the Philippine economy remains disappointingly slow, and there are signs of growing disillusionment with the whole political and economic structure of the Philippines." Four weeks later the embassy added that "the Marcos Administration has concluded its first year in office with little noticeable

[23] *The New York Times,* "The Huks bring terror to the Philippines," March 14, 1965, p. SM28; *FRUS, 1964-1968, Vol. XXVI,* Document 348, "The Huk Resurgence in the Philippines," April 19, 1967; *The New York Times,* "Huks regaining Luzon strength," April 16, 1967, p. 11; *NYT,* "Huks' gains cited as grave threat," May 14, 1967, p. 14; *NYT,* "Christian-Moslem battle kills 26 in the Philippines," August 18, 1968, p. 45; *NYT,* "Philippines denies report of Christian-Moslem battle," August 19, 1968, p. 4.

impact on the southern provinces of the Philippines." In early August 1967 Marshall Wright of the National Security Council staff wrote Rostow to discuss qualities needed in a new ambassador to the Philippines. He noted "The Philippine Republic is stagnant. There is practically no increase in the per capita GNP. The government has failed lamentably to come to grips with the problems in economic and social development. Both the government and the society are shot through with a pervasive and paralyzing corruption. There is a revived subversive Huk movement which is serious, though not yet critical." *U.S. News & World Report* noted "the people are deeply divided – rich against poor. A high birth rate is wiping out economic gains, and a breakdown in law and order is reaching across the nation." [24]

By the end of December the CIA prepared a memorandum, ""Philippine President Marcos' Problems at Midterm." "The problems he faces are serious ones, however, involving the strains of rural poverty and urban unemployment, rising lawlessness, and growing pressures from an emerging generation alienated from the tradition of their parents and seeking a more distinct national identity." The CIA analysis zeroed in on the heart of the problem: "A vast and growing gap exists between the wealth of the few and the poverty of the many. The peasant farmer's subsistence-level existence has been perpetuated by backward agricultural methods, inadequate irrigation, and high loss from uncontrolled pests, particularly in the important rice-growing areas. Initiative for improvements has been discouraged by a feudalistic system of land tenure and by a traditional suspicion of innovation. Progress in land reform and rural development has been generally slow, hampered both by bureaucratic inefficiency and by the interference of landlords who are powerful supporters of both major parties." The CIA analysis noted the role of the Huk movement: "Huk influence is sustained in part by the collaboration of local officials and politicians who recognize the Huk ability to control the vote, in great part through intimidation. To some extent, the Huks have also been able to project a Robin Hood image among peasants disgruntled over bad government and impoverishment." The report concluded

[24] *The New York Times,* "Manila seeks capital in U.S. and Japan," January 20, 1967, p. 55; *NYT,* "Marcos optimistic on solving social ills plaguing Philippines," March 13, 1967, p. 5; NARA, RG 59, CFPF, Box 2428, Pol 15-1 PHIL, 1/1/67, Amembassy Manila to State, #1-449, January 5, 1967; same folder, Amembassy Manila to State, A-540, January 29, 1967; same box, Pol 15-1 PHIL, 2/1/67, Amconsul Cebu to State, A-29, February 23, 1967; *FRUS, 1964-1968, Vol. XXVI,* Document 353, Wright to Rostow, August 2, 1967; *U.S. News & World Report,* "An Asian ally of the U.S. that's heading into trouble," November 13, 1967, p. 112.

somewhat ominously that "Unless the peasant farmer and the urban slum dweller are persuaded that the present system can respond to their needs, their growing apathy could in time turn to rebellion."[25]

The following June there was little improvement as a new National Intelligence Estimate made clear. In advance of the new NIE, George Denney of State's Intelligence and Research division wrote Secretary Rusk that "the Philippines is faced by a host of serious problems, among them widespread poverty and unemployment, rising lawlessness, organized smuggling, corruption from the lowest to the highest levels, a high rate of population growth, an ineffective civil service and low agricultural productivity." Giving Marcos credit for some actions, Denney opined that "the question remains, however, whether rice, roads, schools, and fiscal and monetary reforms are enough to reverse the growing gap between the very few rich and the masses of poor." Similarly, the NIE concluded that "the Philippine political system, despite the trappings of democracy, is dominated by a wealthy and conservative oligarchy, largely unresponsive to the economic and social needs of the vast bulk of the population." When the controversy over Sabah arose again, U.S. officials believed it was a means for Marcos to distract the Philippine people from their nation's real problems.[26]

Thailand's position on the front lines of the Cold War in Asia obviously affected Thai-U.S. relations. In 1959, Hanoi formed groups 559, 759, and 959 to establish land and sea routes to South Vietnam as well as to control the strategic Plain of Jars in Laos. As the fighting expanded into Laos and as North Vietnamese troops moved through southern Laos and eastern Cambodia, Bangkok sought assurances of American determination to win the fight on its doorstep in Southeast Asia. Thai officials worried that this expansion could easily spread to their borders. American officials shared that concern, but also encouraged Thai economic development to maintain support of Thai peasants.

Security issues figured prominently in Bangkok and Washington. U.S. officials realized that "there is some uncertainty among Thai officials that the Kennedy Administration will make clear its strong position against Communism, particularly in Southeast Asia." Within a month of taking office, Kennedy Administration officials worked on an aid package that

---

25 *FRUS, 1964-1968, Vol. XXVI,* Document 362, "Philippine President Marcos' Problems at Midterm," December 7, 1967.

26 NARA, RG 59, CFPF, Box 2428, Pol 15-PHIL, 1/1/67, Denney to Rusk, June 7, 1968; *FRUS, 1964-1968, Vol. XXVI,* Document 367, NIE 56-68, "Prospects for the Philippines," June 20, 1968.

would increase "MAP support up to about 80% of Thai armed strength," and also increase Thai equipment and weaponry. Rusk in turn wrote Kennedy to recommend a letter to Field Marshal Sarit Thanarat, the Thai Prime Minister, "reiterating our intention fully to honor our obligations as an ally and friend," cognizant that Sarit "continues to be gravely concerned over the threat to Thailand's security posed by the troubled situation in Laos and the resulting prospect of a southward thrust of Communist power in Southeast Asia." A month later Rusk cabled the US ambassador in Bangkok, U. Alexis Johnson, to "inform Sarit [that] you [have been] specifically authorized by [the] President to endorse in his name private assurances of US support of Thailand contained in President Eisenhower's letter of last November." Ambassador Kenneth T. Young who followed Johnson wrote Rusk in late May 1961 that "Thailand is not Laos; it is a united, fundamentally stable nation, economically viable and making steady, if slow, progress in improving [the] welfare [of its] people."[27]

The situation in Laos highlighted concerns. By mid-March 1961 Rusk was issuing assurances that "Communist reaction against Thailand in form air strikes at Udorn or Takli would require military response by US." "Posture and capability [of] US forces in Far East, including ability of [the] Seventh Fleet to retaliate swiftly against North Viet-Nam, constitute effective deterrent to Communist action against Thailand." Rusk then wrote Sarit that "Thailand can count on the full military support of the United States in the event that present measures of Thai-United States cooperation and assistance to the Royal Lao Government should result in a Communist armed attack on Thailand." Several days later Kennedy told Thai Ambassador Visutr Arthayukti that "the United States Government is prepared to support Thailand against the dangers it faces on such a long exposed frontier." *Time* magazine began knocking down the dominoes: "if the finger of Laos goes, so too goes the rest of the hand: a complete Communist takeover would endanger Burma, Thailand, Cambodia and South Viet Nam, all of which share Laotian borders. With those countries under the Red flag, India would be dangerously outflanked—pinned down to the east, as it is already bedeviled to the north by Red China. Indonesia,

---

[27] John F. Kennedy Library, National Security File, Country File, Box 163, Thailand, General, 1/61-5/61, "Memorandum: Thai Questions on Southeast Asia Relations," February 6, 1961; *FRUS, 1961-1963, Vol. XXIII,* Document 396, Landon to Rostow, February 16, 1961; p. 840; Document 397, Rusk to Kennedy, February 24, 1961, p. 841; Document 398, Rusk to Embassy in Thailand, March 21, 1961, p 843; for a copy of the "Aide- Mémoire" to Sarit, see Document 399, Attachment, April 3, 1961, pp. 845-846; Document 410, Embassy in Thailand to State, May 27, 1961, p. 863.

already softened by Communist incursions, would be easy plucking. Malaya and Singapore could become steppingstones for further Communist expansion, to the ultimate peril of Australia and New Zealand."[28]

Thai Prime Minister Sarit feared Kennedy might waver in Laos. Rusk wrote Kennedy about a message from Sarit that "reflect[s] a genuine and deep concern over the effect of U.S. decisions and actions on the security of Thailand." Rusk felt Sarit merited "a personal response from you." As late as September, Young cabled Rusk that Thai leaders still "are concerned that US does not publicly identify Southeast Asia more vigorously as [a] critical sector [of] free world which we [are] equally prepared [to] defend."[29]

The Kennedy Administration reiterated its assurances of support. When Lyndon Johnson traveled to Southeast Asia in Spring 1961, he assured Sarit that President Kennedy "explicitly authorized" the stationing of SEATO or U.S. forces in Thailand. Soon thereafter Kennedy wrote Sarit about "my full appreciation of the understandable concern which you and your countrymen feel over developments in Southeast Asia." Kennedy assured Sarit he would not accept "concessions" that would "result in a progressive Communist takeover of the kingdom." It appeared perhaps that Vice President Johnson went too far, and officials in Washington noted that "the character of the dilemma we face in this case is that, partly as a result of the wobbly situation in Thailand resulting from the situation in Laos and partly because of the expectations developed by the Vice President's trip, we are faced by the political need to provide immediate evidence of our support." These officials proposed "endors[ing] the concept of deterring guerrilla warfare in Northern Thailand through a series of economic, political and military measures" while leaving the details to the future. Robert Johnson wrote Walt Rostow of the need "to deal with the 'morbid fear gripping the Thais.'" By July Rusk wrote Young to approach Prime Minister Sarit on behalf of President Kennedy that the "central objective of US policy in Thailand is to assist RTG [Royal Thai Government] to increase national capability to defend Thailand's independence and sovereignty," increase safety, stability, and

---

[28] *FRUS, 1961-1963, Vol. XXIII,* Rusk to Embassy in Thailand, March 21, 1961, p. 843; Document 399, Johnson to Rusk, April 3, 1961, pp. 845-6; Document 400, Memorandum of Conversation, April 6, 1961, p. 847; *Time,* "Laos: Background for Battle," March 31, 1961, http://www.time.com/time/magazine/article/0,9171,872162,00.html.

[29] *FRUS, 1961-1963, Vol. XXIII,* Document 402, Rusk to Kennedy, April 17, 1961, p. 849; JFK Library, NSF, Box 163, Thailand, General, 8/61-9/61, Bangkok to SecState, #449, September 24, 1961.

economic status of strategically important northeast," and "accelerate development of Thai assets and resources for self-sustaining economic and social growth."[30]

The US military also wanted to use bases in northeast Thailand to contest the expanding guerrilla conflicts in Laos and South Vietnam. American officials considered stationing forces in Thailand, as the Deputy National Security Assistant, Walt Rostow, wrote President Kennedy to consider sending a U.S. engineering battalion, increasing U.S. training assistance for Thai armed forces, and/or training U.S. forces with Thai forces on a rotational basis. [31]

The decision to "neutralize" Laos did not please the Thai government, which viewed the decision as retreating before Communist aggression. *Time* reflected the disappointment. "Almost visibly, the U.S. was falling back in Southeast Asia. Emerging from top level meetings, U.S. officials talked not of Laos, but of South Viet Nam and Thailand. Obviously, the concern now was to bolster these countries, who will be acutely exposed when Laos is abandoned to a Communist-dominated neutrality." *Time* did report that "Thailand is in no immediate danger. In the event of trouble, strongman Sarit can call on a 90,000-man army, well-trained and equipped by the U.S. But the Thais, who wanted to send troops to Laos (and actually did beef up the Laotian army with a few volunteers), are angry at what they consider U.S. softness. Officials in Bangkok hinted that Sarit might take the precaution of trading in his pro-Western stand for a more neutralist line."[32]

To demonstrate firmness, the Kennedy Administration increased military and economic assistance for Thailand. Ambassador Young informed Sarit that the United States was committed "to improving the livelihood of the people," for "national unity and social progress are the surest ways in the long run to help prevent Communist expansion in Southeast Asia." Vice President Johnson promised additional aid during his visit, and as late as November 1961 Sarit told Young that he "had been

---

[30] *FRUS, 1961-1963, Vol. XXIII,* Document 406, State to Hong Kong Consulate, May 14, 1961, p. 854; Document 407, Johnson to Bundy, Attachment, May 15, 1961, pp. 855-6; Document 411, Johnson to Rostow, June 23, 1961, p. 868; JFK Library, NSF, Box 163, Thailand, General, 6/61-7/61, "Analysis of Ambassador Young's Report," June 30, 1961; *FRUS, 1961-1963, Vol. XXIII,* Document 414, State to Embassy in Thailand, July 8, 1961, p. 875.

[31] *FRUS, 1961-1963, Vol. XXIII,* Document 418, Rostow to Kennedy, October 2, 1961, p. 886.

[32] *Time,* "Falling Back," May 12, 1961, http://www.time.com/time/magazine/article/0,9171,869872,00.html.

waiting for announcement [of] increased US military and economic assistance program since Vice President left Bangkok." Young noted a bigger issue: Sarit was ill and needed surgery, while Thanat was tired and thus there was a potential leadership vacuum at the top. Kennedy then sent Sarit a letter that "we share your sense of urgency regarding Thailand's development," and "I believe there exists a firm basis for accelerated joint efforts to ensure Thailand's economic and social progress." Kennedy promised increased economic aid, and in January 1962 a letter from Kennedy to Sarit reiterated American promises of economic aid, noting "Thailand has a great potential for economic growth" and "I am pleased you have placed great emphasis on long-range economic planning."[33]

In early October Thai Foreign Minister Thanat Khoman visited Washington. Rostow wrote Kennedy that "the principal problem on Thanat's mind is the inadequacy of the U.S. commitment to the defense of Thailand embodied in the SEATO treaty." In meeting with Rusk, Thanat indicated that Thailand "is not against stationing of foreign forces in Thailand providing there is a function for them to perform." Rusk indicated that, given "the requirement of negotiation and Senate ratification," he wanted to work out Thai-U.S. security arrangements through SEATO rather than a bilateral treaty. The next day President Kennedy told Thanat that "our concern at the security situation in Southeast Asia was equal to our concern over Berlin." Thanat in turn expressed his government's concern for SEATO, and "its failure to act in the Laotian crisis. The discussion about SEATO dominated the meeting, and neither Kennedy nor Undersecretary U Alexis Johnson could ease Thanat's concerns.[34]

A Special National Intelligence Estimate helped make clear the challenge for American foreign policy. SNIE 52-61 concluded that "Thai leaders are now seeking concrete evidence of US determination and ability to halt the Communist advance in Southeast Asia." The SNIE assumed that "Communist policy toward Thailand will probably be directed at moving Thailand away from close association with the US and toward a

[33] JFK Library, NSF Box 163, Thailand, General, Aid & Economy, 10/61, "Memorandum for the Prime Minister," undated; *FRUS, 1961-1963, Vol. XXIII,* Document 421, Embassy in Thailand to State, November 7, 1961, p. 894; JFK Library, NSF Box 163, Thailand, General, 11/61, State to Amembassy Bangkok, #815, November 30, 1961; JFK Library, NSF Box 163A, Thailand, General, 1/62, State to Amembassy Bangkok., #1006,. January 11, 1962.

[34] *FRUS, 1961-1963, Vol. XXIII,* Document 418, Rostow to Kennedy, October 2, 1961, p. 886; Document 419, Memorandum of Conversation, October 2, 1961, pp. 887-8; Document 420, Memorandum of Conversation, October 3, 1961, pp. 890-1.

neutralist position." While the SNIE discussed the threat that nearby Chinese, North Vietnamese and Pathet Lao forces posed, and Bangkok's need for reassurance, it made no mention of economic issues and the appeal of Asian communism to suffering peasant masses.[35]

The deteriorating situation in Laos in Spring 1962 added to the pressure on the Kennedy Administration. In January, Rusk wrote Young that "we all [are] seriously concerned by Thailand's attitude [on] this issue." Rusk continued that "we are determined [to] press ahead with our present course as long as we see [a] reasonable chance [of] achieving [an] acceptable peace settlement." Rusk asked Young to re-explain Washington's position and to conclude that "we have not changed our policies on Laos." Two weeks later, Rusk against wrote Young that "this [is] clearly a case where we reach different conclusions from [the] same facts." Still, given Sarit's "evidently sincere concern for Thai security, we consider he is entitled to fullest possible assurances re US support for Thailand" in case the Laotian proposal fails to hold. Rusk again cabled Young in early February that "you might wish [to] remind RTG that as evidence [of] our good faith and determination [to] safeguard Thailand we have in [the] past raised possibility stationing US combat troops in Thailand but this [is] not acceptable to RTG." A visit by Attorney General Robert Kennedy did little to ease Thai concerns. After the visit, Sarit met with Young and "criticized the U.S. position in Laos" and argued that "the South Vietnam flank (i.e., Laos) is not being protected but instead is being given over to the Communists who will continue to use it as a route into South Vietnam for their troops." He suggested a two-pronged attack into Laos from Thailand and South Vietnam, and Young cabled Rusk that "needless to say, the discussion was heated."[36]

In early March Foreign Minister Thanat Khoman visited Washington and noted Thailand's preference for a bilateral treaty with the United States "similar to that which the US has with The Philippines and several other Far Eastern countries." Premier Sarit, concerned about Laos and South Vietnam, sent Thanat to the American capital for the five days of

---

[35] Lyndon Baines Johnson Library, National Security File, National Intelligence Estimates, Box 7, 52, Thailand, SNIE 52-61, "Thailand's Security Problems and Prospects," 13 December 1961, pp. 1-5.

[36] *FRUS, 1961-1963, Vol. XXIII* Document 422, State to Embassy in Thailand, January 8, 1962, p. 896; Document 424, State to Embassy in Thailand, January 23, 1962, p. 901; Document 427, State to Embassy in Thailand, February 4, 1962, p. 907; see Document 431 for a summary of Robert Kennedy's visit with Sarit, Embassy in Thailand to State, February 20, 1962, pp. 913-4; Document 432, Memorandum for the Record, February 26, 1962, pp. 915-6.

meetings. The resulting joint statement quoted Secretary Rusk as "reaffirm[ing] that the United States regards the preservation of the independence and integrity of Thailand as vital to the national interest of the United States and to world peace," and further promised to "aid Thailand, its ally and historic friend, in resisting Communist aggression and subversion." Sarit was pleased with the communiqué, promising to "double his armed forces," to fulfill his obligation.[37]

Stationing a U.S. army group in Thailand and a naval battle group off shore helped to reassure the Thais. In mid-May the situation was seriously deteriorating in Laos, and senior officials recommended that Kennedy "move the Seventh Fleet task force to the Gulf of Siam and send the 1,000-man U.S. Army battle group from Korat to the Nong Khai near the Thai border with Laos." Thus Rusk cabled Young to "request from Sarit permission to land and deploy in Thailand following U.S. troops," with a variety of missions "to give clear indication [of] US intentions [to] carry out commitments [to] assist in [the] defense [of] Thailand." However, Kennedy told advisors "that he wished to retain the element of reversibility in all military actions." Rusk cabled Young the next day that "purpose of troop movements is to reinforce position and morale of Thailand and to send message to Moscow that major breach of cease fire [in Laos] could be dangerous business." *Time* magazine reported that "Bangkok was barely awake when the marines landed. Wearing canvas-covered helmets and fatigues, burdened with rifles and full field packs, men of the 3rd Battalion, 9th U.S. Marines, walked ashore from two U.S. transports." "It was all business." *Time* further informed readers that "The Marine detachments had been rushed to Thailand to help protect the vital left bank of the Mekong River from the Communist menace." Within several weeks, Ambassador Young cabled Secretary Rusk that reporters already were asking "how long US forces will stay in Thailand and what will be the circumstances permitting the departure." In July senior US officials considered the situation in Thailand and General Harkin and

[37] See JFK Library, NSF Box 163A, Thailand, General, Thanat-Khoman Briefing Book, 3/2-3/5/62, "Scope Paper," noting "recent events in Southeast Asia, particularly Laos, have shaken Thai confidence in SEATO and sapped Thai faith in the efficacy of existing US assurances;" the Scope Paper noted that "we will cite what we are doing in Viet-Nam as evidence of the seriousness of our intentions to assist those countries threatened by indirect aggression which have the will to resist;" *FRUS, 1961-1963, Vol. XXIII,* Document 433, Memorandum of Conversation, March 2, 1962, pp. 918-920; JFK Library, State to Amembassy Bangkok, #1307, March 2, 1962; *Newsweek,* "Southeast Asia: Vulnerable Ally," March 19, 1962, pp. 48-9.

Admiral Harry Felt "expressed the view we should get our forces out of Thailand as soon as possible" to which "McNamara and Ambassador Young agreed." U. Alexis Johnson feared "pulling out US forces had political implications" and reserved the right to discuss the situation with Secretary Rusk. McNamara wrote William Bundy that since "Rusk believes that Sarit would oppose withdrawal of the battle group from Thailand at this time," "I agreed to leave the group or its replacement in Thailand, at least for the present." In October, Foreign Minister Thanat Kohman told Rusk and McNamara that "US forces have created [a] highly favorable impression in Thailand." But he also claimed that "some Asian states are accusing Thailand of being [an] 'occupied' country."[38]

Until late 1963, there was stress in the relationship, and then within two weeks of each other, Kennedy was assassinated in Dallas, Texas and Sarit died in Bangkok. When the Thai ambassador, Visutr Arthayukti, asked to meet with Kennedy, William Brubeck recommended to National Security Advisor McGeorge Bundy that the President emphasize "our firm actions in Thailand and South Viet-Nam to protect interests we regard as vital to our own." In September, Michael Forrestal of the National Security Council Staff wrote Kennedy to explain why "Sarit has become disenchanted with U.S. policy." He noted that Sarit "has become angry at us for not having fought his war in Laos for him." Forrestal agreed with Averell Harriman that "we must not permit ourselves to become Sarit's satellite." Several days later Kennedy met with SEATO Secretary General Pote Sarasin and asked him "to tell Sarit that our assurances to Thailand, the Rusk-Thanat communiqué, the movement of US forces, and the planned logistics program all demonstrate our intention to continue to meet our commitments."[39]

---

[38] *FRUS, 1961-1963, Vol. XXIII,* Document 437, Editorial Note, p. 927; Document 438, State to Embassy in Thailand, May 12, 1962, p. 928; Document 439, Editorial Note, p. 929; Document 441, State to Embassy in Thailand, May 13, 1962, p. 931; Document 448, Embassy in Thailand to State, May 24, 1962, p. 941; *Time,* "Guarding the River," May 25, 1962, http://www.time.com/time/magazine/article/0,9171,896227,00.html; *Time,* "On the Line," May 25, 1962, http://www.time.com/time/magazine/article/0,9171,896218,00.html; *FRUS, 1961-1963, Vol. XXIII,* Document 458, Summary of Discussion at Honolulu Conference, July 23-24, 1962, p. 955; Document 461, McNamara to Bundy, August 13, 1962; JFK Library, NSF, Box 164, Thailand, General, 10/62, State to Amembassy Bangkok, #604, October 3, 1962.

[39] JFK Library, NSF Box 164, Thailand, General, 7/1/62-7/15/62, Brubeck to Bundy, undated; *FRUS, 1961-1963, Vol. XXIII,* Document 464, Forrestal to Kennedy, September 24, 1962, p. 965; see also Document 466 in which Forrestal

At the same time, a Central Intelligence Agency analysis of Thai diplomacy drew attention to "the traditional Thai opportunistic approach to foreign relations," although the analysis believed "the Sarit government is seriously considering embarking on an independent policy mainly because of its disenchantment with U.S. policy, especially as [it] applies to Laos and Cambodia." *Time* explained the strained Thai-Cambodian relationship. A Hindu religious shrine lay along the disputed border, which Bangkok took to the International Court of Justice at The Hague. Equally important, "Thailand is always accusing Cambodia of providing jungle bases for Communist guerrillas. Last fall the two nations severed diplomatic relations after Thailand's Soldier Premier Sarit Thanarit likened Cambodia's Prince Norodom Sihanouk to a pig. In a speech, Sihanouk retorted that though he might look like a pig, Sarit was a fatter pig. If soup were made of the two leaders, sneered Sihanouk, the soup made from Sarit would taste better." Another CIA analysis noted that "the United States handling of the Lao crisis, the abrupt positioning of troops in Thailand and their subsequent withdrawal, and the present delivery of arms to Cambodia" have shaken Sarit's confidence in the United States. In mid-October US officials gathered in Honolulu and agreed that "despite uncertainties in current US-Thai relations, the basic relationship is sound and will probably remain so if Thailand respects our power and needs our resources." Officials also agreed that "it is extremely important to develop programs which will get the Government out to the villagers." The State Department prepared a paper on Thailand for President Kennedy which noted that "Thailand is an essential US operational base in Southeast Asia," and "despite friction on specific issues, the basic US-Thai relationship is sound" "as long as Thailand is convinced of our determination to meet our obligations in Southeast Asia." In early June 1963, the State Department informed the Bangkok embassy of a *Washington Post* front page article that quoted Thanat Khoman: "the show put up by the western nations has deeply shaken the confidence of our people." In November soon after Kennedy was assassinated, Harriman wrote the embassy in Bangkok that "cessation [of] US aid to Cambodia at RKG's request may provide US with better foundation than it had previously for gaining Thai cooperation in dealing with Sihanouk."

suggests Kennedy use Pote Sarasin, SEATO's Secretary General, to send a message to Sarit "indicating your personal concern over the difficulties that have arisen," Forrestal to Kennedy, September 28, 1962, p.967; Document 467, Memorandum of Conversation, September 28, 1962, pp. 968-9; *Time,* "In the Jungle of Love," June 29, 1962, http://www.time.com/time/magazine/article/0,9171,897944,00.html.

Harriman continued that "RTG has long criticized US for being too sensitive to Sihanouk's charges and threats." Harriman concluded that "you are instructed to discuss situation at highest effective level convening US views and soliciting cooperation of Thailand as an ally." Several weeks later Hilsman wrote the embassy that it should "express our willingness and desire to continue our programs of economic and military aid to Thailand uninterrupted." Despite the American efforts to please Bangkok, Thanat stated that "the United States needs Thailand more than Thailand needs the United States." Moreover, "Thai foreign policy will be more assertive than in the past." Thanat even said that "the aid program benefits the United States more than it does Thailand."[40]

Cold War issues overshadowed issues of Thai economic development. In May 1961, A month later, *Time* discussed Thai economic development: Premier "Sarit has cut the price of rice, bus fares and school fees, while boosting exports to $400 million and spurring a healthy 5% annual growth in the national production. U.S. aid, $300 million of it military and $241 million economic, has built a crack 100,000-man army, four main highways, 500 bridges and countless other projects, such as the $14 million power plant that Lyndon Johnson inaugurated last week. Sarit's Cabinet, mostly civilian, is probably the most efficient that the country ever had. Last year Sarit allocated as much money for education as for defense. Corruption, which is a tradition in Asia, is at a conventionalized minimum." In Spring 1962 *Time* reported that "Thailand is a going concern. Under Premier Sarit, the government has built up gold and foreign exchange reserves totaling $451 million, has a hard currency based on the baht (worth about 5¢), a steadily rising export trade. More than $700 million in U.S. aid has gone into roads, bridges and hydroelectric power. Sarit sensibly spends as much on education as on defense." In

---

[40] JFK Library, NSF, Box 164, Thailand, General, 9/62, CIA Intelligence Report, Thailand, 17 September 1962; same box, Thailand, General, 10/62, CIA Intelligence Report, 9 October 1962; *FRUS, 1961-1963, Vol. XXIII,* Document 469, Summary of Discussion, October 11, 1962, p. 973; Document 471, Paper Prepared in the Bureau of Far Eastern Affairs," November 7, 1962, p. 980-1; see Document 472, Paper Prepared in the Embassy in Thailand, undated, pp. 984-6, for a longer restatement of the importance of Thailand and noting the need for "social and economic assistance" and seeking to tie "rural Thailand and its remote areas" to the central government in Bangkok; NARA, RG 59, CFPF, Box 4059, Pol 1, Econ Policy, Background, THAI, State to Amembassy Bangkok, #1779, June 3, 1963; Lyndon Baines Johnson Library, NSF Country Files, Box 282, Thailand, Cables, Vol. I, 11/63-11/64, State to Bangkok, #837, November 25, 1963; same folder, State to Bangkok, #909, December 9, 1963; same folder, CIA report, "Thai Foreign Minister's Comments," 31 December 1963.

January 1963, the State Department sent the Bangkok embassy "the proposed A.I.D. [Agency for International Development] strategy statement for Thailand" and asked for comments. The aid program was part of a broader effort "to strengthen Thailand's capacity to remain independent and to achieve economic and social progress." In turn, "a secure, friendly and developing Thailand is essential to our policy of blocking Communist ambitions in Southeast Asia." [41]

Thereafter, as the U.S. involvement in Vietnam increased, it eased worries of Thai leaders. When Lyndon Johnson succeeded John Kennedy, Bangkok observed with great interest. Graham Martin wrote Rusk that the Thai government "is currently reassessing US commitment in SE Asia, and Thai confidence in that commitment has been shaken by [recent] events." Whatever concerns it had over America's commitment to withstanding Chinese and North Vietnamese expansion, Bangkok approved the commitment of American ground, naval, and air forces throughout 1965 and thereafter during the period that America sought to "win" in Vietnam. The embassy's annual political-economic assessment of February 1964 noted "a substantial portion of the peaceful transfer of power [after Sarit's death] is attributable to Thai confidence in their economic prospects and Thai emulation of the U.S. experience in the tragic days of last November." America's stand in Vietnam caused Thai leaders to pay more attention to regional economic development. Confidence in America's commitment and understanding of the need to cooperate with neighbors helped the Thai economy to increase 6% from the prior year. Equally important, gold and foreign exchange reserves of the Bank of Thailand "now stand at approximately 530 million dollars."[42]

As the situation in South Vietnam and Laos deteriorated, American officials considered deploying U.S. ground forces in Thailand. Bangkok wanted assurances from Washington given its perception of increased Chinese pressure; without such reassurances, the Thai government considered seeking accommodation with Beijing. Thus, Assistant

---

[41] *Time,* "Strong & Popular," May 26, 1961; http://www.time.com/time/magazine/article/0,9171,872456,00.html; *Time,* "Guarding the River," May 25, 1962, http://www.time.com/time/magazine/article/0,9171,896227,00.html; JFK Library, NSF Box 164a, Thailand, General, 1-4/63, "Proposed A.I.D. Strategy Statement for Thailand," January 14, 1963,

[42] LBJ Library, NSF Country Files, Box 282, Thailand, Cables, Vol. I, 11/3-11/64, Bangkok to SecState, #1031, January 8, 1964; NARA, RG 59, CFPF, Box 2697, Pol 2-3, Politico-Economic Rpts THAI, 1/1/64, Amembassy Bangkok to State, A-759, February 24, 1964.

Secretary of State Roger Hilsman "suggested such a move [committing U.S. ground forces] as a signal to North Vietnam and China of U.S. willingness to defend its positions in Southeast Asia" in light of the impending collapse of the South Vietnamese government. Rusk approved having an interagency discussion.[43]

Military strategists opposed deployment for political purposes. During the interagency discussion, Defense Department officials stated that "there was no credibility left in the idea of deploying military forces to Thailand." Even so, the Joint Chiefs wrote CINCPAC that "although the JCS have recommended against introduction of ground forces at this time without specific military or political objectives to b e served, we may be directed to do so on very short notice." Forrestal wrote McGeorge Bundy a few weeks later that the Joint Chiefs of Staff "do not favor the deployment of troops anywhere in Asia unless they are assured that it is part of a larger plan to win a war. In short, it is not the political objectives of the move that they question, but the military usefulness." He wrote again in mid-June to argue for the value of stationing U.S. troops in Thailand.[44]

Thai leaders wanted assurances that the U.S. military had a strategy that would impress Chinese and North Vietnamese leaders. In early May, Thai Foreign Minister Thanat Khoman told reporters that "Thailand has been compelled to move toward a more independent foreign policy to insure that the major powers do not sacrifice her vital interests." He noted for Thais to protect themselves "against possible Communist aggression." Several days later, Graham Martin, the US ambassador to Thailand, cabled the State Department that, although the situation in Laos was deteriorating, "Thai leaders have consistently expressed strong reservations on value redeploying US troops to Thailand merely as isolated deterrent measure." They objected "to deployment in absence [of] other firm measures against [the] Communists." Deputy Defense Secretary Peter Solbert wrote

[43] *The New York Times,* "Chinese Pressure Worries Bangkok," January 2, 1964, p. 9; Department of State, *Foreign Relations of the United States, 1964-1968, Volume XXVII, Mainland Southeast Asia, Regional Affairs,* GPO, Washington, DC, 2000, Document 264, Editorial Note. In part, Bangkok was reacting, as did all of Asia, to Paris' decision to transfer recognition to Beijing; see *The New York Times,* "Impact on Asia: The Feeling Grows that China will now Achieve Dominance in Region," January 26, 1964, p. E3. For another expression of Thai outrage at U.S. policy for Laos, see *The New York Times,* "Thai Leader Assails West,: April 24, 1964, p. 3.

[44] *Ibid.,* Document 264; Document 265, Forrestal to Bundy, March 2, 1964; JFK Library, NSF Box 163A, Thailand, General, 6/1-6/15/62, Forrestal to Bundy, June 14, 1964; LBJ Library, NSF Country Files, Box 282, Thailand, Memos, Vol. I, 11/63-11/64, JCS 5107, February 29, 1964.

Michael Forrestal that "a mere 'show of force' in Thailand without a specific objective would not appear to have the proper effect on the Communists." When Secretary Rusk called on Sarit's successor, Prime Minister Thanom Kittikachorn, there was "frequently indirect but persistent Thai probing for indication of future US course of action in Southeast Asia; Thai questions ranged from significance of [the] Sino-Soviet rift to [the] possibility of diversionary activities against ChiComs elsewhere in Asia." Three weeks later, President Johnson wrote Thanom to offer yet another reassurance: "We regard Communist advances in Laos as a threat to the security of the United States as well as that of Thailand. In accordance with this concept, I have authorized Ambassador Martin to open consultations with you looking toward joint Thai-US military planning of measures to be taken in the event of a Communist drive toward the borders of Thailand." A few weeks later the State Department issued a statement "there can be little doubt in the minds of Communist leaders throughout the Far East and the world that we are prepared to help the Vietnamese repel Communist aggression" and that "our support to Thailand is equally clear."[45]

In the months before the Gulf of Tonkin Incident[s], Bangkok and Washington agreed on joint planning for the defense of Thailand. U.S. officials agreed to increase military assistance. Thai military spending was equal to about 2.5% of GNP, and any more would drag the economy. After several months of meetings of U.S. officials and then joint U.S.-Thai talks, the State Department reported that "during Secretary Rusk's visit to Thailand in May, the Prime Minister and Foreign Minister mentioned several times military defense measures which they were planning in the event of a Communist advance toward the Mekong." Subsequent talks in Honolulu agreed that U.S. officials "would undertake consultations with

[45] *The New York Times,* "Thais Say They Must Take a More Independent Line," May 3, 1964, p. 1; *FRUS, 1964-1968, Vol. XXVII,* Document 268, Embassy in Thailand to Department of State, May 4, 1964; Document 269, Solbert to Forrestal, May 16, 1964; Document 272, Rusk to State Department, May 31, 1964; Document 277, Johnson to Thanom, June 18, 1964. After resigning from the State Department, Roger Hilsman told a television audience that "United States ground forces should be stationed in Thailand on a long-term basis to overcome what he called a 'crisis of confidence' in all of Southeast Asia," *The New York Times,* "Hilsman Favors G.I.'s in Thailand," May 26, 1964, p. 3; "U.S. Confident That Reds Grasp Warnings on Asia," June 23, 1964, p. 1.

the Thai on measures to be taken in the event of such a Communist advance."[46]

Military considerations outranked economic needs. In mid-January, *The New York Times* reported that economic development was proceeding so well that the Thai government was concerned with "the need for coordination of effort to prevent duplication and to avoid a conflict of interests." Two months later, *The Times* claimed that "Thailand, or most of it, is a hot, happy land in which nearly everyone has enough to eat without working too hard for it, and where there is minimal interest in politics." General Prapass Charusathiara, Deputy Prime Minister of Thailand, called on President Johnson in late July. Rusk asked Johnson to "congratulate him on the successful Thai approach to the problem of countering subversion and preventing the outbreak of insurgency" by economic and social programs. Prapass described economic development programs in the northeast near the Laotian border "were being carried out to give the people of Thailand a real incentive to fight against communism."[47]

The so-called Gulf of Tonkin Incidents changed the situation. *The New York Times* reported several days later that "the United States retaliatory attacks on North Vietnam have sent shock waves throughout Southeast Asia." Moreover, "Thailand, which has become America's largest and most active ally in Southeast Asia, has officially cheered the United States' stand." Several days later, *The Times* sought to analyze the issues in Southeast Asia: "the pro-Western Governments of Thailand and Malaysia retain power on thin fabrics of stability that might tear under the strain" of an American defeat in South Vietnam. Ambassador Graham Martin cabled Rusk about Thanom's "obvious pleasure with US actions

---

[46] See *FRUS, 1964-1968, Vol. XXVII*, Document 271, Loftus to McNaughton, May 30, 1964, for a discussion of issues on stationing of either U.S. and/or SEATO forces in Thailand and the threat posed by the North Vietnamese and the Pathet Lao; Document 282, Trueheart to Green, August 5, 1964. Interestingly, *The New York Times* reported on the Honolulu meeting in early June that "the highest diplomatic and military officials of the United States gathered here today for the grim and urgent task of finding a means to deny Southeast Asia to Communism *without directly involving the United States in war there"* [emphasis added], "Top U.S. Officials Meeting in Hawaii on Asia Strategy," June 1, 1964, p. 1. *The Times* also reported that "also under consideration is the sending again of several thousand United States servicemen to Thailand."

[47] *The New York Times,* "Thailand Moving to Consolidation," January 13, 1964, p. 54; LBJ Library, NSF Country File, Box 282, Thailand, Cables, Vol. II, 8/64-3/65, Rusk to President, July 23, 1964; *FRUS, 1964-1968, Vol. XXVII,* Document 279, Memorandum of Conversation, July 24, 1964; Document 285, Memorandum of Conversation, December 11, 1964.

and President's message." Cheering from the sidelines, "Thanat Khoman, Foreign Minister of Thailand, urged today that the United States stand firm against the Communist insurgents in South Vietnam, despite the governmental chaos in Saigon." In December, the Bangkok embassy wrote that "the deterioration of the situation in neighboring countries . . . has added greatly to Thailand's importance to the United States." Happily, "Thailand keeps moving toward higher standards of living, economic diversification, and political integration." "Thailand's current gains in foreign reserves reflect its attractiveness for foreign capital and contribute to it." But the nearby Communist threat makes Thailand's progress "wholly inadequate to cope with a major military threat from the outside." In December 1964, Foreign Minister Thanat called on President Johnson; each was discouraged by the political instability in Saigon, and the resulting difficulties in resisting the Viet Cong. Thanat told Johnson that "any loss of South Viet-Nam would constitute an immediate threat to Thailand, beyond Thailand to Malaysia, and to the rest of the adjacent areas" – a clear statement of the "domino theory." [48]

As the expansion of the Vietnam War continued into 1965 and 1966, Thailand figured prominently in the U.S.-dominated war effort. As the US ambassador in Thailand, Graham Martin, wrote Rusk, "Quite aside from the long list of extraordinarily sensitive activities which the Thai permit us to carry on here and also quite aside from the indirect contributions in artillery, T-28 pilots and "hardnose" operations in Laos, the virtually unrestricted use of Thai bases for US aircraft in Barrel Roll and Rolling Thunder operations has become a pivotal factor in the success of our stepped-up military efforts in SEA. I note, for example, that over half the US aircraft flying in the recent Rolling Thunder missions were from Thai bases." Moreover, he further noted that "our dependence on Thailand, moreover, will clearly increase markedly over the next few months, as witnessed by an ever-growing list of new US requirements for forces and facilities here." Ambassador Martin followed up to Rusk on military requirements in Thailand noting that "it is nevertheless clear that we will need more facilities in the very near future. The faster we can get a start on

---

[48] *The New York Times,* "Asia Reappraises U.S.," August 11, 1964, p. 15; *FRUS, 1964-1968, Vol. XXVII,* Document 283, Embassy in Thailand to State, August, 8, 1964; *The New York Times,* "Much is at Stake in Southeast Asian Struggle," August 16, 1964, p. E4; "Thailand Official Exhorts U.S. To Hold Firm in Vietnam Crisis," August 28, 1964, p. 2; NARA, RG 59, CFPF, Box 2697, Pol 2-3, Politico-Economic Rpts THAI, 1/1/64, Amembassy Bangkok to State, A-455, December 18, 1964; *FRUS, 1964-1968, Vol. XXVII,* ; Document 285, Memorandum of Conversation, December 11, 1964.

them, including the all important business of discussing them with the RTG, the earlier we can get on with the important business of land acquisition and actual construction." William Bundy then wrote John McNaughton at Defense to support "the proposal for add-ons to the Thailand military assistance program for FY 1965 as modified and approved by CINCPAC and the Joint Chiefs of Staff." Bundy warned that if Defense continued to "slash" MAP levels, "if this should prevail, our access to Thai bases would go, our position in Laos would quickly become untenable, our whole strategic position in Southeast Asia would begin to crumble." The Thai government, in turn, supported American policy in the region. According to William Bundy, Thai Foreign Minister Thant Khoman "has continued to speak articulately and effectively in favor of U.S. foreign policy in Southeast Asia." He told a conference that absent U.S. intervention in Vietnam, "the Communists would have by now won there and would be stalking new victims in Asia." In mid-August 1966, *The New York Times* quoted Ambassador Martin on "Thailand's silent but vital role as host to 25,000 American servicemen." As *The Times* stated, "despite traditional Thai suspicion of foreigners, the Kittakachorn regime has bet on Washington's continued willingness to help meet the human and political costs of containing Communism in Southeast Asia." By May 1967, *Business Week* described the "powerful network of [U.S.] air babes and other support systems [in Thailand] for waging war in Vietnam." [49]

Spending to strengthen Thai military capacity also spurred economic development. In January, *The New York Times* editorialized that per capita income in Thailand was less than $100 and that more than 91 percent of the Thai population lived in rural areas and was engaged in agriculture. Six months later change was apparent. Meanwhile Bangkok was planning a huge highway construction program that *The Times* called "welcome news for farmers, resort owners, motorists, and long-distance haulers." In early June 1965, the Bangkok embassy drew attention to the crucial

[49] *FRUS, 1964-1968, Vol. XXVII,* Document 287, Martin to Rusk, March 23, 1965; Document 288, Martin to Rusk, March 31, 1965; Document 291, Bundy to McNaughton, April 24, 1965; NARA, RG 59, CFPF, Box 2697, Pol 7 THAI, 2/17/65, Bundy to Acting Secretary, September 28, 1965; *The New The New York Times,* "A Silent Partner for U.S. in Asia," August 21, 1966, p. 173. The State Department so appreciated Thanat's support that Dean Rusk wrote President Johnson to request that he meet with Thanat in October because of that clear support, see NARA, RG 59, CFPF, Box 2697, Pol 7 THAI, 2/17/65, Rusk to Johnson, undated; and same folder, Bundy to Acting Secretary, October 4, 1965; *Business Week,* "A major U.S. bastion springs up in Thailand," May 13, 1967, p. 38.

weaknesses of Thailand's periphery related to its economic underdevelopment." The report noted that "there are still hundreds of small villages in the border regions whose only ingress is by foot paths," reminiscent of medieval Europe." The next month Laurence Pickering filed a report that William Bundy shared with "even towns well off the path of the highway, such as Rio-et, have reaped clear economic benefits from the ready access to the Capital and its markets, and travel to and from the Capital is much more frequent (witness the appearance of three new hotels in this small provincial town since the Bangkok-Nong Kai road was opened)." "The economic effects of the Northern security road, both in terms of reduced transportation costs and better prices for rice and other produce, are already a matter of record although the road is still under construction and traversing it entails bypassing many bridges still not completed." [50]

Thai security needs dominated Thai-U.S. relations. *U.S. News & World Report* worried about Thailand: "Communist infiltrators are penetrating Thailand's long borders and stirring up trouble." The news magazine favorably described the "new military road – bypassing Bangkok – is being built from amphibious landing stages on Gulf of Siam to the main military depot and air base at Korat." *The New York Times* reported that "groups of Chinese Communists have pushed more than 300 miles into Thailand," and that "terrorist bands have been roaming through the jungles between Malaysia and Thailand for several years." In June *The Economist* focused on the challenges that Thailand faced. North Vietnam "urges the overthrow of the present Bangkok government and the ousting of its 'imperialist' allies." The Thai government made "an impressive beginning" in economic development in the northeast. But "the plateau land is basically poor," and people on both sides of the Mekong are ethnically Lao. In August Thai Deputy Premier Praphas Charusathien "called for greater United States cooperation in defending Thailand's frontiers against Communist activity," and that "the frequency of incidents

---

[50] *The New York Times,* "Key Statistics about Asia," January 18, 1965, p. 38; "Thailand Planning $100 Million Roads to Connect Cities," January 18, 1965, p. 41; NARA, RG 59, CFPF, Box 2697, Pol 2-3, Politico-Economic Rpts THAI, 1/1/64, Amembassy Bangkok to State, A-940, June 4, 1965; *FRUS, 1964-1968, Vol. XXVII,* Document 298, William Bundy to McGeorge Bundy and attachment, July 5, 1965. Interestingly, in late July two American businessmen visited State Department officials to discuss if Thailand was sufficiently stable to merit their company's investing to expand operations, see NARA, RG 59, CFPF, Box 2696, Pol 2, GenRpts& Stat-THAI, 1/1/64, "Situation in Thailand," July 27, 1965.

along Thailand's frontier" "showed that the Communists were beginning an underground war against the country."[51]

The next month the CIA analyzed "The Threat of Communist Subversion in Thailand." The report had its positive and negative comments. "Thailand's chief vulnerability to Communist subversion lies in the northeast region, which borders on Laos." "The chances are good that the government will be able to stay abreast of the likely increase in Communist subversion. The outlook in Thailand would alter greatly, however, if the Communists achieved definitive victory in Laos or South Vietnam." *The New York Times* reported in December that "Asian Communists have accelerated their infiltration of Thailand." "Thai and United States official sources report a substantial increase in Communist guerrilla activity." In January 1966, the CIA reported on the security situation in northeast Thailand: Deputy CIA Director Richard Helms wrote Secretary McNamara that "Thailand [was] being singled out by the Chinese Communist Government as the next country in Asia in which a war of national liberation would most likely develop." Helms praised Thai government efforts "to bring economic and social betterment to its rural population" but believed the government had to do more to gain the allegiance of villagers in northeastern Thailand. *Newsweek* contrasted "the peaceful prosperity of Bangkok and the *carpe diem* atmosphere of the burgeoning base towns in the hinterland." It praised Thailand's "war on poverty" and the government devoting "a whopping 70 per cent of its annual budget to such social-welfare programs as road construction, dam projects, agricultural stations, and schools." A month later, Vice President Hubert Humphrey reported on an official visit to Bangkok. He noted that the Thais were moving firmly against Communist subversion in the northeast, devoting "more than 60 percent of their current income for badly needed social and economic development projects," but they needed increased U.S. aid. [52]

---

[51] *U.S. News & World Report,* "Reds' Next Target in Asia," March 22, 1965, pp. 69-70; *The New York Times,* "Chinese Reported Deep in Thailand," April 25, 1965, p. 11; *The Economist,* "Thailand: West of the Mekong," June 12, 1965, p. 1269; *NYT,* "Thai Minister urges U.S. to aid in Frontier Defense," August 6, 1965, p. 4.

[52] *FRUS, 1964-1968, Vol. XXVII,* Document 303, Special Memorandum prepared by the Board of Estimates, CIA, September 10, 1965; *The New York Times,* "Asian Communists Step up Infiltration in Thailand," December 15, 1965, p. 11; see also "For Thais War Gets Closer," December 26, 1965, p. E3; *Newsweek,* "Thailand: The Anatomy of a Domino," January 31, 1966, pp. 35, 36; *FRUS, 1964-1968, Vol.*

Thailand became so central to the U.S. war effort in Vietnam that Washington provided funds to influence Thai elections. William Colby of the CIA told William Bundy of Thai politicians' requesting funds from Ambassador Martin for the forthcoming national elections. Martin was asking for advice. Bundy and Colby agreed to refer the matter to the 303 Committee. There was concern that the well-organized and well-funded Communist party would dominate the elections with obvious affect on U.S.-Thai relations and the conflict in Southeast Asia. However, "exposure of U.S. financial support to a RTG political party would provide excellent propaganda material for the Communists." Nonetheless, the 303 committee approved funding of a Thai political party. Subsequently, Secretary Rusk gave his approval on November 5, and President Johnson authorized the program on November 11.[53]

By mid-1966, the expanding war in Vietnam affected the security situation in Thailand. William Bundy wrote Secretary Rusk that the Thai request for additional U.S. helicopters for counterinsurgency reflected Thai concern about America's staying power in nearby Vietnam. Defense experts worried about "U.S.-manned helicopters" "fighting Thailand's battle for her." On the other hand, "if Vietnam goes bad," "confidence in the US would be shaken throughout the Far East. If Thailand decides to accommodate, it would then seem likely that, if they had not already done so, Malaysia, Singapore and Burma would change their orientation in the direction of Communist China." Bundy continued to embrace the "domino theory." And so for want of a few helicopters, there could be "another U.S. failure in Southeast Asia."[54]

In July a new NIE assessed the "Communist Insurgency in Thailand." The NIE believed the insurgency did not threaten the Thai government, and, despite several US embassy cables worry about this threat, the local population was generally loyal to the government. Nevertheless a few days later the embassy in Bangkok again reported to the State Department on the "dangerous insurgency threat confronting Thailand." In early August, Rusk wrote McNamara to support a larger MAP because of the increasing insurgency and the strengthened Thai commitment to meeting it. Again, the CIA was not as alarmist in an intelligence memorandum, "Communist Insurgency in Thailand: Strengths and Weaknesses," which concluded that

---

XXVII, Document 307, Helms to McNamara, January 14, 1966; Document 308, Humphrey to Johnson, February 15, 1966.

[53] *FRUS, 1964-1968, Vol. XXVII,* Document 304, Stuart to Hughes, September 10, 1965; Document 305, Memorandum Prepared for the 303 Committee, September 28, 1965; Document 306, Memorandum for the Record, October 8, 1965.

[54] *FRUS, 1964-1968, Vol. XXVII,* Document 313, Bundy to Rusk, May 16, 1966.

"the balance sheet in Thailand does not appear to favor the insurgents." Perhaps the issue was the Thai need for reassurance, especially in the form of a security guarantee. Rusk took advantage of the opening of the 1966 UN General Assembly session to meet with Foreign Minister Thanat who was uneasy about the US bombing campaign over Vietnam that relied on Thai bases. He wanted written assurances, and Rusk demurred because of concerns about the fate of a new mutual defense treaty moving through Congress.[55]

As President Johnson prepared to travel to Asian capitals in October 1966, a Special National Intelligence Estimate stated that "the small-scale Communist insurgencies in northeast Thailand and in the south have virtually no impact on the security situation in Bangkok." After stopping in Manila, the President met with Thanat and Pote Sarasin, and Walt Rostow suggested "a joint statement of mutual assurances" to meet the Thai demand for a bilateral security treaty. There were some disagreements over language, and McNamara and Rusk finally agreed on a statement for President Johnson to read during his visit to Thailand: "Let me assure you in this regard that Thailand can count on the United States."[56]

As part of a tour to Asia, President Johnson met with Thai leaders. Johnson agreed to fly to Manila to meet with America's allies in the Vietnam War. In part Johnson wanted to encourage "several recent initiatives of non-Communist Asian nations to develop closer collaboration on general problems of defending the area and promoting economic cooperation." Ten days later Johnson announced he would add five Asian nations to his Manila itinerary including Thailand. The

---

[55] *FRUS, 1964-1968, Vol. XXVII,* Document 316, NIE 52-66, Communist Insurgency in Thailand, July 1, 1966; Document 317, Martin to Rusk, July 7, 1966; Document 319, Rusk to McNamara, August 6, 1966; Document 321, CIA Intelligence Memorandum, August 11, 1966; see Document 323, Memorandum of Conversation, September 22, 1966; Document 323, Memorandum of Conversation, September 22, 1966 in which Thanat expressed explicit concern about Senators Wayne Morse and J. William Fulbright and to what extent did they represent official and popular views. The next day U. Alexis Johnson cabled Ambassador Graham Martin that Thanat remained "in the foulest mood I have ever seen him," and that he insisted on a bilateral treaty and an agreement on U.S. air bases in Thailand, Document 324, Johnson to Martin, September 23, 1966; Document 326, Rostow to Johnson, October 6, 1966.

[56] LBJ Library, Special National Intelligence Estimate, 40/50-66, "Security Conditions in Five Countries of the Western Pacific Area," 13 October 1966, p. 2; NARA, RG 59, Box 2701, Pol THAI-US, 9/22/66, SecDef to SecState and President, October 21, 1966; same folder, State to Manila [for President and SecState], #70704, October 21, 1966.

president arrived in Bangkok on October 28 to a "restrained, Thai-style welcome."[57]

Despite the flurry of reports worrying about the Communist insurgency and Thai desires for a bilateral security treaty, on balance, the Thai economy was improving and the political system was effective. *The New York Times* explained the dynamic Thai economy: "it has been the millions of United States dollars that have poured into the countryside, because of a score of large American air and military bases, that have been the real spur to Bangkok's expansion." One result was "droves of people into Bangkok to help channel goods to the enriched hinterland and to provide for the thousands of United States servicemen in Bangkok." The American embassy pointed out that "the U.S. military construction program is of importance not only for its physical objectives but also for its impact upon the Thai economy." "About half of the construction will be for ports, roads, airfields, and other infrastructure that will have useful by-products in strengthening Thailand's economic base." Several months later *The Times* reported that Bangkok was "experiencing the pangs of prosperity, Western-style." Bangkok "has attracted enough Western European, Japanese and American investments to launch a conspicuous consumption boom." The result: "the helter-skelter transformation of a once-sedate Oriental river port into a miniature Los Angeles, plus humidity, minus fog." A CIA report on the eve of President Johnson's visit to Asia concluded that "Thailand enjoys a variety of economic and political assets which augur well for its future stability and independence. Guided by skilled and resourceful economic leadership, Thailand has made rapid economic progress in recent years and the prospects are bright for even greater growth and development in the future. In the political sphere, the country has benefited from nine years of stable rule by an autocratic but benevolent military oligarchy."[58]

---

[57] *The New York Times,* "Johnson is Likely to join Six Allies in Manila Parley," September 27, 1966, pp. 1, 3; "Johnson Expands Trip to Far East; to Visit 6 Nations," October 7, 1966, p.1; "Johnson is Given Welcome by Thais," October 28, 1966, p. 1.

[58] *The New York Times,* "U.S. Money for Thailand Bases Spurs Expansion in Bangkok," February 13, 1966, p. 8; NARA, RG 59, CFPF, Box 2701, Pol 3 Thai (BA), Amembassy Bangkok to State, A-876, April 23, 1966; *NYT*, "Boom in Thailand," July 9, 1966, p. 3; *FRUS, 1964-1968, Vol. XXVII,* Document 328, Intelligence Memorandum, October 12, 1966; see Document 333, Memorandum of Conversation, October 23, 1966 and Document 335, Memorandum of Conversation, October 29, 1966. Thailand's international trade and all the visiting businessmen caused a need for additional upscale hotel rooms in Bangkok: see

The Thai government sought to develop regional economic relationships. An embassy report gave credit to Thailand's interest in Southeast Asian regional development and willingness, for example, to work with Japan and thus to benefit from Japanese investment. Embassy officials soon reported on a trip of Thai Economic Affairs Minister, Sunthorn, to Korea and Taiwan. Sunthorn intended to discuss "general trade matters, tax and trade treaties, and joint ventures." Another embassy report commented on Thailand's cooperation in "trade and cultural arrangements, ocean transportation, and telecommunications." It further stated that "Thanat and others have seen propriety and utility of embarking upon meaning cooperative projects" – "economic, cultural and education projects [that] lend 'glue' to evolving regional political groupings." When Minister of National Development [and former SEATO head] Pote Sarasin visited Washington, President Johnson agreed to meet with him because of American "admiration" for the "Thai policy of devoting a very high proportion (over 60%) of the national budget to economic and social development, with special attention to the critical areas of Northeast Thailand."[59]

As the number of U.S. combat troops in Vietnam and the region increased in this period, there was concern for the impact on Thai society and economy. From 1965 to 1968, the number of U.S. ground forces in Vietnam increased to some 550,000 and the number of support forces in nearby Thailand increased as well. In January 1967, Secretary McNamara wrote JCS Chair Earle Wheeler that "I am concerned over the steady growth in the number of U.S. personnel planned for deployment to Thailand." McNamara was particularly concerned about "the very serious implications that a large and growing American presence has for a small and underdeveloped nation such as Thailand" especially given how in Vietnam "economic dislocation can seriously weaken the social fabric of the country and undo much that military actions accomplish." Nonetheless, William Bundy informed Rusk of agreement with Defense about seeking Thai approval for a B-52 base at U Tapao, that is, for expanding the American military presence in Thailand. In late February,

---

U.S. News & World Report, "What U.S. Companies are Doing Abroad," February 13, 1967, p. 99.

[59] NARA, RG 59, CFPF, Box 2698, Pol 15-1 Head of State, Exec Branch, THAI, 1/1/65, Amembassy Bangkok to State, A-1069, June 17, 1966; Box 2697, Pol 7 Thai, 1/1/66, Amembassy Bangkok to State, #2886, June 23, 1966; same folder, Amembassy Bangkok to State, #2560/2, August 29, 1966; same folder, Amembassy Bangkok to State, #2560/1, August 29, 1966; Box 2701, Pol THAI-US, 9/22/66, Rusk to Johnson, October 4, 1966.

U.S. News quoted an American official in Bangkok that "Thailand has a jet-propelled little economy that now has had the afterburner turned on by the Vietnam War." The U.S. construction program helped develop the huge Sattahip port complex, new road and fuel supply facilities, and programs in northeast Thailand. U.S. and Thai officials all hoped the trickle down theory would spread the economic boom in Bangkok to the hinterlands.[60]

American officials remained concerned about the threat of insurgency in the northeast. *The New York Times* reported in December 1966 that ""with men, money and advice, the United States has joined Field Marshal Thanom Kittakachorn's regime in a variety of new civic action programs designed to offset Communist promises and propaganda in northeast Thailand." *The Economist* noted that "Thailand is a one-crop economy," and "eight out of ten farmers grow rice." Thailand needed to export rice to have the funds to improve the economy and connect the isolated northeast with Bangkok. Several months later *The Times* claimed that, "despite all the equipment and plans, the Thai Government's effort is still woefully lacking where it counts in the remote villages." In mid-August 1967, U.S. officials concluded "the Thais were moving in the right direction." Eight months later *Newsweek* reported that "American diplomats are convinced that the Thais can cope with the problem," but it had a map inset titled "Communist onslaught" that clearly overstated the guerrilla threat to Thailand.[61]

As with South Korea, Thailand provided troops for Vietnam, and there were financial and other considerations. In January 1967 *The New York Times* reported the initial Thai contingent – a 1,000 man combat battalion. Over the next two days the Thai government first announced it "had not taken a final decision to send combat troops to South Vietnam" and then that it "would soon send combat troops to South Vietnam." Several months later, Bangkok indicated it "will press the United States for the installation of surface-to-air missiles" because of concern over the

---

[60] *FRUS, 1964-1968, Vol. XXVII,* Document 340, McNamara to Wheeler, January 16, 1967; Document 341, Bundy to Rusk, February 27, 1967; see Document 342, Rostow to Johnson, March 22, 1967, for a discussion acknowledging Thai approval of the base for B-52s; *U.S. News & World Report,* "Thailand: A Fighting Ally for U.S. in Asia," February 27, 1967, pp. 46, 48.

[61] *The New York Times,* "U.S. Helps Thailand at Village Level in Effort to Thwart Reds," December 27, 1966, p. 8; *The Economist,* "Thailand helps itself," May 6, 1967, p. 560; *NYT,* "Thailand Lagging in Guerrilla War," July 4, 1967, p. 4; *FRUS, 1964-1968, Vol. XXVII,* Document 351, Trueheart to Hughes, August 14, 1967; *Newsweek,* "On-Scene in Laos and Thailand," April 22, 1968, p. 47.

possibility of air raids. The incoming Ambassador to Thailand, Leonard Unger, wrote William Bundy that expanding the Thai contingent from 2,300 to more than 10,000 men had serious budget implications. More important, Unger drew Bundy's attention to "the current shortage of non-commissioned officers and company grade officers in the Thai forces" and that increasing the commitment to Vietnam would "accentuate this shortage." Several days later General Maxwell Taylor told Unger that Thai officials suggested that "deploying additional forces to the Northeast to cope with the insurgency" was more important than increasing the troop concentration in Vietnam; Taylor countered additional troops would make the fight seem of more direct concern to Asian nations. The Thais then agreed to provide a 10,800-man brigade, but presented a huge bill for increased American military support. Bangkok told *The New York Times* that it "had agreed to increase its forces in South Vietnam from 2,000 men to a full division." The next month, Clark Clifford meeting with Pote Sarasin noted the "significant drop in popular support for U.S. Vietnam policy" which made "the Thai troop contributions even more important." Thai Foreign Minister Thanat Khoman told President Johnson during a visit to Washington, DC that "Thailand is ready to assume its responsibilities," but "how much additional equipment can be made available for the strengthening of the Thai forces which remain at home?" When Thanat subsequently met with Secretary McNamara, McNamara largely conceded to Thai equipment and assistance demands. Thereafter Washington pressed Bangkok to speed up the schedule for these troops from the original plan to send half by late summer 1968 and the remainder in January 1969. In either case, the forthcoming Communist Tet Offensive rendered the discussion largely moot.[62]

[62] *The New York Times,* "Thai Combat Battalion to be sent to Vietnam," January 4, 1967, p. 6; "Thais Deny a Decision on Troops for Vietnam," January 5, 1967, p. 3; "Thanat Says Thai Units will be sent to Vietnam," January 6, 1967, p. 2; "Thailand to Press U.S. for Missiles," April 1, 1967, p. 4; *FRUS, 1964-1968, Vol. XXVII,* Document 354, Unger to Bundy, September 12, 1967; Document 355, Memorandum of Conversation, September 14, 1967; Document 359, Wright to Rostow, September 19, 1967; NARA, RG 59, CFPF, Box 2526, Pol THAI-US, 1/1/67, Rusk to Johnson, October 4, 1967; *FRUS, 1964-1968, Vol. XXVII,* Document 362, Memorandum of Conversation, October 5, 1967; Document 364, Memorandum of Conversation, October 6, 1967; *The New York Times,* "Thailand Plans Big Increase in Forces in South Vietnam," October 20, 1967, p. 19. Interestingly, Pote told Ambassador Unger that Thailand wanted U.S. military assistance, but not U.S. ground forces, finding the American takeover of the Vietnam conflict in error; as Pote noted, "the American presence has resulted in a reduction of Vietnamese effort and a disposition to leave the fighting to the U.S,"

The Vietnam conflict greatly changed Thailand. Much as American war-related spending pumped the economies of Japan, South Korea, Taiwan, and the Philippines, such dollars expanded service, transportation and construction industries. Jobs in cities and along major transportation routes caused thousands of peasants to move to Bangkok and other major cities for work. American spending helped break down rural society and the traditional family/village structure, although all segments of society did not share in this bounty equally. *The New York Times* reported that the key Thai port of Klong Toi was clogged. "Thailand's consumer boom, fueled by United States spending for base construction and purchases for Vietnam, has spurred imports to a record high." Thai and American officials agreed on the need for a second deepwater port. In August 1967, *The New York Times* reported that "the United States opened a new $43-million deep water port today" in Sattahip, 100 miles south of Bangkok. Nine months later, the United States turned the port over to the Thai government.[63]

In late 1967, American analysts found economic development uneven. Ambassador Unger wrote the State Department that "post-war socio-economic progress has not had time to reach the rural areas – the remote villages in particular, and above all those in the NE. In fact, per capita GNP for the entire country has reached only $135. At the lower end of the scale on the income distribution is, of course, the subsistence farmer in the remote areas. Rice yields for the whole of Thailand are no more than rice yields in India and are less than half that of Taiwan. Rice yields in the northeast are 35 percent below the national average. Per capita GNP in the northeast is less than $65: per capita cash income in the northeast is less than $30." *The New York Times* drew attention to "regional programs to foster orderly growth" especially the newly formed Association of Southeast Asian Nations, including Thailand, "to speed economic growth, social progress and cultural development of the region." A few days later *The Times* reported that "Thailand's economic progress slowed down in 1967" to 6%, down from 9% the prior year but "outstanding compared

see Document 366, Unger to Bundy, October 22, 1967. On the issue of the timing of the troops, see Document 372, Rostow to Johnson, December 8, 1967; Document 374, Wright to Steadman, December 27, 1967; Document 375, McNamara to Johnson, January 12, 1968; and Document 377, Rusk to Johnson, January 20, 1968.

[63] *The New York Times,* "Clogged Port Troubles Thailand," May 13, 1967, p. 45; "U.S. Opens Port in Thailand," August 19, 1967, p. 12; "U.S. Will Present Thailand with a New Port Facility," May 26, 1968, p. 72.

with that of most Asian countries." Development remained uneven, and farmers in the northeast and south did not fully share in the bounty.[64]

The Communist Tet offensive changed the situation in Southeast Asia. On March 31, 1968, Lyndon Johnson told the American people that he would not run for re-election and he would seek peace in Vietnam. A few days later, Thai Premier Thanom Kittakachorn told reporters that, "if the United States changed its Vietnam policy, its honor would be damaged and no one would trust the United States anymore." The next month, *The Times* reported on increased guerrilla activity along Thailand's border and disturbing parallels to Vietnam. On May 6 Thanom visited Washington, DC, and Rusk wrote Johnson that "Thanom will have three major concerns [including] the U.S. commitment to Thailand, particularly after your term of office; where we are headed in Viet-Nam; U.S. support for Thai development and counter-insurgency programs." When Johnson met with Thanom, he noted the Thai commitment of additional troops, as if the Tet offensive and the reversal of American strategy for Vietnam had not occurred. Thanom asked if Johnson was willing to meet with leaders of non-communist nations in the region, and Johnson responded he would keep his schedule flexible for a meeting best scheduled for Honolulu. Johnson asked Thanom for help with America's balance of payments challenge, especially the investing of Thai cash reserves in American long-term securities. Rusk, who met with Thanom and Thanat also made the balance of payments and Thai dollar reserves topics of discussion. Thanom met with Clark Clifford, who replace McNamara as Secretary of Defense, and Clifford re-assured Thanom that the Communists had suffered high losses, "especially in elite units," during the Tet offensive and "the Vietnamese people did not welcome the NVA/VC as liberators in the cities." When Thanom traveled on to Tokyo, he told reporters that "Thailand expects to disprove the validity of the domino theory in relation to the ability of Southeast Asian countries to resist Communist assault." A month later the Bangkok embassy offered a "Policy Assessment for Thailand," and reported that "the Royal Thai Government has been afflicted with growing doubts concerning U.S. staying power." "They reached a peak in early April."[65]

---

[64] *FRUS, 1964-1968, Vol. XXVII,* Document 369, Embassy in Thailand to State, November 6, 1967; *The New York Times,* "War Spurs Economies of a Struggling Asia," January 19, 1968, pp. 49, 53; "Thai Growth Rate Levels Off to 6%," January 19 1968, p. 60.

[65] *The New York Times,* "Thai Warns Against Pullout," April 2, 1968, p. 27; "Thai Insurgency Raises Fears of a New Vietnam," May 5, 1968, pp. 1, 3; *FRUS, 1964-1968, Vol. XXVII,* Document 385, Rusk to Johnson, May 6, 1968; Document 387,

Withdrawal of U.S. forces from Vietnam had many ramifications. Thai leaders sought to strengthen economic relations with the United States, perhaps to compensate for the drawing down of the U.S. military commitment in the region. Pote Sarasin accepted an invitation to speak to the American Management Association in New York in early May and with other groups to encourage investment in Thailand. Pote told the American Chamber of Commerce in Thailand on February 21 that attention to national security cannot "be at the expense of the interruption or cessation of economic development, for the development activity is in fact another essential form of defense." Deputy Prime Minister Praphat visited Korea in mid-March to discuss Asian economic development as well as Asian security. The Senior Interdepartmental Group discussed several key questions at a meeting in May: "How do we handle the withdrawal of U.S. forces from Thailand post-Vietnam without causing the Thai to panic? How serious will the economic effect be of our withdrawal?" The answers were not clear. At the same time, a new NIE evaluated the Communist insurgency in northeast Thailand, and concluded that "the Communist insurgent threat to the stability of the Thai Government has not grown appreciably over the past year despite the appearance of insurgent activity in additional areas of the country." *U.S. News & World Report* claimed that the "big fear of non-Communist countries of Asia is that U.S. pullback in Vietnam would further embolden the Reds;" Thais felt "an unfavorable peace in Vietnam would almost surely increase Communist pressures in the northern Provinces." As Thailand moved to a freer political system in Fall 1968, economic issues continued to increase in visibility. A CIA report noted that "although Thailand has made considerable economic progress under the military regime, and its growth rate compares favorably with that of other nations, the fact remains that its per capita income is still extremely low. There are some people in Thailand, although they are few in number and exercise only marginal influence, who are asking whether the country's economic gains are being made in the right areas and are reaching the right people."

Bundy to Rostow, May 8, 1968; Document 391, May 9, 1968; Document 388, Memorandum of Conversation, May 8, 1968; *The New York Times,* "Thai Leader Doubts the Domino Theory," May 16, 1968, p. 2; NARA, RG 59, CFPF, Box 2526, Pol 1 THAI-US, 1/1/67, Amembassy Bangkok to State, A-1144, June 5, 1968. In the several days between the North Korean seizure of the *USS Pueblo* and the launching of the Tet Offensive, Thanat met with Rusk for reassurance of US commitment to the region; see NARA, RG 59, CFPF, Box 2519, Pol 7 THAI, 1/1/68, "Foreign Minister Thanat's Tour d'Horizon with the Secretary," January 26, 1968.

The New York Times reported Thai government and business leaders traveled to America seeking "a new partnership of progress with the United States." Meanwhile, the Tokyo embassy reported on Thanom's visit to Japan. Thanom discussed the "imbalance of trade between Japan and Thailand," and sought to promote "Thai-Japanese cooperation in economic and technical sectors of both governmental and private level." Thanom apparently "obtained a specific promise from [Japanese Prime Minister] Sato [Eisaku] that Japanese would try to increase imports of agricultural commodities which not competitive with domestic Japanese production." The next month Pote visited Taipei seeking "broad GRC-RTG agreement on economic cooperation," in the fields of "agricultural crops, extension services and general agricultural techniques."[66]

As the Johnson Administration drew to a close, there was a discouraging note. A highly highly-visible columnist, Jack Anderson, asked "are they robbing U.S. blind in Thailand?" In his article in *Parade* magazine on December 29, 1968, Anderson charged that "Thai are profiting from US, but there is little US can do about it;" "American-built roads have crumbled," and "American-made locomotives have broken down." State Department officials worried about the Thai reaction, since Thai leaders had previously complained about American media reporting on Thailand. A year earlier Foreign Minister Thanat complained to State Department officials about "certain elements of the American press" which he repeated two or three times as a "Zionist-liberal conspiracy." He attacked Stanley Karnow of the *Washington Post,* Kim Willenson who was the UPI correspondent in Bangkok, and Robert Moskin, foreign editor of *Look*. Thanat claimed they had written stories "poisonous to U.S.-Thai relations." He also complained about U.S. Senator J. William Fulbright

[66] NARA, RG 59, CFPF, Box 2519, Pol 7 THAI, 1/1/68, Amembassy Bangkok to SecState #5249, February 23, 1968; Box 2521, Pol 15-1 THAI, 1/1/68, Amembassy Bangkok to State, A-860, March 7, 1968; Box 2519, Pol 7 THAI, 1/1/68, Amembassy Seoul to SecState, #9832, March 25, 1968; *FRUS, 1964-1968, Vol. XXVII,* Document 389, Wright to Rostow, May 8, 1968; Document 390, NIE 52-68, Communist Insurgency in Thailand, May 9, 1968; Document 407, Thailand: The Present Political Phase, October 18, 1968; *The New York Times,* "Thais Ask Partnership of Progress," May 7, 1968, pp. 63, 69; *U.S. News & World Report,* "Fear in Asia: a 'Bad' Peace by U.S.," May 6, 1968, pp. 41-42; NARA, RG 59, Box 2519, Pol 7 THAI, 5/1/68, Amembassy Tokyo to SecState, #496, May 23, 1968; same folder, Amembassy Tokyo to SecState, #497, May 23, 1968; same folder, Amembassy Bangkok to Amembassy Taipei, #8364, June 22, 1968.

who had chaired some hearings of the Senate Foreign Relations Committee to question U.S. policy towards Thailand.[67]

[67] NARA, RG 59, CFPF, Box 2526, POL THAI-US, 1/1/68, State to Amembassy Bangkok, December 30, 1968; same folder, Amembassy Bangkok to SecState, #3050, December 30, 1968; same folder, State to Amembassy Bangkok, December 31, 1968; NARA, RG 59, CFPF, Box 2519, Pol 7 THAI, 6/1/67, Conversation with Thai Foreign Minister, December 27, 1967.

CHAPTER SIX

DANGEROUSLY UNSETTLED: MALAYA/MALAYSIA, SINGAPORE, AND INDONESIA

In 1961, Southeast Asia was an unsettled region. Several former British territories considered forming a greater Malaysian Federation. Indonesia and the Philippines each took issue with this arrangement. At the same time, the three countries fell in and out of cooperation, including the short lived "Maphilindo" and the Association of Southeast Asia.

After 1963 the situation changed again, as Malaysia became a success and Indonesia seemed to spiral downward. Although Singapore eventually pulled out of the new federation, Malaysia prospered economically. For years, Indonesia had squandered its natural resources and foreign aid, and by 1965 it seemed to draw ever closer to the People's Republic of China.

As the Johnson Administration drew to a close, the region was developing economically and achieving a welcome degree of regional integration. The failed "Maphilindo" and ASA led to ASPAC, Asian and Pacific Council, and ASEAN, Association of Southeast Asian Nations, and great support for the Asian Development Bank.

The United States government paid relatively scant attention to Malaya and nearby British possessions in the days after Kennedy became president. It is interesting that the State Department's *Foreign Relations* volume begins with a National Intelligence Estimate from mid-July 1962 – evidence that Malaya was a backwater of a sort for American foreign policy in 1961.

Meanwhile, there was increasing interest in a greater Malaysian federation. D.P. Singhal recounted the surprise announcement. Tunku Abdul Rahman visited Singapore on May 27, 1961 and told a group of foreign correspondents that "Malaya, Singapore, and the British territories of North Borneo, Brunei and Sarawak should come together in a single 'Mighty Malaysia.'" Singaporean Prime Minister Lew Kuan Yew responded "independence through merger is now clearly before us and will be achieved sooner than anyone imagined two years ago." *The New York Times* printed an in-depth report on Singapore, and after noting its independence, countered that the Singaporean government "is trying hard to attach Singapore to the thriving Federation of Malaya, across the Johore Strait." Yet "the Western powers, seeing Singapore more as a base or a headquarters than a community of people . . . do not want to risk tainting a friendly, conservative Malaya by the adhesion of a politically unpredictable Singapore." *The Times* also reported Malayan ambivalence because such a merger "would create a Chinese majority in the Federation" which "might give Peiping a wedge jutting into the affairs of the peninsula." Still, a larger federation was "the ultimate solution." At the same time, Prime Minister Lee pressed the U.S. ambassador, William Percy Maddox, for economic aid. He complained about stinginess, claimed the administration did not like him, and threatened to meet with his Cabinet to discuss the matter, but he succeeded in securing U.S. support for his plan to develop Singapore into the entrepôt of the region.[1]

Besides this interest, Malaya also sought to widen diplomatic contacts among Asian and African countries beyond its traditional, close formal relations with Great Britain. Malaya had depended on Britain for defense, trade, and investment. By 1961 it was clear that Great Britain was declining, and Bangkok concluded it made sense to diversify relations and consider union.

There were few pressures for union. For example, Malaya's largely extractive economy – rubber and tin – was in "remarkably good shape." The government budget was strongly positive, as were the value of exports over imports and the increasing foreign exchange reserves. Thomas McHale wrote that the Malayan economy, based on rubber and tin, "has achieved an average per capita income level second to none in Southeast Asia." There was a negative. "While economic specialization in Malaya has brought prosperity, it has done so on a very narrow base that is highly susceptible to forces over which Malayans have little control." Similarly,

[1] D.P. Singhal, "The United States of Malaysia," *Asian Survey, Vol. 1, No. 8,* October 1961, pp. 16-17; *The New York Times,* January 8, 1961, "Jilted by History, Yet Still Historic," p. SM 86; John F. Kennedy Library, NSF Country File, Box 140, Malaya & Singapore, general, 1/61-10/61, Singapore to Secretary of State, #919, section one of two, April 18, 1961; same folder, Singapore to Secretary of State, #921, April 18, 1961; same folder, Singapore to Secretary of State, #926, section two of two, April 20, 1961.

"in such a key market as the United States, natural rubber has steadily lost ground."[2]

The real issue was ethnic diversity, for Malaya was mostly Moslem Malays; Singapore was mostly non-Moslem Chinese; and other islands brought their own degree of diversity to any proposed expansion of the Malayan federation. Singapore's Prime Minister, Lee Kuan Yew, predicted a merger – "inevitable" – by 1963. The Tunku and Lee agreed on Malaya's responsibility for defense, external affairs, and security, and Singapore's commitment to control labor and education within the island. Lee believed that absent a quick merger, Singapore's "future will be chaos." The Tunku complained to American officials about the "apparent British reluctance [to] give [the confederation] plan more positive support." The Malayan leader believed that "dynamic efforts are required to counter effects of Communist pressures from north" and "Greater Malasia [sic] plan is such effort." Secretary of State Dean Rusk signed a telegram to the American embassy in Kuala Lumpur that "department favors [the] concept [of] greater Malaysia confederation if carried out with care and due regard for welfare and interests [of the] Borneo and Singapore peoples." But Rusk carefully noted "this plan must inevitably be [a] British responsibility" in collaboration with local peoples and the "US should not become involved in attempting [to] resolve differences such as timing." [3]

The Malaya-Singapore negotiations continued for months. In mid-October, Undersecretary of State George Ball shared the department's estimate with key embassies and consulates. He noted there was "substantial agreement on [the] general principles [of] confederation between Rahman and Lee, but Department [is] unable [to] judge how far [the] current discussions [are to] achieving substantial progress on technical details." Ball noted that the Tunku remains "suspicious of British," and that the "British Singapore base remains [a] difficult problem." Ironically, Ball concluded the Singapore Prime Minister "Lee is weak and not [a] very attractive or dependable reed upon which to rely" although he dominated Singaporean politics for decades and provided critical stability. Several days later Ball reiterated to the embassy that

---

[2] *The New York Times,* "Reds in Malaya Seek to Gain From Rise in Racial Tensions," May 21, 1961, p. 3; Thomas R. McHale, "The Malayan Economy and Stereo-Regular Rubbers," *Asian Survey, Vol. 1, No. 4, June 1961,* pp. 25-28.

[3] *The New York Times* ,"Singapore's Chief says Merger with Malaya is Likely by 1963," August 25, 1961, p. 9; JFK Library, NSF, Box 140, Malaya & Singapore, General, 1/61-10/61, Kuala Lumpur to Secretary of State, #11, July 11, 1961; same folder, State to Amembassy Kuala Lumpur, #24, July 14, 1961.

"Department believes that our most useful function is to provide general support to British efforts [to] maintain stability [in] Singapore." Further, Ball stated that the "Tunku might be advised [of] our view that any serious trouble arising against British in Singapore can only add to difficulties of all concerned in maintaining [a] barrier to Communist advances in SEA." *Time* reported that in September Prime Minister Lee approached the Tunku "to argue that his situation was deteriorating, and he cannot afford to wait until the Borneo territories [that is, Sarawak, Brunei, and North Borneo] make up their minds." In early December *Time* reported that Malayan Prime Minister Tunku Abdul Rahman "formally proposed the merger to the British, who hastily put their stamp of approval." "Next question: the willingness of three other British-run territories in the area – Sarawak, Brunei, and North Borneo – to join the new political grouping. If they agree, federation could be a fact within two years."[4]

Finances affected both individual economies and the status of federation talks. *The New York Times* reported a Malayan government protest over Washington's decision "to dispose of 5,000 tons of surplus tin." Bangkok claimed that the American decision "greatly disrupted the world tin market," and damaged Malaysian exports, much of which went to the United States. Chester Bowles in Kuala Lumpur wrote Rusk and Ball that the "impact of US stockpile rubber sales here in Malaya is far greater than I had assumed before leaving Washington." "US interest will be seriously damaged in the one really stable nation in the explosive Southeast Asia area" for "Malaya is caught between the deteriorating situation in Vietnam and Laos to the north and potentially explosive situation in Singapore to the south." Returning to rubber sales, Bowles noted that "success of [the] five year plan depends almost wholly on income from rubber and tin." "Personal incomes of three-fourths of all Malayan families are tied directly or indirectly to US rubber prices." Bowles concluded that "it is folly for us to spend billions on economic aid and then allow a situation such as this to get out of hand." Rusk soon responded that "we are much concerned by the serious proportions of the political problem created in Malaya over our rubber disposal program."

---

[4] JFK Library, NSF, Box 140, Malaya & Singapore, General, 1/61-10/61, State to London, #1944 et. al., October 7, 1961; same folder, State to Kuala Lumpur, #211, et. al., October 10, 1961; *Time,* "Precarious Peace," September 8, 1961, http://www.time.com/time/magazine/article/0,9171.87234.00.html; *The New York Times,* "Singapore Ready to Join," September 17, 1961, p. 4; *NYT,* "Union of Singapore and Malaya Pushed,," October 1, 1961, p. 25; .*Time,* "Good Sense Around Singapore," December 1, 1961,
http://www.time.com/time/magazine/article/0,9171,938805,00.html.

Rusk told Bowles that there were other factors forcing the US decision, and thus there was no easy resolution, especially because of the "imperfect understanding and insufficient exchange of information and views." In April 1962, the Malayan government sought assurance that the U.S. government would not sell stockpile tin below $2,680 a ton. If prices fell below that level, Malayan tin mines "will be forced to close." The concern over finances was clear at a March 1962 meeting of the UN Economic Commission for Asia and the Far East. Attending government delegations were worried that "creation of common markets in other parts of the world will squeeze out the products of the underdeveloped nations." [5]

As the discussions continued, Washington considered the situation. In May, the State Department cabled the Bangkok embassy that its "approach to question of aid to Singapore, North Borneo, and Sarawak has been cautious" in part because "we do not wish [to] establish four aid missions where one would do when and if confederation of Malaya with Singapore and British Borneo into Malaysia is realized." A National Intelligence Estimate in July 1962 analyzed "the prospects for achievement of the proposed Federation of Malaysia and for its political and economic viability." The NIE concluded that "the chief threats to the new Federation will be communal antagonisms, easily aroused because of the ethnic diversity found in each of the component states." The analysts gave short shrift to threats from Indonesia and the Philippines, each coveting islands incorporated into the new federation with the mainland state of Malaya. A few days later, President Kennedy asked the Malayan Ambassador, Dato Ong Yoke Lim, about progress towards the federation, and Dato responded that "things were proceeding satisfactorily." In early August the Bangkok Embassy reported that, as the federation came closer, the current Malayan government told embassy officials that Malaysia "will be an applicant for United States aid." Ambassador Charles Baldwin noted that, "on the surface," Malaya did not appear to need external assistance. But bringing in Borneo and Sarawak into the federation would bring about an additional economic burden and there was a likely loss of foreign exchange "from the decreasing price of natural rubber." Baldwin urged serious consideration of any aid request for "Malaya is today a 'showcase'

[5] *The New York Times,* "Malaya Hits Move by U.S. to Sell Tin," September 12, 1961, pp. 45, 50; JFK Library, NSF, Box 140, Malaya & Singapore, General, 11/61-11/62, Kuala Lumpur to Secretary of State, #7107, November 13, 1961; same folder, State Circular Telegram, #921, November 14, 1961, *NYT,* "Malaya to Seek U.S. Assurance on Minimum Sales Price for Tin," April 2, 1962, p. 39; *NYT,* "Nations at Asian Economic Talks See Peril in Rise of Trade Blocs," March 8, 1962, p. 5.

of democracy in an area which is seriously threatened by Communism. The continued existence of a sound and prosperous Malaya will be a constant refutation of Communist propaganda and an example to neighboring countries." Three months later, Baldwin cabled Rusk that the "Tunku told me he very much hoped [the] U.S. Government would be able to lend Malaya [the] amount necessary for a new airport near Kuala Lumpur" "for strategic considerations."[6]

The Philippine and Indonesian governments opposed this federation for each had designs on British-occupied islands to be included. Manila confined its opposition to words. Philippine President Diosdado Macapagal claimed Malaysia "will be ripe for infiltration from Communist China" and thus the claim to British North Borneo. Manila asked Washington to host Vice President Pelaez so he could express Manila's concern over U.S. policy towards the establishment of Malaysia; Manila wanted Washington to await the outcome of the tripartite talks.[7]

Jakarta raided Malaysian islands to disrupt the federation. In March 1963, *Newsweek* reported that "Sukarno seems to be building up for a spoiling attack on the incipient new nation of Malaysia." *Newsweek* repeated Sukarno's charge that "the creation of Malaysia will mean Indonesia's 'encirclement' by 'colonialists and imperialists.'" Not surprisingly, Malayan Prime Minister Abdul Rahman charged that Sukarno "has no good intentions toward Malaya" and Malaya "must consider him a threat." The Tunku claimed that "Soviet aid to Indonesia has to a certain extent helped to change the balance of power out here." He believed that Sukarno's threats to Borneo masked his "real intention to break up Malaysia either before or after it is formed." NIE 55-63 concluded that Sukarno's "sense of national destiny is prompting [him] to seek hegemony over neighboring Malay peoples." "Indonesia almost

---

[6] JFK Library, NSF, Box 140, Malaysia and Singapore, General, 11/61-11/62, State to Amembassy London, #5932, May 7, 1962; Department of State, *Foreign Relations of the United States, 1961-1963, Volume XXIII, Southeast Asia,* Washington, DC, GPO, 1994, Document 327, NIE 54/59-62, Prospects for the Proposed Malaysian Federation, pp. 707-708; Document 328, Greater Malaysia, p. 709; JFK Library, NSF, Box 140, Malaysia and Singapore, General, 11/61-11/62, American Embassy Kuala Lumpur to Department of State, A-71, August 1, 1962; same folder, Kuala Lumpur to Secretary of State, #285, Sections 1 and 2, November 6 and 7, 1962.

[7] *Newsweek,* "Clouds in the South Seas," March 4, 1963, p. 42; NARA, RG 59, CFPF, Box 3976, POL 7, Visits, Mtgs-Malaysia, Manila to SecState, #1157, April 19, 1963.

certainly intends to annex Portuguese Timor when the time is propitious, probably within the next two or three years."[8]

As Sukarno committed to upsetting the status quo with Malaysia and in Dutch New Guinea, which he called West Irian, Washington worried that instability could lead to Communist gains. Washington sought to pressure Sukarno to modify his behavior. *The New York Times* reported that the U.S. government "suspended shipment of weapons and ammunition to Indonesia" because of Sukarno's "hostile attitude toward Malaysia." At the same time, Washington withdrew from a proposed international consortium that was arranging a $500 million long-term development credit to Indonesia. [9]

Kuala Lumpur, Manila, and Bangkok flirted with the idea of a Southeast Asian union. In mid-February 1961, Thai Foreign Minister Thanat Khoman met with Philippine Foreign Secretary Felixberto Serrano and Malayan Prime Minister Tunku Abdul Rahman in Kuala Lumpur about "an association of Southeast Asian states." The Thais wanted a larger association; the Filipinos and Malayans were seeking a smaller, more limited union. Six months later *The New York Times* editorialized that the initials of the new Association of Southeast Asia "spell a word that means 'hope' in all three languages of its member states." The three partners, all small nations, were seeking "ways to pool their limited capacities into a combination important for Southeast Asia." An accompanying declaration noted ASA sought "to establish a firm foundation for common action to further economic and social progress in Southeast Asia." [10]

Discussions continued into 1962. In April the second ASA meeting occurred in Kuala Lumpur, and the three foreign ministers discussed cooperation in eighteen fields. The Tunku told delegates that they will be "converting plans on paper into reality, concerting our efforts to make them successful." The foreign ministers eventually agreed on "a multilateral agreement on trade and navigation," "abolition of visa requirements for officials and waiver of visa fees for other nationals of a

---

[8] *U.S. News & World Report,* "A New 'Sea of Troubles' in Southeast Asia," February 11, 1963, p. 46; *Newsweek,* "Clouds in the South Seas," March 4, 1963, p. 42; *USN&WR,* "Malaya Sees Sukarno as Danger for Southeast Asia," March 18, 1963, p. 80; "National Intelligence Estimate, "Indonesia's International Orientation," 55-63, 10 April 1963, www.foia.cia.gov/browse.

[9] *NYT,* "U.S. Scales Down Help to Indonesia," November 22, 1963, p. 1.

[10] *The New York Times,* "3 Asian Countries will Discuss Ties," February 11, 1961, p. 2; "3 Asian Nations Form Non-Communist Group," August 1, 1961, p. 12; "A Southeast Asia Grouping," August 7, 1961, p. 22.

member country," "joint promotion of tourism," "early consideration of establishing special reduced charges for press telegrams," "through railway service between Kuala Lumpur and Bangkok," and "a micro-wave telecommunications link between Kuala Lumpur and Bangkok." *The New York Times* reported that 'participants in the conference were confident that, as concrete projects adopted at the four-day meeting are implemented, more countries will want to join" the regional efforts "to raise living conditions in emerging states." *The Times* editorialized that the new association "has embarked on a remarkably concrete and promising program." "They have made a hopeful beginning in a venture that over the years should become increasingly important in the Southeast Asian picture."[11]

The idea soon died, a victim of the ambitions of its partner governments. The issue was the islands that Malaya sought to incorporate into a greater Malaysian federation. About the time of the ASA meeting, the Philippine government resurrected a claim to British Borneo, which the Sultan of Sulu once nominally ruled until 1940 when the Sultanate ceded the archipelago to the Philippines, and Manila threatened to take the sovereignty issue to the International Court of Justice. Two months later President Diosdado Macapagal claimed Philippine sovereignty over British North Borneo, and indicated Manila wanted to negotiate to acquire that territory. Several months later Great Britain rejected the Philippine claim, and announced it would merge North Borneo into the new Federation of Malaysia. Then, as *U.S. News* reported, "now Sukarno wants all of Borneo, too." By year's end, both Indonesia and the Philippines looked covetously at North Borneo and supported the Sultan of Brunei's effort to remain independent. Diplomats, *The New York Times* reported, considered this external support for an uprising in Brunei "an upsetting development in Southeast Asia." As a consequence of what Bangkok perceived as meddling in its internal affairs, it postponed the next planned meeting of the A.S.A. Philippine Defense Secretary Marcario Peralta justified the Philippines claim to North Borneo that "they could handle communist subversion there. They did not wish to see a communist-penetrated Malaysia on their southern border."[12]

---

[11] *The New York Times,* "3 Countries Open Talks in Malaya," April 4, 1962, p. 6; *NYT,* "New Asian Group Spurs Projects," April 7, 1962, p. 5; *NYT,* "3 Nations in Asia Set Up Self-Help," April 8, 1962, p. 2; *NYT,* "Good Beginning for A.S.A.," April 16, 1962, p. 28.

[12] *The New York Times,* "Malaysia Merger Faces Obstacles," April 15, 1962, p. 5. *The New York Times* reported Malayan political hardball: Malaya warned "the granite causeway linking Singapore to the Federation of Malaya would be closed at

Despite this background noise, negotiations for a greater Malaysia moved ahead. Malaya wanted Sarawak and North Borneo for their native Malay populations would help balance the largely Chinese and non-Moslem population of Singapore. Negotiators had to strike a balance between national power and local autonomy. London appointed a Royal Commission led by Lord Cobbold, a former governor of the Bank of England, to help resolve these and other issues. *Time* reported "Merger is a Must," and that it would "prevent Singapore from becoming an Asian Cuba off Malaya's coast." Happily, in early August Great Britain announced agreement but without "the schedule for establishing the Federation of Malaysia or any of the precise terms of the agreement." Britain ignored a Philippine request for a looser confederation including the Philippines.[13]

The British and Malayan governments kept the Kennedy Administration well informed. In mid-February 1963, Dean Rusk brought John Kennedy up-to-date. He noted that "the British have been developing the Malaysia concept for the last three years." "While the United States has not participated in the negotiations," Washington has "followed these developments closely" and the British have assumed American approval given the lack of objections. Rusk told Kennedy that "we have informed the British that we do not intend to give any military assistance or economic assistance" to Malaysia. Ambassador Baldwin in Kuala Lumpur provided an analysis to the State Department and recommended Washington should continue to support Malaysia, encourage Malaya and Singapore to "sell" Malaysia in the Asian-African world, seek to "prevent Indonesia and Malaya from reaching the point of open conflict," and do all this "without alienating Indonesia or the Philippines." A few days later, a

---

the end of this year if Singapore rejected the proposed political merger," April 16, 1962, p. 14; *NYT,* "Philippines Claims Sovereignty in British-Ruled North Borneo," June 23, 1962, p. 1; *NYT,* "Manila Rebuffed on North Borneo," August 8, 1962, p. 8; *NYT,* "Singapore in Favor of Joining Malaya," September 2, 1962, p. 1; *NYT,* "Leader of Malaya Warns Indonesia Not to Meddle," September 25, 1962, p. 6; *NYT,* "Manila Imperils Ties to Malaya by Support of Revolt in Brunei," December 19, 1962, p. 1; *U.S. News & World Report,* "On-the-Scene Report," December 24, 1962, p. 31. See also *The Economist,* "Philippines: Getting Unhooked," January 26, 1963, p. 316 on the background of the Philippine claim to North Borneo; NARA, RG 59, CFPF, Box 3975, POL-POLAFF&REL Malaya, Discussion on Indonesia, Malaysia, North Borneo, February 5, 1963.

[13] *The New York Times,* "Malaysia Merger Faces Obstacles," April 15, 1962, p. 5; *Time,* "Merger is a Must," July 27, 1962, www.time.com/time/magazine/article/0,9171,827471,00.html; *NYT,* "Accord Reached on Malay Union," August 1, 1962, p. 1.

Special National Intelligence Estimate noted the British and Malayans promoted the new federation "as a means of checking the Communist threat in Singapore" and "providing the UK with an acceptable alternative to its present colonial position in northern Borneo." The SNIE warned that "Indonesia is the biggest threat to the establishment of the Malaysian Federation" and "has provided political, financial, and limited military support to the Brunei rebels." "The Philippines is an added though lesser threat." Finally, "US political support for the Federation would tend to strengthen it by diminishing its sense of threat from hostile neighbors." In late April Malayan Deputy Prime Minister Tun Abdul Razak told Kennedy that "the Indonesians were seriously concerned about the contrast between the record of prosperity and success which Malaya had achieved since independence and the series of mistakes and difficulties which had beset Indonesia." "He was convinced that the Malayans and Filipinos could settle the differences [i.e., North Borneo] between them." [14]

Perhaps the concern the SNIE evidenced was overly pessimistic, for there seemed to be progress in regional cooperation. In March, Jakarta and Manila agreed to meet with Bangkok to discuss "Malaya's program to absorb three British territories in Borneo," for they "contend that the formation of the expanded state involved the security of Indonesian and the Philippines." Opposition to the proposed Malaysian Federation helped bring, at least temporarily, Jakarta and Manila closer together. They hoped that Malaya would find a loose regional confederation more attractive than a federation only with British colonies in Borneo. Indonesia feared

[14] *FRUS, 1961-1963, Vol. XXIII,* Document 329, Rusk to Kennedy, February 17, 1963, pp. 710-711; NARA, RG 59, CFPF, Box 3976, POL-POLAFF&REL Malaysia-A, Considerations Affecting United States Policy Toward the Malaysian Area, February 11, 1963; a month later Baldwin cabled Harriman to question "unequivocal US decision not give military or economic assistance to Malaysia," same box, POL 7 Visits, Mtgs – Malaysia, Manila to SecState, #986, March 11, 1963; *FRUS, 1961-1963, Vol. XXIII,* Document 330, SNIE 54/59-63, February 20, 1963, pp. 712-714; Document 331, Memorandum of Conversation, April 24, 1963, pp. 718-719; NARA, RG 59, CFPF, Box 4036, POL 2-1, Joint Weekas-Sing, Singapore Weeka NR 14 of April 1963, April 12, 1963; same box, POL 2-3, Politico-Economic Rpts-SING, Politico-Economic Assessment, 8 June 1963; Alden Cutshall, "The Political Geography of Indonesia and Malaya," *United Asia, Vol. 15, No. 3, March 1963,* pp. 245-250. A report from the American consulate in Singapore noted "it is difficult to predict the course of development of Singapore's economy during the next year, in view of the uncertainties concerning [1] economic aspects of Malaysia and [2] Indonesian attitudes; see NARA, RG 59, CFPF, Box 4036, POL 2-3 Politico-Economic Rpts SING, Politico-Economic Assessment, 8 June 1963.

subversion of Indonesian Borneo while the Philippines feared "leftists from Singapore might make Northern Borneo a Communist enclave a few miles from southern Philippine islands." Malaya agreed to meet with Indonesia and the Philippines "in an honest endeavor to iron out difficulties and remove any misunderstandings which may exist, or are likely to arise, in order to pave the way toward harmony and cooperation among the three countries." But *Time* reported that "the acrid dispute between Indonesia, the Philippines, and Malaysia added an undertone of tension to the otherwise calm meeting of the Association of Southeast Asia." At the same time, Malaya, Thailand and the Philippines sought a free-trade region that eventually would become "a Far Eastern counterpart of the European Common Market." They also agreed to form a "consultative council" to restrain "Chinese expansionism" in the area.[15]

The resolution became an agreement on a UN-sponsored plebiscite of peoples on Borneo. In early June "Indonesia and the Philippines relaxed today their firm opposition to the proposed merger of Malaya, Singapore, and three British-held territories on the island of Borneo," *The New York Times* reported. *Business Week* stated that "Sukarno scored a tactical victory this week at his 'summit' meeting" by having the UN verify elections in Sarawak and North Borneo. Indonesian Foreign Minister Subandrio told Ambassador Howard Jones that he was "convinced that

[15] *The New York Times,* "Parley is Proposed on Malaya's Plans," March 11, 1963, p. 3; *NYT,* "Indonesia Builds Ties with Manila," March 16, 1963, p. 3; *NYT,* "Malaya Agrees to Discussions with Philippines and Indonesia," April 5, 1963, p. 3; *NYT,* "Malayan Picture Continues Bright," April 5, 1963, p. 77; *NYT,* "New Bloc Gaining in Southeast Asia," April 7, 1963, p. 3; *NYT,* "Malaya and Philippines Want Talk with Sukarno," April 30, 1963, p. 37. *The Economist* was surprisingly appreciative of the Philippine position about North Borneo and the proposed Malaysian Federation, see "Filipinos on Stage," May 11, 1963, p. 650. Although Tunku Abdul Rahman and Sukarno met informally in Tokyo in early June, the Tunku noted "Malaysia is our domestic affair; it is not the concern of anyone else," *Time,* "Posies for Brickbats," June 7, 1963, www.time/com/time/magazine/article/0,9171,874745,00.html. To be sure, *U.S. News & World Report* claimed in February that Sukarno was "a man in a hurry" and that "Britain, Malaya, Philippines, and even the U.S. are disturbed by Sukarno's appetite for empire," "A New 'Sea of Trouble' in Southeast Asia," February 11, 1963, p. 46; *Time,* "The Man Who," April 12, 1963, www.time.com/time/archive/printout/0,23657,828097,00.html; *NYT,* "3 Nations Advance Free-Trade Region For Southeast Asia," April 4, 1963, p. 17; *NYT,* "3 Asian Lands Act to Block Chinese," June 11, 1963, p. 1; *NYT,* "Asian Lands Back Anti-Peking Pact," June 12, 1963, p. 1; *Time,* "Triplets Reunited," June 21, 1963, www.time.com/time/magazine/article/0,9171,874896,00.html.

UN survey team report will be inconclusive re Sarawak and if so this will create [a] new situation in which Malaysia cannot be established on September 16." The Philippines repeated its suggestion of a "confederation" of the three nations, and that the Philippine claim to North Borneo "could be most justly and expeditiously settled within the framework of a Malay confederation." The result was interest, for a brief time, in an amalgam titled "Maphilindo," for Malaya, the Philippines, and Indonesia. The media gave the Philippines and Macapagal the credit for Maphilindo, noting their "international prestige has soared." Moreover, the Philippines "secured assurance [that] North Borneo claim will be heard fairly and settled amicably." *The Economist* gave credit to the Tunku for knowing "when to compromise." While Dean Rusk traveled to Moscow for the signing of the Limited Test Ban Treaty, Assistant Secretary Roger Hilsman provided him with background: "The primary issue at Manila is that of determining the attitude of the Borneo Territories toward their inclusion in Malaysia;" there was also the British defense agreement with the various territories and the Philippine proposal for Maphilindo. Kennedy soon cabled British Prime Minister Harold MacMillan to postpone the planned August 31 establishment of Malaysia and the British turnover of the two North Borneo territories. He concluded that "this is your show, but I feel we ought to place our worries frankly before you." At another meeting in early August, the three heads of government asked U Thant, Secretary General of the United Nations, to ascertain the views of the populations of the North Borneo territories. Malaya agreed to UN action as long as it completed its work and made its report by August 31, the date that Britain would transfer sovereignty to the new Malaysian Federation. At the same time as discussions of uniting Malay people into the loose grouping of Maphilindo moved forward, President Sukarno of Indonesia seemingly supported military action – guerrilla activity, "menacing gestures," and the like – towards the British colonies in North Borneo. Sukarno apparently worried about the economic success of Malaysia so close to his country's tottering economy, about what he claimed was renewed British colonialism in forming this "super Malay state," and perhaps his ambition to dominate all the islands of the Southwest Pacific. Within a few days, negotiators agreed to give U Thant extra time for the survey if needed before Malaya and Britain moved ahead with the forming of Malaysia. Sukarno claimed victory that "nothing could be done around her [Indonesia's] borders without her approval." [16]

---

[16] *The New York Times,* "Indonesia and Philippines Relax Stand Against Malaysia

Malaya made clear it would move ahead on September 16. In April, Malayan Foreign Minister Tun Razak visited Washington, and indicated his government's belief about "sustained Indonesian opposition after formation Malaysia." He stressed the contrast between Malayan achievements and communist-leaning Indonesian failures. Bangkok issued a declaration on August 29 fixing the date, in part reflecting U Thant's comment that the UN teams would complete their surveys and report by September 14. It seemed somewhat in opposition to the spirit of Maphilindo and Malay solidarity. Predictably, "Indonesia filed a strong protest against Malaya's insistence on forming the Federation of Malaysia Sept. 16," calling it a "reckless and premature decision" and "a unilateral act contravening the letter and spirit of the Manila Summit agreements." At the same time, London asked Washington to support U Thant's report on Malaysia, "assuming it is favorable." Undersecretary of State Averell Harriman agreed "the U.S. would issue a public statement citing U Thant's report," "welcoming the creation of Malaysia." Meanwhile, Jakarta and Manila recalled their Ambassadors and refused to recognize the new federation. Rusk cabled key embassies that "Department believes our position should be cool silence in [the] face of Indo-Phil actions."[17]

Merger," June 8, 1963, p. 1; *Newsweek,* "And Now Maphilindo," June 24, 1963, p. 63; *Business Week,* "International Outlook," August 10, 1963, p. 54; JFK Library, Roger Hilsman Papers, Box 2, Malaysia, 1963-64, Manila to SecState, # 193, August 7, 1963; *FRUS, 1961-1963, Vol. XXIII,* Document 332, Hilsman to Rusk, August 2, 1963; Document 333, Kennedy to MacMillan, August 3, 1963; *NYT,* "Asian Chiefs Differ on U.N. Role in Malaysia Issue," August 2, 1963, p. 4; *NYT,* "Sukarno's Ambition Clouding Malaysia's Future," August 4, 1963, p. 133; *NYT,* "Asia Chiefs Reach Malaysia Accord," August 5, 1963, p. 1; *Time,* "Then the Lights Went Out," August 9, 1963,
www.time.com/time/magazine/article/0,9171,874745,00.html;
Newsweek, "Philippines: On and On," August 12, 1963, p.p. 37-8; *The Economist,* "Malaysia: When to Compromise," August 10, 1963, p. 498; *NYT,* "Sukarno Adjusts Malaysia Policy," August 17, 1963, p. 5; *NYT,* "New Role for Thant," August 18, 1963, p. 153. See *NYT,* "Sukarno Says He Will Heed People on Malaysia," August 29, 1963, p. 4; NARA, RG 59, CFPF, Box 3977, Pol 3 Orgs & Alignment-Malaysia, September 10, 1963.

[17] NARA, RG 59, CFPF, Box 3939, POL Indon-Malay, Malaya and Malaysia, April 23, 1963; Box 3976, POL 7 Visits, Mtgs-Malaysia, April 24, 1963; same folder, State Outgoing Telegram re visit of Tun Razak, April 26, 1963; *The New York Times,* "Malaya Promises a Federation Regardless of Findings by U.N.," August 30, 1963, p. 1; *NYT,* "Indonesia Protests Malaya's Insistence on Forming Malaysia on Sept. 16," September 4, 1963, p. 6. Members of the UN team found the work hot, boring, and at times threatening; see *Time,* "Tunku Yes, Sukarno No," September 6, 1963,

Matters came to a head with the formal creation of the Malaysian Federation in late September 1963. *The New York Times* reported "with fireworks and lantern parades, with games and speeches, the birth of a new nation will be celebrated." The next day *The Times* noted "the country of Malaysia came into being this morning with the raising of her new flag and the release of 101 white pigeons." *The Economist* reported that, external threats notwithstanding, "the most serious threats to Malaysia will come from within – from internal jealousies, racial suspicions and mistrust, and from political and economic tension." It noted the need "to assimilate by persuasion and tolerance the powerful Chinese community," among other challenges. One of the first acts of the new federation was to break relations with its neighbors and fellow Malay states, Indonesia and the Philippines. One day after its founding, "the federation severed normal ties with its larger neighbors to the west and east" in response to opposition by those countries. Angry mobs stormed the Malaysian and British embassies in Jakarta and the Indonesian embassy in Kuala Lumpur. *The New York Times* called the severing of relations "a severe setback to two potentially significant regional organizations of Asian states." It noted the damage to the Association of Southeast Asia and to Maphilindo, founded only six weeks earlier. Indeed, Philippine Foreign Minister Lopez told Adlai Stevenson that Manila would not oppose the UN report on North Borneo because it "would almost surely be [the] end of Maphilindo" to which the Macapagal administration attached great importance. Meanwhile Sukarno "declared that Indonesia was endangered by Malaysia and that she would have to 'fight and destroy' the new federation." But Indonesian Deputy Foreign Minister Sudjarwo explained to U.S. diplomats "at some length [the] reasons why Indonesia would find it difficult [to] accept SYG's [UN survey team's] findings." [18]

---

www.time.com/time/magazine/article/0,9171,870460,00.html; *FRUS, 1961-1963, Vol. XXIII,* Document 334, Memorandum of Conversation, September 10, 1963; NARA, RG 59, CFPF, Box 3977, Pol 3 Orgs & Alignment-Malaysia, State outgoing telegram #306, September 14, 1963.

[18] *NYT,* "Birth of a Nation in Asia," September 15, 1963, p. 234; "Malaysia's Birth Marked in 4 Lands," September 16, 1963, p. 1; *The Economist,* "Malaysia: Brave New State," September 21, 1963, p. 993; *The New York Times,* "Malaysia Breaks Ties to 2 Nations," September 18, 1963, p. 1; *NYT,* "Southeast Asian Setback," September 19, 1963, p. 2; *NYT,* "Sukarno Pledges Fight to Achieve Malaysia Doom," September 26, 1963, p. 1; *Time,* "Wild Actions, Wilder Threats," October 4, 1963, www.time.com/time/archive/printout/0,23657,875246,00.html. At the UN, Indonesia claimed the British originally conceived of Malaysia "as a perpetuation of their sphere of influence in a strategic area," while Britain and Malaysia forcefully disagreed; see *NYT,* "Indonesia Scores Britain at U.N.,"

As its neighbors continued to harbor misgivings, Malaysia moved ahead. While Sukarno apparently pulled back from military action, Indonesia continued to show little interest in resuming negotiations with Malaysia or in encouraging the Philippines to recognize the new federation. Jakarta continued to reinforce troop units along its side of the border with Sarawak and Sabah. Great Britain remained concerned and when British Foreign Secretary Lord Home met with President Kennedy, Home said "the last thing the British wanted was a conflict with the Indonesians. It was difficult to tell what Sukarno would do," and "the U.S. would have to put the squeeze on him." Kennedy and Home discussed American economic aid to Indonesia; Kennedy was reluctant to cut it, telling Home that "this was a card that could only be played once." More important, matters were not as simple as Home implied. Kennedy agreed to have the US ambassador in Kuala Lumpur deliver an oral message to the Tunku that "developments in your area have been of deep concern to me," and "the best chance of bringing about a real reconciliation between the Maphilindo powers seems to lie in the restoration of contacts between you." Despite Kennedy's comment, by year's end the State Department noted "US has stopped any consideration of additional aid." "In addition, US has cut out of ongoing programs all arms and ammunition." The Manila embassy noted that Macapagal alternated between the long-term goal of "constraining Indonesians and influencing them toward the Free World" with "protecting GOP North Borneo claim." Undersecretary George Ball cabled Ambassador William Stevenson in Manila that he "should see Macapagal and inform him that as part of [the] President's efforts [to] reduce tensions in [the] Malaysia dispute, President had been in touch with Tunku." Robert Komer of the National Security Council Staff wrote National Security Advisor McGeorge Bundy that "only the US has the leverage in this situation to have any influence on Sukarno," that "obviously, we must support Malaysia," but if the U.S. government allowed matters to drift, "we may practically push him into Communist hands." Komer proposed "some more Presidential diplomacy" to avoid losing "Indonesia to the [Communist] Bloc." Several days later, Benjamin Read of the State Department sent Bundy a memorandum proposing quiet U.S. diplomacy with each of the parties – the Tunku, Sukarno, and Macapagal. Philippine Foreign Minister Salvador Lopez visited Washington in October 1963 and stated Manila would recognize Malaysia if the new federation put assurances in writing that it would assume all

September 28, 1963, p. 4; NARA, RG 59, CFPF, Box 3977, Pol 3 Orgs & Alignment-Malaysia, USUN New York to Sec State, #786, September 12, 1963; same folder, USUN New York to Sec State, #787, September 12, 1963.

obligations and responsibilities of Malaya, including North Borneo. Michael Forrestal of the NSC Staff wrote Bundy with his concern at "a developing stalemate in our diplomatic activities in the Far East." He stated that "we have allowed the Indonesian confrontation with Malaysia to rock along without any initiative on our part," and, as the Indonesian military build-up continued, Forrestal concluded "this is a situation where coordinated initiatives are required in four capitals: Manila, K.L., Jakarta, and London." Komer in another memo to Bundy agreed: "I am more convinced than ever that inertia, plus the nationalistic emotionalism of Sukarno, the Tunku, Macapagal, and the British, is carrying us inescapably toward a big Malaysia flap." Malaysia, at least in the short term, had to regard its larger neighbors warily.[19]

As Malaysia struggled into existence, Indonesia charted an uncertain course that, at times, seemed to threaten war with its neighbors. Unlike Malaya in 1961, American foreign policymakers focused on Indonesia from the outset of the Kennedy Administration. *The New York Times* reported that more than "the permanent threat of a nuclear Communist China," "the most immediate threat to the peace in this corner of the world is the new flare-up of tensions between Indonesia and the Netherlands over West New Guinea." Ambassador Howard Jones cabled Dean Rusk in January that it was time for a reassessment of U.S. policy and to deal with the increasing Communist influence in Indonesia. The issue was the status of Dutch [West] New Guinea, which Indonesia called West Irian. Jones

---

[19] *The New York Times,* "Indonesia Easing 'War' on Malaysia," December 7, 1963, p. 2; JFK Library, NSF, Box 423, Robert W. Komer, Indonesia, 1961-1963 (folder 1 of 3), White House to Sec State, September 31, 1963; *FRUS, 1961-1963, Vol. XXIII,* Document 339, Memorandum of Conversation, October 4, 1963; NARA, RG 59, CFPF, Box 3980, POL 16 Independence, Recognition-Malaysia, Manila to SecState, #442, September 2, 1963; same box, Pol-PolAff&Rel Malaysia-A, October 5, 1963; same folder, State outgoing telegram, October 11, 1963; *FRUS, 1961-1963, Vol. XXIII,* Document 341, Komer to Bundy, October 9, 1963; Document 342, State to Kennedy, October 14, 1963; NARA, RG 59, CFPF, Box 3980 POL 16, Independence, Recognition, Malaysia, Malaysia-Indonesia Dispute, October 16, 1963; same box, POL-POLAFF&REL, Malaysia-A, State Outgoing Telegram, October 18, 1963; *FRUS, 1961-1963, Vol. XXIII,* Document 346, NIE 54/55-63, The Malaysian-Indonesian Conflict," October 30, 1963; .Document 347, Forrestal to Bundy, November 18, 1963; Document 348, Komer to Bundy, December 7, 1963; LBJ Library, NSF Country File, Box 246, Indonesia, Cables, Vol. I, 11/63-11/64, State Outgoing Telegram 683, December 20, 1963; J.M. van der Kroef, "The New Malaysia and its Neighbors," *United Asia, Vol.15, No. 10, October 1963,* p. 688.

wanted Washington to seize the initiative, find a resolution, and "convince Sukarno we are interested in working with him to achieve [a] peaceful solution." Jones wanted President Kennedy to develop a personal relationship with the Indonesian. He concluded that "we must take positive action to restore relations between the US Executive and Indonesia as one element in coordinated program to keep Indonesia out of Communists' hands."[20]

They needed to find a compromise on Papua New Guinea. The Dutch government wanted to prepare Papuans for self-determination; Indonesia viewed it [along with Portuguese-controlled East Timor] as part of a greater Indonesia. The Dutch wanted American support, which would complicate relations with a region very conscious of its colonial heritage. The situation forced Washington to choose between a NATO ally and the most populous country in the region – truly the horns of a dilemma! Various proposals – including UN trusteeship – failed because Sukarno was determined to take West Irian. [21]

Sukarno's visit to Washington did little to improve U.S.-Indonesian relations. Sukarno invited himself to the United States as part of a tour in which he would visit the Soviet Union; Kennedy agreed to extend a formal invitation. An SNIE of early March noted the stakes: The Soviet offensive to gain influence in Indonesia "appears to be making significant progress." Richard Bissell of the CIA wrote McGeorge Bundy in late March that "Indonesia's growing vulnerability to communism stems from the distinctive bias of Sukarno's global orientation." Moreover, "economic factors are likely to play a decisive role in making Indonesia ripe for a Communist takeover." "A continuing and accelerated decline in the economic life of Indonesia is very probable." The unofficial CIA paper held Sukarno responsible for Indonesia's economic decline, offered no proposal to mediate the West New Guinea dispute, but believed Kennedy needed to convince "Sukarno of the firmness of the United States position."[22]

---

[20] *The New York Times*, "The Chinese Threat: Reports from Asia," January 15, 1961, p. E5; *FRUS, 1961-1963, Vol. XXIII,* Document 143, Jones to Rusk, January 25, 1961, pp. 302-304; Document 144, Jones to Rusk, January 25, 1961, pp. 305-307.

[21] *FRUS, 1961-1963, Vol. XXIII,* Document 145, Memorandum of Conversation, January 31, 1961, p. 308; Document 149, Rusk to Bowles, February 18, 1961, p. 313. See Document 158, Rusk to Kennedy, The Problem of West New Guinea (West Irian), April 3, 1961, pp. 336-338.

[22] *FRUS, 1961-1963, Vol. XXIII,* Document 147, Rusk to Kennedy, February 14, 1961, p. 311; Document 149, Jones to Rusk, February 23, 1961, p. 314; Document

The visit was full of pomp but little substance. Chester Bowles prepared President Kennedy, indicating the need to "help improve the cordial but still somewhat distant tone of our relations with Indonesia," indicate Washington's interest in a peaceful settlement of the West New Guinea dispute, increase Sukarno's understanding "of our position in the Cold War," and thus "dispel his evident belief that we oppose him personally." Sukarno told Kennedy that "the crux of the attitude of the peoples of Asia is nationalism," that they "are longing and fighting for freedom." Sukarno claimed that "long before the Dutch came, West Irian was Indonesian territory."[23]

The tension over West New Guinea/Irian continued for months. In early September Robert Johnson reported to Walt Rostow on the "latest Indonesian reaction" to U.S. proposals, and it was "not an encouraging message." Later that month, the Netherlands offered to transfer control over West New Guinea to the United Nations. Three weeks later Rostow wrote Kennedy that he needed to press for Indonesian control, "otherwise the issue will continue to divert Indonesian attention from the constructive tasks of economic development." A Dutch effort to negotiate through the United Nations ran into an opposition group of mostly Asian and Soviet bloc delegates. McGeorge Bundy wrote Kennedy that Rusk's dislike, which Kennedy shared, for Sukarno was influencing policy, and the result "can only help the Communists."[24]

151, SNIE 55-61, Outlook in Indonesia with Special Reference to West New Guinea," March 7, 1961, pp. 318-319; Document 155, Bissell to Bundy, March 27, 1961, pp. 328-332. Robert Komer, who was remarkably forthright as a staff member on Bundy's National Security Council Staff, took offense at Bissell's study, but offered no real alternative, see Document 156, Komer to Bundy, March 27, 1961, pp. 333-334, and later took equally strong offense at a State Department paper on the West Irian situation, see Document 159, Komer to Rostow, April 5, 1961, p. 340. The Dutch viewed Sukarno as "a dangerous opportunist," and that "Netherlands relations with Indonesia had deteriorated in direct ratio to the growth of power of Sukarno over the past ten years," see Document 162, Memorandum of Conversation, April 10, 1961, p. 345. Indonesia's poor economic performance continued to worry U.S. analysts; see Document 186, Johnson to Rostow, Indonesian Economic Development, September 8, 1961, pp. 419-421.

[23] *FRUS, 1961-1963, Vol. XXIII,* Document 168, Bowles to Kennedy, April 20, 1961, pp. 368-369; Document 170, Rusk to Kennedy, April 22, 1961, pp. 378-379; Document 171, Rostow to Kennedy, April 22, 1961, pp. 380-382; Document 172, Memorandum of Conversation, April 24, ,1961, pp. 382-384.

[24] *FRUS, 1961-1963, Vol. XXIII,* Document 185, Johnson to Rostow, September 2, 1961, p. 416; see Document 193, Editorial Note, p. 434; Document 197, Rostow to Kennedy, October 13, 1961, pp. 440-441; *NYT,* "Dutch Again Urge New Guinea

The media combined concern for West New Guinea/Irian and for Sukarno's orientation in the Cold War. *Newsweek* reported on Indonesia's "tilt toward Moscow" to counter what its military chief, General Abdul Haris Nasution, claimed was the "provocative marshalling of Dutch military power" in West New Guinea. Three months later *Newsweek* had a map of the region with a vice grip "squeezing out the Dutch." *U.S. News & World Report* noted Sukarno "has Soviet arms" and "like Nehru in Goa, Sukarno has Moscow's blessing." That is, the news magazine reduced the issues to the existing Cold War bipolarity which, of course, predetermined the U.S. response. *U.S. News* followed up arguing that "it's Indonesia that's set for a grab of territory" but "a Sukarno war will not be a cinch. He could be headed for disaster – dragging the U.S., Russia and others into a conflict nobody really wants." Two weeks later, the news magazine stated "a war between Indonesia and Holland over West New Guinea would be one of the silliest wars ever fought." *Newsweek* quoted Sukarno telling his parliament that Indonesia will speak "with the language of guns." [25]

By early January 1962 Indonesia seemed to turn to military action. The Dutch navy claimed to have sunk at least one Indonesian torpedo boat and forced the invading units to turn away. *Time* reported on three Indonesian torpedo boats attacking several Dutch frigates. Sukarno claimed that "we've got the ships, we've got the men,' we've got the money, too" even though he lacked all of them. *The New York Times* warned that "it could be a bitter war," and that the conflict "has extended cold war considerations to embrace one of the most primitive lands on earth." As the two combatants backed away from further military action, Komer urged the U.S. to convince the Dutch the real issue was "the importance of retaining a western presence in Indonesia" rather than continuing Dutch occupation of West New Guinea. A few weeks later, the Dutch government indicated it would turn over administration of West New Guinea if Indonesia would

Talks," November 29, 1961, p. 5; *FRUS, 1961-1963, Vol. XXIII*, Document 205, Bundy to Kennedy, December 1, 1961, p. 463. See *Time,* "Fight over the Papuans," December 29, 1961, www.time.com/time/magazine/article/0,9171,827197,00.html.

[25] *Newsweek,* "Indonesia: Tilt Toward Moscow," January 30, 1961, p. 36; "Indonesia: In the Middle," April 24, 1961, p. 55; *NYT,* "Dutch Again Urge New Guinea Talks," November 29, 1961, p. 5; "Indonesia Makes New Guinea Offer," December 29, 1961, p. 4; *U.S. News & World Report,* "Dutch New Guinea: Next to Be 'Liberated?'", January 1, 1962, pp. 22-23; "If Sukarno Chooses War," January 29, 1962, p. 30; "A War Over This?" February 8, 1962, p. 44; *Newsweek,* "Indonesia: Language of Guns," April 9, 1962, p. 50.

permit the local population an opportunity to vote. At the same time, the Dutch told American officials they were considering marines as reinforcements and asked if they could use U.S. military bases to transport their troops. The Dutch also sent two destroyers and two submarines to the U.S. West Coast [through the Panama Canal] perhaps on their way to the southwest Pacific.[26]

The continuing confrontation with The Netherlands overshadowed virtually all foreign and domestic issues for Indonesia. A new National Intelligence Estimate in early March noted that "Sukarno will probably draw even closer to the [Communist] Bloc position on major international issues." At the same time, "the economic outlook for Indonesia over the next year or so is definitely unfavorable" owing to "the intensification of inflation and the continued decline of foreign exchange reserves." Amry Vandenbosch wrote that the first twelve years of Indonesian independence "have been hectic; economically they have brought little but suffering." He further noted that "the political and economic deterioration which began so early has never been more than momentarily arrested. The country is now in a desperate plight."[27]

Talks began in mid-March although neither side offered to compromise. Indonesian negotiators could only accept the transfer of West Irian; Dutch negotiators refused without Indonesian guarantees about the Papuan people. As the talks stalled with mutual recriminations and Dutch

---

[26] *FRUS, 1961-1963, Vol. XXIII,* Document 221, Rusk to Jones, January 15, 1962, p. 221; *Time,* "Setback for Sukarno," January 26, 1962, www.time.com/time/magazine/article/0,9171,972869,00.html; "By Jingo," February 9, 1962, www.time.com/time/magazine/article/0,9171,938310,00.html; *NYT,* "New Guinea Crisis Grows," January 21, 1962, p. 154; *FRUS, 1961-1963, Vol. XXIII,* Document 225, Komer to Kaysen, February 2, 1962, pp. 512-3; Document 230, Ball to AG Kennedy, February 12, 1962, p. 521; Document 240, Tyler to Rusk, February 27, 1962, pp. 542-543. See President Kennedy's meeting with Dutch Foreign Minister Joseph Luns, March 2, 1962, Document 244, pp. 549-552, which Robert Komer characterized as "painful." *FRUS, 1961-1963, Vol. XXIII,* Document 249, Ball to Harriman, March 14, 1962, p. 558. *Time* noted that 'for all Sukarno's impassioned denunciations of Dutch 'imperialism,' indignation was mainly directed at the U.S.," "Into Space," January 19, 1962, www.time.com/magazine/article/0,9171,895825,00.html.

[27] *United Asia, Volume 14, No. 2, February 1962,* "Special Review of West Irian Dispute," pp. 97-132; *FRUS, 1961-1963, Vol. XXIII,* Document 247, NIE 55-62, The Prospects for Indonesia, March 7, 1962, pp. 555-556; Amry Vandenbosch, "'Guided Democracy' in Indonesia," *Current History, December 1961,* pp. 329-331. See also, Justus M. van der Kroef, "Indonesia in the Cold War," *Current History, February 1960,* pp. 88-93.

anger at the U.S. government, the CIA reported "a number of indications that the Indonesians may be planning large scale attacks in the West New Guinea area in the near future." *Time* reported that "warfare flared again along the coast" of the disputed island. The fighting caused the Dutch to demand guarantees for the native population, and the Indonesian delegation "rose and left for home." [28]

The talks re-started in mid-July. *Newsweek* reported that "Sukarno's vaunted 'invasion' of Dutch New Guinea seemed to be getting nowhere," and "under heavy diplomatic pressure, the Dutch announced they were ready to accept a U.S. proposal 'as the basis for negotiation.'" U.S. Ambassador Ellsworth Bunker served as an "honest broker," and with a Dutch commitment to transfer administration to the United Nations and an Indonesian commitment to permit some "act" of self-determination by the Papuans. Even the skeptical Robert Komer wrote President Kennedy that the talks "are going well so far." Several weeks later Ambassador Jones informed Rusk that "Sukarno has accepted terms of preliminary understanding on [the] West New Guinea issue." [29]

In response to the good news, Kennedy issued National Security Action Memorandum 179 asking key departments and agencies to "review their programs for Indonesia and assess what further measures might be useful." The goal was to "capitalize on the US role in promoting this settlement." There were immediate challenges. The "very large and complex problems of Indonesian balance of payments and internal inflation" reflected "repayment of outstanding foreign debts which are largely Soviet." As Michael Forrestal of the NSC pointed out, "the political repercussions of even indirectly paying off debt incurred for military equipment in the Soviet Union would be deafening." Nonetheless, two weeks later, George Ball forwarded the State Department's proposal

---

[28] See *FRUS, 1961-1963, Vol. XXIII,* Documents 250-257, pp. 559-573; Document 269, Knochel to McCone, May 22, 1962, pp. 595-596; *Time,* "Pacific Snowball," April 6, 1962, www.time.com/time/magazine/article/0,9171,896033,00.html; "Dutch Squeeze," April 13, 1962, www.time.com/time/magazine/article/0,9171,827260,00.html; *The Economist,* "Holland and Indonesia: The Unlikely Remarriage," April 22, 1962, p. 224.

[29] *Newsweek,* "Indonesia: The Easy Way," June 11, 1962, p. 46; *U.S. News & World Report,* "Dutch Fending Off Sukarno, But Time and Russia are on His Side," June 11, 1962, p. 74; *FRUS, 1961-1963, Vol. XXIII,* Document 274, Rusk to Kennedy, July 10, 1962, pp. 603-604; Document 276, Komer to Kennedy, July 20, 1962, p. 607; *Time,* "Toward West Irian," August 24, 1962, www.time.com/time/magazine/article/0,9171,896515.00.html. On the possible breakdown of talks, see Document 281, Memorandum of Conversation, July 26, 1962, pp. 618-620.

to President Kennedy which called for expanding U.S. programs for food and fiber, technical assistance, the Peace Corps, and for persuading Indonesia and Free World nations to join in a major economic stabilization and development program. Ten days later Kennedy approved the "recommendations for emergency assistance" but not any others.[30]

It soon became clear that agreement on Papua New Guinea did not improve Indonesian foreign relations. Averell Harriman noted that "the U.S. and the U.K. differed somewhat in assessing the likelihood that Sukarno would deliberately join the Soviet Bloc." But both agreed that Sukarno wanted to expand against his neighbors. While Ambassador Howard Jones reported in February on "favorable prospects for econ[omic] stabilization," the embassy's semi-annual assessment reported that "the economy [is] currently deteriorating perceptibly." Perry Ellis wrote that "Indonesian production cannot be restored to anything like the pre-World War II level." Interestingly he claimed that "weird contradictions continue to accompany severe inflation." Jones sent a discouraging cable to Undersecretary Averell Harriman in early March 1963 that the "next few weeks may be critical ones for Indonesia." Indonesian leaders recognized the desperate economic situation and the need for reforms, but Sukarno cared more for his image as a revolutionary leader allied with the People's Republic of China and the Soviet Union than accepting the harsh economic medicine the United States and the International Monetary Fund proposed. *U.S. News* reported that "inside Indonesia, the economy is skidding downhill faster and faster" and perhaps that influenced Sukarno's apparent commitment to a guerilla war with Malaya over Borneo.[31]

At the same time, Jakarta was seeking to expropriate assets of two American oil companies, and that complicated prospects for American economic assistance. Embassy officials reported in April that "the hoped for improvement in the economy has yet to materialize." *Business Week* reported that "Reds' attempt to make archipelago a Communist arsenal

---

[30] *FRUS, 1961-1963, Vol. XXIII,* Document 285, Embassy in Indonesia to State, August 3, 1962, p. 624; Document 287, NSAM 179, August 16, 1962, p. 627; Document 290, Forrestal to Harriman, September 25, 1962; Document 291, Ball to Kennedy, October 10, 1962, pp. 634-637; Document 294, NSAM 195, October 22, 1962, p. 647.

[31] NARA, RG 59, CFPF, Box 3941, POL Indon-USSR, Memorandum of Conversation, January 17, 1963; Box 3937, POL 2-1, JointWeekas, Indon, 2/1/63, Jakarta to Secretary of State, #1229, February 9, 1963; same box, POL 2-3, Politico-Economic, Indon, 2/1/63, Amembassy Jakarta to State, February 13, 1963; *FRUS, 1961-1963, Vol. XXIII* Document 302, Jones to Harriman, March 1, 1963, pp. 659-662.

poses a threat to other countries in Southeast Asia – and to U.S. foreign policy" and printed a map with the caption, "Soviet-armed Indonesia on the march in Southeast Asia." In mid-May James D Bell wrote Undersecretary Roger Hilsman wondering "why are we giving money to that swine Sukarno when Indonesia has already swung over into the Communist camp?" Equally important, "what proof do we have that Sukarno won't try to have Indonesia expand its borders to include British Borneo, Portuguese Timor or Australian New Guinea." Finally, "do we have any hope of success in getting Indonesia to embark on a sound economic stabilization program?" By mid-summer, Sukarno "retreated abruptly from the good feeling established in Tokyo and Manila among the Malayans, the Indonesians and the Filipinos. His recent attacks on the Tunku have been violent." The situation deteriorated, and in late September Secretary Rusk told Subandrio that he was "increasingly concerned" over "disturbances against the British and Malaysian representation, owing to the announcement of the new Federation of Malaysia. As the date for the new Malaysian Federation neared, the embassy in Jakarta cabled the State Department that "Indonesia has been at what might be characterized as a fork in the road." It contrasted "a further turn toward the Sino-Soviet Bloc" with a turn "toward the West with an attempt to stabilize the economy with assistance from the IMF and the DAC countries." "The economic situation," the embassy reported, "is still very serious" and "which could have been prevented."[32]

---

[32] NARA, RG 59, Box 3937, Pol 2-3, Politico-Economic Indon, 2/1/63, AmConsul Surabaya to State, #A-73, April 9, 1963; *U.S. News & World Report,* "Worldgram," March 4, 1963, p. 58. On the oil company negotiations, see Documents 305-309, pp. 666-675. *FRUS, 1961-1963, Vol. XXIII*, Document 312, Forrestal to Kennedy, July 23, 1963, p. 678; Document 315, Memorandum of Conversation, September 24, 1963, pp. 686-687. A Japanese diplomat, Hidemichi Kira, reported a conversation with an Indonesian economic official; he quoted the Indonesian as saying "if Indonesia did not get U.S. assistance, it would turn to the USSR and Red China." The Indonesian further challenged Kira that Japan could not afford to get out of Indonesia because her raw material assets and her market for consumer items made Indonesia indispensable to Japan," NARA, RG 59, CFPF, Box 3939, POL Indon-Jap, Amembassy Jakarta to State, #A-1013, March 15, 1963; Box 3940, POL Indon-US, Five Questions on Indonesia, May 11, 1963; *Business Week,* "Indonesia-Another Cuba?" April 27, 1963, p. 59. The Indonesian government was sensitive to U.S. media criticism of the Indonesian economy and it complained to the government in Washington: see NARA, RG 59, CFPF, Box 3940, POL Indon-US, Memorandum of Conversation, May 6, 1963; same folder, Indonesian Embassy Officers Discussion of U.S. Press Criticism of Indonesia," May 10, 1963. Media criticism, nonetheless, continued. *The New York Times*

When Johnson succeeded Kennedy, Indonesia's relations with its neighbors and with the United States continued to deteriorate. Philippine President Macapagal seemed to think that Sukarno was "bewildered." Macapagal "was convinced Sukarno wanted to move toward the West and the United States but a way would have to be found that he could do so without endangering his domestic political position." From other sources, American policymakers believed that the Indonesian government needed reassurance. The embassy reported on an editorial in the *Indonesian Herald* which praised the "fruitful results" of General Nasution's visit to Washington, DC. The embassy concluded that the "editorial seems to reflect the need for self-reassurance by Indo[nesian] leadership and elites that [the] death of President Kennedy does not prejudice Indo[nesian] chances [to] gain objectives vis-à-vis U.S." Several days latter Ambassador Frank Galbraith reported that Indonesian Foreign Minister Subandrio "contested my assertion that economic confrontation [with Malaysia] was costly to Indonesia." *The Indonesian Herald,* considered to represent the views of the Foreign Ministry, editorialized that "confrontation is a logical outgrowth of Indonesia's consistent policy for true national freedom in all former colonial territories," and that "US concern that confrontation against Malaysia may delay Indonesia's economic rehabilitation 'is not entirely misplaced.'" Johnson told McNamara that "I don't think we ought to encourage this guy [Sukarno] to do what he is doing there. And I think that any assistance just shows weakness on our part." [33]

---

editorialized that "Indonesia seems inexorably addicted to one nationalistic excess after another." It criticized the seizure of West Irian, the pressure on American oil companies, and the deteriorating economy," "Crossroads for Sukarno," May 30, 1963, p. 11; NARA, RG 59, CFPF, Box 3937, POL 2-3 Politico-Economic Indon, 2/1/63, Amembassy Jakarta to State, A-245, September 13, 1963. *The New York Times* hailed a "stopgap financial plan to stabilize Indonesia's economy" that required Indonesian fiscal austerity as well as broad international support, "Indonesia Moves to Spur Economy," June 30, 1963, p. 18; *Time* represented media opinion when it stated that "of the 79 nations receiving help under the U.S. foreign aid program, none is so exasperating as Indonesia. Despite $881 million in U.S. handouts since 1946, Indonesia is an economic shambles," October 25, 1963, "Hoodwinked," www.time.com/time/magazine/article/0,9171,830486,00.html.

[33] NARA, RG 59, CFPF, Box 3940, POL Indon-P, Indonesia and Malaysia Dispute, November 27, 1963; same box, POL Indon-US, Jakarta to SecState, #1184, December 4, 1963. During his visit, Nasution argued that "Malaysia under British domination and not truly independent" and that Malaysia "would fall under domination of resident Chinese and thus provide Communist Chinese beachhead., NARA, RG 59, CFPF, Box 3937, POL 7 Visits & Mtgs-Indon, 2/1/63, State to

For many months thereafter, American officials worried about an Indonesian invasion of the island units of the new Malaysian Federation. Rusk cabled Ambassador Jones that "latest Indonesian actions such as Kalabakan raid, renewed statements GOI intention [to] "crush" Malaysia, Sukarno and Saleh treatment of SVN Liberation Front make it questionable whether we will be able [to] continue existing ongoing aid let alone increase it or take on new obligations." The situation was so serious that Rusk asked Johnson "whether a Presidential Determination on aid to Indonesia should be signed," which would cut U.S. aid and perhaps force Indonesia further into Soviet and Chinese arms. National Security Advisor McGeorge Bundy followed up that "we should have a cool and firm policy of increasing opposition to Sukarno, if he goes on lifting the level of force used against Malaysia." In early May, Assistant Secretary of State William Bundy warned Indonesia that the United States might cut its remaining aid programs if Jakarta continued its aggression.[34]

Mediation efforts did little to ease tensions between Indonesia and Malaysia. *Newsweek* reported Sukarno "running true to form" as he "shouted out his determination to 'crush Malaysia.'" Sukarno traveled to Manila to meet Macapagal, but could not move the Philippine government beyond its existing non-recognition policy and claim to North Borneo. Sukarno "flatly refused to withdraw guerrillas on Malaysian territory except in [the] context [of a] political settlement." In May 1964, the Philippines and Malaysia established consular relations, a first, step, perhaps, to establishing embassies. *The Economist* worried that Washington's desire for a resolution might reward Indonesian intransigence. *U.S. News* quoted a "senior British field commander" who stated "these raids [into Borneo] are just a curtain raiser for what's bound to be a long, hard and costly war." Attorney General Robert Kennedy traveled to Asia

---

Jakarta, #626, December 7, 1963; Lyndon Baines Johnson Library, NSF, Box 246, Indonesia Cables Vol. I, 11/63-11/64, Jakarta to SecState, #1212 [One of Two], December 9, 1963; NARA, RG 59, CFPF, Box 3980, POL-POLAFF&REL Malaysia-A, Amembassy Jakarta to State, #A-567, December 24, 1963; Department of State, *Foreign Relations of the United States, 1964-1968, Volume XXVI, Indonesia; Malaysia-Singapore, Philippines,* GPO, Washington, DC, 2001, Document 1, Telephone Conversation Between Johnson and McNamara, January 2, 1964, p. 1.

[34] For an example of yet more efforts at negotiation, see NARA, RG 59, CFPF, Box 3980, POL 16, Independence, Recognition-Malaysia, Malaysia-Indonesia Dispute, October 16, 1963; *FRUS, 1964-1968, Vol. XXVI,* Document 2, State to Indonesia, January 4, 1964, p. 2; Document 4, Rusk to Johnson, January 6, 1964, p. 5; Document 6, Bundy Memorandum, January 7, 1964, p. 13; *NYT,* "U.S. Warns Indonesia on Anti-Malaysia Policy," May 6, 1964, p. 5.

and the Thai and Philippine governments also offered their "good offices." *U.S. News* claimed Britain only worried that "Kennedy's special mission might not get results" for "Britain can't get rid of its empire fast enough" and "London will be delighted if U.S. will share Britain's headaches." Kennedy told Sukarno "that the policy of military confrontation which he is pursuing against Malaysia will have disastrous consequences for our relations with his country." Kennedy appeared to have succeeded, for Sukarno "agreed to stop military confrontation on Kalimanitan border as preparatory step to holding tripartite meeting of representatives of Malaysia, Indonesia, Philippines." U.S. officials described a subsequent breakfast as "extremely friendly even lighthearted." Kennedy then secured support from Philippine President Diosdado Macapagal who agreed to urge the Tunku to cooperate to ease regional tensions. Within four weeks, Michael Forrestal wrote Assistant Secretary of State Roger Hilsman that "I am getting concerned that the agreement to negotiate the difference in this dispute is beginning to come unstuck." Forrestal noted Sukarno's unwillingness to withdraw guerrilla forces and the Tunku's unwillingness to engage in serious talks before such a withdrawal. Rusk agreed several days later in a cable to the Indonesian embassy: "on eve Bangkok meeting, prospects major progress not promising." Rusk sent a telegram to the embassies in Jakarta and Kuala Lumpur explaining the only remaining action for the U.S. government was to reduce aid to Indonesia. *Newsweek* noted an "inauspicious beginning" for the conference – "no set agenda" and the "building's air conditioning promptly collapsed." At a meeting of White House staff on March 4 Bundy noted "there are reports that discussions between Sukarno and the Tunku have been broken off." *Newsweek* reported that "the conference broke up over a single issue: the refusal of Sukarno to withdraw his infiltrators from the Malaysian Borneo territories." *Newsweek* stated that "with bland intransigence, Indonesia's Sukarno refused to abandon his guerrilla raids across the 970-mile border which separates Indonesian Borneo from Malaysian Borneo." Six weeks later American diplomats despaired over re-starting the talks. In mid-June the three Asian leaders met in Tokyo but Prince Abdul Rahman "would not agree to cooperate with any commission so long as President Sukarno kept his guerrillas on Malaysian territory" and Sukarno "pledge his nation" to destroy the Malaysian Federation. By August, there were new raids on the western coast of Malaya, a scant 30 miles across the Straits of Malacca from Indonesian Sumatra. For the remainder of 1964, State Department officials tried to bring Sukarno and the Tunku back to the bargaining table without luck.[35]

While the talks stalled, the fighting continued. *U.S. News* claimed that "Sukarno is using his harassing tactics to try to get Malaysia's share of another big island – Borneo." While Sukarno sent paratroopers, seaborne raiders, and guerrillas into Borneo, Indonesia was "a shocking mess of mismanagement, graft and corruption. His cities and towns are rat-ridden. Millions of his people are diseased, close to starvation." *U.S. News* worried that Sukarno's "war" might involve the United States in another

---

[35] *Newsweek,* "Malaysia: The Bully Boy," January 13, 1964, p. 34; *NYT,* "Sukarno Cancels Appeal to Manila," January 9, 1964, p. 3; *NYT,* "Malaysia Parley Closes in Manila," January 11, 1964, p. 3; NARA, RG 59, CFPF, Box 2581, POL 7, Visit,Mtgs,PHIL, 1/1/64, Amembassy Jakarta to Department, #A-698, February 5, 1964; same folder, Manila to SecState, #1290, March 1, 1964; same folder, Manila to SecState, #1299, March 2, 1964; Box 2589, POL 17, PHIL-Malaysia, 3/9/64, Amembassy Manila to State, A-973, May 27, 1964; *The Economist,* "Confronting Sukarno," January 25, 1964, pp. 281-282; *USN&WR,* "Borneo: Where a New War is Heating Up," January 27, 1964, p. 58; *Business Week,* "International Outlook," February 1, 1964, p. 62; *FRUS, 1964-1968, Vol. XXVI,* Document 14, Forrestal to Johnson, January 13, 1964, p. 33; Document 17, Embassy in Japan to State, January 17, 1964, p. 37; Document 18, Forrestal to Bundy, January 18, 1964, p. 38; Document 21, Embassy in the Philippines to State Department, January 20, 1964, p. 43. For summaries of Kennedy's mission, see Document 23, Embassy in Indonesia to State Department, January 23, 1964, pp. 45-49 and Document 27, US Mission to the UN to State Department, January 28, 1964, pp. 53-54. See also *NYT,* "Robert Kennedy in Tokyo to Seek Malaysia Accord," January 17, 1964, p. 1; "Malaysia and Philippines will Discuss Dispute," January 22, 1064, p. 11; "Sukarno Accepts Malaysian Truce," January 23, 1964, p. 1; "U.S. Sees 'Last Chance' to Prevent Malaysia War," January 31, 1964, p. 9; *Time,* "Seaweed & Soothing Words," January 24, 1964, www.time.com/time/magazine/article/0,9171,875656,00.html; *USN&WR,* "Worldgram," February 3, 1964, p. 54; *NYT,* "Malaysia Pact Still Far Off," February 9, 1964, p. E4; *Newsweek,* "Malaysia: Difficult and Delicate," February 17, 1964, p. 46; *FRUS, 1964-1968, Vol. XXVI,* Document 31, Forrestal to Hilsman, February 19, 1964, p. 60; Document 32, Rusk to Jones, February 29, 1964, p. 62; Document 34, Memorandum for the Record, March 4, 1964, pp. 67-68, *Newsweek,* "Malaysia: No Solution," March 16, 1964, p. 52; LBJ Library, NSF Country File, Box 246, Indonesia, Cables, Vol. I, 11/63-11/64, State Outgoing Telegram, #946, March 3, 1964; *NYT,* "Asians Balked in Asia," June 22, 1964, p. 2; "Sukarno Presses His Malaysian Campaign," August 23, 1964, p. E5; *Time,* "State of Emergency," September 18, 1964, www.time.com/time/magazine/article/0,9171,830717,00.html. See, for example, Document 43, Embassy in the Philippines to State Department, April 17, 1964, pp. 88-91 and for the remainder of 1964 see FRUS, *1964-1968, Vol. XXVI,* pp. 96-188.

worsening conflict in Southeast Asia. *Newsweek* reported that at the United Nations "the Indonesians made not even a pretense of denying the Malaysian charge" of Indonesian aggression on Malaysian Borneo. A Special National Intelligence Estimate concluded that "recent Indonesian paramilitary landings in Malaya are part of Sukarno's long-range campaign to break up Malaysia." "Should there be an escalation of overt hostilities between Indonesia and UK/Malaysia, the Soviets and the Chinese Communists would of course support Indonesia with extensive propaganda and diplomatic activity." These conclusions led the U.S. government to call for negotiation and for United Nations condemnation of Indonesia's resorting to force against a U.N. member nation. By early 1965 Britain transferred troops, ships, and aircraft and, along with Malaysian armed forces, they were able to contain the Indonesian threat.[36]

Sadly, the Indonesian economy continued to stall while Jakarta focused on the Malaysian Federation. In January 1964, *The New York Times* filed a long analysis of Sukarno and Indonesia. It contrasted "new government buildings, monuments, hotels, sports stadiums and statues" with "the wretchedness that surrounds them;" an accompanying photograph showed "the glittering, modern Hotel Indonesia rising behind a crowded row of hovels in Jakarta." Reporter Seth King wrote "the country's problems are staggering. Indonesia is fiscally bankrupt." Worse, "the government is plagued with corruption throughout its ranks. Industries are producing only a fraction of their capacities. The transportation system is falling apart." King noted "in a country where it is literally possible to eat the scenery, the Sukarno government is obliged each year to spend $75 million – 12 per cent of its foreign currency earnings – on imported rice." By November there was no progress. *Time,* in summarizing the situation in Asia, described Indonesia "in economic shambles under Dictator Sukarno, with the world's third-largest Communist Party waiting in the wings."[37]

---

[36] *USN&WR,* "Worldgram," September 14, 1964, p. 63; "Sukarno's War-Will it Involve U.S.?" September 21, 1964, p. 63; *Newsweek,* "Malaysia: What's the Fuss?" September 21, 1964, p. 50; Special National Intelligence Estimate 54/55-64, 16 September 1964, www.foia.cia.gov/browse; *Department of State Bulletin,* "U.S. Calls for Negotiation of Malaysia-Indonesia Dispute," September 28, 1964, pp. 448-449; *Newsweek,* "Malaysia: Wolf! Wolf!" January 11, 1965, p. 36; *Business Week,* "Malaysia feels bite of war threat," January 16, 1965, p. 58.

[37] *NYT,* "Sukarno Stirs Up Another Asian Storm," January 19, 1964, pp. SM14+; "U.S. Warns Indonesia on Anti-Malaysia Policy," May 6, 1964, p. 5; "Sukarno Presses His Malaysia Campaign," August 23, 1964, p. E5; *Time,* "Waiting for Evolution," November 13, 1964, www.time/com/time/magazine/article/0,9171,898230,00.html.

Before long, the continuing tension with Malaysia seemed less important than the threat of a communist takeover of the Indonesian archipelago. As early as September 1963, *Business Week* warned that "Indonesia slides – and fast – toward Communist camp." In February, *U.S. News* warned that "under Sukarno's regime, Indonesia's Communist Party has become one of the world's biggest." Thus, the news magazine questioned "the official U.S. assumption that Sukarno is a bulwark against Communism." Sukarno had long accepted Soviet military assistance, incurring significant loan debt to Moscow; he also made many public statements indicating philosophic agreement with Beijing. *The New York Times* editorialized about the Moscow-Jakarta axis, noting that "now Soviet Russia joins in what could become a Communist pincer movement in the Far East." Moscow apparently supported Jakarta's commitment to crushing Malaysia, and "promise[d] Indonesia further massive shipments of Soviet arms that may include missiles." *U.S. News* stated that "more and more it looks as though Indonesia and Red China are becoming axis partners in a massive squeeze play against the U.S. and Britain in Southeast Asia." "Mao's long range objective," the news magazine claimed, "is to drive the U.S. off the Asian mainland, out of South Vietnam, Cambodia, Laos, and, eventually, Thailand." In May, the National Security Council discussed Indonesia, and noted "Indonesia is a major difficulty" and the economy "continues to deteriorate." A new NIE in July 1964 concluded that "Sukarno remains virtually all-powerful" and "there is almost no chance that his rule or his policies will be effectively challenged by any group, movement, or individual during his lifetime." Of greater concern, "over the past year Sukarno has tended to reinforce the position of the Indonesian Communist Party." "The Communist cause will be the chief beneficiary of the economic, social, and political disarray he will bequeath to Indonesia." In late 1964, the Indonesian Communist Party emerged as the most powerful political faction in Indonesia, and thus the stage seemingly was set for the establishment of a regime favorable to Mao's China in a critical region of the world.[38]

Malaysian-Philippine relations flowed and ebbed depending on the Manila's interest in pressing the tenuous claim to Sabah; see NARA, RG 59, CFPF, Box 2589, POL-POLAFF&REL, PHIL-Malaysia, 1/1/64, Philippine-Malaysian Relations, October 6, 1964.

[38] *Business Week,* "International Outlook," September 28, 1963, p. 112; *USN&WR,* "Worldgram," February 17, 1964, p. 57; "Squeeze Play on U.S. in Asia: The Mao-Sukarno Axis," May 18, 1964, p. 72; *The New York Times,* "Moscow-Jakarta Axis," July 2, 1964, p. 30; *Newsweek,* "Malaysia: Confrontation Continued," July 6, 1964, p. 34; LBJ Library, NSF Country File, Box 246, Indonesia, Cables &

Sukarno had accepted Soviet military assistance for years, and now it appeared he was drawing closer to the Chinese-influenced Indonesian Communist Party. *The New York Times* headlined "Sukarno moves toward Peking." In January 1965 Indonesia resigned from the United Nations, "pushing Indonesia nearer to her gigantic and truculent neighbor to the north." *Newsweek* reported that Beijing offered little support beyond slogans. *U.S. News* warned readers in February that "Sukarno is making headway on plan to force U.S. out of all Southeast Asia." He intended "to make Indonesia a pro-Communist, anti-Western base that will outflank U.S. in Vietnam at same time it outflanks Britain in Malaysia." At the same time *Time* quoted Chinese Premier Zhou Enlai who "proposed the creation of a new U.N – a 'revolutionary' one" "free from 'the manipulation of U.S. imperialism.'" *Time* worried about "a new Peking-Djakarta axis that raises some disturbing problems for both East and West." *The New York Times* noted the "large-scale aid program and stabilization fund" the U.S. government proposed if Sukarno "would concentrate on long-range economic development" and leave Malaysia alone, and the outcome where Sukarno looked closer to Beijing and the Indonesian Communist Party.[39]

The specter of Indonesia going communist worried the American news media. Sukarno increasing issued "expressions of support for the Communist cause in Vietnam." Indonesia then announced it was seizing American-owned rubber plantations in North Sumatra, a move *The New York Times* lumped with "the closing of American libraries, withdrawal from the United Nations and the strengthening of economic ties with Communist China." *U.S. News* evaluated the result of U.S. diplomacy towards Indonesia and concluded: "defiance from Sukarno, Indonesia drawing closer to the Communists, and another defeat for the U.S. in Asia." The news magazine claimed that "Sukarno is preparing to join Red

---

Memos (2 of 2), Vol. II, 5/64-8/64, Paper for NSC Discussion of Indonesia, May 12, 1964; National Intelligence Estimate 55-64, "Prospects for Indonesia," 22 July 1964, www.foia.cia.gov/browse.

[39] *NYT,* "Sukarno Moves Toward Peking," January 17, 1965, p. E4; *Business Week,* "Indonesia steps closer to the brink," January 16, 1965, pp. 52-54; *Newsweek,* "Indonesia: Waiting for a Letter," January 18, 1965, p. 27; "Indonesia: The Ritual Dance," January 25, 1965, p. 40; "Indonesia: The Old Game," February 8, 1965, p. 38; *USN&WR,* "Worldgram," February 8, 1965, p. 67; *Time,* "The Asian Axis," February 5, 1965, www.time.com/time/magazine/article/0,9171,839226,00.html; *NYT,* "Indonesia: Looking Toward China," February 7, 1965, p. E3. Sukarno fascinated the media; see *Newsweek,* "Sukarno: Headman to a Nation," February 15, 1965, pp. 40-46 for a detailed look at his life, goals, and achievements.

China in a drive to dominate all of Southeast Asia." Two months later *U.S. News* reported that "Indonesia's Sukarno collaborates with Red China in efforts to force Britain and U.S. out of Southeast Asia." "Sukarno has powerful sponsorship: Red China. A new Peiping –Jakarta axis has been created with allies in North Vietnam and North Korea. Together they hope to become the rallying point for violent, racist, aggressive agitation against the *status quo* throughout the world." A new NIE concluded that "ties with Communist China are likely to become closer, since Sukarno sees no immediate Chinese threat to Indonesian ambitions." "President Sukarno of Indonesia has reached an understanding with Communist China," *The New York Times* reported, "that will bring increasing pressure to bear on the defenses of the Western powers in Southeast Asia." "In a speech on August 17, Sukarno spoke of building an axis linking Indonesia, North Vietnam, Communist China and North Korea." [40]

More importantly, that prospect greatly concerned American diplomats and their allies. In May 1964, Ambassador Howard Jones reported on a meeting with Sukarno and Foreign Minister Subandrio; Subandrio said "relations between our two countries were approaching a new all time low." Jones noted "so long as Indonesia appeared in the role of aggressor, things would continue difficult." To which Subandrio replied, the "principal reason for GOI economic difficulties was a failure of U.S. to fulfill its promises re balance of payments assistance." Jones "took grim satisfaction in demolishing this accusation in Sukarno's presence" but the very charge indicated the increasing gap between the two governments. In late August 1964, Dean Rusk asked Johnson to approve deferring military assistance, reducing military training, yet continuing some economic aid because of Sukarno's recognition of North Viet-Nam on August 10 and continuing, anti-American speeches; Johnson approved all the recommendations. In October, Rusk wrote key embassies that "our basic objectives with regard Indonesia continue to be to do what we can to keep Indonesia out of communist control, to restrain Indo military and foreign policy excesses" and "to get through current period without open break

---

[40] *NYT,* "In the Neutral World," February 21, 1965, p. E3; "Indonesia Seizes Rubber Estates of U.S. Concerns," February 27, 1965, p. 1; *USN&WR,* "End of the Road for U.S. in Indonesia," March 15, 1965, p. 49; "Another Asian Country in a Weird War with Reds," May 3, 1965, p. 75; "Another Big Country About to go to the Reds," May 17, 1965, p. 80; National Intelligence Estimate 54/55-65, Prospects for Indonesia and Malaysia, 1 July 1965, p. 1; *The Economist,* "What Are We Doing There?" August 14, 1965, p. 586; *NYT,* "Sukarno Acts With China to Outflank West in Asia," August 25, 1965, pp. 1, 3; "The U.S. and Indonesia—A Tragedy in Diplomacy," August 29, 1965, p. SM26+.

between US and Indonesia." Rusk's memo noted "we can anticipate Indos will become progressively more hostile to US." In December, an intelligence analysis found "faint stirrings of an anti-Communist movement Indonesia" but carefully qualified it with "it is too early to measure the movement's strength or effectiveness." Ambassador to Malaysia James Bell wrote Rusk that "our difficulties with Indonesia stem basically from deliberate, positive GOI strategy of seeking to push Britain and the US out of Southeast Asia. If this is the case, growing Indonesian alignment with Communist countries should be seen as outgrowth such strategy."[41]

When Sukarno sought an invitation with President Johnson, Deputy Assistant Secretary of State Marshall Green wrote William Bundy that "to favor Sukarno with a presidential invitation at this time would convince Sukarno all the more that he can play his pro-Communist iconoclastic role in world affairs without fear of reaction from the Americans." The CIA focused on Sukarno's illness, the seriousness of which was not clear, and concluded that "if this ailing dictator should indeed die in the near future, his bequest to Indonesia would be international outlawry, economic near-chaos, and weakened resistance to Communist domination. Yet if Sukarno lives on for some time to come, the chances of the Communist Party to assume power will probably continue to improve." In February Rusk cabled the embassy in Jakarta noting the "crescendo of harassments against USG establishment in Indonesia, culminating in attacks on Jakarta and Medan libraries." Rusk indicated Washington would reduce US AID funds to demonstrate "concern over mistreatment US diplomatic establishments abroad." By mid-March Undersecretary George Ball wrote Lyndon Johnson that "our relations with Indonesia are on the verge of falling apart. Sukarno is turning more and more toward the Communist PKI." Johnson accepted Ball's recommendation, and asked Ellsworth Bunker to visit Jakarta, and file an assessment of the situation. Bunker gave Johnson a report in late April that a variety of factors keep Indonesian-American relations from improving, including U.S. support for Malaysia, America's "intervention" in South Vietnam, "Sukarno's ambition to solidify the Afro-Asian nations" and "to occupy himself a dominant position in the struggle," "the influence of the PKI which looks

[41] LBJ Library, NSF Country File, Box 246, Indonesia, Cables & Memos (1 of 2), Vol. II, 5/64-8/64, Amembassy Jakarta to SecState, #2323, May 9, 1964; same box, Indonesia, Cables & Memos (2 of 2), Vol. II, 5/64-8/64, Assistance Programs for Indonesia, August 30, 1964; *FRUS, 1964-1968, Vol. XXVI,* Document 89, Intelligence Memorandum, December 2, 1964; Document 95, Embassy in Malaysia to State, December 17, 1964.

to Peking for inspiration." Bunker recommended reducing the U.S. presence where it "provides targets easily exploitable by the PKI" but "maintain as much contact with as many other elements in Indonesia as circumstances permit." The NIE of July 1965 noted earlier concluded that "the principal development in Indonesia over the past year has been the sharply accelerated growth of the Communist Party role in government." Ominously, the NIE believed "this trend is likely to continue as long as Sukarno is in control." A month later the new Ambassador to Indonesia, Marshall Green, reported that "Sukarno is deliberately promoting Communism's cause in Indonesia," "Indonesia has become an almost completely closed society," and "U.S. officials in Indonesia are becoming increasingly isolated." Another month later a new SNIE concluded that "Communist fortunes in Indonesia will probably continue to prosper so long as Sukarno stays in power." "In the event of Sukarno's early death or incapacity, the PKI drive to power would probably be slowed for a time." Given the heritage of anti-colonialism in the islands, the NIE was unsure how much direction a victorious PKI might accept either from Beijing or Moscow.[42]

A dramatic and violent army coup jerked Indonesian politics to the right. On September 30, 1965, army officers allegedly sympathetic to the Indonesian Communist Party staged a "palace revolution," placed Sukarno in "protective custody," and established a "Revolutionary Council." The next day the army struck back. While it was not immediately apparent, the army turned on communists and Chinese Indonesians and there was a bloodbath. Some scholars continue to insist there was CIA involvement, although the proof is scant. Two weeks later the American media had questions about the reasons for the coup. Was the Communist Party threat real, or was it an excuse for army officers to seize power? Whether the treat was real or not, by the end of October "Indonesia's large Communist

---

42 *FRUS, 1964-1968, Vol. XXVI,* Document 100, Green to Bundy, January 20, 1964; LBJ Library, NSF Country File, Box 246, Indonesia, Cables (1 of 2), Vol. III, 9/64-2/65, State Circular Telegram, #714, October 22, 1964; *FRUS, 1964-1968, Vol. XXVI,* Document 103, Special Memorandum Prepared by Director of ONE of the CIA, January 26, 1965; LBJ Library, NSF Country File, Box 246, Indonesia, Cables (2 of 2), 9/64-2/65, State Outgoing Telegram to Jakarta, # 727 , February 20, 1965; Box 247, Indonesia, Memos, Vol. IV, 3-9/65, Diplomatic Moves to Resolve Indonesian Crisis, 10 March 1965; *FRUS, 1964-1968, Vol. XXVI* , Document 118, Ball to Johnson, March 18, 1965; Document 121, Bunker to Johnson, undated; Document 126, NIE 54/55-65, July 1, 1965; Document 131, Embassy in Indonesia to State, August 8, 1965; Document 137, SNIE 55-65, Prospects for and Strategic Implications of a Communist Takeover in Indonesia," September 1, 1965.

party and its many front organizations were in full retreat this week, hunted and harried by military leaders bent on eliminating them." The coup leaders ordered virtually every government department "to cleanse itself of all persons connected with the 30th of September movement." The anti-communist cleansing continued for months. Ball told McNamara that "the business in Indonesia has a very bad smell." He felt that "this may be the first step toward a Communist takeover."[43]

As anti-communist generals seemingly seized control, American officials followed events closely. By October 4 intelligence analysts reported "growing antagonism between the Army and the groups that supported the 30 September Movement." Green reported from Jakarta that "events of the past few days have put PKI and pro-Communist elements very much on defense" while "at the same time we seem to be witnessing what may be the passing of power from Sukarno's hands to a figure or figures whose identity is yet unknown." The CIA's Office of Current Intelligence analyzed that "the Indonesian army, having countered what appears to have been a leftist coup on 1 October, is for the time being firmly in control of Indonesia." OCI believed Sukarno "hopes to conciliate the leftists and return the Communist Party to the favorable political position it enjoyed prior to the events of 1 October." OCI noted that "many questions remain unanswered about the '30 September Movement'" and that "most revolve around Sukarno."[44]

Within two weeks, the larger issue of future American policy dominated the documents. Rusk asked Green for advice on "our attitudes toward recent and current developments." Green soon replied that "many basic issues [in Indonesia] will remain unresolved," "Sukarno's image has been damaged," but "no dramatic changes in Indonesia's foreign policy are likely" despite the army's belief in Beijing role in the "30 September

---

[43] *USN&WR,* "Blowup in Indonesia: What It Means to U.S. and Reds," October 11, 1965, pp. 43-44; *NYT,* "Indonesian Coup Still a Mystery," October 17, 1965, p. 1; "Setbacks for Indonesia' P.K.I.," October 31, 1965, p. E3; *The Economist,* "Indonesia: Rings on a tree trunk," November 6, 1965, p. 594. For a summary of the coup timeline, see *Newsweek,* "Indonesia: The Confused Coup," October 11, 1965, pp. 51-53 and *The New York Times,* "'65 Uprising in Indonesia: Study in Red Blundering," August 23, 1966, pp. 1, 2. "Show" trials of alleged coup leaders drove home the anti-communist message, see *The Economist,* "Indonesia: Trial by shadow," November 26, 1966, pp. 907-908. See also *NYT,* "The Great Purge in Indonesia," May 8, 1966, pp. SM13+ and "Indonesia Wobbles Toward Recovery," October 1, 1967, pp. 238+.

[44] *FRUS, 1964-1968, Volume XXVI,* Document 146, Blouin to NcNaughton, October 4, 1965; Document 147, Embassy in Indonesia to State, October 5, 1965; Document 149, Intelligence Memorandum, October 6, 1965;

Movement." The embassy was isolated in Jakarta and it needed time to "realize that Indonesia was undergoing a full scale purge of PKI influence and that these killings were overlaid with long standing and deep ethnic and religious conflicts." Within a month it became clear that there were two Indonesian governments: "the Sukarno-led Dwikora Cabinet" and "the Indonesian military" which was encouraging Moslem support to counter Communist influence. The CIA faced the main question – should the U.S. government provide requested aid to the Indonesian military to continue attacking the PKI even though military leaders did not constitute the internationally-recognized government. The CIA concluded if Washington so desired it could supply requested items "in discreet fashion." But Green counseled that, "US and allies should be extremely cautious about offering help to Generals at this time" until the "army move[s] against Sukarno." Green wrote Rusk in late December that "Indo politics has continued to move in 'right' direction since our last assessment. PKI is no longer a significant political force and Djakarta-Peking axis is in tatters." Rusk wrote Green that before the U.S. government could provide requested economic assistance, "we must be sure we are dealing with cohesive and effective GOI which can and will use it effectively" and "we can only deal openly and publicly with Indonesian Government on matter of aid," thereby killing the idea of covert assistance through the CIA to the Indonesian military. Green returned to Washington for consultations and Robert Komer of the National Security Council Staff asked President Johnson to meet Green and to approve needed economic assistance through the military. Johnson somewhat sidestepped, telling Green he should "make specific recommendations as to the timing and conditions under which the United States might extend assistance to Indonesia." Finally, in March 1966 Sukarno tried to regain power, and the military moved decisively against him, ending the two governments-system that caused such concern in previous months. [45]

---

[45] *FRUS, 1964-1968, Volume XXVI,* Document 153, State to Embassy in Indonesia, October 13, 1965; Document 156, Green to State, October 17, 1965; Document 162, Editorial Note; Document 167, Cuthell to Bundy, November 3, 1965; Document 172, Memorandum Prepared by the CIA, November 9, 1965; Document 177, Embassy in Indonesia to State, November 19, 1965; Document 186, Embassy in Indonesia to State, December 22, 1965; Document 189, State to Embassy in Indonesia, January 20, 1966; Document 192, Komer to Johnson, February 15, 1966; Document 194, Memorandum of Conversation, February 15, 1966. See *FRUS, 1964-1968, Volume XXVI,* Documents 200-204 and NARA, RG 59, CFPF, Box 2206, POL 2-1, INDON, 1/1/67, Amembassy Jakarta to SecState, #4316, March 16, 1967, in which embassy notes Sukarno "has now faded from view and

To western diplomats, Indonesia's new leaders needed to end the conflict with Malaysia, renew relations with neighbors, and secure western financing all to rebuild the deteriorating economy. But "army leaders either feel sincerely that they cannot drop their campaign against nearby 'neocolonialism' – or they dare not drop it for political reasons." Meanwhile, "the end of the line is finally in sight, with complete exhaustion of the hidden assets piled up during the Dutch colonial period." *U.S. News* suggested the army "has got to stop runaway inflation," "it's got to bring some sense of order in the country," and it had to end the confrontation with Malaysia.[46]

In fits and starts, Indonesia moved towards peace with its smaller neighbor. In January 1966 *U.S. News* reported "Indonesia's war against Malaysia is simmering down." Soon thereafter, Suharto "reiterated Indonesia's complaints against Malaysia and that Indonesia was compelled to continue a policy of confrontation." But his indication of "peaceful methods" held out hope for a settlement. Several days later, Indonesian Foreign Minister Adam Malik told reporters his country "would take steps to end her policy of confrontation against Malaysia." Malaysia responded positively two weeks later, and the two foreign ministers agreed to meet in Bangkok although the outcome was not clear. The Bangkok talks went well, and the two foreign ministers agreed "on the principles on which practical steps to restore friendly relations should be based," although "they did not announce resumption of normal diplomatic relations." Despite the positive atmosphere, Malaysia remained adamant on the status of Sabah and Sarawak on North Borneo, Indonesia balked at normalizing relations without a face-saving gesture on the fate of North Borneo. Finally, in early August the Indonesian government announced that "the Malaysia issue will reach a stage of settlement in which physical confrontation can be ended." Several weeks later *U.S. News* reported "Indonesia and Malaysia are at peace after signing an agreement in Jakarta." Interestingly, *U.S. News* asked "What impact will this have on the war in Vietnam?" Finally, in late August 1967 Indonesia and Malaysia

---

Box 2209, POL 15-1, Indon, 1/1/67, Amembassy Moscow to State, March 28, 1967, in which embassy reported "Soviets have for some time been progressively disengaging from Sukarno" and after the legislature stripped him of all power Moscow "wrote Sukarno off as a liability.

[46] *USN&WR,* "Indonesia – the Reds are on the run, but," November 1, 1963, pp. 63-64; "The Red 'Paper' – Failure in Indonesia," November 22, 1965, pp. 82-83.

restored full diplomatic relations "a year after agreeing to end three years of armed confrontation." [47]

Although the continuing confrontation remained, at best, bothersome, the government in Washington supported the new military rulers in Jakarta. In mid-April Washington agreed to sell 50,000 tons of PL-480 Title IV rice to Indonesia. "This limited resumption of aid marks a turning point on the road back to cooperative relations now that Sukarno's power has been circumscribed." In turn, Jakarta was considering returning seized U.S. rubber estates to their owners. Washington was willing to provide raw cotton [made available because of Asian textile imports into the United States] to "meet bona fide Indo emergency needs." But, as Ambassador Green told Suharto, to approve a resumption of U.S. aid programs, Congress would want "improving relationships and improved handling of Indo economic problems." A State Department analysis noted and then dismissed the more than 300,000, mostly Chinese Indonesians dead in the resulting counter-coup, and then praised Indonesia's commitment to economic reform and development and the need to contain Chinese influence in the region's largest and potentially most prosperous nation. At the National Security Council meeting on August 4, President Johnson pointed out the changes in the past year since the government cut off most U.S. aid to Indonesia and after discussion participants agreed to support Suharto and his regime. Marshall Green, noting that Indonesia officially ended the three-year confrontation with Malaysia, requested approval for a short-term, emergency aid program.[48]

---

[47] *USN&WR,* "Worldgram," January 17, 1966, p. 60; *NYT,* "Suharto Adamant Against Malaysia," April 10, 1966, p. 1; "Indonesia to Seek Malaysian Accord," May 4, 1966, p. 5; "Malaysia and Indonesia Moving Toward Talks," May 19, 1966, p. 4; "Weekend Parley on Malaysia Set," May 26, 1966, p. 20; "Malaysia and Indonesia in Accord on Steps to Ties," June 2, 1966, p. 9; *Time,* "An Uproar of Peace," June 10, 1966, www.time.com/time/magazine/article/0,9171,942007,00.html; *Newsweek,* "Indonesia: Peace Talks," June 13, 1966, p. 52; .*NYT,* "Malaysia is Firm on Borneo Issue," June 5, 1966, p.5; "Indonesians Balk on Malaysian Pact," June 9, 1966, p. 6; "Malaysia Continues Talk with Indonesia," June 14, 1966, p. 6; "Jakarta Expects Early End of Anti-Malaysia Policy," August 5, 1966, p. 4; *USN&WR,* "Worldgram," August 22, 1966, p. 43; *NYT,* "Diplomatic Links Restored by Indonesia and Malaysia," August 31, 1967, p. 2.

[48] *FRUS, 1964-1968, Volume XXVI,* Document 206, Ropa to Rostow, April 18, 1966; Document 207, Thomson to Rostow, May 4, 1966; Document 209, Embassy in Indonesia to State, May 27, 1966; Document 210, Rostow to Johnson, including Attachment, June 8, 1966; Document 217, Notes of the 563rd Mtg. of the NSC, August 4, 1966; *NYT,* "Renewed U.S. Aid to Jakarta Urged," August 27, 1966, p. 2.

Efforts at economic development began in mid-1966. The government changed billboards and slogans from "Crush Malaysia" to "advertising spark plugs and cooking utensils." New Foreign Minister Adam Malik indicated that Indonesia needed "to stretch out Indonesia's debts" and needed emergency rice and funds to rebuild the decaying transportation system. The embassy in Jakarta wrote that "in past nine months Indonesia has made one of the most dramatic changes in recent history of Far East. From being important nation on verge communist control, it has switched to strongly anti-communist state." To the embassy, these changes merited a "major policy statement" of support. Japan quickly offered emergency aid to purchase 10,000 tons of rice and 5,000 bales of cotton, hoping, perhaps, to encourage trade once the Indonesia economy revived. *Business Week* reported that "Jakarta's military-backed regime talks about encouraging private business and several months later approvingly reported "the military-backed leadership of Indonesia – struggling to pull the big Asian nation out of the economic morass created by President Sukarno – is moving faster to make foreign businessmen welcome." Ambassador Marshall Green again requested approval for a short-term assistance program and planning for a multi-national aid program including the newly formed Asian Development Bank. He wanted to move before Indonesian Foreign Minister Adam Malik traveled to Moscow and then Washington seeking such assistance. In late September Malik visited Washington and gained the assurances he sought. Rusk said "there was understanding and sympathy for Indonesia's problems" and "the IMF and the creditor nations are organizing for a cooperative effort to help." In a meeting with President Johnson, Malik listened as Walt Rostow outlined current measures, including "the role of the Fund and the Bank in advising Indonesia on its stabilization program, the outcome of the Tokyo meetings on debt rescheduling, and close cooperation" with other countries.[49]

A new NIE concluded that "the Indonesian economy cannot quickly recover from a decade and more of ruinous mismanagement, but it is probable that economic conditions will at least cease to deteriorate and

---

[49] *NYT,* "After Sukarno, the Headache," September 11, 1966, p. 239; "Indonesia Seeks Economic Help," April 5, 1966, p. 7; "Indonesia Needs $400-Million Aid," April 8, 1966, p. 6; *The Economist,* "Indonesia: Japan to the Rescue," April 2, 1966, p. 76; *Business Week,* "International Outlook," May 7, 1966, p. 133; *USN&WR,* "Indonesia: 'Hope . . . Where Once There Was None," June 6, 1966, pp. 70-72; NARA, RG 59, CFPF, Box 1897, POL-POLAFF&REL, Asia, 1/1/64, Amembassy Jakarta to SecState, #159, July 11, 1966; *Business Week,* "Hopes rise for Indonesia," July 20, 1966, pp. 92-94; "Indonesia dusts off welcome mat," December 31, 1966, p. 24.

begin to improve within a year or two." The promised aid came in the form of additional emergency relief under P.L. 480 and support for economic restructuring and development. By February 1967, Rostow told Johnson the debt rescheduling was close to agreement, the Indonesian government was pursuing a "pragmatic economic policy," and "we should push for economic assistance." In late June 1967 Nicholas Katzenbach reported "a resounding vote of confidence at Scheveningen meeting where intergovernmental group agreed to provide $200 million gap in Indonesia's balance of payments as projected by IMF." After returning from a trip to East Asia, Vice President Hubert Humphrey informed Johnson of his talks with Prime Minister Eisaku Sato of Japan and of Ambassador Green's first extensive conversation in five months with Indonesian leader Suharto. Humphrey noted Suharto's "hopes for considerable foreign assistance from the United States." Rostow followed up a few days later that "Indonesian expectations of American aid vastly exceed anything we are going to be able to come up with." But "we will keep digging until we find" a solution.[50]

By summer 1967 the worst was averted, and efforts moved from relief to recovery. The State Department concluded that "progress in domestic economic reform had been considerably greater than was anticipated in August of last year. An ambitious and reasonably effective stabilization program was put into effect." American-trained, Indonesian economists deserved the credit. Non-communist nations agreed to reschedule some $300 million of debts, and to provide $200 million in new assistance to provide vital foreign exchange.[51]

---

[50] NIE 55-67, "Prospects for Indonesia," 15 February 1967, www.foia.cia.gov/browse; *FRUS, 1964-1968, Volume XXVI,* Document 219, Embassy in Indonesia to State, August 13, 1966; Document 223, Memorandum of Conversation, September 27, 1966; Document 224, Memorandum of Conversation, September 27, 1966; *FRUS, 1964-1968, Volume XXVI,* Document 231, Rostow to Johnson, February 21, 1967; Document 235, State to Embassy in Indonesia, June 27, 1967; Document 237, Humphrey to Johnson, July 14, 1967; Document 2329, Rostow to Johnson, July 22, 1967.

[51] *FRUS, 1964-1968, Volume XXVI,* Document 241, Paper Prepared in the Department of State, August 4, 1967. The military government felt sufficiently in control by March 1967 that it removed Sukarno as chief of state; there was little public reaction to the news, see *Time,* "The New Order," March 24, 1967, www.time.com/time/magazine/article/0,9171,836881,00.html; *Newsweek,* "Indonesia: Ultimatum for Sukarno?" January 9, 1967, p. 31; *The Economist,* "Indonesia: Slow curtain for Sukarno," January 7, 1967, pp. 34-35; "The End for Sukarno," January 28, 1967, p. 303; Indonesia: How many friends has Sukarno got?" February 18, 1967, p. 610.

Through the end of the period, Indonesia made gradual progress, rising from the economic abyss of the Sukarno years. *The Economist* explained the dilemma: "foreign debt approaches U.S. $2,500 million; foreign exchange reserves are effectively nil. What foreign exchange is earned by the country's declining export industries is immediately swallowed by emergency imports." But, "the astonishing fact is that Indonesia's creditors are showing every sign of coming back for more." *U.S. News* noted the dilemma of "a poor people living in a rich land." This included "per capita income of [only] $65 a year in a country with the Far East's largest petroleum reserves" and "malnutrition, even occasional starvation, in a land that could feed other nations in addition to itself." American experts explained that Indonesia faced two separate problems: to fulfill the stabilization program, the U.S. government had to increase its commitment and planners had to devise a sufficiently rapid economic development program to retain popular support for the Suharto government. Indonesia needed U.S. rice, but so did South Vietnam and neither was willing to accept bulgur wheat, which America had in surplus. Indonesia wanted more U.S. financial assistance, but the Johnson Administration worried that Congress would simply shift aid from Latin America to Indonesia. At the same time, diplomats in Jakarta reported "over-sized Indonesian aid expectations." Suharto told Ambassador Green one figure, $100 million, and soon thereafter his aide, Colonel Sutikno, mentioned the figure as $150 million. About the same time, General Alamsjah, Suharto's principal aide, expressed "dismay" to U.S. officials "over what he felt was inadequate evidence of current and future US support."[52]

Despite the possible games-playing, Lyndon Johnson was impressed with Indonesia and wanted to help. The U.S. embassy at year's end summarized the situation and concluded that "we believe Indonesia's overall performance during 1967 was adequate to justify continued optimism that the nation has set out on the long and probably tortuous road to modernization." There were few good alternatives, and Rostow asked Johnson to approve increased U.S. assistance as part of a $325 million IMF program. Johnson approved, writing Rostow that "I want to do everything I can for Indonesia – as quickly as I can. Send me a program." Finally, at year's end, a new NIE noted "the Suharto government has

---

[52] *The Economist,* "Indonesia After Sukarno," July 9, 1966, pp. 159-160; NARA, RG 59, CFPF, Box 2212, POL INDON-US, 1967, Amembassy Jakarta to SecState, #5771 [Section 1 of 3], May 26, 1967; *FRUS, 1964-1968, Volume XXVI,* Document 242, Guad and Freeman to Johnson, August 8, 1967; Document 243, Rostow to Johnson, August 8, 1967; Document 244, Memorandum for the Record, August 9, 1967; Document 245, Wright to Rostow, September 27, 1967.

adopted a moderate pragmatic approach to Indonesia's serious economic problems." Equally important, "there is likely to be a continuation of the present trends toward improved relations with neighboring countries and the free world, cool relations with the USSR, and hostility toward Communist China." By March 1968 *Time* reported that "though the country still has a long way to go, encouraging signs are multiplying." "Some 45 new investment projects have been approved, at least in principle, and within the past four week, 15 foreign banks have received the nod to open branches in Jakarta." Still, Indonesia asked for increased American aid in "the wake of a 57% December-March increase in the Jakarta consumer price index" and "a second quarter expansion in the budget deficit which threatens to exceed ceilings set by the IMF." The analysis for President Johnson noted that "this clear need for more aid presents the United States with a dilemma." In mid-June US officials gave Johnson a proposed aid program to meet Indonesia's needs. Still Rostow wrote Johnson that "Indonesia's needs are greater than ever. Despite the government's responsible policies, the stabilization program has thus far failed to work." Rostow urged Johnson to approve a package that Bill Gaud and Orville Freeman proposed, which Johnson did. A few months later *U.S. News* returned to the dilemma: "this island nation, rich in potential but now tangled in economic troubles, is becoming a major test of how – or even whether – the underdeveloped "third world" can turn poverty into progress." The CIA reported that "the economy of Indonesia is slowly recovering from the severe damage wrought by more than a decade of mismanagement under Sukarno." "Progress is not assured, and the next few years will be crucial." On December 31, 1968 a new NIE concluded that Suharto and the army effectively controlled Indonesia, that the government had "adopted a moderate, pragmatic approach to Indonesia's serious economic problems," "there is likely to be a continuation of the present trends toward improved relations with neighboring countries and the free world, cool relations with the USSR, and hostility toward Communist China." [53]

[53] *FRUS, 1964-1968, Volume XXVI,* Document 246, Record of Cabinet Meeting, October 18, 1967; LBJ Library, NSF Country File, Box 249, Indonesia, Memos (1 of 2), Vol. VIII, 6/67-8/68, Rostow to Johnson, November 17, 1967; same box, Indonesia, Memos (2 of 2), Vol. VIII, 6/67-8/68, Johnson to Rostow, November 21, 1967; *Time,* "Indonesia Waits," November 10, 1967, www.time.com/time/archive; *USN&WR,* "Indonesia: Poor People in a Rich Land," December 25, 1967, pp. 50-54; *FRUS, 1964-1968, Volume XXVI,* Document 251, Embassy in Indonesia to State, January 12, 1968; Document 253, Embassy in Indonesia to State, February 21, 1968; Document 258, Rostow to Johnson, June

The Malaysian Federation did not survive. At first, the Malaysian people seemed to come together. In April 1964 the Tunku's Alliance party won "a smashing victory" – 87 of 104 seats in the Malaysian Parliament. It seemed an endorsement of his "Greater Malaysia" and opposition to Sukarno's efforts to break the federation. The semi-annual review from the U.S. embassy noted the Malaysian economic outlook is "generally favorable," and should result in "a prosperous, stable, anti-Communist Malaysia." Malaysia also reported an improving economy despite the confrontation with Indonesia and a drop in the price of rubber. The Tunku visited Washington in July 1964, and William Bundy wrote Dean Rusk

---

18, 1968; Document 262, NIE 55-68, Indonesia, December 31, 1968; *Time,* "After the Hangover," March 15, 1968, www.time.com/time/archive; LBJ Library, NSF Country File, Box 249, Indonesia, Memos (2 of 2), Vol. VIII, 6/67-8/68, Memorandum for the President, May 27, 1968; same box, Indonesia, Memos (1 of 2), Vol. VIII, 6/67-8/68, Aid to Indonesia, June 12, 1968; McNamara in his new capacity as World Bank president visited Indonesia to help with putting together an economic plan, see LBJ Library, NSF Country File, Box 249, Indonesia, Cables, Vol. VIII, 6/67-6/68, Amembassy Jakarta to SecState, #6579, June 17, 1968; same box, Indonesia, Memos (1 of 2), Vol. VIII, 6/67-8/68, Aid to Indonesia, June 18, 1968; LBJ Library, Papers of Henry H. Fowler, Box 69-70, International Classified Material - Countries: Indonesia, Aid to Indonesia, June 19, 1968; LBJ Library, NSF Country File, Box 249, Indonesia, Memos (1 of 2), Vol. VIII, 6/67-8/68, Indonesia: Prospects for Economic Stability, July 1968; *USN&WR,* "Developing an Asian Nation: Test Case in Indonesia," August 12, 1968, pp.76-77; LBJ Library, NSF Country File, Box 249, Indonesia, 1/64-1/69, NIE, Indonesia, No. 55-68, 31 December 1968. Katzenbach cabled in Kuala Lumpur that "if Suharto has doubts or questions about U.S. policy it is desirable he resolve them directly with you rather than using complicated and unreliable mechanism of intermediaries" and Katzenbach rejected "criticism circulating in Jakarta that U.S. support of Indonesian stabilization effort has been slow" and he offered details to use in discussions with Suharto." See NARA, RG 59, CFPF, Box 2212, POL INDON-US, 1967, State to Jakarta, #216750, June 27, 1967. About the same time Lee interestingly told the Institute for Strategic Studies in London that "there is no substitute at present for western military power as counterweight to China," "U.S. must continue its resistance to Hanoi aggression," and "China's growing nuclear capability is not decisive factor in Asian power balance," LBJ Library, NSF Country File, Box 281, Singapore, Memos, Vol. I, 8/65-7/67, Roche to Johnson, June 29, 1967. Despite the hopes of non-communist governments, the Soviet Union believed Suharto "in the medium term will fail to cope successfully with Indonesia's multitude of social, economic, and political problems;" see NARA, RG 9, CFPF, Box 2209, POL 15-1, INDON, 1/1/68, Soviet Policy Towards Indonesia, April 30, 1968. See Justus M. Van Der Kroef, "Suharto's Indonesia," *United Asia, Volume 20, No. 2, March-April 1968,* pp. 67-76.

that "our problem is to reaffirm our support for Malaysia and make some tangible gesture of encouragement without involving the United States in the substance of this dispute or in substantial new commitments in Southeast Asia, and without needless aggravation of our relations with Indonesia." Bundy believed "Malaysia has a relatively good economic situation," and in saying nothing about Malaysian-Singaporean relations must have found them sufficiently warm and effective. Rusk in turn wrote President Johnson that "the Tunku is deeply troubled by almost two years of Indonesian hostility to Malaysia." In return for American support, the Malaysian leader likely would make clear his anti-Communist stance.[54]

The Tunku met with Johnson and topics included relations with the Philippines and Indonesia, but again nothing about Singapore. But there were stresses, more political and economic than racial, from heavily-Chinese Singapore. Singaporean Finance Minister Goh Keng Swee told U.S. Ambassador James Bell that "the recent ban on barter trade with Indonesia is a severe blow to Singapore's economy." The ambassador reported his belief that economic issues were more serious. *The Economist* reported that the two leaders – Lee Kuan Yew, Chinese, and Tunku Abdul Rahman, Malay – "themselves typify the enduring stresses inside Malaysia. They do not at heart really like or trust each other." This lack of trust was pronounced in policy differences, including foreign affairs, internal taxes, and the respective roles of Malays, Chinese, and Indians in the federation. In February, the Singapore consulate reported British officials in Hong Kong feared that the Tunku "has had enough of Lee" and "might decide to oust Singapore." By June Prime Minister Lee "suggested that Malaysia be partitioned if the country's Malay leaders did not accept what he called a 'Malaysian Malaysia.'" "If the ultranationalists among the Malays continue to call for a communal approach to all our problems," Lee told reporters, "then the people of Singapore, Sarawak and Sabah, where non-Malays are in a majority, must consider alternative arrangements." *The Economist* feared "this experiment in multi-racialism could collapse from within." "Over the past months, tension between the mainly Malay leadership in Kuala Lumpur and the mainly Chinese leadership of the People's Action party, which governs Singapore, has

[54] *NYT,* "Malayan Regime Wins Heavy Vote," April 26, 1964, p. 28; "Malayan Election Heartens Regime," April 27, 1964, p. 7; NARA, RG 59, CFPF, Box 2452, POL 2-3, Malaysia, 1/1/64, Semi-Annual Politico-Economic Assessment, February 19, 1964; *NYT,* "Malaysia Shows Gains In Economy," April 6, 1964, p. 45; NARA, RG 59, CFPF, Box 2455, POL 15-1, Head of State, Executive Branch Relations, 6/1/64, Bundy to Rusk, July 13, 1964; *FRUS, 1964-1968, Vol. XXVI,* Document 264, Rusk to Johnson, July 20, 1964.

been increasing until today both sides openly accuse each other of playing racial politics." *Newsweek* stated that "the conflict between Malaysia's Malay and Chinese citizens is even more of a threat to the twenty-month-old state than the marauding guerrillas whom Indonesia's President Sukarno ships in." [55]

In August 1965, Singapore withdrew from Malaysia to become an independent city-state. A year earlier, the embassy in Malaysia was reporting "the problem of worsening relations between the central government of Malaysia and the Singapore state government." The next month it noted concern with "Malaysia's slow progress towards national consolidation." In late October it drew attention to the Singapore-Kuala Lumpur "power struggle." By mid-December, the State Department learned from Toh Chin Chye, Singapore's Deputy Prime Minister of the "grim picture of relations between the Kuala Lumpur and Singapore governments and between the leaders of the UMNO and PAP. Toh said the tensions "raised real questions about the future of Malaysia and referred several times to possible disintegration of the federation." The American embassy in Kuala Lumpur in its regular semi-annual summary predicted "the odds favor Malaysia hanging together." "With few exceptions," the embassy reported, "Malaysians throughout the country have shown themselves to be loyal to the nation." However, "Kuala Lumpur-Singapore relations remain dangerously strained." "Although the occasionally rumored separation of Singapore from Malaysia is unlikely as there is no attractive alternative to union, it would be in the U.S. interest to see this debilitating squabble ended." In May, the embassy in Kuala Lumpur reported "the verbal jousting and political jockeying between Kuala Lumpur and Singapore have now continued intermittently for a year or so. In the past month or two, the din of debate has been growing steadily louder." In June, Rusk met with Prime Minister Robert Menzies

---

[55] NARA, RG 59, CFPF, Box 2458, POL-POLAFF&REL, Malaysia-PHIL, 1/1/64, President's Second Meeting with the Prime Minister of Malaysia, July 23, 1964; Box 2452, POL 7, Visits, Mtgs, Malaysia, 7/1/64, Conversation with Malaysian Secretary for External Affairs, July 23, 1964; same folder, Visit of Prime Minister of Malaysia, Part I of II, July 27, 1964; same folder, State Outgoing Circular Telegram, #182, July 30, 1964; Box 2450, POL 2, Gen Rpts & Stat-Malaysia, 1/1/64, Amembassy Kuala Lumpur to State, A-143, August 21, 1964; *The Economist,* "Malaysia: No Bridge Across the Straits," January 23, 1965, p. 326; NARA, RG 59, CFPF, Box 2450, POL 1, Gen Policy, Background, Malaysia, 1/1/64, Singapore to SecState, #274, February 12, 1965; *NYT,* "Threat of Partition Raised in Malaysia Dispute," June 2, 1965, p. 15; *The Economist,* "Malaysia: People's Enemy?" June 5, 1965, pp. 1138-1139; *Newsweek,* "Malaysia: A Promise Threatened," June 21, 1965, p. 43.

of Australia and Menzies stated the Tunku and Lee "are engaged in a shooting match. The Tunku six months ago spoke of the need for a fundamental revision of Malaysia in order to change the status of Singapore." Three weeks before the split, the consulate in Singapore recommended permitting Lee to meet with senior U.S. officials during a possible visit to America. "Exposure to appropriate U.S. officials in Washington," the consulate wrote, "should pay dividends in increasing understanding and support for U.S. position." Rusk replied the president's schedule was busy, but he, Rusk, would certainly meet with Lee. *The New York Times* editorialized that 'what made their conflict irreconcilable was Lee's challenge to the basic power structure of Malaya, where the urban Chinese who dominate the economy have left control of the Government to the rural Malays." The Tunku told his Parliament that "my dream is shattered," even though he ordered Lee without forewarning to take Singapore out of the federation. Malaysian press releases quoted the Tunku as stating "separation should be regarded as member of family leaving to set up own home, but Singapore still member of 'Greater Malaysia Family.'" Singapore and Malaysia agreed to develop a "treaty on external defense and mutual assistance" and to "establish a Joint Defense Council." The political division notwithstanding, "the flow of commerce, transport, and people between Malaysia and Singapore is continuing."[56]

[56] NARA, RG 59, CFPF, Box 2450, POL 2, Gen Rpts & Stat, Malaysia, 1/1/64, Amembassy Kuala Lumpur to State, A-88, August 7, 1964; Box 2452, POL 2-3, Malaysia, 1/1/64, Amembassy Kuala Lumpur to State, A-174, September 11, 1964; Box 2450, POL 2, Gen Rpts & Stat, Malaysia, 1/.1/64, Amembassy Kuala Lumpur to State, A-330, October 30, 1964; same folder, Viability of Malaysia, December 16, 1964; Box 2452, POL 2-3, Malaysia, 1/1/64, Amembassy Kuala Lumpur to State, A-652, March 5, 1965; Box 2455, POL 15, Malaysia, 5/12/65, Amembassy Kuala Lumpur to State, A-859, The Kuala Lumpur-Singapore Debate Sharpens, May 12, 1965; Box 2450, POL 1, Gen Policy, Background, Malaysia, 1/1/64, Situation in Malaysia, June 7, 1965; Box 2453, POL 7, Malaysia, 4/28/65, Amconsul Singapore to SecState, #10, July 20, 1965; State to Singapore, #23222, August 5, 1965; *NYT,* "Malaysia's Crack-up," August 11, 1965, p. 34; "Singapore Ends Tie of Federation with Malaysia," August 9, 1965, p. 1; *Newsweek,* "Malaysia: My Dream is Shattered," August 23, 1965, p. 33; NARA, RG 59, CFPF, Box 2455, POL 15-1, Malaysia, 6/4/65, Amembassy Kuala Lumpur to SecState, #223, August 21, 1965; *NYT,* "The Future of Malaysia," August 11, 1965, p. 2; *Time,* "One of Our Islands is Missing," August 20, 1965, www.time.com/time/magazine/article/0,9171,841960,00.html. Sukarno told reporters that Malaysia was "beginning to fall apart from the inside," *Time,* "Malaysia: The Art of Dispelling Anxiety," August 27, 1965, www.time.com/time/magazine/article/0,9171,828327,00.html.

There were obvious issues. Singapore asked "to remain in the British Commonwealth." Singapore needed to become an even greater entrepôt of the region. Great Britain, its economy drained by the military commitment to defend the federation, had to determine its relations with the remainder of Malaysia and the new city-state of Singapore, especially the fate of Britain's naval base in Singapore. There was concern that Singapore's departure might separate the three remaining states of the federation. Malaysia faced the same challenge "in developing the economically backward states of Sabah, which was formerly North Borneo, and Sarawak." Britain "feared that the Singapore secession changed the real political and strategic balance in Southeast Asia." And, in light of continuing economic challenges, the U.K. Government "would have to consider readjustment of its defense priorities in the Far East," putting more pressure on the U.S. Government increasingly involved in Vietnam. Washington "strongly challenged the British assumption that secession of Singapore called for urgent contingency planning regarding the maintenance of the British position." The Consulate in Singapore believed, if the British downgraded their base at Singapore, "British (and our) position in Singapore will deteriorate with almost incredible swiftness." [57]

But, in the aftermath of the division and the counter-coup in Indonesia, now-independent Singapore and the federation each moved forward. Almost immediately, the two nations "appeared ready for close cooperation in trade." Malaysia fundamentally was an extractive economy, exporting rubber and tin; Singapore was "an industrializing island emporium, needing trade outlets in Malaya." At the same time, Singapore considered trade with every nation in the region, including the People's Republic of China, and asked the U.S. government for understanding. It

---

[57] *NYT,* "Singapore Asks Tie to Commonwealth," August 11, 1965, p. 2; "The Future of Malaysia," August 11, 1965, p. 2; *U.S. News & World Report,* "Business Around the World," August 23, 1965, p. 81; *NYT,* "Trade is Crucial in Singapore Life," August 12, 1965, p. 3; "Singapore's Move Poses Wide Range of Problems for Britain," August 10, 1965, p. 7; "Malaysia Begins Survival Fight," August 11, 1965, p. 1; "Malaysia's Problems Remain," August 13, 1965, p. 3; "Malaysia: New Era, New Problems," August 21, 1966; *Newsweek,* "Southeast Asia: Still Good Friends," August 30, 1965, p. 37; *The Economist,* "Malaysia: much ado about what?" August 20, 1966, p. 759; "Tin and the Tunku," January 8, 1966, pp. 116-117; NARA, RG 59, CFPF, Box 2459, POL-POLAFF&REL, Malaysia-Singapore, 4/8/65, Singapore-Malaysia, September 8, 1965; same folder, Malaysia-Singapore, September 8, 1965; LBJ Library, NSF Country File, Box 281, Singapore, Memos, Vol. I, 8/65-7/67, Amembassy London to SecState, September 9, 1965; LBJ Library, NSF Country File, Box 281, Singapore, Cables, Vol. I, 8/65-7/67, Amconsul Singapore to Sec State, 136, September 6, 1965.

also engaged in the "Jurong program" or plan for industrial development. Singaporean officials believed the United States would "have to assist Singapore by providing a market for its industrial products" or "risk the disaster of a Communist takeover in Singapore by denying Singapore access to the United States textile market."[58]

The U.S. government reviewed policy for Malaysia and Singapore in the aftermath of the break-up and the countercoup in Indonesia. In December 1965, a new NIE found cause for concern. "The entire area is more unstable now than at any time in the past decade." "Singapore is more exposed than before; Malaysia is less certain of the loyalty of its Borneo components." "Mutual suspicions between Malays and ethnic Chinese will cloud Malaysia-Singapore relations. The embassy in Malaysia noted six months after the separation of Singapore "mutual antagonism remains strong and up to now cooperation has been minimal." Nonetheless, "1965 was a year of continued economic progress in Malaysia." Sabah and Sarawak fully participated in the economic development. The embassy applauded the 1966-1970 development plan for "providing more jobs for youths and raising rural incomes." Fortunately, "much of the heat has gone out of Indonesian confrontation," and Malaysia sought to cultivate relations with its Southeast Asian neighbors. Encouragingly for U.S. policy, Malaysia has taken "an

---

[58] *NYT,* "Singapore Nearing Accord on Revival of Malaysia Trade," August 20, 1965, p. 4; "Singapore Asks U.S. Tolerance," September 8, 1965, p. 17; "Singapore Seeks Expanded Trade," September 9, 1965, p. 8; NARA, RG 59, CFPF, Box 2653, POL POLAFF&REL, Singapore-US, 1/1/65, Singapore Defense Minister's Views on U.S. Policy Toward Singapore, October 25, 1965. Again, in April 1967, Ambassador to Singapore Francis Galbraith wrote Rusk that "I am apprehensive re possible effect on USG-GOS relations of recent USG decisions detrimental to Singapore textile industry." "I feel that for sake small sop to U.S. textile interests, we may lose benefit of our efforts of past several months to convince Singapore that cooperation with U.S. is to mutual benefit, LBJ Library, NSF Country File, Box 281, Singapore, Memos, Vol. I, 8/65-7/67, Amembassy Singapore to SecState, #1730, April 22, 1967; Bundy held firm in a meeting with Ambassador Wong Lin Ken of Singapore, explaining that "U.S. domestic pressures precluded the United States being more forthcoming than it has been," see NARA, RG 59, CFPF, Box 2481, POL Singapore-US, 1/1/67, Singapore Ambassador Pays Courtesy Call, April 27, 1967; Rusk followed up to the embassy in Singapore that "we have been under intense pressure over past several months from textile industry and its congressional supporters" over the downturn in and future prospects for the U.S. industry; see LBJ Library, NSF Country File, Box 281, Singapore, Cables, Vol. I, 8/65-7/67, State to Amembassy Singapore, #184000, April 28, 1967.

increasingly clear-cut stance against communist expansion in Asia." Given economic progress and a lessening of tensions with Indonesia, Malaysian-American relations were becoming "progressively closer."[59]

The real issue was "whether or nor to give more economic assistance," for "Malaysians are resentful of our seeming unresponsiveness to their need." Related to aid issues, Malaysia was concerned with U.S. restraint levels for anticipated textile exports [also a concern to Singapore for its exports]." The embassy believed "we should seek ever-expanding American contacts with Malaysia," "offer substantially greater economic aid," "deal as generously and sympathetically as possible with Malaysia on trade issues," and "encourage Malaysia's revitalized interest in Southeast Asian affairs." At the same time, the consulate in Singapore concluded that Singapore was focused on "economic and political survival" and "for the long term, re-merger with Malaysia." The consulate noted the alpha and omega: "Singapore is a potential source of regional instability" and "Singapore could make a major contribution to regional cooperation in Southeast Asia." The consulate was convinced that serious political and economic dislocation in Singapore would greatly affect Malaysia, too, since the two countries "continue to be one economic unit." The challenge was economic: Singapore's economy depended "on temporary sources of income," including British base expenditures and U.S. procurement for Vietnam and the "Vietnam R&R program." Given these considerations the consulate recommended encouraging Singapore's exporting of goods to the United States and other developed countries, "encourage the Singapore Government's interest in regional projects," and

[59] *FRUS, 1964-1968, Vol. XXVI,* Document 270, NIE 54/59-65, Prospects for Malaysia and Singapore, December 16, 1965; NARA, RG 59, CFPF, Box 2452, POL 2-3, Malaysia, 1/1/64, U.S. Policy Assessment, February 18, 1966; same folder, Policy Assessment Working Papers, March 22, 1966; same folder, Policy Assessment Working Paper – Economic, April 12, 1966; Box 2651, POL 6, Singapore, 1/1/65, Singapore Policy Assessment, February 25, 1966. On the eve of Deputy Prime Minister Razak's visit to Washington, the embassy in Kuala Lumpur noted Malaysian desire in U.S. economic aid and suggested responding that the U.S. was committed in Vietnam, etc., and had to rely on the Commonwealth to assist Malaysia, see NARA, RG 59, CFPF, Box 2453, POL 7, Malaysia, 6/10/66, Amembassy Kuala Lumpur to SecState, #956, Sections 1 and 2, September 15, 1966. Yet within 10 days, the embassy followed up with a major report that, in light of the "significant reduction in the British role in Malaysia," "the U.S. should assume a considerably more active role in ensuring that the present political stability and economic progress of Malaysia is maintained."

support Singapore's foreign policy even when it criticizes the U.S. government.[60]

For Singapore, until regional economies expanded, there was limited inter-regional trade for it to help move and market. Within several months of the breakup of Malaysia, the Singaporean economy faced real challenges: "widespread unemployment, dwindling trade, and tense relations with Malaya." Singapore told U.S. officials it wanted "to resume its profitable $500 million-a-year trade with Indonesia" after the military coup there. Prime Minister Lee recognized the challenge: "unless we succeed in industrializing, Singapore is going to be overflowing with youngsters demanding work and that can be very dangerous." Despite earlier efforts, economic relations between Malaysia and Singapore were poor, and both nations placed tariffs on the goods of the other. By mid-1966, Singapore gave up any hope for re-merger with Malaysia and committed to working with neighboring states. About the same time, Indonesia moved to recognize Singapore, and Singaporeans hoped to regain the quarter of their trade that took place with Indonesia prior to its

---

[60] The embassy argued for increased U.S. economic assistance as part of a larger package of support from non-communist, industrialized nations, see NARA, RG 59, CFPF, Box 2460, POL 1, Malaysia-US, 1/1/64, Amembassy Kuala Lumpur to State, A-114, September 23, 1966. Also see *FRUS, 1964-1968, Vol. XXVI,* Document 273, Rostow to Johnson, October 4, 1966: Rostow told Johnson that Razak likely will ask for military assistance, economic aid, and help maintaining international rubber prices. President and Mrs. Johnson visited Malaysia on October 30, 1966 but spent most of his time in "ceremonial activities" and did not have private meetings with Malaysian leaders; see *FRUS, 1964-1968, Vol. XXVI,* Document 275, Editorial Note. Nonetheless, when Malaysia presented an Aide-Memoire seeking U.S. loan and grant assistance, William Bundy replied it "did not provide sufficient quantitative specificity to permit the USG to take meaningful decisions on the request." "In light of U.S. commitments elsewhere and the general shortage of U.S. assistance funds, no meaningful case could be made in support of the GOM's request, see NARA, RG 59, CFPF, Box 2459, POL-POLAFF&REL, Malaysia-US, 1/1/64, Malaysian-American Relations, November 30, 1966. In late December, Washington relented and offered to "facilitate Malaysian commercial purchase of 15 American-manufactured helicopters from Sikorsky, see LBJ Library, NSF Country File, Box 281, Singapore, Cables, Vol. I, 8/65-7/67, State to Singapore, #108434, December 24, 1966. Helicopters aside, U.S. tin surplus disposal and rubber purchases mattered more; see NARA, RG 59, CFPF, Box 2321, POL-Malaysia, 1/1/67, Malaysian Ambassador Makes Courtesy Call, February 9, 1967 and Box 2322, POL 7, Malaysia, 1/1/67, Problems of the Rubber Market and Other Matters, April 13, 1967; Box 2481, POL Singapore-US, 1/1/67, The Singapore Textile Industry in the Context of US-Singapore Relations, June 13, 1967.

confrontation with Malaysia. As the Indonesian economy revived with international assistance, exports from smaller Indonesian ports would move to and through Singapore for transshipment to the United States, Japan, and Europe. By October 1967 Singapore-Indonesia relations continued to improve, and Singapore was "notably conciliatory in its dealings with Indonesia." Still, the Singaporean execution of two Indonesian marines in October 1968 for a crime committed in early 1965 showed the fragile nature of the developing relations in the region. Within a year the Singaporean economy revived, marked by construction of eight large hotels, mostly for business travelers, additional air line connections, and new restaurants and other amenities. Perhaps the specter of improved Singaporean-Indonesian relations broke the logjam, but Malaysia and Singapore announced "currency interchangeability" when they issued separate currencies, in part to support trade between the two. [61]

Throughout this period, the U.S. government had "no official policy paper for Singapore and no authoritative definition of U.S. policy interests" there while needing to reappraise policy toward Malaysia. But, Prime Minister Lee will "look to the United States as his principal source of political and economic support." The embassy believed that "Singapore has an importance to the region and to the United States, for good or evil, out of proportion to its size." It occupied a strategic location; it was a Chinese ethnic outpost in a largely Malay ethnic region, and thus possessed "trouble-making potential;" it could serve as a positive example to overseas Chinese against the negative example of the People's Republic of China. The embassy recommended Washington "continue indirect efforts to help Singapore economically," avoid actions or public

---

[61] *Time,* "The Boom That Went Bust," January 7, 1966, www.time.com/time/magazine/article/0,9171,834961,00.html; *NYT,* "Singapore Fights to Spur Growth," February 1, 1966, p. 18; NARA, RG 59, CFPF, Box 2459, POL POLAFF&REL, Malaysia-Singapore, 4/8/65, Singapore and Malaysia Relations One Year After Separation, August 26, 1966; *NYT,* "Indonesia Seeks Singapore Tie," June 4, 1966, p. 60; "Indonesia-Singapore Tie Reported to Be Imminent," August 16, 1966, p. 2; *The Economist,* "Indonesian trade: Can Singapore get it back?" August 20, 1966, p. 763; *NYT,* "Indonesia to Renew Singapore Trade," September 11, 1966, p. 9; "Singapore's Strides," February 26, 1967, p. X43; "Indonesia and Singapore Move to Resume Trade," March 1, 1967, *NYT,* "Singapore Reaches Malaysian Accord," June 6, 1967, p. 67; NARA, RG 59, CFPF, Box 2210, POLAFF&REL, INDON-S, Singapore-Indonesia Relations, October 6, 1967; same folder, Indonesian-Singapore Relations, October 17, 1968; same folder, Potential Effects of Current Singapore/Indonesian Difficulty, October 23, 1968; same folder, Amembassy Kuala Lumpur to SecState, #5054, October 24, 1968.

statements that might tend to compromise Lee Kuan Yew's non-aligned image," avoid any appearance of taking sides between Malaysia and Singapore, and encourage regional cooperation with Singapore as the central point in such an economic arrangement. Ambassador Galbraith believed Lee would "attempt to keep open as many options" as he could, but Washington should continue to befriend him even if he seemed at times to turn his back. At the same time, the embassy in Kuala Lumpur wrote that "Malaysia continues to remain remarkably stable in comparison to most developing countries in the area." However, rubber prices declined seriously, the political-security situation in Sarawak deteriorated, and the British drastically reduced aid to the federation, forcing Washington "to play a considerably more active role in Malaysia." Whereas the prior year the embassy recommended "the U.S. no longer deal with Malaysia through the British," in Spring 1967 the embassy recommended Washington "assume a more active role than in the past," "quietly encourage Malaysia to participate in appropriate cooperative regional efforts," hope but not expect improvement in Malaysia-Singapore and Malaysia-Indonesia relations, and not press Kuala Lumpur into too much support for the war in Vietnam. Henry Owen wrote Walt Rostow in June 1967 about security issues in the region, and attached a paper that Ralph Clough had written earlier in February. Clough stated the United States had "important interests in this area which would be endangered were any of these states – Indonesia, Malaysia, and Singapore – to fall into hostile hands. He believed that "regional association offers the best hope for creating a sense of security which would enable the British to withdraw without unsettling effects." Clough concluded that "to ensure the continued security of the Indonesia-Malaysia-Singapore area, the United States should continue to contain Communist China and stabilize the frontier with Communism in Southeast Asia, urge the British to stay on in Singapore as long as necessary, and support appropriate regional association as an eventual substitute for the British presence."[62]

---

62 NARA, RG 59, CFPF, Box 2478, POL Singapore, 1/1/67, U.S. Policy Assessment for Singapore, April 28, 1967; Box 2321, POL 2-3 Malaysia, 1/1/67, Annual Policy Assessment – Malaysia, May 2, 1967; LBJ Library, NSF Country File, Box 281, Singapore, Memos, Vol. I, 8/65-7/67, Memorandum for Mr. Donald Ropa, May 4, 1967; same box, Singapore, Cables, Vol. I, 8/65-7/67, State to Amembassy Singapore, #189351, May 5, 1967; Box 276, Malaysia, Memos, Vol. IV, 1965-1968, Memorandum for Mr. Rostow, May 9, 1967; Box 281, Singapore, Cables, Vol. I, 8/65-7/67, Amembassy Singapore to SecState, #1941, May 24, 1967; Box 276, Malaysia, Cables, Vol. IV, 1965-1968, Amembassy Kuala Lumpur

Policy considerations moved ahead as the date for an official state visit by Singapore Prime Minister Lee Kuan Yew neared. In August, Thomas Hughes, Director of Intelligence and Research in the State Department, wrote Rusk on the eve of Lee's first visit to the United States as prime minister of an independent Singapore that Lee will see "to make personal contact with the leaders of a great power he now regards as vital to Singapore's future economic stability and security." This represented a change from 1965 when Lee was "critical of the United States to the press." Lee believed "it vital to Singapore that American should continue in Vietnam" as well. On the eve of Lee's visit, William Bundy wrote Rusk that Lee wanted to discuss Singapore's cotton textile quota and U.S. use of Singapore bases because "the bases currently provide roughly 20% of Singapore's GNP and – directly or indirectly – some 40,000 jobs, all of which could be lost unless alternative uses are found following British withdrawal". A scope paper concluded that Lee "will probably express a desire for increased access to American markets for Singapore, increased American investment in Singapore, and American use of the Singapore Naval base." Rusk told Johnson that Lee "really wants to discuss the future of Southeast Asia frankly with you and assess American policy there." The press release following the meeting noted Johnson and Lee "had a frank and useful exchange of views" and "their talks reflected the cordial relations existing between Singapore and the US." Lee later told Ambassador Galbraith that Lee gained "a deeply favorable impression of the President" and wanted "to be helpful to the President on Viet-Nam." [63]

---

to SecState, #4547, May 27, 1967; NARA, RG 59, PPS Subject & Country File, 1965-1969, Asia-1967, Owen to Rostow, June 6, 1967.

[63] NARA, RG 59, CFPF, Box 2479, POL 7 Singapore, 1/1/63, Hughes to Rusk, August 9, 1967; Box 2478, POL Singapore, 1/1/67, Singapore's Foreign Relations, September 29, 1967; same box, POL 7 Singapore, 10/1/67, Galbraith to Rusk, October 3, 1967; Box 2481, POL Singapore-US, 1/1/67, Amembassy Singapore to SecState, #1193, September 2, 1967. Malaysian Ambassador Ong agreed in an interview in *Reader's Digest,* stating that "the United States' withdrawal from Vietnam under present circumstances would confirm the fear of many Asian leaders that China is the wave of the future" and "in Vietnam you have at stake the independence of more than 200 million people in South East Asia; the rice bowl of the world; vast supplies of rubber, tin, and oil; strategic control of critical sea lanes; and the integrity of a great nation, the United States," LBJ Library, Confidential File, Box 13, CO333, Malaysia, Federation of, Marvin to LBJ, September 14, 1967; NSF Country File, Box 282, Singapore, Visit of PM Lee, 10/17-18/67, Bundy to Rusk, October 13, 1967; same folder, Memorandum for the President, October 13,1967; LBJ Library, Confidential File, Box 11 (1 of 2), CO266, Singapore, "Scope Paper, Visit of Prime Minister Lee," October 10, 1967;

As Singapore's economy revived, it received a quick, dramatic shock from its former colonial master. Britain could no longer afford to maintain military forces east of Suez, and announced it would withdraw the 20,000 servicemen from Singapore by the end of 1971. They both helped to defend Singapore, and also were significant consumers of goods and services, hence spurring the economy. With the Great Proletarian Cultural Revolution peaking in China, investment funds had been moving from Hong Kong to Singapore for greater stability, and Britain's withdrawal might affect the image of Singaporean stability. As *The Economist* noted, Britain's decision increased pressure on Malaysia and Singapore to "develop a workable level of mutual tolerance by the time British forces leave Singapore in 1971." *Newsweek* told readers, likely fixated on the Communist Tet Offensive in Vietnam, that "Singapore and Malaysia are current facing serious problems of their own," namely withdrawal of the British. Singaporeans, by contrast, clearly focused on President Johnson's March 31, 1968 announcement that he would not seek re-election but would seek peace in Vietnam. They wondered about American staying power, and if America withdrew, would the nations of the region be sufficiently strong to resist the lure of China. Singapore's response, in part, became the famed "rugged society," where Singaporeans and foreign visitors, sacrificed personal freedoms to obtain great economic success. Still, Singapore sought to replace British troops with British investment, and the effort was only partially successful. [64]

---

same folder, Suggestions on Approaching the Singaporeans and Topics of Conversation, October 10, 1967; NARA, RG 59, CFPF, Box 2481, POL Singapore-US, 1/1/67, US Mission to UN to SecState, #7701, October 16, 1967; same folder, Memorandum of Conversation, October 17, 1967; same folder, Memorandum of Conversation, October 18, 1967; LBJ Library, NSF Country File, Box 282, Singapore, Visit of PM Lee, 10/17-18/67, Wright to Rostow and attachment, November 28, 1967. The Malaysian Government "maintained a strict silence in public" concerning Lee's visit to Washington but embassy staff reported government officials had "undisguised admiration tinged with envy over Lee's performance," see NARA, RG 59, CFPF, Box 2479, POL 7 Singapore, 11/1/67, Malaysian Reaction to Lee Kuan Yew's Visit to the United States, December 4, 1967.

[64] *The Economist,* "Singapore: No reassurance from Healey," April 29, 1967, p. 447; "Singapore: The burden they have to pick up," January 20, 1968, p. 69; "Malaysia and Singapore: After sunset," January 20 1968, p. 34; "Singapore and Malaysia: Four years to be friends again," January 27, 1968, p. 22; *Newsweek,* "Southeast Asia: Withdrawal Symptoms," March 4, 1968, pp. 37-38; *NYT,* "Singapore is Afraid That Time is Running Out," April 28, 1968, p. SM28+; *The Economist,* "Singapore: Road to Bali," June 8, 1968, p. 78; *Newsweek,* "Singapore:

In March 1968, the embassy provided a positive policy assessment for Singapore. It noted that Singapore enjoyed "continued economic growth, improved relations with near neighbors Malaysia and Indonesia, increased interest and participation in regionalism, and reduction to near impotence of the strength of the Communist-oriented political opposition." Given the good news against the backdrop of Britain's military withdrawal by 1971, embassy staffers believed American policy was appropriate. Singapore recognized for Indonesia to accept Singapore, "Singapore should assist in helping the Suharto government solve Indonesia's economic problems." In December 1968, Prime Minister Lee paid a courtesy visit to President Johnson; they spoke equally about the recent U.S. presidential election and Singapore's prospects after Britain's withdrawal in 1971. Importantly, the conversation was relaxed, perhaps indicating that the crisis had passed.[65]

As Singapore moved towards accommodation with its neighbors, Malaysia continued to progress. The Tunku told the media that "Malaysia is neutral and does not want to be 'tied up with anybody.'" He believed that "Britain will come to Malaysia's aid when required even after her withdrawal from Malaysia." Malaysia and the Soviet Union were moving with "deliberate speed" to establish trade and diplomatic relations. Embassy officials reported that "a desire to strengthen its position vis-à-vis Communist China" motivated Malaysia. At the same time, Malaysian officials sought concessions on cotton textile, tin, and rubber exports as well as so-called Food for Freedom transfers under Public Law 480.[66]

The Rugged Society," August 19, 1968, pp. 44-45; *The Economist,* "Singapore and Malaysia: Glad but doubtful," August 24, 1968, pp. 22-23; "Which Way for Singapore?" August 24, 1968, pp. 42-43; *NYT,* "Singapore, Facing British Withdrawal in 1971, Fights for Prosperity and Survival," November 8, 1968, p. 12; *The Economist,* "Singapore: More export aids," November 16, 1968, p. 79.

[65] NARA, RG 59, CFPF, Box 2481, POL Singapore-US, 1/1/67, U.S. Policy Assessment for Singapore, March 15, 1968; Box 2210, POLAFF&REL, INDON-S, Singapore-Indonesia Relations, April 5, 1968; same folder, State to Jakarta and Singapore, #157678, May 3, 1968; same folder, Improvement in Singapore's relations with Indonesia, April 18, 1969: the next year the embassy reported that "the most significant development in Singapore during the past year has been the general rapprochement with Indonesia.;" *FRUS, 1964-1968, Vol. XXVI,* Document 292, Bundy to Johnson, December 10, 1968; Document 293, Editorial Note.

[66] NARA, RG 59, CFPF, Box 2321, POL-Malaysia, 1/1/67, Amembassy Kuala Lumpur to SecState, #4246, May 21, 1968; same folder, Amembassy Kuala Lumpur to SecState, #4282, May 24, 1968; same folder, Bean to Bundy, Malaysian Roundup, July 11, 1968.

There was talk of a new grouping of Southeast Asian nations, a larger Maphilindo, or perhaps a customs union to assist economic development and resist the lure of communism. With the Communist tide receding in Indonesia by early 1966 and with hopes for peace between Malaysia, the Philippines, and Indonesia, and with the encouragement of the strong American stand in Vietnam, the time seemed right. At first, Thailand, Malaysia, and the Philippines considered reviving the Association of Southeast Asia, which collapsed in 1963 with the formation of Malaysia. In early May leaders of the three former ASA members met, and invited neighbors to join with them. About the same time, Indonesia was approaching Malaysia discussed earlier, leading to some talk of a revival of Maphilindo. Signs were so encouraging that, in mid-June 1966, *The New York Times* reported "optimism" that Southeast Asia outside Vietnam "was really moving toward harmony and regional cooperation." Nine non-Communist governments met and formed the Asian and Pacific Council [ASPAC], declaring their common "determination to preserve their integrity and sovereignty in the face of external threats." While the signatories to the declaration "avoided the abusive language of the cold war in the communiqué," they left no doubt they had come together "to turn back the Marxist challenge." Indonesia was interested in joining with its nine regional neighbors, giving real impetus to the grouping. ASPAC, along with the Asian Development Bank and the Association of Southeast Asian Nations brought mostly western-oriented, capitalist economy nations of the region together, a true goal of America's involvement in Vietnam.[67]

---

[67] *NYT,* "Malaysia Has Problems – But Promise, Too," June 5, 1966, p. 206; "Hope for Asian Market Seen," January 4, 1966, p. 2; "Southeast Asia Group Meets," March 3, 1966, p. 25; *USN&WR,* "Business Around the World," April 4, 1966, p. 100; *NYT,* "Southeast Asians Revive Joint Unit," May 1, 1966, p. 13; *Newsweek,* "Indonesia: Maphilindo Again," May 30, 1966, pp. 53-54; *NYT,* "4 Nations in Asia Plan a New Union," June 3, 1966, p. 1; "Southeast Asia Talks of Cooperation, Not Confrontation," June 12, 1966, p. 210; "New Asian Council Supports Saigon," June 17, 1966, p. 8; "Southeast Asians are Heartened by Rising Trend Toward Unity," June 18, 1966, p. 4; "Asians Inch Toward a Regional Defense System," June 20, 1966, p. 2; *Time,* "A New Alliance, and More Help for Viet Nam," June 24, 1966, www.time.com/time/magazine/article/0,9171,835789,00.html; Peter Braestrup, "A Larger 'Maphilindo,'" *Current, August 1966,* pp. 26-27; *NYT,* "Indonesia Hints at Joining Regional Organization," August 24, 1966, p. 16; "Indonesia Reports Major Steps Toward Rejoining International Institutions," September 18, 1966, p. 16; Narciso Ramos, "Association of Southeast Asia and The Philippines," *United Asia, Vol. 18, No. 6, Nov./Dec. 1966,* pp. 295-298. Interestingly, as much as Washington favored Southeast Asian cooperation,

Discussions continued into 1967. *Time* congratulated "the sudden blooming of regional cooperation among countries that for centuries were divided by animosity." It quoted Japanese Prime Minister Eisaku Sato that "blood is thicker than water. We are all brothers, born and raised in Asia." *Time* further stated that "there would be economic sense in further Asian groupings," even if it meant bringing Japan back into the region, a leftover problem of the Second World War. *The New York Times* gave credit to "the sudden spectacle of the Chinese giant thrashing and gasping in a violent wrestling match with itself" [the Cultural Revolution] and "the Johnson Administration's policy in Vietnam" for these Southeast Asian groupings. The idea is to "place the relatively backward nations on more equal terms with Japan and Korea, and all of them in a stronger position to cope with China." In April some 40 nations came together in Tokyo for the UN Economic Commission for Asia [ECAFE], "the beginning of more regional coordination in economic planning," according to the UN Commission. The Philippines invited its neighbors to establish a free-trade area, negotiating tariff concessions.[68]

Having agreed on the attractiveness of a regional bloc, governments needed additional time to come together. In July ASPAC ministers met for the second time, and they considered "how much of an 'activist' economic role the council should or could play." Japan and Australia feared other nations would expect them to finance "broad joint economic ventures." Other nations did not want to duplicate the Asian Development Bank or the revived ASA. So they agreed "to move slowly on joint economic projects and avoid a hard anti-communist line" despite the urgings of South Korea and Nationalist China. A month later Indonesia, Singapore, the Philippines, Malaysia and Thailand meeting in Bangkok founded the Association of Southeast Asian Nations [ASEAN] to promote regional economics and cultural exchange. The document contained only five

---

Singapore viewed the "possible revival of 'Maphilindo' as a general term to describe Pan-Malayanism in all its manifestations," and the embassy in Kuala Lumpur agreed; see NARA, RG 59, Box 2459, POL POLAFF&REL, Malaysia-Singapore, 4/8/65, Amembassy Singapore to Sec State, #798, May 31, 1966; same folder, Amembassy Kuala Lumpur to SecState, #1434, June 2, 1966; same folder, Amembassy Singapore to SecState, #820, June 7, 1966.

[68] *Time,* "Regional Groupings: Islands of Hope," February 3, 1967, www.time.com/time/magazine/article/0,9171,901973,00.html; *NYT,* "Southeast Asia: The Hope of Counterweight," February 9, 1967, p. 38; "Economic Parley Beginning in Asia," April 3, 1967, p. 48; "Manila Talks Open on Free-Trade Area," May 30, 1967, p. 13; "Philippines and Indonesia Plan New Regional Alliance," May 31, 1967, p. 3; *The Economist,* "South-East Asia: Looking for ties that bind," June 10, 1967, p. 1112.

articles concerning economic, social, cultural, technical, and educational cooperation. *The New York Times* reported favorably on ASEAN's founding, calling it part of "a healthy trend in the South Pacific," where governments "are now getting together in economic, cultural and scientific fields." *The Economist* approved ASEAN for "bringing Indonesia back into the regional community." The news weekly noted that the ASEAN declaration did not call for "a common market or a free trading area," but did promise "more effective collaboration in industry and agriculture." Perhaps a sign of ASEAN's prospects for the future was the quick condemnation from the People's Republic: ASEAN "cannot possibly save the whole lot from approaching doom." Beijing charged that ASEAN was "an out-and-out counterrevolutionary alliance against China, Communist and the people." [69]

In the eighteen months before the Tet Offensive that marked the American high tide in Vietnam, what appeared to be America's forthright stand encouraged these regional, western-oriented groupings. *Time* stated in September 1966 that America's "determined moves" in Vietnam "have created a new atmosphere of hope and confidence throughout Asia's southern crescent of nations shoring up and strengthening Red China's fearful neighbors." The American effort in Vietnam "has bought time for an Asian future that will be more and more mastered by the Asians themselves." More specifically, "a new Asian cooperativeness is already emerging." "Given time, the free Asians should be able to act together to speed up their own development, aided by U.S. money, technical assistance and encouragement." Seven months later *Time* followed up with another positive report. "While China has been thrashing in economic disorder, her neighbors have by and large prospered and plucked up their courage, partly because of the U.S.'s determined stand in South Viet Nam." *Time* noted the countries with thriving economies – Japan, Taiwan, and South Korea – and noted that "if other Asian economies are less thriving, most are reversing the downward spiral." *The New York Times*

---

[69] *NYT,* "9-Nation Asian Unit Meets Amid Discord on Role," July 6, 1967, p. 5; "Asia-Pacific Council Ends Bangkok Talks," July 8, 1967, p. 3; "Asian Nations Form New Economic Role," August 9, 1967, p. 55; "Cooperation in Asia," August 9, 1967, p. 38; *The Economist,* "South-east Asia: Asean togetherness," August 1, 1967, p. 569; *NYT,* "Chinese Reds Score New Asian Grouping," August 13, 1967, p. 20; "Planning by New Southeast Asian Association Is Delayed by a Protocol Problem," August 17, 1967, p. 4; *Time,* "Sports-Shirt Diplomacy," August 18, 1967, www.time.com/time/archive; *NYT,* "Three Members to Dissolve Southeast Asia Association," August 30, 1967, p. 8; "Sato To Take Aid to Southeast Asia," September 1, 1967, p. 7.

agreed: "non-communist nations of Southeast Asia appear to be more confident about their future as a result of the United States' stand in Vietnam and the political convulsions in Peking." On the eve of the Tet Offensive, Takeshi Watanabe, President of the Asian Development Bank, had a long commentary in *The New York Times* that noted the progress of the past year and the distance left to travel. *The Times* noted the war in Vietnam "has served to stimulate the economies of noncombatant neighbors." Donald Zagoria, writing in *The New York Times* in April 1968 argued that "although the domino theory may have had some relevance to a world in which Communism was monolithic, it is no longer even remotely a satisfactory guide to American policy." That is, even if American peace efforts in Vietnam failed, Asia would continue on its largely non-Communist and non-Chinese dominated path.[70]

Nonetheless, there were continual challenges to strengthened Southeast Asian regional cooperation. *The New York Times* pointed out that "there are at least 10 regional organizations in various stages of development in Asia." "In hard economic terms, Southeast Asia's new regional groups have produced little in the way of joint endeavor, or even agreement on joint endeavor." Regional economies "are competitive rather than complementary." That is, they export the same commodities, principally tin, rubber, rice, and timber, providing a very real stumbling block to cooperation. In summer 1968 the status of Sabah, the former North Borneo, part of Malaysia, still claimed by the Philippines, again rose to prominence. The two capitals, Kuala Lumpur and Manila, hurled invective at one another, and, as *The Economist* commented, "the flare-up over Sabah has shown that for all the progress regionalism has made in the last few years, the governments of southeast Asia are not yet ready to subordinate nationalist interests to it." The dispute over Sabah continued until the end of the year when Malaysia and the Philippines agreed to set it

[70] *Time,* "America's Permanent Stake in Asia," September 23, 1966, www.time.com/time/printout/o,8816,842805,00.html; "The News – Mostly Good – Beyond Viet Nam," April 7, 1967, www.time.com/time/magazine/article/0,9171,843504,00.html; *NYT,* "Non-Red Nations In Asia Take Hope," April 30, 1967, p. 1; "Viewpoint: Asia Needs Help to Keep Hope Alive," January 19, 1968, p. 61; "War Spurs Economies Of a Struggling Asia," January 19, 1968, p. 49; Ricardo P. Llardizabal, "Economic Growth of South-East Asia," *United Asia, Vol. 20, No. 1, Jan-Feb 1968,* pp. 39-42; Donald S. Zagoria, "Who's Afraid of the Domino Theory?" *New York Times,* April 21, 1968, pp. SM28+.

aside for a year, postponing any resolution into the early months of the Nixon Administration.[71]

As the Johnson administration was drawing to a close, the U.S. government produced a National Policy Paper on the future for Indonesia, Malaysia, and Singapore. It concluded that the forthcoming British withdrawal from the region "will remove a stabilizing presence," and there likely will be an "increase in unemployment in Singapore, communal strains and economic vulnerabilities in Malaysia and both economic and political weaknesses in Indonesia." To help the region resist the People's Republic of China, the National Policy Paper proposed that Washington "contribute to the economic development of Indonesia, Malaysia and Singapore," "urge Japan to expand its responsibilities in the subregion," "quietly encourage increased economic and political cooperation among the three states and their immediate neighbors outside the subregion," and

---

[71] *NYT,* "Asian Unity Periled By Stumbling Blocs," January 19, 1968, p. 60; *The Economist,* "South-east Asia: Much ado about Sabah," June 22, 1968, pp. 29-30; NARA, RG 59, CFPF, Box 2521, POL 15-1 THAI, 1/1/68, Amembassy Bangkok to SecState, #9318, July 26, 1968 in which Thai Foreign Minister Thanat Khoman "was pleased" that Malaysia reacted "mildly" when the Philippines recalled its diplomatic mission over the Sabah dispute; same folder, Amembassy Bangkok to SecState, #580, September 13, 1968; *Newsweek,* "Southeast Asia: Claims on Sabah," July 29, 1968, p. 40; *NYT,* "Five Asian States Meeting in Jakarta," August 6, 1968, p. 5; "A 'Cooling-Off' Period Over Sabah Reported," August 7, 1968, p. 3; "Malaysian Leader Welcomes Philippine Accord," August 8, 1968, p. 3; "Sabah on Ice," August 8, 1968, p. 32; *Time,* "A Victory for Regionalism," August 16, 1968, www.time.com/time/magazine/article/0,9171,838550,00.html; *Newsweek,* "Southeast Asia: Confrontation Again," September 30, 1968, pp. 54-55; *The Economist,* "Malaysia and the Philippines: Sabah blows up again," October 19, 1968, p. 50; *NYT,* "Asian Experiment in Regionalism," November 1, 1968, p. 2; *The Economist,* "South-east Asia: Humph," November 9, 1968, p. 37; *Time,* "Family Quarrels," November 15, 1968, www.time.com/time/magazine/article/0,9171,723859,00.html; *NYT,* "Sabah Dispute Continues to Simmer in Malaysia," November 18, 1968, p. 5; "Malaysia and Philippines Agree To Drop Sabah Issue for a Year," December 14, 1968, p. 5; NARA, RG 59, CFPF, Box 2519, POL & THAI, 5/1/68, Amembassy Bangkok to SecState, #2689, December 14, 1968; Thanat told American diplomats that "he did not foresee immediate direct bilateral negotiations between Manila and KL but that 'a definite and positive cooling-off period may be observed by both sides;" same folder, Amembassy Manila to SecState, #6148, December 16, 1968; *The Economist,* "Sabah: The dog is barking," December 21, 1968, pp. 16-17.

where appropriate "express approval of future regional security arrangements, such as might, for example, be based on ASEAN."[72]

How does one evaluate U.S. relations with this region? In the closing days of the Johnson Administration, the State Department wrote an administrative history and found policy generally achieved its goals. "East Asia, like Europe, was one of the two great focal areas of US foreign policy concern throughout the Johnson Administration." "During the Johnson years our twofold task in Asia of helping hold back aggression, while assisting weak nations to become strong, grew more complicated and burdensome but also showed encouraging results." "Gains were in large part due to our help and protection." "Virtually all the non-communist nations of the area came into their own as ongoing national units," and "in the economic sphere alone the developments of the recent past have been dramatic." "There has emerged in East Asia a sense of regional interdependence and cooperation – a development of historic significance." The history noted ASPAC, ASEAN, and the ADB as evidence of "multilateral cooperative efforts to development Southeast Asia as projected in President Johnson's speech at Johns Hopkins University." Johnson had said that "the first step [to improve life in Southeast Asia] is for the countries of Southeast Asia to associate themselves in a greatly expanded cooperative effort for development." Closely related, "the question of trade preferences became one of the major issues of US foreign economic policy, requiring the personal attention of the President." Developing countries in the sub-region depended heavily "on primary products with generally poor growth prospects" and worried that new industries could not compete with established industries in highly developed countries without clear trade preferences, which the U.S. government granted despite the economic cost at home. While facing such pressures, Washington also had to deal with the Kennedy Round, the ongoing balance of payments challenge, and "pressures for a special US-Latin American trade arrangement." Although U.S. involvement and influence with the sub-region "historically have been limited," both were "significantly greater in late 1968 than they were in late 1963." The history acknowledged that Malaysia "hoped the United States would be a significant contributor to its economic development" but it noted "Malaysia does not qualify" "because of its relatively good economic health and its ability to acquire development funds from

[72] NARA, RG 59, PPS-Subject & Country File, 1965-1968, Asia-1968, National Policy Paper, Indonesia, Malaysia and Singapore Subregion, September 1968.

international institutions." U.S. disposal of surplus tin and rubber and U.S. quotas on Malaysian textile imports were sources of continuing stress. Singapore-U.S. relations began with Prime Minister Lee's personal attacks and then demands for "preferential US access to its products." Washington satisfied Lee's concerns with various programs and Lee also sought "to attract American investment in Singapore as well as gain access to American markets for Singapore products." Still, "the United States can play only a limited role in assisting Malaysia and Singapore to deal with the economic problems stemming from British withdrawal." Meanwhile "Indonesia's transition from a nation moving steadily toward Communist control to a responsible member of the free community is one of the major success stories of recent years." Following the coup, Washington's policy included "a multilateral approach, a carefully tailored economic aid program, a modest Military Assistance Program, a low-keyed information and cultural effort, and a good measure of personal diplomacy. Our influence during the years 1966-1968 was significant and sometimes crucial for Indonesia's well-being."[73]

[73] LBJ Library, Administrative History of the Department of State, Box 3, Chapter 7 (East Asia), Sections A-D, "A: Overview: Asian Trends and U.S. Policy," pp. 1-5; "B: East Asian Regionalism," pp. 11-12, "C: Trade Preferences For Development Countries," pp, 1, 3, 10; same box, Chapter 7 (East Asia), Sections E-L, "J: Malaysia/Singapore," pp. 1, 5-6, 9, 10, 11-12, 15; "L: Indonesia," p. 1, 29.

CONCLUSION

SUCCESS YET FAILURE

In 1961, the prospects for the free nations in East Asia greatly concerned American policymakers. Japan had recovered from the devastation of the Second World War but had difficult relations with its neighbors in the region. South Korea and Taiwan focused more on their respective civil wars against North Korea and the People's Republic of China than political stability and economic development. Other nations in the region suffered from political corruption and economic weakness.

Most free nations in East Asia agreed that mainland China represented a threat to regional stability. China was the unspoken constant at the back of every discussion. The excesses of the 1950s and the resulting widespread starvation and suffering, costing millions of lives, shocked and amazed governments and peoples on China's periphery. Moreover, Mao Zedong and the People's Republic espoused a revolutionary philosophy that threatened violent overthrow of the existing order. Yet, in this period where limited and uneven economic development meant relative poverty for many millions of people, governments feared that China's revolutionary philosophy might attract the allegiance of those without economic stake in their respective societies.

The United States did not have an entirely free hand in meeting the challenges. The troubling and continuing balance of payments deficit indicated weaknesses in the American economy. Yet the region needed not only U.S. economic assistance but increased access to American markets to earn the foreign exchange they needed to finance their respective economic developments. This economic challenge would have been sufficiently daunting, but the Vietnam War, especially in its dislocations for the U.S. economy and boon times for regional economies made U.S. foreign policy all the more complicated.

The expanding conflict in Vietnam though not the subject of this monograph was the other constant in regional discussions. Free nations in East Asia needed a sign of America's commitment to resist Communist aggression and to contain China, thus, the oft-misunderstood domino theory. America's allies needed the United States to stem what many perceived as a Chinese-inspired, Chinese-supplied, and perhaps Chinese-run insurgency in Indochina so they could expand economies, stabilize societies, and develop effective if not democratic polities. While most Americans in the 1960s believed that Presidents John F. Kennedy and Lyndon Johnson were determined to secure a free South Vietnam, the government in Washington really sought only time and a shield behind which its allies could sufficiently develop to reject the appeal and pressure of the presumably aggressive government in Beijing.

China seemed threatening. Mao's philosophy espousing peasant overthrow of the ruling classes potentially held real appeal to poor farmers throughout East Asia; China implicitly encouraged radical threats to the existing order. There were guerrilla groups of varying numbers and power, proclaiming allegiance to Beijing, in virtually every country in the region.

The so-called domino theory, properly stated, had real power in this era. The phrase has always appeared to suggest a scene of millions of tiny black rectangles standing close to one another where pushing the first one leads quickly and inevitably to the toppling of thousands and even millions of subsequent dominoes. But the real domino theory summarized a widely held belief that, absent a strong U.S. presence in Eastern Asia, the various governments would either fall under the sway of Beijing or succumb to internal communist-led revolutionary movements. Inevitability not speed was the key.

The Kennedy administration recognized the challenges, but weaknesses in the U.S. economy constrained its responses. From a position of economic dominance in 1946, by 1961 the U.S. economy faced strains and stresses that caused Kennedy and his advisors much concern. American experts concentrated on balance of trade and balance of payments issues with Western Europe. The Trade Expansion Act of 1962 and the subsequent Kennedy Round of tariff adjustments, which Kennedy's successor, Lyndon Johnson, secured, to the existing GATT treaty focused squarely on economic relations with Europe. There was little American trade with African nations, and the quick announcement of the Alliance for Progress in March 1961 indicated Washington was committed to spending billions of dollars to assure economic development in Latin America, in part to contain Castro's hemispheric threat in Cuba.

At the same time, the dominance of Cold War thinking caused the Kennedy and Johnson administrations to downplay contentious trade issues in favor of strengthening free nations to confront the challenge of "Red China" along its East and Southeast Asian periphery. Textiles exemplified the challenge of negotiating foreign policy and foreign economic policy. While such economic officials as Johnson era Treasury Secretary Henry Fowler pressed for a firmer U.S. policy on Asian exports to and imports from America, State Department officials won the internal policy debates and focused on strengthening regional economies and polities to contain the People's Republic of China. The risks of weak East Asian economies seemingly outweighed the dislocations that the balance of payments deficit and the dwindling balance of trade surplus were causing.

Moreover, countries mattered differently to U.S. policymakers. Japan was the anchor of the American position in East Asia, and, as the Japanese economic boom continued, Washington wanted Tokyo to take a larger role and contribute far more to East Asian development to compensate for Japan's small defense posture. South Korea and Taiwan were natural allies of Japan, and Washington wanted Tokyo to befriend Seoul and Taipei.

The two administrations placed great faith in the so-called Kennedy Round to resolve the issues. In 1962, Congress passed the Trade Expansion Act, which gave President Kennedy authority to lower U.S. tariffs and other impediments to imports in return to similar reductions by America's trading partners; the act expired in five years, and the clock ticked louder as mid-1967 approached. Fear of U.S. trade barriers caused developed nations to agree to the so called Kennedy Round reductions and promises of special conditions and economic assistance assuaged concerns of developing nations. Administration economists believed that foreign tariff barriers had caused America's weakening international trade position, not a declining competitiveness of the American economy.

The costs of the expanding American presence in Vietnam exerted increasing yet differing impacts on the American and East Asian regional economies. The Kennedy Round agreement seemed to augur improvements in the U.S. balance of payments, and U.S. promises of economic assistance reflected a delicate balancing of support for developing East Asian economies while concern for the state of the U.S. economy. But, as Treasury Secretary Fowler told President Lyndon Johnson, spending on the war in Vietnam dramatically affected the balance of payments. There was spending on the war in the Vietnam War zone, purchases of goods and services in the region, spending on bases in neighboring countries, and spending of servicemen and women on so-called R&R in the region – the total effect topping $4 billion annually – a significant sum given that era – and sending more U.S. dollars abroad.

For America, the Vietnam War placed additional pressure on the balance of payments deficit that so concerned successive Secretaries of the Treasury. Historians have well-documented Lyndon Johnson's commitment to "guns" and "butter." He wanted to believe Hanoi would either end its aggression in South Vietnam or accept his offer of economic development assistance. In either case, he did not adjust the U.S. government budget or America's spending abroad until the situation was too far along for small steps to have great impact. That is, in addition to leaving the ending of the war in Vietnam to his successor, Richard Nixon, Johnson also left a weakening U.S. international trade position.

For the region, America's war in Vietnam helped expand economies and provided access to the American market. American manufacturers concentrated on military procurement and that left openings for foreign manufacturers to gain market share. Local industries benefited from America's purchases of goods and services in the region to support the war effort in Vietnam. The effect reached from nearby Thailand all the way to more distant Japan.

There were additional concerns about America's staying power against the People's Republic of China, indicated, perhaps, by the limited involvement in Laos in 1961 and 1962. The situation in Laos was complicated and easily and perhaps even purposefully misunderstood. At one level, it posed a challenge to SEATO, the Southeast Asian Treaty Organization, and SEATO proved wanting. Thailand in particular criticized the timidity it perceived keeping France and Great Britain from taking stronger stands to defend Laotian territorial integrity. America's allies in the region wanted Washington to make clear its commitment, and the hesitant response to the North Vietnamese-supported Pathet Lao worried free nations of East Asia. But, as Kennedy and his advisors considered options after Kennedy's summit with Khrushchev in Vienna, the Berlin Wall, and the Bay of Pigs fiasco in Cuba, Vietnam with its long coastline –easier to reach and supply – seemed a more logical choice for a stand than Laos.

When Johnson succeeded Kennedy, the issues still seemed in doubt. U.S. assistance to South Vietnam had steadily increased from 1961 to 1964 but the situation continued to deteriorate. If South Vietnam either was neutralized or fell to the communist Viet Cong, the domino theory would advance, with Thailand surrounded on several sides, Malaysia now threatened, and Beijing driving on the ultimate goal of resource-rich, heavily populated Indonesia. America's allies as well as the United States itself did not easily differentiate between a possibly indigenous communist insurgency in South Vietnam, the communist government in North Vietnam seeking to unify Vietnam, the communist rulers of the People's Republic of China seeking regional hegemony, and the communist government in the Soviet Union expanding in another theater of the Cold War.

The expanding American involvement in Vietnam seemingly demonstrated American commitment to meet the Communist threat in East Asia. From 1961 through 1963, the number of American combat advisors increased to nearly 32,000; from 1965 through 1968, Lyndon Johnson committed some 550,000 Americans to Vietnam and tens of thousands more on board ships and at bases in neighboring countries. Much as the Pentagon reported progress to the American people, Washington reported similar progress to its allies, who believed the news and achieved a degree of confidence about the depth of America's support.

All of this found a unifying theme of a sort through the Vietnam War and a fear of Chinese expansionism. Until the Great Proletarian Cultural Revolution shocked and saddened the world, China loomed as a threat to its neighbors, its revolutionary ideology committed to overthrowing the existing order. But beginning in 1965 and continuing until the end of the Johnson years, China was caught up in its latest sorrow, and as young people clashed with each other and as army troops fought to restore order in key cities, the threat of Chinese aggression faded for many years, replaced, to some extent, by fear of Japanese economic imperialism.

The strong U.S. stand in Vietnam and China's seemingly self-destruction changed the situation in the mid-1960s. Japan had become an economic juggernaut; South Korea gained stability and enjoyed economic growth; Taiwan had stopped taking U.S. economic assistance; Malaysia survived its birthing and Singapore managed to accommodate its Malay neighbors while thriving as an entrepôt outpost of Chinese Singaporeans. Only Indonesia troubled American officials, for its economy suffered while its leader, Sukarno, was seemingly leaning toward Communist China.

Japan's economy boomed. When Prime Minister Ikeda Hayato announced his famous "income doubling" plan at the start of this period, critics abounded; as the years passed, the Japanese economy more than doubled, exports expanded even faster, the balance of trade moved into surplus, and Japan became the envy of its neighbors. More important, the Japanese economy was making a transition from light manufactures – mostly textiles – and small electronics into heavy industry. Steel produced rose dramatically; Japanese shipyards turned out massive supertankers; other companies moved into television and radio manufactures, and towards the end of the decade Japanese companies began to organize for a concerted effort in automobile exports.

International trade was critical to Japan's economic success. Rich only in human resources, Japan needed to import raw materials from surrounding nations and export finished goods of increasing sophistication and quality to developed nations. Japan wanted to help its neighbors develop their extractive industries and develop sufficiently to absorb Japan's light manufactures; in turn, Japan also needed access to markets of industrialized nations for its better quality, more value added exports. Europe remained resistant; Canada, Australia and other industrial nations simply did not have capacity to absorb vast quantities of Japanese exports; that left the United States. This led to a Faustian bargain of a sort whereby Japan supported America's Cold War objectives while the U.S. government looked past Japan's import barriers and export practices that caused the American economy so much trouble.

With America committed to South Vietnam, Washington policymakers began a long-term process of seeking to involve Japan in regional economic development initiatives to make Japan bear some regional responsibilities. The so-called MacArthur Constitution limited Japan's military expenditures and defense posture, and Tokyo's continuing reluctance to acknowledge fully and apologize for its excesses during the Second World War made a military role for Japan in the region, including Vietnam, virtually impossible. But Japan's phenomenal economic success and growing balance of trade surpluses made Japan a potential banker for regional development, assuming that its neighbors would take aid without fear of a new Greater East Asia Co-Prosperity Sphere defended with American military might.

Washington sought to involve Tokyo in taking the lead in the Asian Development Bank and other measures. Japan joined America as primary funders of the ADB, and a Japanese official, served as the first president of the bank. While the ADB was headquartered in Southeast Asia, site of its greatest need, Japan provided much of the definition for bank activities. East Asian nations had great hopes for the ADB but the bank had made few loans and had little impact by the end of the Johnson presidency. Japan supported the Association of Southeast Asian Nations [ASEAN], as well as helping Indonesia rebuild after the army countercoup crushed the PKI and eventually removed Sukarno from power.

Washington pressured Tokyo to make concessions to achieve an accommodation with Seoul, which eventually it did. In dealing with Seoul and with other governments in the region, Tokyo had to face the issue of "blood" money, of those governments demanding financial advantages to compensate them for the ravages of the war that Japan visited upon them twenty years earlier. Japan's neighbors insisted on such payment, while

Tokyo refused to feel guilt for actions of a Japanese government those two decades earlier. Still, if only in fits and starts, Tokyo and Seoul reached agreement on their difficult relationship, fisheries, economic assistance, and their respective views of the Cold War in Asia.

South Korea and Taiwan stopped receiving U.S. assistance, and enjoyed strong growth rates and strengthened political stability. At first, American diplomats despaired that Seoul could not achieve a measure of political stability and clamp down on the endemic corruption that retarded economic development. But the military government of Park Chung-hee traded economic growth and rising prosperity for some political freedoms. It is possible the North Korean attempt to assassinate Park and then seize the USS *Pueblo* reflected Kim Il-song's frustration at South Korea's development. Similarly, while Jiang Jieshi remained fixated on retaking the mainland and seeking signs of Communist disintegration or declining U.S. support, government technocrats curtailed inflation, cut government deficits, and stopped taking U.S. economic aid.

By mid-decade Korea became a leader in regional cooperation. President Park Chung-hee was interested in regional security arrangements and tried to revive the idea of a Pacific Pact dating back to 1949; he also deeply involved Korea in the new Asian Development Bank, in the Association of Pacific and Asian Countries, and widened Korean diplomatic relations in part to provide opportunities for Korean exports as the economy expanded.

Perhaps as a consequence, Kim Il-song accepted that his efforts to overthrow the government in Seoul had failed. Throughout the 1960s North Korean irregulars tried to cross the heavily-defended 38th parallel or infiltrate by sea into South Korea. While there were some firefights and some damage in the south, generally speaking these efforts achieved little. Eventually Kim recognized that his great gamble in 1950 had failed and South Korea had become a stunning Asian success story, mentioned typically right after Japan.

In Taiwan, Jiang focused on regaining the mainland. Successive American ambassadors and secretaries of state tried to have Jiang focus on economic development, on securing allegiance from the native Taiwanese people who outnumbered mainland refugees by four to one. They failed, for Jiang was committed to eliminating the communist regime, and followed every twist and turn of Maoist policy like reading tea leaves swirling in a half-empty cup. He also watched Washington with equal fervor to ferret out changes in American policy toward China, constantly seeking assurances of American support.

But with increasing success, Taiwanese technocrats developed the economy, and removed Taiwan from U.S. foreign aid. Within a few years, a group of technocrats managed to reduce corruption, strengthen the economy, develop export products, and Taiwan became another Asian success story often mentioned in the same breath as South Korea.

Spurred in part by U.S. regional spending for the Vietnam War, Thailand and the Philippines also enjoyed economic growth while improving their respective political systems. In 1961 such growth seemed a distant dream, for corruption and unrepresentative hierarchies in power characterized both governments. American diplomats feared a void in Thailand after Prime Minister Sarit, who was in declining health for some time, died; at the same time, diplomats were disappointed again and again as new Philippine leaders proved as ineffective as those they succeeded in reducing corruption, and securing allegiance of peoples at a distance from the capital.

Corruption was a major stumbling block to political reform and economic development in the Philippines. Perhaps Washington deserved some of the blame for the colonial legacy, but Philippine politics was corrupt, and that corruption distorted the economy, weakened the political system, and helped disaffect the general population. By the end of the 1960s, Manila had reduced the level of corruption, reached a *modus vivendi* with Malaysia, and became a contributing member to the various Asian security and economic groupings.

Thailand was surprisingly stable given its proximity to the expanding Vietnam conflict. Bangkok and Washington had concerns about North Vietnamese aggression across the Mekong River and Communist-inspired guerrillas operating out of the jungles of northern Malaysia. Thai leaders sought U.S. military assistance in quantities that American officials believed exceeded Thai needs and capacity to use effectively. Other signs of American support, including economic aid and access to American markets, satisfied Thai needs for reassurance.

But security issues, not economic development, dominated Thai-American diplomacy. In the early 1960s Thai leaders fixated on what they perceived as a Beijing-directed, Hanoi-supplied Communist insurgency in neighboring Laos. Thai leaders wanted a strong American commitment, not a momentary movement of U.S. armed forces to the region. For most of the Johnson years Bangkok approved the American effort in Vietnam and accepted Washington's claims of success. When the Communist Tet offensive seemingly shattered American claims of success, Thailand had strengthened its economy and no longer feared an imminent movement of Chinese-inspired revolutionaries further into Southeast Asia.

Malaya and Singapore joined together, then separated, yet began prospering and living well with their neighbors by the end of the Johnson administration. The Kennedy and Johnson administrations deferred to Great Britain since Malaya and Singapore as well as Borneo were long-time British colonies. But the looming presence of the People's Republic, the fighting in Laos and increasing in tempo in Vietnam, and concerns of America's long-time colony and now ally, the Philippines, created an American interest. Washington approved of plans for the Malaysian Federation, and had concerns for Singapore's separation. As Britain retreated east of Suez owing to budget challenges, the United States stepped into the breach.

Malaya drove discussions for a greater Malaysia. The Tunku wanted to unite with Singapore and as much of Borneo as possible [given concerns of the Sultan of Brunei], and create a stronger, more viable state, to interact with its near and regional neighbors. While most of the peoples in the proposed federation were ethnic Malays, there were significant differences in religion, economic status, and social organization to make the federation, at least initially, rather challenging.

At the same time, Malaysia appeared a target for expansionist neighbors. Sukarno in Indonesia coveted Malaysia which had perhaps 10% of the population and less natural wealth than his nation; it was unclear if he only wanted to add to Indonesia's territory on Borneo or take mainland Malaya as well. Successive administrations in the Philippines advanced a weak claim to Sarawak but told American diplomats they were concerned that a weak Malaysian federation could invite Communist subversion and penetration into the southern Philippines where Manila's hold over the population was weaker and where Moro Moslem values clashed with Spanish-brought Catholicism of the northern islands.

Indonesia initially was one of America's greatest challenges, but, after the failed coup of October 1965, became a strong American ally and recipient of U.S. economic assistance. Sukarno was a threat, having first threatened the Dutch in Irian Java and then taking it; he also threatened the new Malaysian Federation, and continued a long, draining guerrilla war on Malaysia's island provinces. He seemed to ally with the People's Republic and criticized Great Britain and the United States and, through them, their regional allies, as colonial powers holding back the will of the free peoples of the region. In addition to foreign adventurism that threatened the regional status quo, he also drove a resource-rich economy into bankruptcy causing suffering for Indonesian people throughout the 3,500 mile long chain of islands making up the nation.

In October 1965, the tables turned rather dramatically. Apparently some government officials with support of the Indonesia Communist Party sought power, the Army resisted, and that began a more than year long witch hunt for communists and, frankly, Indonesians of Chinese descent whose loyalty was suspect by the largely Malay officer corps. When the Army finally secured power, it turned against Beijing, supported Washington's Cold War position, and sought international economic assistance to develop Indonesia's natural resources and industrial development. By the end of the Johnson administration, Indonesia had turned the corner and had begun the takeoff phase for its international development.

In general, American foreign policy succeeded in its larger goal. Washington wanted to sufficiently strengthen western-oriented and neutral regimes in the region so they could resist the pressure of the People's Republic of China and its call for violent, nationalist revolutions to overthrow the existing order. By 1969, the region was experiencing an economic development boom, spurred in part, by American spending on the Vietnam conflict. Stronger economies helped strengthen the political allegiance of peoples to their respective governments, and it helped these nations resist any turn to the PRC.

This success helped create additional problems that became clear to the American public with Richard Nixon's announcement of dramatic economic measures on August 15, 1971. The Kennedy and Johnson administrations accepted a balance of payments challenge to support East and Southeast Asian economic growth and thereby to achieve Washington's political goals of continuing the isolation of the People's Republic of China. By 1971, America's balance of payments deficit had worsened, and an existing balance of trade surplus was turning negative. Secret diplomacy with Beijing and more public diplomacy with Moscow helped ease concerns about the Cold War in Asia; secret diplomacy with Hanoi appeared to offer the "time" the Nixon administration needed to separate America from the Vietnam conflict. The lessened threat of Cold War in Asia helped Nixon and his advisors face the very real weaknesses in America's international economic position and make his rather dramatic announcement of a "New Economic Program."

The confluence of foreign policy and foreign economic policy is a critical matter for diplomats then and scholars now. While mainland China was the threat looming quietly in the distance, America's concern for regional economic development affected the American home front as well as its foreign policy in the region. The tradeoffs between assuring the soundness of the American economy and strengthening economies in the region, of securing the free nations of Asia from Chinese influence and maintaining America's capacity to provide a security umbrella posed difficult challenges for American policymakers. Once they decided that the Cold War in East Asia mattered most, that decision determined their acceptance of some economic dislocations in exchange for stronger regional economies supporting American foreign policy goals in the region.

Perhaps the real price of America's foreign economic policy will soon take place. Christopher Martin writing in *The Whitehead Journal of Diplomacy and International Relations* noted that ASEAN countries called for an East Asian Free Trade Area with host Philippine President Gloria Arroyo declaring last August that "East Asian countries must 'draw up a collective response.'" East Asia, Martin stated, "is quietly coming together." He pointed out that "the U.S. was not invited to attend the East Asian Summit," and that "to date, the U.S. has pursued no comprehensive policy towards the possible emergence of EAFTA." During the Kennedy and Johnson years, the United States sacrificed to contain the People's Republic and to help economies of free nations in East Asia develop; the call for an EAFTA is a triumph for U.S. foreign policy at the same time it poses a dilemma for U.S. foreign economic policy, a situation that began during this period.[1]

Lyndon Johnson's National Security Advisor, Walt W. Rostow, best summarized the purpose of U.S. foreign policy towards the non-Communist nations in East Asia. In *Parameters, Winter 1996-1997,* Rostow responded to former Defense Secretary Robert McNamara's book, *In Retrospect: The Tragedy and Lessons of Vietnam.* After discussing McNamara's emerging belief that Vietnam was "a problem with no solution," and, based on an analysis by CIA Director Richard Helms, further believed that the risks of withdrawal "are probably more limited and controllable than most previous argument has indicated." Rostow concluded his summary of McNamara's argument by repeating the question "were such high costs justified?"[2]

Rostow, perhaps unsurprisingly, responded in the affirmative. "Dean Rusk, Walter Rostow, Lee Kwan Yew, and many other geopoliticians

---

[1] Christopher Martin, "Crafting a US Response to the Emerging East Asia Free Trade Area," *The Whitehead Journal of Diplomacy and International Relations, Winter/Spring 2007,* pp. 73-84.

[2] W.W. Rostow, "The Case for the Vietnam War," *Parameters, Winter 1996-1997,* pp. 39-50.

across the globe to this day answer yes." He then moved to re-instating the domino theory: "they conclude that without US intervention in Vietnam, communist hegemony – both Soviet and Chinese – would have spread farther through South and East Asia to include control of Indonesia, Thailand, and possibly India." Rostow focused on 1965 as the key year, and the "local people [in Asia] knew that a dangerous crisis was taking place in 1965 which could go one way or the other." Rostow recalled that, when Johnson "went through Asia for three weeks at the end of 1966, he spoke at least 90 percent of the time about the need for Asia to unite and organize, not about the struggle in Vietnam."

Rostow noted the lack of concern in 1975 as North Vietnamese tanks rolled up to the Presidential Palace in Saigon. The Malaysian foreign minister noted that, as Saigon fell, "ASEAN by then had seven solid years of living in neighborly cooperation." "There were no falling dominoes in Southeast Asia following the fall of Saigon to the communists, and the United States withdrawal from Southeast Asia." "Both the NICs and the ASEAN members roughly quadrupled their real GNP between 1960 and 1981. They were, socially and politically as well as economically, quite different countries than they had been when Southeast Asia went through the crises of 1965." While Rostow's main argument, not repeated, concerned the correctness of Johnson's Vietnam policy, he made the case for U.S. policy towards the free nations of Asia.

Assuming Rostow's recollection accurately summarized American policy from 1961 to 1969, the question remains whether the benefits outweighed the costs. As long as key leaders and their aides in free nations in Asia and the developed world viewed China as a threat and as long as they could not alter that view, the policy of sacrificing the American economy to underwrite Asian economic development was simply an extension of America's Cold War burden. And given the great power triangle between the United States, the Soviet Union, and the People's Republic of China, there were few opportunities to test assumptions of Chinese aggressiveness and to alter policy.

BIBLIOGRAPHY

Government Documents/Publications

John F. Kennedy Library
National Security Files.
President's Office Files.
Papers of James C. Thomson, Jr.
Lyndon Baines Johnson Library
Administrative History of the Department of State.
Confidential File
National Security Files.
Papers of William P. Bundy
Papers of Henry H. Fowler.
Papers of Edward K. Hamilton.
Papers of Walt W. Rostow.
Papers of Bromley K. Smith.

National Archives and Records Administration

Records of the Department of State
RG 59, Central Foreign Policy Files.
RG 59, Policy Planning Staff, Subject and Country Files.
Central Intelligence Agency, National Intelligence Estimates and Special National Intelligence Estimates, 1961-1969, see http://www.foia.cia.gov/search.asp?pageNumber=1&freqReqRecord=nic_geo_ea.txt.
Department of State. *Bulletin*. Washington, DC: GPO, 1961-1969.
Department of State. *Foreign Relations of the United States, 1961-1963, Volume IX, Foreign Economic Policy*. Washington, DC: GPO, 1995.
—. *Foreign Relations of the United States, 1961-1963, Volume XXII, China, Korea, Japan*. Washington, DC: GPO, 1996.
—. *Foreign Relations of the United States, 1961-1963, Volume XXIII, Southeast Asia*. Washington, DC: GPO, 1997.
—. *Foreign Relations of the United States, 1964-1968, Volume VIII, International Monetary and Trade Policy*. Washington, DC: GPO, 1998.

—. *Foreign Relations of the United States, 1964-1968, Volume XIV, The Soviet Union.* Washington, DC: GPO, 2001.

—. *Foreign Relations of the United States, 1964-1968, Volume XXVI, Indonesia; Malaysia-Singapore; Philippines.* Washington, DC: GPO, 2001.

—. *Foreign Relations of the United States, 1964-1968, Volume XXVII, Mainland Southeast Asia; Regional Affairs.* Washington, DC: GPO, 2000.

—. *Foreign Relations of the United States, 1964-1968, Volume XXIX, Part I, Korea.* Washington, DC: GPO, 1999.

—. *Foreign Relations of the United States, 1964-1968, Volume XXIX, Part II, Japan.* Washington, DC: GPO, 2006.

—. *Foreign Relations of the United States, 1964-1968, Volume XXX, China.* Washington, DC: GPO, 1998.

Books

Addington, Larry H. *America's War in Vietnam: A Short Narrative History.* Bloomington: Indiana University Press, 2000.

Allen, G.C. *Japan's Place in Trade Strategy: Larger Role in Pacific Region.* London: The Atlantic Trade Study, 1968.

Anderson, David L. *The Vietnam War.* New York: Palgrave Macmillan, 2005.

Anderson, Terry H. *The Sixties.* New York: Pearson/Longman, 2004.

Barfield, Claude. *Korea in Asia: Korea's Development, Asian Regionalism, and U.S.-Korea Economic Relations.* Washington, DC: Korea Economic Institute, 2003.

Barnouin, Barbara. *Chinese Foreign Policy During the Cultural Revolution.* New York: Kegan Paul International, 1998.

Bhattacharjee, G.P. *Southeast Asian Politics: Malaysia & Indonesia.* Calcutta, India: Minerva Associates, 1976.

Brands, H.W., Editor. *The Foreign Policies of Lyndon Johnson: Beyond Vietnam.* College Station: Texas A&M University Press, 1999.

Brant, Ed. *The Last Voyage of the USS Pueblo.* New York: W.W. Norton & Co., 1969.

Bucher, Lloyd M. and Mark Rascovich. *Bucher: My Story.* Garden City, NY: Doubleday & Co., 1970.

Buckley, Roger. *US-Japan alliance diplomacy, 1945-1990.* New York: Cambridge University Press, 1992.

Buhite, Russell, Editor. *A Documentary History of United States Foreign Policy, 1945-1973, Volume IV, The Far East.* New York: McGraw-Hill Book Company, 1973.

Bunge, Frederica M., Editor. *Thailand: A Country Study.* Washington, DC: GPO, 1981.

Bush, Richard C. *At Cross Purposes: U.S.-Taiwan Relations since 1942.* Armonk, NY: M.E. Sharpe, 2004.

Chaffee, Frederic H., et. al. *Area Handbook for Japan.* Washington, DC: GPO, 1969.

—. *Area Handbook for the Philippines.* Washington, DC: GPO, 1969.

Chen Jian. *Mao's China and the Cold War.* Chapel Hill: University of North Carolina Press, 2001.

Cohen, Stephen D. *Fundamentals of U.S. foreign trade policy: economics, politics, laws, and issues.* Boulder, CO: Westview Press, 1996.

Cohen, Warren I. and Nancy Bernkopf Tucker. *Lyndon Johnson Confronts the World: American Foreign Policy, 1963-1968.* New York: Cambridge University Press, 1994.

Cusumano, Michael A. *The Japanese Automobile Industry: Technology and Management at Nissan and Toyota.* Cambridge, MA: Harvard University Press, 1985.

Dahm, Bernhard [Translated by P.S. Falla]. *History of Indonesia in the Twentieth Century.* New York: Praeger Publishers, 1971.

Dallek, Robert. *Flawed Giant: Lyndon Johnson and His Times, 1961-1973.* New York: Oxford University Press, 1998.

Davids, Jules, Editor. *Documents on American Foreign Relations, 1964.* New York: Harper & Brothers, 1965.

Davids, Jules. *The United States in World Affairs, 1964.* New York: Harper & Row, Publishers, 1965.

Dietrich, William S. *In the shadow of the rising sun: the political roots of American economic decline.* State College, PA: The Pennsylvania State University, 1991.

Edmonds, Anthony O. *The War in Vietnam.* Westport, CT: Greenwood Press, 1998.

Edström, Bart. *Japan's evolving foreign policy doctrine: from Yoshida to Miyazawa.* New York: St. Martin's Press, Inc., 1999.

Emmerson, John K. *The Eagle and the Rising Sun.* Reading, MA: Addison-Wesley, 1988.

Foot, Rosemary. *The Practice of Power: U.S. Relations with China since 1949.* New York: Oxford University Press, 1995.

Gaddis, John Lewis. *Strategies of Containment: A Critical Appraisal of American National Security Policy During the Cold War.* New York: Oxford University Press, 2005.

—. *The Long Peace: Inquiries into the History of the Cold War.* New York: Oxford University Press, 1987.

—. *We Now Know: Rethinking Cold War History.* New York: Oxford University Press, 1997.

Gallery, Daniel V. *The Pueblo Incident.* Garden City, NY: Doubleday & Co., 1970.

Garson, Robert. *The United States and China Since 1949: A Troubled Affair.* Madison, NJ: Fairleigh Dickinson University Press, 1994.

Garver, John. *The Sino-American Alliance: Nationalist China and American Cold War Strategy in Asia.* Armonk, NY: M.E. Sharpe, 1997.

Gavin, Francis J. *Gold, dollars, and power: the politics of international monetary relations, 1958-1971.* Chapel Hill: The University of North Carolina Press, 2004.

Goh, Evelyn. *Constructing the U.S. Rapprochement with China, 1961-1974.* New York: Cambridge University Press, 2005.

Hellmann, Donald C. *Japan and East Asia: The New International Order.* New York: Praeger Publishers, 1972.

Henderson, John W. *Area Handbook for Malaysia.* Washington, DC: GPO, 1970.

Henderson, John W., et. al. *Area Handbook for Indonesia.* Washington, DC: GPO, 1970.

Herring, George C. *America's Longest War, Fourth Edition.* New York: McGraw-Hill, Inc. 2002.

Hersh, Jacques. *The USA and the rise of East Asia since 1945: dilemmas of the postwar international political economy.* New York: St. Martin's Press, 1993.

Hillman, Jimmye S. and Robert A. Rothenberg. *Agricultural Trade and Protection in Japan.* London: Gower, 1988.

Hixson, Walter L., Editor. *Military Aspect of the Vietnam Conflict.* New York: Garland Publishing, 2000.

Holt, Richard D. *The Reluctant Superpower: A History of America's Global Economic Reach.* New York: Kodansha America, Inc., 1995.

Hook, Glenn D., et. al. *Japan's international relations: politics, economics and security.* New York: Routledge, 2001.

Hsing, Mo-huan. *Taiwan: Industrialization and Trade Policies.* London: Oxford University Press, 1971.

Huff, G.W. *The Economic Growth of Singapore: trade and development in the twentieth century*. New York: Cambridge University Press, 1994.
Jain, Rajendra Kumar. *China and Japan, 1949-1980, 2nd Edition*. Atlantic Highlands, N.J.: Humanities Press, 1981.
Johnson, Lyndon Baines. *The Vantage Point: Perspectives of the Presidency, 1963-1969*. New York: Holt, Rinehart and Winston, 1971.
Kajima, Morinosuke. *Modern Japan's Foreign Policy, 2nd Edition*. Rutland, VT: Charles E. Tuttle Company, Publishers, 1970.
Kaplan, Edward S. *American trade policy, 1923-1995*. Westport, CT: Greenwood Press, 1996.
Karnow, Stanley. *Vietnam: A History*. New York: Viking Press, 1983.
Kawashima, Yutaka. *Japanese foreign policy at the crossroads*. Washington, DC: The Brookings Institution, 2003.
Kim, Dong-Hi and Yong-Jae Joo. *The Food Situation and Policies in the Republic of Korea*. Paris: Organization for Economic Cooperation and Development, 1982.
Kiyosaki, Wayne S. *North Korea's Foreign Relations*. New York: Praeger Publishers, 1976.
Kunz, Diane B., Editor. *The Diplomacy of the Crucial Decade: American Foreign Relations During the 1960s*. New York: Columbia University Press, 1994.
LaFeber, Walter. *The clash: a history of U.S.-Japan relations*. New York: W.W. Norton & Company, Inc., 1997.
Langdon, F.C. *Japan's foreign policy*. Vancouver: University of British Columbia Press, 1973.
Lee, Kenneth B. *Korea and East Asia: the story of a Phoenix*. Westport, Ct: Praeger Publishers, 1997.
Leifer, Michael. *Indonesia's foreign policy*. Winchester, MA: Allen & Unwin Inc., 1983.
—. *Singapore's foreign policy: coping with vulnerability*. New York: Routledge, 2000.
LePoer, Barbara Leitch, Editor. *Singapore: a country study*. Washington, DC: Federal Research Division, Library of Congress, 1991.
Lerner, Mitchell B. *The Pueblo Incident: A Spy Ship and the Failure of American Foreign Policy*. Lawrence: University of Kansas Press, 2002.
Ma Jisen. *The Cultural Revolution in the Foreign Ministry of China*. Hong Kong: The Chinese University Press, 2004.
MacFarquhar, Roderick. *Sino-American Relations, 1949-1971*. New York: Praeger Publishers, 1972.

Maga, Timothy P. *John F. Kennedy and the New Pacific Community, 1961-1963.* New York: MacMillan Press, Ltd., 1990.

Matray, James Irving. *Japan's Emergence as a global power.* Westport, CT: Greenwood Press, 2001.

Murphy, Edward F. *Semper Fi Vietnam: from Da Nang to the DMZ.* Novato, CA: Presidio Press, 1997.

Muscat, Robert J. *Thailand and the United States: development, security, and foreign aid.* New York: Columbia University Press, 1990.

National Unification Board. *A Comparative Study of South and North Korea.* Seoul, Republic of Korea: 1982.

Nester, William R. *Power across the Pacific: a diplomatic history of American relations with Japan.* New York: New York University Press, 1996.

Nuechterlein, Donald E. *Thailand and the Struggle for Southeast Asia.* Ithaca, NY: Cornell University Press, 1965.

Olson, Lawrence. *Japan in Postwar Asia.* New York: Praeger Publishers, 1970.

Palmer, Bruce. *The 25-Year War: America's Military Role in Vietnam.* Lexington: University of Kentucky Press, 1984.

Palmer, Ingrid. *The Indonesian Economy since 1965.* Totowa, NJ: Frank Cass and Company, Ltd., 1978.

Park, Eul Yong. *The Economics and Politics of the United States-Japan Trade: 1953-1971.* Seoul, Korea: Seoul National University, 1971.

Park, Hongsuk H. *American politics and foreign economic challenges.* New York: Garland Publishing, Inc., 1990.

Parsons, Robert A. *Congress and the politics of U.S. foreign economic policy, 1929-1976.* Berkeley, University of California Press, 1980.

Paterson, Thomas G., Editor, *Kennedy's Quest for Victory: American Foreign Policy, 1961-1963.* New York: Oxford University Press, 1989.

Randolph, R. Sean. *The United States and Thailand. Alliance Dynamics, 1950 1985.* Berkeley: University of California Press, 1986.

Rostow, Walt W. *The Process of Economic Growth.* New York: W.W. Norton & Co., 1952.

Rusk, Dean with Richard Rusk and Daniel S. Papp. *As I Saw It.* New York: W.W. Norton & Co., 1990.

Sanderson, Fred H. *Japan's food prospects and policies.* Washington, DC: The Brookings Institution, 1978.

Schoenbaum, Thomas J. *Waging War and Peace; Dean Rusk in the Truman, Kennedy, and Johnson Years.* New York: Simon and Schuster, 1988.

Schulzinger, Robert D. *American Diplomacy in the Twentieth Century, Third Edition,* New York, Oxford University Press, 1994.

Smith, Dennis B. *Japan since 1945: the rise of an economic superpower.* New York: St. Martin's Press, 1995.

Smith, Harvey H., et al. *Area Handbook for Thailand.* Washington, DC: GPO, 1968.

Solomon, Robert. *The international monetary system, 1945-1981.* New York: Harper & Row, Publishers, Inc., 1982.

Stebbins, Richard P. *The United States in World Affairs, 1961.* New York: Harper & Brothers, 1962.

—. *The United States in World Affairs, 1962.* New York: Harper & Brothers, 1963.

—. *The United States in World Affairs, 1963.* New York: Harper & Brothers, 1964.

—. *The United States in World Affairs, 1965.* New York: Harper & Brothers, 1966.

—. *The United States in World Affairs, 1966.* New York: Harper & Brothers, 1967.

—. *The United States in World Affairs, 1967.* New York: Simon and Schuster, 1968.

Stebbins, Richard P., Editor. *Documents on American Foreign Relations, 1961.* New York: Harper & Brothers, 1962.

—. *Documents on American Foreign Relations, 1962.* New York: Harper & Brothers, 1963.

—. *Documents on American Foreign Relations, 1963.* New York: Harper & Brothers, 1964.

—. *Documents on American Foreign Relations, 1965.* New York: Harper & Brothers, 1966.

—. *Documents on American Foreign Relations, 1966.* New York: Harper & Brothers, 1967.

—. *Documents on American Foreign Relations, 1967.* New York: Harper & Brothers, 1968.

—. *Documents on American Foreign Relations, 1968-69.* New York: Harper & Brothers, 1969.

Summers, Harry G. *On Strategy.* Novato, CA: Presidio Press, 1982.

Togo, Kazuhiko. *Japan's Foreign Policy, 1945-2003: The Quest for a Proactive Policy.* Boston, MA: Brill, 2005.

Turley, William S. *The Second Indochina War.* Boulder, CO: Westview Press, 1986.

Uchino, Tatsurō. *Japan's postwar economy.* New York: Harper & Row, Publishers, Inc., 1983.

Vreeland, Nena, et. al. *Area Handbook for Singapore.* Washington, DC: GPO, 1977.

—. *South Korea: a country study.* Washington, DC: GPO, 1982.

Walton, Richard J. *War and Counter Revolution: The Foreign Policy of John F. Kennedy.* New York: Viking Press, 1972.

Wilcox, Wayne Ayres. *Asia and United States Policy.* Englewood Cliffs, NJ: Prentice-Hall, Inc., 1967.

Yamazawa, Ippei. *Economic development and international trade: the Japanese model.* Honolulu, HI: East-West Center, 1990.

Zeiler, Thomas W. *American Trade and Power in the 1960s.* New York: Columbia University Press, 1992.

—. *Dean Rusk: Defending the American Mission Abroad.* Wilmington, DE: SR Books, 2000.

Zhang Shu Guang. *Economic Cold War: America's embargo against China and the Sino-Soviet alliance, 1949-1963.* Washington, DC: Woodrow Wilson Center Press, 2001.

Articles in Edited Books

Baldwin, Robert E. "The Changing Nature of U.S. Trade Policy since World War II," in Robert E. Baldwin and Anne O. Krueger, Editors, *The structure and evolution of recent U.S. trade policy.* Chicago: University of Chicago Press, 1984, pp. 5-25.

Barnhart, Michael A. "From Hershey Bars to Motor Cars: America's Economic Policy Toward Japan, 1945-1976," in Akira Iriye and Robert A. Wampler, *Partnership: The United States and Japan, 1951-2001,* New York: Kodansha International, 2001, pp. 201-222.

Fosberg, Aaron. "America and the Japanese Miracle: The Economic Nexus, 1945-2000," in Richard Jensen, et. al., Editors, *Trans-Pacific relations: America, Europe, and Asia in the twentieth century.* Westport, CT: Praeger Publishers, 2003, pp. 249-2xx.

Gallicchio, Marc. "Occupation, Dominion, and Alliance: Japan in American Security Policy, 1945-1969," in Akira Iriye and Robert A. Wampler, *Partnership: The United States and Japan, 1951-2001,* New York: Kodansha International, 2001, pp. 115-134.

Hahn, Bae Jo. "Policy Toward Japan" in Youngnok Koo and Sŭng-ju Han, Editors, *The foreign policy of the Republic of Korea.* New York: Columbia University Press, 1985, pp. 167-197.

Han, Sung-Joo. "Policy Toward the United States," in Youngnok Koo and Sŭng-ju Han, Editors, *The foreign policy of the Republic of Korea.* New York: Columbia University Press, 1985, pp. 139-166.

Haslam, Jonathan. "The Pattern of Soviet-Japanese Relations since World War II" in Tsuyoshi Hasegawa, Jonathan Haslam, and Andrew Kuchins, editors, *Russia and Japan: an unresolved dilemma between distant neighbors.* Berkeley: University of California Press, 1993, pp. 3-48.

Johnson, Chalmers. "MITI and Japanese International Economic Policy" in Robert A. Scalapino, Editor, *The Foreign Policy of Modern Japan,* Berkeley: University of California Press, 1977, pp. 227-247.

Kanemitsu, Hideo. "U.S.-Japanese Trade Relations, 1955-1982," in Akira Iriye and Warren I. Cohen, Editors, *The United States and Japan in the postwar world.* Lexington: The University of Kentucky Press, 1989, pp. 145-170.

Kato, Hiroshi. "Japan's Foreign Trade Policy" in Leon Hollerman, Editor, *Japan and the United States: economic and political adversaries.* Boulder, CO: Westview Press, Inc., 1980, pp. 79-96.

Kim, Ipyong J. "Policies Toward China and the Soviet Union," in Youngnok Koo and Sŭng-ju Han, Editors, *The foreign policy of the Republic of Korea.* New York: Columbia University Press, 1985, pp. 198-218.

Kislenko, Arne. "The Vietnam War, Thailand, and the United States" in Richard Jensen, et. al., Editors, *Trans-Pacific relations: America, Europe, and Asia in the twentieth century.* Westport, CT: Praeger Publishers, 2003, pp. 217-245.

Klein, Lawrence R. "US-Korea trade and economic relations" in Kim Youn-Suk and Oh Kap-Soo, Editors, *US-Korea Economic Partnership: Policy Directions for Trade and Economic Co-operation.* Brookfield, VT: Ashgate Publishing Company, 1995, pp. 9-14.

Kosaka, Masataka. "The International Economic Policy of Japan" in Robert A. Scalapino, Editor, *The Foreign Policy of Modern Japan,* Berkeley: University of California Press, 1977, pp. 207-226.

Krasner, Stephen and Daniel Okimoto. "Japan's Evolving Trade Posture," in Akira Iriye and Warren I. Cohen, Editors, *The United States and Japan in the postwar world.* Lexington: The University of Kentucky Press, 1989, pp. 117-144.

McMahon, Robert J. "Ambivalent Partners: The Lyndon Johnson Administration and its Asian Allies," in H. W. Brands, Editor, *The foreign policies of Lyndon Johnson: beyond Vietnam.* College Station: Texas A&M University Press, 1999, pp. 168-186.

Moskowitz, Karl. "Issues in the Emerging Partnership" in Karl Moskowitz, Editor, *From Patron to Partner.* Lexington, MA: LexingtonBooks, 1984, pp. 1-18.

Park, Eul Yong. "Foreign Economic Policies and Economic Development," in Youngnok Koo and Sŭng-ju Han, Editors, *The foreign policy of the Republic of Korea.* New York: Columbia University Press, 1985, pp. 106-138.

Rha, Woong Bae. "The future of US-Korea cooperation in the Asia-Pacific area" in Kim Youn-Suk and Oh Kap-Soo, Editors, *US-Korea Economic Partnership: Policy Directions for Trade and Economic Co-operation.* Brookfield, VT: Ashgate Publishing Company, 1995, pp. 15-24.

Rostow, Walt W. "Basic National Security Policy," in Gordon Chang, *Friends and Enemies.* Stanford, CA: Stanford University Press, 1990.

Sasagawa, Takeo. "Japanese-U.S. Relations in Science and Technology," in Leon Hollerman, Editor, *Japan and the United States: economic and political adversaries.* Boulder, CO: Westview Press, Inc., 1980, pp. 39-56.

Saxonhouse, Gary R. "The World Economy and Japanese Foreign Economic Policy," in Robert A. Scalapino, Editor, *The Foreign Policy of Modern Japan,* Berkeley: University of California Press, 1977, pp. 281-295.

Schaller, Michael. "Altered States: The United States and Japan During the 1960s," in Diane B. Kunz, Editor, *The diplomacy of the crucial decade: American foreign relations during the 1960s.* New York: Columbia University Press, 1994, pp. 251-282.

Tucker, Nancy Bernkopf. "Threats, Opportunities, and Frustrations in East Asia" in Warren I. Cohen and Nancy Bernkopf Tucker, Editors, *Lyndon Johnson confronts the world: American foreign policy, 1963-1968.* New York: Cambridge University Press, 1994.

Wang, Peter Chen-main. "A Bastion Created, A Regime Reformed, An Economy Reengineered, 1949-1970," in Robinson, Murray A., Editor, *Taiwan: A new history.* Armonk, New York: M.E. Sharpe, Inc., 1999, pp. 320-338.

Articles in Scholarly Journals

Albinski, Henry S. "Australia Faces China." *Asian Survey, Vol. 2, No. 2, April 1962,* pp. 16-28.

Aliber, R.Z. "Planning, Growth, and Competition in the Japanese Economy." *Asian Survey, Vol. 3, No. 12, Dec. 1963,* pp. 596-608.

Amsden, Alice H. "Taiwan's Economic History: A Case of Etatisme and a Challenge to Dependency Theory. *Modern China, Vol. 5, No. 3, July 1979,* pp. 341-379.

Amuzegar, Jahangir. "Nationalist vs. Economic Growth." *Foreign Affairs, Vol. 44, No. 4, July 1966,* pp. 651-661.

Anderson, Robert B. "The Balance of Payments Problem." *Foreign Affairs, Vol. 38, No. 3, April 1960,* pp. 419-432.

Anonymous. "Peking on Coexistence." *Foreign Affairs, Vol. 38, No. 4, July 1960,* pp. 676-681.

Aquino, Benigno S., Jr. "What's Wrong with the Philippines?" *Foreign Affairs, Vol. 46, No. 4, July 1968,* pp. 770-779.

Armstrong, Hamilton Fish. "The Troubled Birth of Malaysia." *Foreign Affairs, Vol. 41, No. 4, June 1963,* pp. 673-693.

—. "Thoughts Along the Chinese Border: Will Neutrality be Enough?" *Foreign Affairs, Vol. 38, No. 2, Jan. 1960,* pp. 238-260.

Ashton, Nigel. "Uncertain Decade: US-Soviet relations, 1961-1968." *Diplomacy & Statecraft, Vol. 14, No. 1, March 2003,* pp. 195-202.

Ayal, Eliezer B. "Some Crucial Issues in Thailand's Economic Development." *Pacific Affairs, Vol. 34, No. 2, Summer 1961,* pp. 157-164.

Bowles, Chester. "The 'China Problem' Reconsidered." *Foreign Affairs, Vol. 38, No. 3, April 1960,* pp. 476-488.

Brackman, Arnold C. "Indonesia: 'Another Communist Disaster.'" *Current History, Vol. 56, No. 331, March 1969,* pp. 156-160+.

Brigham, Robert K. "Resolve and Credibility in Southeast Asia." *Diplomatic History, Vol. 25, No. 4, Fall 2001,* pp. 713-718.

Brown, Lester R. "The Agricultural Revolution in Asia." *Foreign Affairs, Vol. 46, No. 4, July 1968,* pp. 688-698.

Brzezinski, Zbigniew. "Threat and Opportunity in the Communist Schism." *Foreign Affairs, Vol. 41, No. 3, April 1963,* pp. 513-525.

Buszynski, Leszek. "The United States and Southeast Asia: A Case of Strategic Surrender." *Journal of Southeast Asian Studies, Volume XIV, Number 1, March 1983,* pp. 225-233.

Butwell, Richard. "Southeast Asia: How Important—To Whom?" *Current History, Vo. 52, No. 305, January 1967,* pp. 3-7.

—. "The Philippines: Changing of the Guard." *Asian Survey, Vol. 6, No. 1, Jan. 1966,* pp. 43-48.

—. "The United States and the Philippines: Misunderstandings of The Relationship." *United Asia, Vol. 17, No. 4, July-August 1965,* pp. 301-304.

Chakravarti, P.C. "Indian Non-Alignment and United States Policy." *Current History, Vol. 44, No. 259, March 1963,* pp. 129-137.

Chang, David W. "U.S. Aid and Economic Progress in Taiwan." *Asian Survey, Vol. 5, No. 3, March 1965,* pp. 152-160.

Chao, Kang. "Economic Aftermath of the Great Leap in Communist China." *Asian Survey, Vol. 4, No. 5, May 1964,* pp. 851-858.

Cohen, Stephen P. "India's China War and After: A Review Article." *The Journal of Asian Studies, Vol. 30, No. 4, Aug. 1971,* pp. 847-857.

Crawcour, Sydney. "Progress and Structural Change in the Japanese Economy." *Asian Survey, Vol. 1, No. 6, Aug. 1961,* pp. 3-9.

Cullather, Nick. "'Fuel for the Good Dragon': The United States and Industrial Policy in Taiwan, 1950-1965." *Diplomatic History, Vol. 20, No. 1, Winter 1996,* pp. 1-25.

Cumings, Bruce. "The Political Economy of Chinese Foreign Policy." *Modern China, Vol. 5, No. 4, Oct. 1979,* pp. 411-461.

Cutshall, Alden. "The Political Geography of Indonesia and Malaya." *United Asia, Vol. 15, No. 3, March 1963,* pp. 245-250.

Dai, Shen-Yu. "Peking and the 'Third World.'" *Current History, Vol. 49, No. 289, September 1965,* pp. 142-149.

Daquila, Teofilo C. "Japan-Asia Economic Relations: Trade, Investment, and the Economic Crisis." *East Asia, Autumn 1999,* pp. 88-115.

Darling, Frank C. "Marshal Sarit and Absolutist Rule in Thailand." *Pacific Affairs, Vol. 33, No. 4, December 1960,* pp. 347-360.

—. "Thailand: Stability and Escalation." *Asian Survey, Vol. 8, No. 2, February 1968,* pp. 120-126.

—. "The Geopolitics of American Foreign Policy in Asia." *United Asia, Vol. 15, No. 4, May 1963,* pp. 370-376.

Dartford, Gerald P. "The Communist Threat to Malaya and Singapore." *Current History, Vol. 40, No. 222, February 1960,* pp. 82-87.

Diebold, William, Jr. "New Horizons in Foreign Trade." *Foreign Affairs, Vol. 45, No. 2,* pp. 291-303.

—. "Trade Policies Since World War II." *Current History, Vol. 42, No. 250, June 1962,* pp. 356-361.

Dobbs, Charles M. "The Pact That Never Was: The Pacific Pact of 1949." *The Journal of Northeast Asian Studies,* Winter 1985.

Dorfman, Robert. "An Economic Strategy for West Pakistan." *Asian Survey, Vol. 3, No. 5, May 1963,* pp. 217-223.

Douglas, William A. "South Korea's Search for Leadership." *Pacific Affairs, Vol. 37, No. 1, Spring 1964,* pp. 20-36.

Dudley, Leonard and Peter Passell. "The War in Vietnam and the United States Balance of Payments." *The Review of Economics and Statistics, Vol. 50, No. 4, November 1968,* pp. 437-442.

Easter, David. "'Keep the Indonesian Pot Boiling': Western Covert Intervention in Indonesia, October 1965-March 1966." *Cold War History, Vol. 3, No. 1, February 2005,* pp. 55-73.

Eckstein, Alexander. "On the Economic Crisis in Communist China." *Foreign Affairs, Vol. 42, No. 4, July 1964,* pp. 655-668.

Emery, Robert F. "Recent Economic Developments in Communist China." *Asian Survey, Vol. 6, No. 6, June 1966,* pp. 303-309.

—. "The Japanese Measures to Restore Economic Equilibrium." *Asian Survey, Vol. 2, No. 4, June 1962,* pp. 33-39.

Emery, Robert F. and Henry F. Lee. "Economic Trends in Asia in 1966." *Asian Survey, Vol. 7, No. 11, Nov. 1967,* pp. 807-823.

Emmerson, John K. "Japan: Eye on 1970." *Foreign Affairs, Vol. 47, No. 2, Jan. 1969,* pp. 348-362.

Engelbrecht, Hans-Jürgen and Brent Kelsen. "Economic Growth and Convergence Amongst the APEC Economies, 1965-1990." *Asian Economic Journal, Vol. 13, No. 1,* pp. 1-3.

Fall, Bernard, B. "Red China's Aims in South Asia." *Current History, Vol. 43, No. 253, September 1962,* pp. 136-141, 181.

Fallows, James, "Containing Japan." *The Atlantic Monthly, May 1989,* pp. 40-50.

Fitzgerald, C.P. "China in Asia." *Current History, Vol. 53, No. 313, September 1967,* pp. 129-134+.

Forsberg, Aaron. "Eisenhower and Japanese Economic Recovery: The Politics of Integration with the Western Trading Bloc, 1952-1955." *The Journal of American-East Asian Relations, Spring 1996, Vol. 5, No. 1,* pp. 57-76.

Gardner, Richard N. "Strategy for the Dollar." *Foreign Affairs, Vol. 38, No. 3, April 1960,* pp. 433-445.

Garthoff, Raymond L. "Unconventional Warfare in Communist Strategy." *Foreign Affairs, Vol. 40, No. 4, July 1962,* pp. 566-575.

Garver, John W. "Food for Thought: Reflections on Food Aid and the Idea of Another Lost Change in Sino-American Relations." *The Journal of American-East Asian Relations, Vol. 7, Nos. 1-2, Spring-Summer 1998,* pp. 101-106.

Gavin, Francis J. "The Gold Battles within the Cold War: American Monetary Policy and the Defense of Europe, 1960-1963." *Diplomatic History, Vol. 26, No. 1, Winter 2002,* pp. 61-94.

—. "The Gold Battles within the Cold War: American Monetary Policy and the Defense of Europe, 1960-1963." *Diplomatic History, Vol. 26, No. 1, Winter 2002,* pp. 61-94.

Girling, J.L.S. "Thailand's New Course." *Pacific Affairs, Vol. 42, No. 3, Autumn 1969,* pp. 346-359.

Goldman, Marshall I. "A Balance Sheet of Soviet Foreign Aid." *Foreign Affairs, Vol. 43, No. 2, January 1965,* pp. 349-360.

—. "Communist Foreign Aid: Success and Shortcomings." *Current History, Vol. 51, No. 300, August 1966,* pp. 78-87+.

Gordon, Bernard K. "Economic Impediments to Regionalism in Southeast Asia." *Asian Survey, Vol. 3, No. 5, May 1963,* pp. 235-244.

Graebner, Norman A. "China: Unanswered Challenge." *Current History, Vol. 42, No. 245, January 1962,* pp. 36-42.

Gurtov, Melvin. "Communist China's Foreign Aid Program." *Current History, Vol. 49, No. 289, September 1965,* pp. 150-154+.

—. "Taiwan in 1966: Political Rigidity, Economic Growth." *Asian Survey, Vol. 7, No. 1, Jan. 1967,* pp. 40-45.

Hahm, Pyong Choon. "Korea's 'Mendicant Mentality'? A Critique of U.S. Policy." *Foreign Affairs, Vol. 43, No. 1, Oct. 1964,* pp. 165-174.

Harries, Owen. "Should the U.S. Withdraw from Asia?" *Foreign Affairs, Vol. 47, No. 1, Oct. 1968,* pp. 15-25.

Hasluck, Paul. "Australia and Southeast Asia." *Foreign Affairs, Vol. 43, No. 1, October 1964,* pp. 51-63.

Hellmann, Donald C. "Basic Problems of Japanese-South Korean Relations." *Asian Survey, Vol. 2, No. 3, May 1962,* pp. 19-24.

—. "Japan's Relations with Communist China." *Asian Survey, Vol. 4, No. 10, Oct. 1964,* pp. 1085-1092.

Hornbeck, Stanley K. "The 'Asia Policy' – yes and no – of the United States." *World Affairs, Vol. 129, No. 1, Apr/May/June 1966,* pp. 7-12.

—. "United States Policy Regarding China: What Did Mr. Hilsman Disclose at San Francisco?" *World Affairs, Vol. 126, No. 4, Winter 1963-64,* pp. 238-243.

Humphrey, Don D. "Indonesia's National Plan for Economic Development." *Asian Survey, Vol. 2, No. 10, Dec. 1962,* pp. 12-21.

Ike, Nobutaka. "Japan, Twenty Years after Surrender." *Asian Survey, Vol. 6, No. 1, Jan. 1966,* pp. 18-27.

Itagaki, O. "India-Japan Relations." *United Asia, Vol. 18, No. 2, March-April 1966,* pp. 86-89.

Jackson, Barbara Ward. "Foreign Aid: Strategy or Stopgap?" *Foreign Affairs, Vol. 41, No. 1, October 1962,* pp. 90-104.

—. "India on the Eve of its Third Plan." *Foreign Affairs, Vol. 39, No. 2, Jan. 1961*, pp. 259-270.

Jan, George P. "Japan's Trade with Communist China." *Asian Survey, Vol. 9, No. 12, December 1969,* pp. 90—918.

Jansen, Marius B. "Japan Looks Back." *Foreign Affairs, Vol. 47, No. 1, Oct. 1968,* pp. 36-50.

Johnstone, William C. "Political Commitment in Southeast Asia." *Current History, Vol. 54, No. 317, January 1968,* pp. 1-6.

—. "The United States in Southern Asia." *Current History, Vo. 48, No. 282, February 1965,* pp. 65-68+.

—. "U.S. Policy in Southeast Asia: What's Ahead?" *Current History, Vol. 50, No. 294, February 1966,* pp. 106-111+.

—. "United States Policy in Southern Asia." *Current History, Vol. 46, No. 270, February 1964,* pp. 65-70+.

Jones, Matthew. "U.S. Relations with Indonesia, the Kennedy-Johnson Transition, and the Vietnam Connection, 1963-1965." *Diplomatic History, Vol. 26, No. 2, Spring 2002,* pp. 249-281.

Kahin, George McT. "Malaysia and Indonesia." *Pacific Affairs, Vol. 37, No. 3, Autumn 1964,* pp. 253-270.

Kallgren, Joyce K. "Nationalist China: Political Inflexibility and Economic Accommodation." *Asian Survey, Vol. 4, No. 1, Jan. 1964,* pp. 638-645.

—. "Nationalist China: Problems of a Modernizing Taiwan." *Asian Survey, Vol. 5, No. 1, Jan. 1965,* pp. 12-17.

Kang, Jean S. "Firmness and Flexibility: Initiations for Change in US Policy toward Communist China, 1961-1963." *The American Asian Review, Vol. 21, No. 1,* pp. 142.

—. "Food for Communist China: A U.S. Policy Dilemma, 1961-1963." *The Journal of American-East Asian Relations, Vol. 7, Nos. 1-2, Spring-Summer 1998,* pp. 39-72.

Kauffman, Kenneth M. "The Indian Economy: Some Recent History and Near Term Prospects." *Asian Survey, Vol. 7, No. 6, June 1967,* pp. 405-422.

Kaufman, Burton I. "Trade Policy." *Diplomatic History, Vol. 21, No. 1, Winter 1997,* pp. 117-125.

Kennan, George F. "Japanese Security and American Policy." *Foreign Affairs, Vol. 43, No. 1, October 1964,* pp. 14-28.

Keunho, Park. "The Vietnam War and the 'Miracle of East Asia.'" *Inter-Asia Cultural Studies, Vol. 4, Number 3, 2003,* pp. 372-399.

Khoman, Thanat. "Which Road for Southeast Asia?" *Foreign Affairs, Vol. 42, No. 4, July 1964,* pp. 628-639.

Kim, C.I. Eugene. "Korea in the Year of Ulsa." *Asian Survey, Vol. 6, No. 1, Jan. 1966,* pp. 34-42.

Kim, Hong N. "The Sato Government and the Okinawa Problem," *World Affairs, Volume 134, Number 3, Winter 1971,* pp. 220-233.

Kim, Joungwon A. "Korean Participation in the Vietnam War." *World Affairs, Vol. 129, No. 1, Apr/May/June 1966,* pp. 28-35.

Kim, Roy U.T. "Sino-North Korean Relations." *Asian Survey, Vol. 8, August 1968,* pp. 708-722.

Ko, Seung K. "South Korean-Japanese Relations Since the 1965 Normalization Pacts." *Modern Asian Studies, Vol. 6, No. 1, 1972,* pp. 49-61.

Kochavi, Noam. "Kennedy, China, and the Tragedy of No Chance." *The Journal of American-East Asian Relations, Vol. 7, Nos. 1-2, Spring-Summer 1998,* pp. 107-116.

Koo, Anthony Y.C. "Economic Consequences of Land Reform in Taiwan." *Asian Survey, Vol. 6, No. 3, March 1966,* pp. 150-157.

Koo, Shou-eng. "The Role of Export Expansion in Hong Kong's Economic Growth." *Asian Survey, Vol. 8, No. 6, June 1968,* pp. 499-515.

Ladejinsky, Wolf. "Agrarian Reform in Asia." *Foreign Affairs, Vol. 42, No. 3, April 1964,* pp. 445-460.

LaFeber, Walter. "China and Japan: A Matter of Options." *Current History, Vol. 55, No. 325, September 1968,* pp. 153-158+.

Langer, Paul F. "China and Japan." *Current History, Vol. 45, No. 265, September 1963,* pp. 150+.

—. "Growing Pains of a Changing Japan." *Current History, Vol. 43, No. 255, November 1962,* pp. 283-289.

Lardizabal, Ricardo P. "Economic Growth of Southeast Asia." *United Asia, Vol. 20, No. 1, Jan-Feb 1968,* pp. 39-42.

—. "Philippines' Stand on Crucial World Issues." *United Asia, Vol. 21, No. 2, March-April 1969,* pp. 83-85.

Lee, Chae-Jin. "The Politics of Sino-Japanese Trade Relations, 1963-68." *Pacific Affairs, Vol. 42, No. 2, Summer 1969,* pp. 129-144.

Lerner, Mitchell. "A Dangerous Miscalculation: New Evidence from Communist Bloc Archives about North Korea and the Crises of 1968." *Journal of Cold War Studies, Vol. 6, No. 1, Winter 2004,* pp. 3-21.

Levi, Werner. "China's Asian Policy." *Current History, Vol. 51, No. 301, September 1966,* pp. 153-158.

—. "Chinese-Indian Competition in Asia." *Current History, Vol. 38, No. 222, February 1960,* pp. 65-68, 81.

Lindblon, Charles E. "Has India an Economic Future?" *Foreign Affairs, Vol. 44, No. 2, Jan. 1966,* pp. 239-252.

Linebarger, Genevieve Collins. "The Netherlands-Indonesian Dispute." *World Affairs, Vol. 125, No. 1, Spring 1962,* pp. 30-35.

Linebarger, Paul M.A. "America's Okinawa Policy." *World Affairs, Vol. 126, No. 2, Summer 1963,* pp. 85-91.

—. "America's Okinawa Policy." *World Affairs, Vol. 126, Summer 1963, #2,* pp. 85-91.

—. "The New Japan in a Troubled Asia." *Current History, Vol. 41, No. 244, December 1961,* pp. 355-359, 367.

—. "The Republic of China on Taiwan: A Descriptive Appraisal." *World Affairs, Vol. 126, Spring 1963, #1,* pp. 5-16.

Lockwood, David E. "The U.S. Aid Program in Asia." *Current History, Vol. 49, No. 291, November 1965,* 257-261+.

Lyman, Princeton N. "Economic Development in South Korea: Prospects and Problems." *Asian Survey, Vol. 6, No. 7, July 1966,* pp. 381-388.

Maddox, William P. "Singapore: Problem Child." *Foreign Affairs, Vol. 40, No. 3, April 1962,* pp. 479-488.

Malik, Adam. "Promise in Indonesia." *Foreign Affairs, Vol. 46, No. 2, Jan. 1968,* pp. 292-303.

—. "Some Important Aspects of Indonesia's Foreign Policy." *United Asia, Vol. 19, No. 1, Jan/Feb 1967,* pp. 27-33.

Manglapus, Raul S. "Asian Revolution and American Ideology." *Foreign Affairs, Vol. 45, No. 2, January 1967,* pp. 344-352.

—. "The State of Philippine Democracy." *Foreign Affairs, Vol. 38, No. 4, July 1960,* pp. 613-624.

McDougall, Derek. "The Evolution of Australia's Defense Policy in relation to Malaysia-Singapore, 1964-1971." *Journal of Southeast Asian Studies, Volume III, Number 1, March 1972,* pp. 97-110.

McHale, Thomas R. "The Malayan Economy and Stereo-Regular Rubbers." *Asian Survey, Vol. 1, No. 4, June 1961,* pp. 25-28.

McLane, Charles B. "U.S.S.R. Policy in Asia." *Current History, Vol. 49, No. 290, October 1965,* pp. 214-220+.

McNelly, Theodore. "Japan: Potential for Peace." *World Affairs, Vol. 128, No. 1, Apr/May/June 1965,* pp. 28-35.

—. "Japan's Role in South Asia." *Current History, Vol. 49, No. 291, November 1965,* pp. 284-293+.

Means, Gordon P. "Malaysia—A New Federation in Southeast Asia." *Pacific Affairs, Vol. 36, No. 2, Summer 1963,* pp. 138-159.

Mendel, Douglas H. Jr. "Japan's Taiwan Tangle." *Asian Survey, Vol. 4, No. 10, Oct. 1964,* pp. 1073-1084.

—. "Japanese Views of Sato's Foreign Policy: The Credibility Gap." *Asian Survey, Vol. 7, No. 7, July 1967,* pp. 444-456.

Miki, Takeo. "Japan in Asian Pacific Sphere." *United Asia, Vol. 20, No. 4, July-August 1968,* pp. 231-233.

Milne, R.S. "Singapore's Exit from Malaysia: the Consequences of Ambiguity." *Asian Survey, Vol. 6, No. 3, March 1966,* pp. 175-184.

—. "The New Administration and the New Economic Program in the Philippines." *Asian Survey, Vol. 2, NO. 7, Sept. 1962,* pp. 36-42.

Mosely, Philip E. "Soviet Policy in the Developing Countries." *Foreign Affairs, Vol. 43, No. 1, Oct. 1964,* pp. 87-98.
Mozingo, David P. "China's Relations with Her Asian Neighbors." *Current History, Vol. 47, No. 277, September 1964,* pp. 156-161+.
Mukherji, Sudhansu Bimal. "Cold War in South-east Asia." *United Asia, Vol. 15, No. 6, June 1963,* pp. 423-427.
Murphey, Rhoads. "China and the Dominoes." *Asian Survey, Vol. 6, No. 9, Sept. 1966,* pp. 510-515.
Neal, Alfred C. "New Economic Policies for the West." *Foreign Affairs, Vol. 39, No. 2, Jan. 1961,* pp. 247-258.
Neuchterlein, Donald E. "Thailand: Another Vietnam." *Asian Survey, Vol. 7, No. 2, February 1967,* pp. 126-130.
—. "Thailand after Sarit." *Asian Survey, Vol. 4, No. 5, May 1964,* pp. 842-850.
—. "Thailand: Year of Danger and Hope," *Asian Survey, Vol. 6, No. 2, February 1966,* pp. 119-124.
Olsen, Edward A. "Changing U.S. Interests in Northeast Asia," *World Affairs, Volume 143, Number 4, Spring 1981,* pp. 346-365.
Ozaki, Robert S. "Economics and Economists in Japan." *Asian Survey, Vol. 4, No. 6, June 1964,* pp. 873-879.
—. "Japan's 'Price-Doubling' Plan?" *Asian Survey, Vol. 5, No. 10, Oct. 1965,* pp. 515-521.
—. "Japan's Role in Asian Economic Development." *Asian Survey, Vol. 7, No. 4, April 1967,* pp. 237-244.
Paauw, Douglas S. "Economic Progress in Southeast Asia." *The Journal of Asian Studies, Vol. 23, No. 1, Nov. 1963,* pp. 69-92.
Packard, Georg R., III. "Living with the Real Japan." *Foreign Affairs, Vol. 46, No. 1, Oct. 1967,* pp. 193-204.
Paige, Glenn D. "1966: Korea Creates the Future." *Asian Survey, Vol. 7, No. 1, January 1967,* pp. 21-30.
Palmer, Norman D. "The Challenge for Aid in Asia." *Current History, Vol. 51, No. 299, July 1966,* pp. 7-13+.
Paltridge, Shane. "Australia and the Defense of Southeast Asia." *Foreign Affairs, Vol. 44, No. 1, October 1965,* pp. 49-61.
Parish, H. Carroll. "Thailand—Cornerstone of Peace in Southeast Asia." *World Affairs, Vol. 123, Summer, No. 2, 1960,* pp. 46-48.
Park, No-Yong. "Should We Impose Democracy on Korea?" *Current History, Vol. 41, No. 244, December 1961,* pp. 341-349+.
Parmer, J. Norman. "Malaysia: Changing a Little to Keep Pace." *Asian Survey, Vol. 7, No. 2, Feb. 1967,* pp. 131-137.

Patil, Mrs. S.R. "Economic Co-operation in Asia." *United Asia, Vol. 20, No. 4, July-August 1968,* pp. 189-193.

Patrick, Hugh T. "Dollar, Dollar, Who Has the Dollar?—Relationship between the Japanese and American Balance of Payments." *Asian Survey, Vol. 6, No. 8, Aug. 1966,* pp. 434-447.

—. "Japanese Influences on the United States Balance of Payments." *Asian Survey, Vol. 3, No. 5, May 1963,* pp. 224-234.

Pauker, Guy J. "Indonesia: Internal Development or External Expansion?" *Asian Survey, Vol. 3, No. 2, Feb. 1963,* pp. 69-75.

—. "Indonesia: The Year of Transition." *Asian Survey, Vol. 7, No. 2, Feb. 1967,* pp. 138-150.

—. "Political Doctrines and Practical Politics in Southeast Asia." *Pacific Affairs, Vol. 35, No. 1, Spring 1962,* pp. 3-10.

—. "The Soviet Challenge in Indonesia." *Foreign Affairs, Vol. 40, No. 4, July 1962,* pp. 612-626.

Peritz, Rene. "The United States, Communist China and Indonesia's Confrontation Policies." *United Asia, Vol. 17, No. 4, July-August 1965,* pp. 294-300.

Pincus, John A. "What Policy for Commodities?" *Foreign Affairs, Vol. 42, No. 2, Jan. 1964,* pp. 227-240.

Piquet, Howard S. and Elden E. Billings. "Japan Still Has a Trade Problem." *World Affairs, Vol. 123, Summer, No. 2, 1960,* pp. 52-54.

Plath, David W. "Will Success Spoil the Japanese?" *Asian Survey, Vol. 1, No. 9, Nov. 1961,* pp. 27-31.

Pombhejara, Vichitvong N. "The Second Phase of Thailand's Six-Year Economic Development Plan, 1964-1966." *Asian Survey, Vol. 5, No. 3, March 1965,* pp. 161-168.

Poole, Peter Andrews. "Communist China's Aid Diplomacy." *Asian Survey, Vol. 6, No. 11, Nov. 1966,* pp. 622-629.

Prybyla, Jan S. "Communist China's Economic Relations with Africa, 1960-1964." *Asian Survey, Vol. 4, No. 11, Nov. 1964,* pp. 1135-1143.

—. "Communist China's Strategy of Economic Development, 1061-1966." *Asian Survey, Vol. 6, No. 10, Oct. 1966,* pp. 589-603.

Pye, Lucian W. "Coming Dilemmas for China's Leaders." *Foreign Affairs, Vol. 44, No. 3, April 1966,* pp. 387-402.

Quigg, Philip W. "Japan in Neutral." *Foreign Affairs, Vol. 44, No. 2, Jan. 1966,* pp. 253-263.

Rahman, Tunku Abdul. "Malaysia: Key Area in Southeast Asia." *Foreign Affairs, Vol. 43, No. 4, July 1965,* pp. 659-670.

Ramos, Narciso. "Association of Southeast Asia and The Philippines." *United Asia, Vol. 18, No. 6, Nov/Dec 1966,* pp. 295-298.

Reischauer, Edwin O. "Our Dialogue with Japan." *Foreign Affairs, Vol. 45, No. 2, Jan. 1967,* pp. 215-228.

Rhee, T.C. "Japan and the Soviet Union," *World Affairs, Volume 133, Number 3, December 1970,* pp. 240-256.

Romulo, Carlos P. "The Philippines since Independence." *Current History, Vol. 40, No. 235, March 1961,* pp. 139-146+.

Roseman, Alvin. "Foreign Aid Under Lyndon Johnson." *Current History, Vol. 50, No. 298, June 1966,* pp. 335-341+.

—. "U.S. Economic Commitment in Southeast Asia." *Current History, Vol. 54, 317, January 1968,* pp. 7-14, 52.

Roucek, Joseph S. "The Geopolitics of Formosa (Taiwan)." *United Asia, Vol. 15, No. 4, April 1963*, pp. 305-308.

—. "The Geopolitics of Japan." *United Asia, Vol. 15, No. 4, April 1963,* pp. 297-301.

—. "The Geopolitics of Korea." *United Asia, Vol. 15, No. 4, April 1963,* pp. 302-304.

Roy, Raj. "The Battle for Bretton Woods: America, Britain and the International Financial Crisis of October 1967-March 1968." *Cold War History, Vol. 2, No. 2, January 2003*, pp. 33-60.

Rusk, Dean. "Development for Survival." *United Asia, No. 2, Vol. 19, March-April 1967,* pp. 77-79.

—. "The President." *Foreign Affairs, Vol. 38, No. 3, April 1960,* pp. 353-369.

Sarantakes, Nicholas Evan. "Continuity through Change: The Return of Okinawa and Iwo Jima, 1967-1972." *The Journal of American-East Asian Relations, Vol. 3, No. 1, Spring 1994,* pp. 35-53.

—. "In the Service of Pharoah? The United States and the Deployment of Korean Troops in Vietnam, 1965-1968." *Pacific Historical Review, Vol. 68, No. 3, August 1999,* pp. 425-449.

Sato, Kazuo. "Rapid Growth, 1952-1974." *The Japanese Economy, Vol. 30, Nos. 4-5, July/October 2002,* pp. 136-160.

Scalapino, Robert A. "Moscow, Peking and the Communist Parties of Asia." *Foreign Affairs, Vol. 41, No. 2, Jan. 1963,* pp. 323-353.

—. "Which Route for Korea?" *Asian Survey, Vol. 2, No. 7, Sept. 1962,* pp. 1-13.

Schran, Peter. "Economic Planning in Communist China." *Asian Survey, Vol. 2, No. 10, Dec. 1962,* pp. 29-42.

Shimizu, Sayuri. "Perennial Anxiety: Japan-U.S. Controversy over Recognition of the PRC, 1952-1958." *The Journal of American-East Asian Relations, Fall 1995, Vol. 4, No. 3,* pp. 223-248.

Sieg, Kent S. "Marshall Green and the Reverse Course in Indonesia, 1965-1966." *The American Asian Review, Vol. 15, No. 2, Summer 1997,* pp. 101-125.

Singh, L.P. "Thai Foreign Policy: The Current Phase." *Asian Survey, Vol. 3, No. 11, No. 1963,* pp. 535-543.

Singhal, D.P. "The United States of Malaysia." *Asian Survey, Vol. 1, No. 8, Oct. 1961,* pp. 16-22.

Sobhan, Rehman. "The Problem of Regional Imbalance in the Economic Development of Pakistan." *Asian Survey, Vol. 2, No. 5, July 1962,* pp. 31-37.

Sodhy, Pamela. "Malaysian-American Relations during Indonesia's Confrontation against Malaysia, 1963-1966." *Journal of Southeast Asian Studies, Volume XIX, Number 1, March 1988,* pp. 111-136.

Solarz, Stephen. "US and Taiwan Trade Relations." *The American Asian Review, Vol. 3, No. 4, Winter 1985,* pp. 133-138.

Soukup, James R. "Japanese-African Relations: Problems and Prospects." *Asian Survey, Vol. 5, No. 7, July 1965,* pp. 333-340.

Spector, Ivar. "Soviet Policy in Asia: A Reappraisal." *Current History, Vol. 43, No. 255, November 1962,* pp. 257-262.

Starner, Frances L. "Philippine Economic Development and the Two-Party System." *Asian Survey, Vol. 2, No. 5, July 1962,* pp. 17-23.

Sternberg, David T. "The Philippines: Contour and Perspective." *Foreign Affairs, Vol. 44, No. 3, April 1966,* pp. 501-511.

Stockwell, Anthony J. "Malaysia: The Making of a Grand Design." *Asian Affairs, Vol. 34, No. 3, November 2003,* pp. 227-242.

Sundstrom, Harold Walter. "The United States and Indonesia." *United Asia, Vol. 14, No. 2, February 1962,* pp. 115-122.

Tacuber, Irene B. "Japan's Population: Miracle, Model or Case Study?" *Foreign Affairs, Vol. 40, No. 4, July 1962,* pp. 595-604.

Takane, Masaaki. "Economic Growth and the 'End of Ideology' in Japan." *Asian Survey, Vol. 5, No. 6, June 1965,* pp. 295-304.

Tate, Gordon. "China's Asian Targets." *United Asia, Vol. 21, No. 2, March-April 1969,* pp. 60-62.

The Editor. "Malaysia: An Economic Challenge." *United Asia, Vol. 14, No. 3, March 1962,* pp. 175-176.

Thomas, John R. "Soviet Russia and Southeast Asia." *Current History, Vol. 55, No. 327, November 1968,* pp. 275-280+.

Trager, Frank N. "A U.S. Program for Southern Asia." *Current History, Vol. 40, No. 235, March 1961,* pp. 129-138.

—. "The United States, SEATO and the Defence of Southeast Asia: A Forward Look." *United Asia, Vol. 17, No. 4, July-August 1965,* pp. 278-286.

Unger, Leonard. "Changing American Perceptions of Taiwan, 1949-1979." *The American Asian Review, Vol. 1, No. 3, Fall 1983,* pp. 1-26.

Vandenbosch, Amry. "'Guided Democracy' in Indonesia." *Current History, Vol. 41, No. 244, December 1961,* pp. 329-334+.

Van der Kroef, Justus M. "Indonesia in the Cold War." *Current History, Vol. 38, No. 222, February 1960,* pp. 88-94.

—. "Suharto's Indonesia." *United Asia, Vol. 20, No. 2, Mar-April 1968,* pp. 67-76.

—. "The New Malaysia and its Neighbours." *United Asia, Vol. 15, No. 10, October 1963,* pp. 682-689.

—. "The U.S. and the Future of Malaysia." *United Asia, Vol. 15, No. 12, December 1963,* pp. 813-817.

Vellut, J.L. "Japanese Reparations to the Philippines." *Asian Survey, Vol. 3, No. 10, Oct. 1963,* pp. 496-506.

Vernon, Raymond. "A Trade Policy for the 1960s." *Foreign Affairs, Vol. 39, No. 3,* pp. 458-470.

Viner, Jacob. "Economic Foreign Policy on the New Frontier." *Foreign Affairs, Vol. 39, No. 4, July 1961,* pp. 560-577.

Weatherbee, Donald E. "Interpretation of *Gestapu,* the 1965 Indonesian Coup. *World Affairs, Vol. 132, No. 4, 1969-1970,* pp. 305-317.

Wilson, David A. "Bongkok's Dim View to the East." *Asian Survey, Vol. 1, No. 4, June 1961,* pp. 13-17.

Wit, Daniel. "The Sino-American Clash of Interests in Southeast Asia." *United Asia, Vol. 17, No. 4, July-August 1965,* pp. 287-293.

Wolf, Charles, Jr. "Economic Planning in Korea." *Asian Survey, Vol. 2, No. 10, Dec. 1962,* pp. 22-28.

—. "Public Policy and Economic Development in the Philippines." *Asian Survey, Vol. 1, No. 10, December 1961,* pp. 35-38.

Wong, John. "Rice Exports: A New Dimension in China's Economic Relations with Southeast Asia." *Journal of Southeast Asian Studies, Volume X, Number 2, September 1979,* pp. 451-469.

Wu, Yuan-Li. "Economics, Ideology and the Cultural Revolution." *Asian Survey, Vol. 8, No. 3, March 1968,* pp. 223-235.

Wurfel, David. "A Changing Philippines." *Asian Survey, Vol. 4, No. 2, February 1964,* pp. 702-710.

—. "The Philippines: Intensified Dialogue." *Asian Survey, Vol. 7, No. 1, January 1967,* pp. 46-52.

Yamamura, Kozo. "Growth vs. Economic Democracy in Japan—1945-1965." *The Journal of Asian Studies, Vol. 25, No. 4, Aug. 1966,* pp. 713-728.

Yi, Kil J. "In Search of a Panacea: Japan-Korea Rapprochement and America's 'Far Eastern Problems.'" *Pacific Historical Review, Vol. 71, No. 4,* pp. 633-662.

Zhai, Quang. "China and America: A Troubled Relationship." *The Journal of American-East Asian Relations, Vol. 7, Nos. 1-2, Spring-Summer 1998,* pp. 93-99.

On-line Articles

Barnhart, Michael A. "A Secondary Affair: American Economic Foreign Policy and Japan, 1952-1968. Working Paper No. 9. The National Security Archive, U.S.-Japan Project. http://www.gwu.edu/~nsarchiv/japan/barnhartwp.htm, 5/2/2006.

Gallacchio, Marc. "Japan in American Security Policy: A Problem in Perspective. Working Paper No. 10." The National Security Archive, U.S.-Japan Project. http://www.gwu.edu/~nsarchiv/japan/gallicchiowp.htm, 5/2/2006.

Zeiler, Thomas W. "U.S. Foreign Economic Policy and Relations with Japan, 1969-1976. Working Paper No. 1. The National Security Archive, U.S.-Japan Project. http://www.gwu.edu/~nsarchiv/japan/zeiler.htm, 5/2/2006.

Unpublished Dissertations

Pellegrin, Charles J. "United States Military and Diplomatic Relations with the Republic of China in the Era of the Vietnam War, 1961-1969," unpublished Ph.D. dissertation, Mississippi State University, 2005.

Newsmagazines

Business Week, 1960-1969.
Newsweek, 1960-1969.
The Economist, 1960-1969.
The New York Times, 1960-1969.
Time, 1960-1969.
U.S. News & World Report, 1960-1969.

INDEX